TROUT FLIES

OF

BRITAIN AND EUROPE

A study in concentration – the author fishing the dry fly.

TROUT FLIES
OF
BRITAIN AND EUROPE

The Natural Fly and
Its Matching Artificial

JOHN GODDARD

F.R.E.S.

Robert Hale • London

ISBN 0 7090 6968 5

Robert Hale Limited
Clerkenwell House
Clerkenwell Green
London EC1R 0HT

2 4 6 8 10 9 7 5 3 1

DEDICATION
To my beloved daughter
Susan Jane Overend
and my grandson, Christopher

Printed in Great Britain by
Butler & Tanner Ltd, Frome

CONTENTS

ACKNOWLEDGEMENTS

A lot of the information included in this new volume originally appeared in the first two books I wrote, 'Trout Fly Recognition' and 'Trout Flies of Stillwater' so I should like to take this opportunity to thank once again all those good friends and kind people who assisted me so many years ago in the preparation of these.

So far as this present volume is concerned I should like to thank the following for permission so kindly given to reproduce certain articles and/or illustrations Keys etc; The editor of the Trout & Salmon magazine for two recent articles written for them. The British Biological Association and the Authors of 'A Key to the Adults of the British Ephemeroptera' for allowing me to reproduce some of the illustrations appearing in their handbook. Richard publishing Co Ltd; and Janet Harker the author of 'Mayflies' for permission to reproduce some of the keys to the Ephemeroptera appearing in this handbook. To the Royal Entomological Society and Norman E. Hickin the author of 'Caddis Larvae' for permission to reproduce certain illustrations of caddis larvae.

When I was first approached by my publishers Messrs A & C Black and asked to produce this volume not only on the flies of the British Isles but also the whole of Europe I considered this not only a daunting but all but impossible task. Fortunately over the years I had built up through correspondence friends in many European countries with a specialised knowledge of angling entomology and it is thanks to these good people and the assistance that they so kindly and freely offered that I was able to finally accept a contract to produce this new book. I should therefore like to take this opportunity to thank most sincerely all those that have helped in this project and in particular the following.

First of all I should like to thank my very good friend Preben Torp Jacobsen of Denmark for his great help and the knowledge of European species that he has passed on to me over the years. I should also like to thank his friend Frank Jensen of the University of Aarhus for all the information he supplied on the distribution of many North European species. My grateful thanks also go to my good colleague Piero Lumini in Italy who has been so helpful with Southern European species and also Docteur J. Manach of Sizun France who assisted with the Upwinged species in his and surrounding areas. In Scandinavia I was most fortunate in obtaining the services of Tommy Bengtsson of Lund and his friend Dr Bjorn Malmquist in the Dept; of Ecology Zoology of Umec University.

Finally I should like to offer great thanks to my old friend Ivan Tomka of Switzerland who is one of the leading authorities in Europe on the Upwinged flies for his very considerable assistance in formulating the simple keys to the Upwinged flies appearing in Chapter 4, for his help in the descriptions of the European species of Upwinged flies appearing in Chapter 5 and also for his great generosity in supplying the colour photographs of many of the European species of upwinged flies and nymphs that appear in the colour plates: 1 to 11 and also photographs numbered 107, 121, 145 to 147, 153 to 156, 162, 169 to 176, 183 to 188.

I should also like to offer grateful thanks to the following for photographs supplied. To Keith Whitehead for the photographs No 181, 182, 232, 240, 276, 277 and 279. To Piero Lumini for No's 228, 230, 231, 233, 235, 236, 238, 239, 243, 247, 250, 251, 261 and 267. Also to my old friend Taff Price for No's 245, 249 and 254.

COLOUR PLATES
(between pp.146–7)

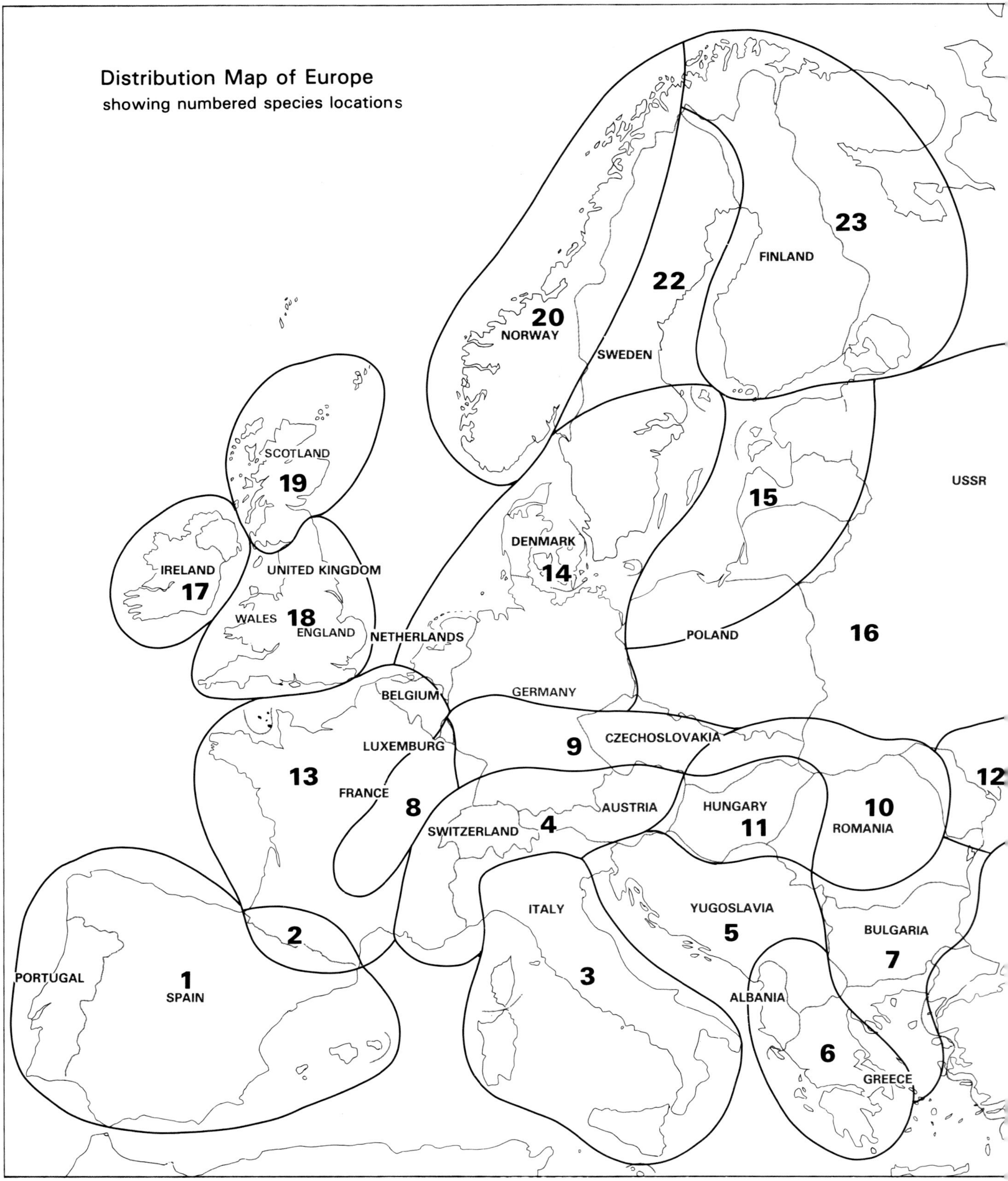
Distribution Map of Europe
showing numbered species locations
NORWAY
20
SWEDEN
22
FINLAND
23
USSR
SCOTLAND
19
IRELAND
17
UNITED KINGDOM
WALES
18
ENGLAND
NETHERLANDS
DENMARK
14
15
POLAND
16
BELGIUM
GERMANY
LUXEMBURG
CZECHOSLOVAKIA
9
13
FRANCE
8
SWITZERLAND
4
AUSTRIA
HUNGARY
11
10
ROMANIA
12
ITALY
YUGOSLAVIA
5
BULGARIA
7
2
PORTUGAL
1
SPAIN
3
ALBANIA
6
GREECE

INTRODUCTION

It was in the very early 50's that I succumbed to the spell of fly fishing, the one branch of our most facinating sport that I have still remained faithful to over all the intervening years. In those early days I quickly became convinced that exact imitation was the key to success. At the time I had a rod on the Abbott's Barton stretch of the River Itchen, the same stretch of this famous chalk stream that the grand old master of the nymph G.E.M. Skues fished for most of his life. This stretch of river without doubt is one of the most demanding dry fly streams in the world, the gin clear water combined with a relatively slow flow allows the trout all the time in the world to thoroughly inspect your offering before deciding whether or not to accept it.

This type of water is of course rather unique and does demand if not an exact imitation certainly a close imitation and during the many years that I fished here I developed several new patterns that have since proved very effective on many trout streams throughout the world. Since those early and nevertheless informative years I have learned with experience that at times on most waters a general pattern to imitate the insects hatching will suffice, as to-day I am convinced that the approach of the fly fisher to his quarry, and the presentation of the fly, particularly if it is a dry fly, is of far more importance than the appearance of the fly itself. It is however important to get the basic colour and size of the artificial correct.

To-day I no longer strive for or think in terms of exact imitation for any new patterns I develop, as I consider close imitation is far more appropriate, particularly if one exaggerates a certain key factor or features of the natural fly you are trying to imitate.

Now how important is a knowledge of angling entomology to the average fly fisher? To be perfectly honest in many instances it will be a little or no value at all. Particularly during those periods when the trout are hungry and feeding indiscriminately on any insects that present themselves. During my long fly fishing life I have known or met many very successful fly fishers who have had no knowledge of entomology at all, but they have all had other equally important aspects tuned to a fine degree, such as casting, presentation, patience and the ability to spot trout or their rises. However, I am quite certain that they would have been more accomplished and successful with even a basic knowledge of entomology. On many rivers and even more so on most lakes and reservoirs the angler who is able to identify the insect or fauna on which the trout are feeding will definitely have the edge on the angler who lacks this knowledge. The reason for this is at certain times many trout become preoccupied feeding on a certain species to the exclusion of all others, and at such times your best chances are to offer them a fairly close imitation. Let us now look briefly at such selective feeders.

SELECTIVE FEEDERS

At certain times during the season or even brief periods during any given day many trout in both rivers and stillwaters will often become very selective, feeding upon one particular species of fly or fauna to the exclusion of all others. When this occurs they are often extremely difficult to catch unless one is able to offer them a fairly close representation of the natural upon which they are feeding. It is at this time that a good basic knowledge of entomology will pay dividends. First of all it will be necessary to capture a specimen of the species of food that the trout are feeding upon in order to identify it. On rivers this is usually a fairly simple operation as it is only necessary to station oneself immediately downstream of the feeding trout where one can observe the water closely to establish on what type of food the trout are feeding. With experience the species can often be identified by sight, but if in doubt it will be necessary to capture a specimen, and this can be achieved with a small insect net. I always carry a small folding net in my pocket for such eventualities. On lakes and reservoirs it is often much more difficult as in this medium not only do the trout spend much more time feeding well below the surface, but they also have a greater variety of fauna to select from, and to compound the problem you have no strong current to drift the food down to where you can see or capture it. Under these circumstances you will have to rely upon a knowledge of what food should be present in the type of water you are fishing combined with the area and the month of the season. This will at least narrow the field to some degree and you will be able to try several different patterns with at least some degree of confidence. These days I tend to return most of the trout I catch, but in the above situation I will always kill the first trout I catch, and with a marrow scoop remove the contents of the trout's stomach for investigation. With the help of this book it should then be a fairly simple matter to identify precisely upon what species the trout is feeding. Mind you it is not always this difficult as on most stillwaters sometimes during the day, but nearly always in the early morning or late evenings a good surface rise will occur at which times one can usually observe the food just below or on the surface. With experience you can also often identify the type of food on which the trout are feeding by the rise form. This applies to both rivers and stillwaters while it is often particularly helpful upon the latter. The following are a few typical examples: Violent splashy rises during the early evenings from mid–summer on will often indicate trout feeding upon ascending sedge pupae, or a similar rise during the mornings particularly close to shore are made by trout feeding upon damosel nymphs on their shoreward migration to hatch. In late summer large splashy swirls near the shore or weed beds are usually made by trout feeding upon fry. From late June onwards in the late evenings if you see trout rising with their heads out of the water they will be taking adult sedges off the surface. During the day a quiet sip type rise is made by trout feeding upon tiny midge pupae in the surface film. Under calm conditions early mornings or evenings a slow head and tail rise nearly always indicates trout feeding in the surface film upon hatching midge pupae. However this is not always the case as this rise form also applies although less frequently to trout feeding upon upwinged spinners, or hatching caenis duns.

On very rare occasions this typical head and tail rise can also be activated by trout feeding upon another type of food of which they are inordinately fond. I can still remember most vividly being caught out in no uncertain manner by such a rise on Chew valley lake in Somerset many years ago. I was there for a weekend's fishing, and by Saturday evening had experienced one of the most frustrating day's fishing in my life. All day long the trout had been head and tailing and for most of the day I had been fishing with midge pupae patterns in various colours and sizes as I was quite convinced they were taking hatching midge pupae in the surface film. Later in the day in desperation I tried various spinner patterns and even caenis although I could seen none on the water or in the air. The following morning the trout were still rising in the same manner so for several hours I again persevered with pupae patterns all to no avail. By late morning I observed a few caenis in the air so again switched to a caenis pattern but fared no better. At midday I did what I should have done on the previous morning, I waded out into the lake as far as I could to search the water in an effort to ascertain on what these cussed trout were feeding. After studying the surface for some considerable time I was still non the wiser, and it was only when in desperation I was looking directly down into the water to see if there was anything below the surface, that I suddenly became aware of the answer staring me in the face. A snail!!! The water was liberally covered with fairly small water snails hanging shell downwards in the film with their pad uppermost, and the only way you could see these was by looking directly down onto the surface. At certains times of the year usually in August during hot sultry conditions there is a mass migration of snails from the bottom to the surface, where they often remain for several days. Now trout absolutely adore snails and when they leave their hiding places on or near the bottom and ascend to the surface they provide rich pickings and the trout will happily feed upon them all day long.

There are many other instances of selective feeding in stillwater that I could quote, but I will mention just one other situation that often occurs on a pretty regular basis throughout the latter half of the summer. On many of our rich lowland reservoirs on those evenings conducive to good hatches of fly the trout will become very selective indeed. On a typical evening you will often find at least three types of food in which the trout are interested, ascending sedge pupae, adult sedges and hatching midge pupae. Most of the trout will start feeding on the ascending sedge pupae, but at some period during the evening they will all suddenly switch to either the adult sedges or the midges and then later on switch yet again. If you can anticipate these switches correctly and change to the right pattern you may have a ball, on the other hand it is all too easy to have a blank if you make the incorrect choices.

On rivers selective feeding often adopts a different format. Most of us who have fished rivers for any length of time will have come across what are generally termed smutting trout. These are trout that will often feed selectively and happily all day on tiny reed smuts, termed the anglers curse or the black curse in many old angling books as it is generally recognised that when trout are taking these minute insects they are all but impossible to tempt with an artificial fly. If you spot a trout in a river lying very close to the surface and sipping down apparently invisible flies with incredible regularity then you are probably observing a trout feeding on reed smuts. This is what I thought until three or four years ago I undertook some serious research into this phenomenon. I soon found out to my surprise that small midge pupae were even more common in most river than reed smuts, and that furthermore those impossible to catch trout taking reed smuts were most of the time also feeding upon tiny midge pupae drifting down to them in the surface film.

After trying several different midge pupae patterns with no great success, I decided to adapt one of my own patterns that over the years had proved to be extraordinarily successful on stillwaters. This was my "Suspender Hatching Midge" pattern dressed on size 12 or 14 hooks. Dressing a slightly modified pattern on size 16 and 18 Roman Moser arrow point hooks with either green or brown bodies I found to my delight these were incredibly effective. These have now been tested out over a long period on many different rivers by various friends and have proved to be so successful that we now look upon smutting trout as easy meat. As explained previously it is usually fairly easy to establish what trout are feeding upon in a river, but there are a few instances where it can be quite difficult unless you are really fully alert. For instance most spinners of the many species of upwinged flies float along on top of the surface, but in the case of a few of the Baëtis species that lay their eggs below the surface these float downstream beneath the surface film.

Some evenings the trout will become preoccupied feeding upon these and unless you spot this and present a spinner pattern dressed sparsely and fished just below the film you will not catch many trout. At other times particularly on nice days when there are good hatches of fly you will find several different species of upwinged flies hatching at the same time. When this occurs some trout will become very selective picking out one species to the exclusion of all the others. Finally I should like to mention those trout that become selective not by choice but due to heavy fishing pressure. On many trout rivers today that are heavily fished it is not uncommon to come across a trout that is ostensibly rising regularly to hatching duns drifting down to him on the surface and that in practice appears impossible to catch. It is very easy to be fooled by such a fish as he appears to be rising to nearly every dun that drifts over him. However, very careful observation will reveal that he is not touching any of newly hatched duns but only taking stillborn or emerging duns either in or just below the surface film. This trout has learnt from bitter experience that an apparently innocuous fly floating on the surface can conceal a very sharp hook, so he has become selective to the extent that he will only accept flies in or below the surface.

WHICH FLY

Which artificial fly to use at any given period or under any particular situation is a question that has vexed fly fishers since the beginning of time. How often have many of us been witness to a situation where one fly fisher on the banks of a lake has been hauling in trout after trout while the man next to him has not had a touch. Eventually in desperation the fishless angler will approach him and ask him on what fly is he catching the fish. After being told he will walk away shaking his head as although he now has the required information he will not have a clue as to what the pattern looks like or indeed even if he has one in his fly box. On the other side of the coin we have the gentleman with a good knowledge of artificials but none on natural flies, so he also is unable to "Match the Hatch". Obviously the fly fisher who knows his artificials and also has a comprehensive knowledge of entomology will have a tremendous advantage over his peers, but unfortunately few of us have either the time or the inclination to study this subject in depth. In any case a deep knowledge of entomology is certainly not necessary to increase the chances of filling your creel. A basic understanding is really all that is required and will suffice in most situations, and it is my sincere hope that this volume will provide this and also a deeper knowledge where it may be required. It is certainly a most facinating subject and it does open up a whole new world and at the same time provide an additional interest during those often boring periods when the fish are not feeding.

If used correctly this volume should enable you to accurately and fairly quickly identify any insects or fauna captured while fishing anywhere in Europe. In addition to this it not only recommends several matching artificials for most species mentioned but also provides coloured photographs of them which will be found in the special alphabetical section at the back of this book. In most cases I have given the reader a choice of both general and imitative patterns but feel I must point out that many of them are my personal choice. Many thousands of artificial patterns exist and as it is obviously quite impractical to list all of them I can only apologise if I have omitted any particular favourites.

HOW TO IDENTIFY A NATURAL FLY

1.   Once you have obtained your specimen turn to page [1] and establish to which group it belongs.

2.   Having established to which group it belongs, turn to the appropriate section of colour photographs in order to match it. Once this has been achieved it is advisable to also check the size and main identification features in the section of text appertaining to the particular species you think it is. In the case of upwinged flies it is advisable to identify it through the keys appearing on page [26].

3.   When you have established positive identification you can choose an artificial from the recommended list for that particular species and then turn to the appropriate section of this book where you will find colour photographs of all the artificials listed in alphabetical order.

4.   If a specimen cannot be obtained refer to the monthly emergence charts as these should assist to some extent in making a choice or at least narrowing the field.

WARNING NOTE

The colour photographs provided in this book are not to scale as, in most cases, the subject has been enlarged as much as possible to assist in identification.

An upwinged fly – *Ephemeroptera*

A fly with roof-shaped wings – *Trichoptera*

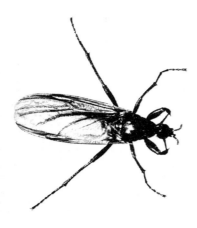

A flat-winged fly – *Diptera*

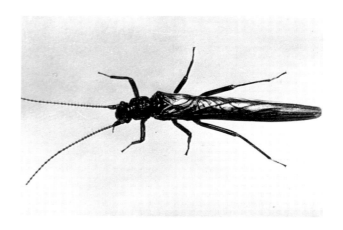

A hard-winged fly – *Plecoptera*

CHAPTER 1

THE FOUR MAJOR GROUPS

CLASSIFICATION AND LIFE CYCLE

The entomological Orders of Ephemeroptera, Diptera, Trichoptera and Plecoptera include most of the insects which are of importance to the fly fisherman, and for simplicity these Orders can be described as Upwinged flies, Flat-winged flies, Flies with Roof-shaped wings, and Hard-winged flies.

The first step in the identification of any given fly is to establish to which of the following groups the specimen belongs:

1. The Upwinged flies (Ephemeroptera)
All flies in this Order have a segmented body, two or three long tails and two large upright transparent or opaque wings. Almost all have two small hindwings.

2. The Flat-winged flies (Diptera)
The flies of this Order have two rather short transparent wings which lie flat along the top of the body (except *Tipulidae* spp., which hold wings at right angles to body). They have no tails and in general appearance, though not always in size, are somewhat similar in many cases to the common house-fly.

3. Flies with Roof-shaped wings (Trichoptera)
These flies have four wings, and when at rest the wings lie close along the body in an inverted V shape. The wings appear to be soft, as they are covered completely in very tiny hairs. They are without tails.

4. The Hard-winged flies (Plecoptera)
The wings, of which there are four, are long and rather narrow when the fly is at rest, and lie flat along and slightly over the body; they are hard and shiny or horny. Some of the larger species have tails. The wings of the male of many of these larger species are often very short and useless for flight.

A simplified explanation of the life cycle of flies in these Orders may be of interest, and as the first group (although it is the smallest) is of more importance to the average river fly fisher than the other three, it is intended to give here a more detailed life history of the Upwinged flies than of those of other Orders.

THE UPWINGED FLIES (*EPHEMEROPTERA*)

Flies in this Order are known as the Upwinged flies. To quote a reference in many angling books, when a hatch of these occurs 'they look like a fleet of miniature yachts sailing down the river'. This is a relatively small order.

The Egg
The egg stage is the first in the life cycle of flies of this Order. Eggs of most species are deposited by the adult female on the surface of the water, when they sink to the bottom and attach themselves naturally to weeds, stones, etc. Certain other species, such as some of the *Baëtis* genus, crawl down projecting weeds, stones,

posts, etc., and deposit the eggs directly (see Plate 26 No's 206-207). The egg stage of development lasts anything from a matter of days to many months, according to species and time of year.

The Nymph

The nymphal stage is the second in the cycle, following the hatching out of the egg. This period may last from two to twelve months or even longer, according to species and the time of year the egg was laid. During this stage the nymph lives on or near the bottom. Some species hide in or on various weeds, others cling to stones and rocks, while certain other species actually burrow in the river bed.

It develops from a small nymph through progressively larger stages, each change or instar accompanied by a moult. The growing nymph feeds mainly on decaying vegetable matter although some are carnivorous. Some Genera like the Ephemera have but one generation every two years while most of the Genera have one generation a year while some of the smaller Genera such as some of the Bactis species may have two or more generations a year.

The Sub-imago or Dun

When the nymph is fully grown it is at last ready to change into the winged insect known as the sub-imago, or dun. This emergence takes place fairly rapidly. The mature nymph ascends to the surface, where the nymphal case splits (see Plate 26 No 205) and the fully winged fly emerges on to the surface film, resting on this film while its wings dry and it gathers strength to fly off. Some species emerge via emergent vegetation, stones or posts etc.

On hot, dry days or in fast broken water this emergence is very rapid, as the wings dry very quickly and the insect flies off almost at once. The dun is slower to take wing on wet, damp, cold days. Certain species seem able to become airborne much faster than others. The dun stage usually lasts between twelve and thirty-six hours, much less in the case of flies belonging to the family Caënidae, where the transpositions from nymph to dun and dun to spinner may both take place in a matter of minutes.

The Imago or Spinner

The final stage in the life cycle of flies of this Order is after the change from the rather dull-looking dun to the beauty and perfection of the imago or spinner. It is during this final stage of its life, which may last only a matter of hours, that the fly engages in the procreative processes before it dies. The spinner can easily be distinguished from the dun as the latter with a fine coating of hair on parts of its body is rather drab or dun-coloured, as its name implies. The wings are dull and opaque, and the trailing edges are usually lined with very fine hairs which can be clearly seen under a low-power magnifying glass. On the other hand, the spinner's body is very bright and shiny, with transparent shiny wings, now devoid of the fine hairs along the trailing edges; (apart from some species of Caënis) the tails and forelegs are also considerably longer.

The final stage of transposition from dun to spinner is accomplished fairly quickly in much the same way as the earlier stage from nymph to dun. This usually takes place in the bank herbage, any thing from a few hours to a day or two after the appearance of the winged dun. The change from dun to spinner can actually be observed, with patience. If a dun can be successfully taken home alive, it should be deposited in a cool place, or better still kept overnight in an ice box or refrigerator, which usually results in slowing or halting the metamorphosis. On the following morning, place the fly in a warm spot in direct sunlight if possible, and within a fairly short time if you are fortunate the final transposition can be observed.

Duns at rest hold their wings upright and together, and usually the first indication of the forthcoming transposition is when the wings open out until they are spread wide apart. The dun sometimes spends several minutes in this position, quivering slightly from time to time, before the wings finally appear to fold slowly along the body. It is at this stage that the skin splits along the top of the thorax, and the fully adult fly or spinner emerges. See Plate 12 (93 to 96).

The cast-off skin retains the shape of the original insect, with the exception of the wings, which are too frail.

The fly now, as a spinner, is able to mate, and copulation usually takes place in flight. After this act, the spent male dies over land, but in some cases dies over and falls on to the water. The female, after extruding or depositing her eggs, on or in some cases under the water, then dies almost immediately.

Finally, it should be explained that all flies in this Order have either two or three long tails, a segmented body, six legs and upright wings. Most of them have two large forewings and two smaller hindwings. In some cases the latter can be clearly seen, as in the Mayfly or Blue Winged Olive, but in other species, such as the Small Spurwing, they are so small that a magnifying glass is required to detect them. In a few species the hindwings are absent altogether.

THE FLAT-WINGED FLIES (*DIPTERA*)

This is an extremely large Order of insects, which includes all the true flies, such as house-flies, mosquitoes, dung-flies, crane-flies, etc., and is considerably larger than all the other three Orders put together. Despite this, relatively few of these flies are of significance to the fly fisherman.

Of the few flies in this Order that are of interest to anglers, the majority are aquatic. They can be divided into three main sections: Reed Smuts, Gnats and Midges. The latter, it should be mentioned, are very much more important to the lake than to the river angler. The vast majority of the two-winged flies in this Order are non-aquatic, and with a few notable exceptions (including some of the Gnats mentioned above) are of no importance to the angler.

Reed Smuts

The adult female insects in this section mainly lay their eggs in masses of jelly on protruding vegetation, stones, posts, etc., and may in some case crawl down these projections and lay their eggs under water. The eggs usually hatch within a week or so, and small wormlike larvae emerge. These larvae moult at intervals, gradually increasing in size. Finally, the larvae spin a cone-shaped case, usually attached to weeds, in which to pupate. When the adult fly is ready to emerge from its pupal case, it burst out and ascends to the surface in a bubble of gas. (It is this feature combined with their small size which makes it so difficult to deceive a fish when it is feeding on these creatures.) As a result of this phenomenon the fly emerges at the surface quite dry, and quickly takes off.

3

Gnats and Midges

Most of the flies in these two sections are larger than the very tiny Reed Smuts of the previous one. The eggs of the Midges are usually laid by the adult females on the surface, in small or large clusters, forming rafts of eggs which attach themselves to weed or other projections.

The small larva which at length emerges swims to the river or lake bed, where it lives in the mud or silt. Eventually the larva transforms into a pupa which, unlike the previous species, is of the free-swimming variety, similar to the nymphs of the Olives. When the adult fly is ready to emerge the pupa ascends to the surface where it remains suspended for some little time in the surface film (depending on weather and water temperature). The winged insect then emerges and flies away.

All flies in this section are fully adult immediately after emerging from their pupal case, and pass only through the one-winged stage before they mate and die. It should be noted that most of the Gnats are terrestrial.

All flies in the Diptera Order are tailless, and have two short flat transparent wings similar to the common house-fly, which belongs to this same Order.

FLIES WITH ROOF-SHAPED WINGS (*TRICHOPTERA*)

The Caddis or Sedge-flies

This again is a fairly large Order of flies, about 190 different species having been recorded in these islands with at least a further 500 species known in Europe. The majority of these are of little interest to the angler; many are very small, while many others are very uncommon or locally distributed.

However, the few species of Sedge-flies that are common are very important indeed to anglers. They have roof-shaped wings (when at rest), four in number, which are covered with a layer of tiny fine hairs. These are sometimes difficult to see with the naked eye, but show up clearly with a magnifying glass. Superficially, they are similar to moths, but these latter have a covering of tiny scales on their wings instead of hairs. Also Sedges when at rest are considerably slimmer, particularly across the thorax.

Many Sedge-flies have particularly long antennae, in some cases over twice the length of their bodies. The mouthparts include two pairs of jointed protuberances called palps, which are set one behind the other. The front ones, the 'maxillary palps', sometimes vary between male and female, and in a few families the male palps consist of three to four segments and the female's of five segments. In most families, however, both male and female palps consist of five segments.

The female Sedge-fly lays her eggs in one of three ways according to the species:

(a)   On the water surface.
(b)   By crawling under water and depositing the eggs.
(c)   On herbage or vegetation overhanging the water.

The several hundred eggs are often laid in one gelatinous mass which adheres to any vegetation with which it comes in contact.

There are four well-marked stages in the life of the Sedge-fly: egg, larva, pupa and the adult winged fly.

The Eggs

These begin to hatch into larvae after ten to twelve days and most species construct cases to protect their relatively soft bodies.

The Caddis Larvae

These are a familiar sight to most anglers, as practically every clump of weed pulled from the river bed will have its attendant host of Caddis cases in various shapes and sizes. In days gone by these used to be a popular bait with bottom fishermen, and even today are still much used in Ireland. The larvae form their tubular cases see Plate 27 (211 to 215) from all manner of debris from the bed of the river or lake, including particles of gravel, shells, bits of leaf, decaying vegetation and even small sticks. In fast flowing water the larvae usually choose heavy materials such as small stones, gravel, etc., to help prevent them being swept away by the current. On the other hand, the species found in still water tend to use semi–buoyant materials which facilitate movement.

The majority of flies in this Order form cases as described, but a few free-swimming species see Plate 27 (210) form shelters on the undersides of stones or plants. After the larva is fully developed, it pupates within its case or shelter, and after a period varying from days to weeks, according to species and the time of year, during which its does not eat, the pupa emerges see Plate 27 (216). At this stage it is still enclosed in its pupal envelope and is equipped with a pair of powerful paddle-like legs which enable it to swim to the surface, or to climb up plant or weed stems above water where it hatches out into the fully adult fly. In some species the pupa swims directly to the surface, where it immediately hatches out. Large Cinnamon Sedges are typical of this latter group, and many anglers with be familiar with the disturbance they cause as they hatch on the surface and skitter about in a frantic effort to become airborne.

Sedge–flies in the winged state, perhaps because they are able to absorb liquid, live for a much longer period than flies of the Ephemeroptera group.

Finally, it should be noted that while some of these flies commence mating or coupling on the wing most of them mate while at rest, and therefore it is usually the female of the species that is sometimes taken by the trout when she returns to lay her eggs.

THE HARD-WINGED FLIES (*PLECOPTERA*)

Commonly called the Stoneflies, this is also quite a small Order of flies consisting of a little over thirty different species in the U.K., with a further 300 or so species occuring throughout Europe. However, like the Sedge–flies the vast majority of these are scarce or very local in their distribution. Nevertheless, where the more common species occur in abundance, they are important to anglers. This is mainly in the North Country or Europe in rivers that have gravelly or stony beds. They are of course found in some of our southern rivers, including many of the chalk streams here and in France, but seldom in sufficient quantities to be of interest to anglers. Some species are also to be found in stillwater.

The flies in this group vary considerably in size, from the large Stonefly, see Plate 33 (261 to 264) which is well over an inch long, to the small Willow-fly, and even smaller Needle-fly, the smallest fly in the Order. They all have four wings and when at rest the wings are long and narrow and lie close to the body. These wings are hard and shiny, prominently veined and considerably longer than the body of the fly, except in some males as mentioned earlier. They are poor fliers and in flight appear considerably larger than they really are. The adult fly is, like its nymph counterpart, active on its feet.

The life span of the flies in this Order varies considerably, the average being about a year, but in some cases lasting as long as two to three years.

The Egg
The time taken for the eggs to hatch out, again, varies from a few days to many weeks. The nymphs of Stoneflies are very robust and active creatures. Many anglers will be familiar with some of the larger nymphs in this group which are popularly known as creepers and in some circles are much in demand as bait for bottom fishing.

The Nymph
These nymphs can easily be distinguished from the nymphs of the Ephemeroptera as they have two claws on each leg and the two antennae on the head are quite long. In the latter stage of the life of these nymphs the wing cases are quite prominent see Plate 33 (257 to 260). When the adult winged fly is ready to emerge from its nymphal case, the mature nymph crawls on to dry land where the transition takes place. The life of the Stone-flies in the winged state can be anything from a few days to a few weeks according to species, and they never wander very far from water, and mate at rest.

In many of the larger flies in this Order, the wings of the male are little better than stumps, and these insects are quite incapable of flight see Plate 33 (262).

The females return to the water to lay their eggs, and the method of doing so varies a little according to the species. So far as can be ascertained, however, they all lay their eggs actually on the surface. With some of the larger species, they will alight on the water and release the eggs while swimming or fluttering along. In doing so they create quite a disturbance, and make an attractive target for any hungry trout in the vicinity.

Other species fly out over the water and literally fall down on the surface, releasing all their eggs in one mass, while some dip up and down on the water in a similar manner to some of the Upwing spinners, depositing a few eggs at a time. The eggs when released by the female on the surface sink to the bottom where they attach themselves to stones, rocks, etc.

N.B. In the following chapters it will be noted that the emphasis on identification heavily favours the Ephemeroptera. The reason is that most of the flies in this Order hatch in very large regular numbers, floating on the surface as duns and returning to the water as spent spinners. Therefore correct identification is more important in this than in other Orders.

However, it is also appreciated that in certain areas this Order of flies may be of less importance and I ask for the indulgence of anglers in those areas for the sake of the majority.

The Orders or Classes of interest to fly-fishermen as as follows. They are listed according to importance.

Ephemeroptera	Upwinged flies.
Trichoptera	Sedge-flies
Diptera	Midges, Gnats, etc.
Plecoptera	Stoneflies
Crustacea	Shrimps, Water-louse, etc.
Megaloptera	Alder-flies
Hemiptera	Water-bugs, Corixids, etc.
Odonata	Dragon flies and Damselflies
Coleoptera	Beetles

Arachnidae   Spiders
Lepidoptera   Moths, etc.
Neuroptera   Lacewings, etc.

All the above with the exception of Crustacea and Arachnidae belong to the Class Insecta.

For the fly-fisher intending to make a superficial study of entomology, it is important to note that all insects are divided into Orders, which in turn are divided into Families, and then into Genera, and finally into the Species. The following table shows how two different Orders of insects are classified.

	MAYFLY	**BLACK GNAT**
CLASS	*INSECTA*	*INSECTA*
ORDER	*EPHEMEROPTERA*	*DIPTERA*
FAMILY	*EPHEMERIDAE*	*BIBIONIDAE*
GENUS	*EPHEMERA*	*BIBIO*
SPECIES	*DANICA*	*JOHANNIS*

CHAPTER 2

THE UPWINGED FLIES (EPHEMEROPTERA)

THE PHYSICAL STRUCTURE WITH DETAILED NAME KEY

In the opening stages of Chapter 1, the life cycle of this Order has been dealt with fairly concisely, and it is not felt necessary to elaborate further for fear of confusing the reader. However, there are many other features and facts about this interesting and fascinating group of flies which, if explained in a straightforward and simple manner, can be of considerable interest to the angler. It is therefore proposed to deal with them step by step as we go along.

It should first be explained that although the winged flies in this group are important from the angler's or fly-fisherman's point of view, they are not necessarily of so much importance from the trout's point of view, as they may not form a substantial part of its diet. Trout feed on a great variety of food; snails, shrimps, crayfish, caddis and the larvae of other aquatic insects such as Smuts and Midges. In addition, trout are not averse to feeding on the smaller specimens of their own kind. Minnows, Sticklebacks and the fry of other fish also form an important part of their diet in many waters, as do the nymphs or larvae of the other three orders. On occasions, also, both trout and grayling are fortunate in coming across such tit-bits as tadpoles, caterpillars, beetles, wasps, and various other land-bred insects which find their way on to or into the water. Therefore with this large variety of food to choose from, it is sometimes surprising that trout ever bother to rise at all to small Ephemeropteran duns or spinners. It is very fortunate for the fly-fisher that trout and grayling feed regularly on surface flies; they do so probably because these flies are conveyed by the current to the positions where the fish lies, thus enabling the latter to feed heartily with the expenditure of minimum effort. Another possibility, of course, is that adult flies supply a deficiency in the trout's diet and are necessary to its well-being, or perhaps it looks upon them as either an *hors-d'oeuvre* or a *dessert*

Let us now consider the physical structure or characteristics of flies in this Order:

The Head
This is often wider than its length, the major portion consisting of the eye structure; there is no mouth as such, the duns being incapable of eating or drinking. This may account for their very short life span in the final winged state. The head also has a small pair of antennae like miniature horns, which are usually plainly visible.

The Eyes

The head carries a pair of large compound eyes or oculi, one on each side, and in most cases the eyes of the male are considerably enlarged and extend over the top of the head, and are divided into two distinct areas, in the lower area they face sideways and downward and in this structure the eye is specialised for observing detail. In the upper structure the eyes face upward and are capable of seeing any rapid movements. In several species these two upper structures are further accentuated as they are raised well above the lower eyes and these are known as turbinate eyes. These upper eyes in the males are probably provided by nature to enable it to locate the female of the species, which usually approach the male swarms from a higher level.

The Thorax

The head is connected by a short neck to the thorax of the fly, which is made up of three segments. The middle segment is by far the largest, and carries the forewings and the middle pair of legs. The front segment carries the forelegs and the rear segment the hindwings (if any) and rear pair of legs.

The Abdomen

This, the main body of the fly, is divided into ten distinct segments. The last segment carries the tails and the ninth segment carries the claspers of the male fly. The top of the abdomen will be referred to as the dorsum, and the under surface as the venter.

The Tails

They are usually long and slender. In some species there are two and in others three. In many cases these tails are very short when the dun is freshly hatched, but they rapidly lengthen with age. In the spinner stage the tails are usually considerably longer, particularly in the case of the males as they assist the fly in flight when swarming.

The Wings

As previously explained, these are fairly large with extensive veining and are always carried upright. Most of the flies in this group have hindwings of various sizes and shapes, but several species have no hindwings at all.

The Legs

These are six in number, the front or anterior legs being normally longer than the remaining four, which are referred to as the median and posterior legs respectively. The anterior legs of the males are usually a little longer than those of their female opposites; in the spinner stage they are often longer still. Each leg consists of five main joints; the most important of these are the femure (thigh joint), tibia (shin joint) and tarsus (foot).

So much for the physical structure of these flies, but before we proceed further let us consider from the angler's point of view the simplest way of determining the sexes. This can be achieved by two methods, the first of which concerns the eyes. In the male these are usually very prominent, and to clarify this the following sketches should be studied. The first sketch shows the eyes of a typical female, and the second those of the male. (See figs 1 and 2)

9

It must be pointed out, however, that to identify the males by the eye characteristics alone is not conclusive. In certain of the larger families of flies in this Order, this difference in structure is not so apparent. Therefore for conclusive evidence the second method is infallible. All male flies in this Order have a pair of forceps or claspers to enable the male fly to attach itself to its chosen mate during copulation. These are situated underneath the fly just behind the tail on the ninth segment (see figs 3 and 4). They can usually be seen with the naked eye, but a small magnifying glass will show them quite clearly. In conclusion, it should be noted that in nearly all cases the male fly is smaller than the female of the same species.

1 Eyes of a typical female

DIFFERENCE IN SIZE AND COLOUR

It is probably not generally realized how much variation it is possible to find in the colour and size of Ephemeropteran flies of the same species. This, of course, can greatly increase the difficulties of positive identification, as we automatically tend to recognise certain flies by their general size and colour. Therefore these variations must be kept very much in mind. But fortunately these variations seem to occur only occasionally and it is possible to work to average sizes and colours in most cases with reasonably accurate results. Let us first discuss the question of colour.

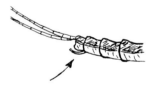

2 Turbinate eyes of a typical male (*Baëtidae* Spp.)

Colour

As a general rule the temperature of the air is thought to affect the coloration; the colder the day, the darker the colour of the fly. To follow this temperature effect further, flies that hatch in the spring or early in the year are darker than flies of the same species that hatch during the summer. Then, when the weather begins to get colder in the autumn, the colour is again darker. Another point also to be borne in mind is that the male is usually darker than the female. Apart from the above, the colours of the same species of fly can vary in different localities. However, where a colour variation does occur, it is more a lightening or darkening of the basic colour. One notable exception is the Blue Winged Olive. When this fly first appears in early June the body colour of the female is sometimes quite a bright olive green, but in October the colour is often quite different, being a distinct shade of rusty brown. Little has been written on the subject of size and coloration in the past, and during the preparation of this book hundreds of colour photographs have been taken and many thousands of specimens have been examined, and it has been during this time that these variations have been noticed.

3 Claspers of male fly viewed from the side

Having dealt briefly with colour as applicable to the duns, let us now consider colour in respect of spinners. With these the variation in colour seems to be very much greater, and is much more noticeable in certain species than in others. Whether or not air temperature plays much part in coloration in the spinners is not definitely known, but it is generally accepted that the older the spinner the darker the colour. This is particularly noticeable in the females, and they seem to darken very rapidly after copulation. Although this progressive darkening with age seems fairly constant, it does not bear any relation to the final colour of any particular spinner, as this seems to depend more on the original colour of the spinner when it changes from the dun stage. The following two examples may help to illustrate this point:

(a) The female spinner of the Medium Olive (*Bäetis vernus*)—this often first appears with a greenish-brown body, and, when it is spent, with a dark brownish

4 Close-up of male claspers viewed from beneath

body, tinged red. The more common coloration, however, is a brownish body to start with, finishing up in the spent stage with a distinctly reddish body. It will be appreciated that the variation here between these two varieties is not so great.

(b)   The female (Sherry) spinner of the Blue Winged Olive seems to be subject to a very large variation, and on more than one occasion I have seen swarms of these spinners ranging in colour from a pale olive-brown to a deep lobster-red. So far as I have been able to ascertain the exact cause of this variation in colour is unknown. Dr Michael Wade suggests that mutant factors might ensure a mixture of colours in each generation so that against different coloured backgrounds some will be less conspicuous to predators and thus more likely to survive.

Difference in Size

Fortunately from the point of view of identification this variation in size, apart from the difference between males and females, seems to be the exception to the rule, and it is only the odd fly here and there that is either very considerably smaller or larger than the norm. If there is a variation it is more likely that the specimens will be smaller than average rather than larger. It is quite common to encounter complete hatches of the various species in this Order that vary in size slightly. Once again one can only theorise on the reason for this, and in all probability it is simply a lack or an abundance of food during their early stages of life under water. There are it should be noted, two species Cloëon Simile and C. Dipterum that always seem to vary in size. Those that hatch in the early summer being much larger than those which hatch in the late summer. Furthermore the females are often considerably larger than the males. This variation in size between the males and females seems to apply to most species in this Order.

It must also be borne in mind that a small variation in size can be accounted for by a natural tendency of all living creatures to differ in this respect. To give a comparison of this as against human beings, half a millimetre difference in the length of a B.W.O. (which is quite common) would be roughly equivalent to a difference in a man's height of about eight inches. Therefore a variation of up to one millimetre or more would not be abnormal in a fly.

MATING AND FLIGHT

Mating

Although this was dealt with superficially in Chapter 1 it is felt that a little more detail would be of general interest. In most cases mating takes place in the air. Once a male has located a female of the species, he approaches her from underneath and with the aid of his long front legs and forceps (claspers) he attaches himself to her. Copulation then immediately takes place, during which the female endeavours to keep both herself and her mate airborne. The pair may slowly sink towards the ground, but in most cases copulation has been effected before they actually reach it. After mating has taken place the female will usually fly out over the water in preparation for laying her eggs and the male will return to its swarm, possibly preparatory to mating with other females. Eventually the males when fully spent will return inland where they die. Few males actually fall spent on the water in any quantity. However, there are exceptions to this, and three that immediately come to mind are the Small Spurwing, the Iron Blue and the Blue Winged Olive. The males in these cases sometimes fall spent on the water in considerable numbers. The actual reason for this seems difficult to pinpoint, but from observations I have made, it would appear that these particular species often mate over the water, whereas most of the other species in this Order usually copulate over land.

Flight

The male spinners of the Ephemeroptera usually form themselves into swarms of varying size. Each swarm may be composed of several hundred or even several thousand individuals. Each different species seems to have its own favourite area or locality for swarming. For instance, the Pale Evening spinner is usually found swarming along the edges of rivers and seldom inland. On the other hand, the Small Red spinner is often to be found inland, sometimes as much as sixty or seventy yards from the water. Also, apart from the location of the individual swarms, the actual flight pattern or behaviour of flies of the different species varies. From the above it will be apparent that with experience the keen observer may eventually be able to recognise and identify some of the different species of spinners while in flight or by their location. For the angler, a little knowledge of the behaviour of these spinner swarms can be important. Certain species fall spent on the water earlier than others, and as most swarms form late in the afternoon and seldom fall spent till early or late evening, the correct identification of spinners in a swarm can assist the angler to be in the right place at the right time with the right artificial. Spinners, however, are very susceptible to a change in weather conditions, especially to a drop in temperature, and indeed on cold days they are often absent. Also if a cold wind blows up in the evening, bringing about a temperature drop, the swarms which might have formed throughout the afternoon will suddenly disappear to await a more favourable opportunity. This may not arise until the next day.

On some rivers the banks vary between open meadows and sheltered woodland. In inclement weather, the exposed open meadows will be deserted, and the spinner swarms may then often be located in the sheltered lee of the trees and shrubs.

DETAILED NAME KEY FOR THE EPHEMEROPTERA GROUP
BRITISH AND EUROPEAN SPECIES (WITH COMMON ANGLING NAMES)

CURRENT ANGLING NAME	OLD ANGLING NAME	ENTOMOLOGISTS. NAME	POPULAR NAME FOR FEMALE SPINNER
MAYFLY	Green Drake	*Ephemera danica* *Ephemera vulgata* *Ephemera lineata*	Spent Gnat. Drake mackerel
LARGE DARK OLIVE	Large Spring Olive or Blue dun	*Baëtis rhodani*	Large Dark Olive spinner or Large Red spinner.
IRON BLUE	Iron Blue	*Baëtis muticus* or *Baëtis niger*	Iron Blue spinner or Little Claret spinner.
MEDIUM OLIVE	Medium Olive	*Baëtis vernus* or *Baëtis buceratus*	Medium Olive spinner or Red Spinner.
SMALL DARK OLIVE	Summer Olive, July dun or Pale Watery	*Baëtis scambus*	Small Red spinner or Small Dark Olive spinner.
PALE WATERY	Pale Watery	*Baëtis fuscatus*	Golden spinner or Pale Watery spinner.
DARK OLIVE	—	*Baëtis atrebatinus*	Dark Olive spinner.
YELLOW EVENING DUN	Yellow Evening dun	*Ephemerella notata*	Yellow Evening spinner.
BLUE WINGED OLIVE	Blue-winged Olive	*Ephemerella ignita*	Sherry spinner.
SMALL SPURWING	Little Sky-blue or Pale Watery	*Centroptilum luteolum*	Little Amber spinner.
LARGE SPURWING	Blue-winged Pale Watery or Pale Watery	*Pseudocentroptilum·pennulatum*	Large Amber spinner.
PALE EVENING DUN	—	*Procloëon bifidum*	Pale Evening spinner or Golden spinner.
POND OLIVE	Pond Olive	*Cloëon dipterum*	Pond Olive spinner or Apricot spinner.
MARCH BROWN	March Brown	*Rhithrogena germanica*	March Brown spinner.
OLIVE UPRIGHT	Olive Upright	*Rhithrogena semicolorata*	Yellow Upright.
YELLOW MAY DUN	Little Yellow May dun or Yellow Hawk	*Heptagenia sulphurea*	Yellow May spinner.
DUSKY YELLOWSTREAK	Dark dun	*Electrogena lateralis*	Dusky Yellowstreak spinner.
TURKEY BROWN	Turkey Brown	*Paraleptophlebia submarginata*	Turkey Brown spinner.
PURPLE DUN	—	*Paraleptophlebia cincta*	Purple spinner.
DITCH DUN	—	*Habrophlebia fusca*	Ditch spinner.
CLARET DUN	Claret dun	*Leptophlebia vespertina*	Claret spinner.
SEPIA DUN	—	*Leptophlebia marginata*	Sepia spinner.
AUTUMN DUN	August dun	*Ecdyonurus dispar*	Autumn spinner.
LARGE BROOK DUN	—	*Ecdyonurus torrentis*	Large Brook spinner.
LARGE GREEN DUN	Large Green dun	*Ecdyonurus insignis*	Large Green spinner.
LATE MARCH BROWN	Late March Brown or False March Brown	*Ecdyonurus venosus*	Great Red spinner.
LARGE SUMMER DUN	Summer Mayfly	*Siphlonurus lacustris* *S. alternatus* *S. armatus.*	Great Red spinner.
BROWN MAY DUN	—	*Heptagenia fuscogrisea*	Brown May spinner.
CAENIS OR BROADWING	Angler's Curse or White Midge	*Caënis* and *Brachycercus spp.*	Caënis spinner or Broadwing spinner.

EUROPEAN SPECIES ONLY ARE NOT INCLUDED AS THEY HAVE NO ANGLERS COMMON NAMES

With regard to the above list, it should be explained that in the early days of fly-fishing most of the species of the *Baëtis* genus apart from the Iron Blue (*Baëtis pumilus* or *niger*), were referred to generally as Olive duns. In addition the two flies from the *Centroptilum* genus and one of the flies from the *Baëtis* genus, the Pale Watery (*Baëtis fuscatus*), were all referred to as Pale Watery. This has led to a certain amount of confusion in the past, and therefore in this name key and the indentification keys I have designated them in accordance with contemporary thought. It must be pointed out, however, that the above insects are very similar in general appearance and are far from easy to identify positively. In fact in most cases the difference is so slight that it is very doubtful indeed whether correct identification is of any help at all to the angler.

Finally it must be emphasized, as mentioned in the introduction, that the above list does not include all the insects in the Ephemeroptera Order. Those flies that are seldom seen or confined only to local areas have been omitted for fear that their inclusion might lead to some confusion.

CHAPTER 3

THE UPWINGED FLIES
(Continued)

CONSTANT PHYSICAL FEATURES TO ASSIST IN IDENTIFICATION OF SOME COMMON SPECIES

So far as the dry fly fisherman is concerned The Upwinged flies (Ephemeroptera) are by far the most important group and furthermore the only group out of the four major groups where precise identification of a species can sometimes make the difference between success and failure during a day's fishing. Generally speaking the faster more turbulent and coloured a river the less important identification. On this type of water a general pattern providing it is the correct size will usually suffice. The clearer and slower flowing a river the more important identification becomes. It never ceases to amaze me how often the older and wiser trout on such rivers are able to pick out with unerring accuracy one Upwing species from another, particularly when perhaps two or even three very similar species are hatching. That they can do this is now an undisputed fact, but how or even why they do this has not been fully established. Maybe to the pallet of the trout there is a subtle difference in taste from one species to another, and maybe their close up vision is better than ours and they can appreciate the minor differences which we often have so much difficulty with. Whatever the reason the one aspect that is abundantly clear on this type of water is that your ability to identify the species and to then match the hatch will give you a big advantage over your fellow angler.

Before we proceed to the next chapter where you will find the main identification keys for all the different species let us look at some of the physical features which in some cases can lead to instant identification and in others to at least a narrowing of the field. Two typical examples are as follows:- You may happen to notice after a cursory examination of the specimen you have caught that there is a distinctive yellow mark or streak each side of the body on the thorax below the wing root. In another instance you may have noticed after a close examination of the fly you have caught that it has small oval shaped hindwings with a distinct spur. Now had you managed to memorise all the various physical features listed in this chapter you would immediately realise that the former fly could be none other than "The Dusky Yellowstreak" as this is the only species that has this distinctive mark. The small oval spur shaped hingwings of the latter fly would have alerted you to the fact that it must be one of the "Baëtis" species.

While in some cases it may be advantageous to identify a specimen down to the actual species, in most situations identification as far as the Genera will suffice, so the reader will have to make his own decision as to how far in this direction he feels he needs to go, depending on the type of water he regularly fishes. While not absolutely necessary a small low power pocket magnifying glass is a distinct

15

advantage at the waterside when examining a specimen, as unless one has excellent eyesight I do assure you it will prove very difficult to for example study the venation of the wings, or to find and identify the shape of the hindwings on some of the very small olives.

It should be pointed out that all trained entomolgists rely mainly on a close examination of the sexual appendages of most insects for positive identification of a species, as this is apparently one section of the anatomy that is constant yet varies from one species to another. Such a study requires of course specialised laboratory equipment which is beyond the scope of the average fly fisher. Fortunately for the fisherman most of the physical features mentioned here are fairly obvious and in most cases will lead to a reasonably positive I.D.

WING VENATION OF THE UPWINGED FLIES

The following sketches and photographs of the fore-wings and hindwings of the Ephemeroptera are included in order to assist the angler/entomologist to identify specimens more positively; this can be done by studying the venation, or veining and in some cases also the shape of the wings, particularly with some of the more difficult types, where it is an essential point of reference.

HINDWINGS (not to size)

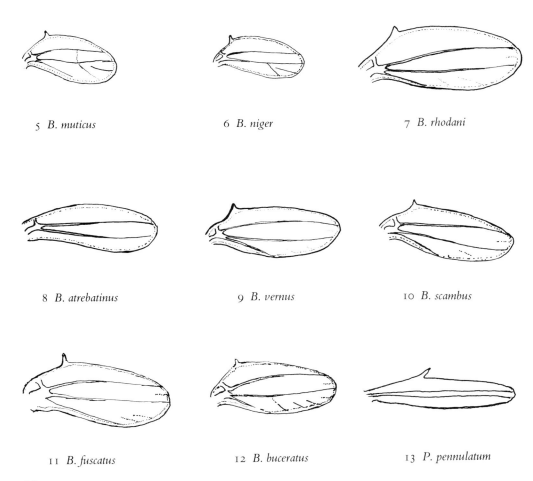

5 B. muticus   6 B. niger   7 B. rhodani

8 B. atrebatinus   9 B. vernus   10 B. scambus

11 B. fuscatus   12 B. buceratus   13 P. pennulatum

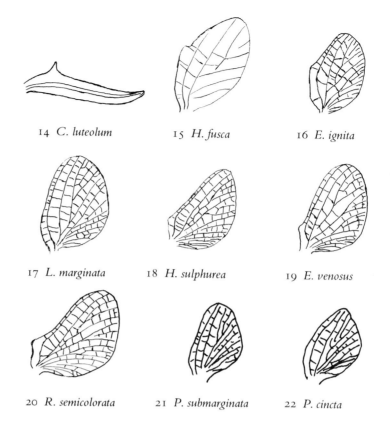

14 *C. luteolum*   15 *H. fusca*   16 *E. ignita*

17 *L. marginata*   18 *H. sulphurea*   19 *E. venosus*

20 *R. semicolorata*   21 *P. submarginata*   22 *P. cincta*

THE FOREWINGS (not to size)

The following drawings and photographs showing venation and shape of wings have been provided to assist the amateur angler/entomologist to confirm the identity of some species where there may be doubt.

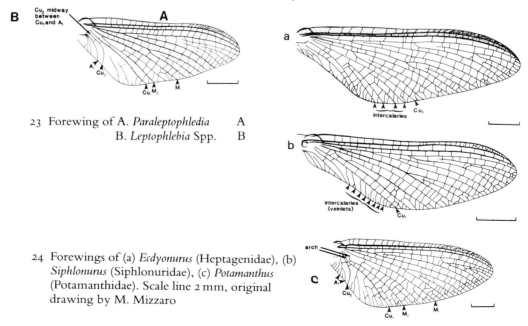

23 Forewing of A. *Paraleptophledia*   A
      B. *Leptophlebia* Spp.   B

24 Forewings of (a) *Ecdyonurus* (Heptagenidae), (b) *Siphlonurus* (Siphlonuridae), (c) *Potamanthus* (Potamanthidae). Scale line 2 mm, original drawing by M. Mizzaro

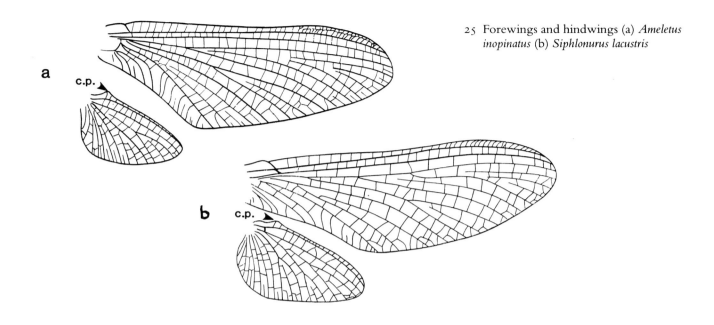

25 Forewings and hindwings (a) *Ameletus inopinatus* (b) *Siphlonurus lacustris*

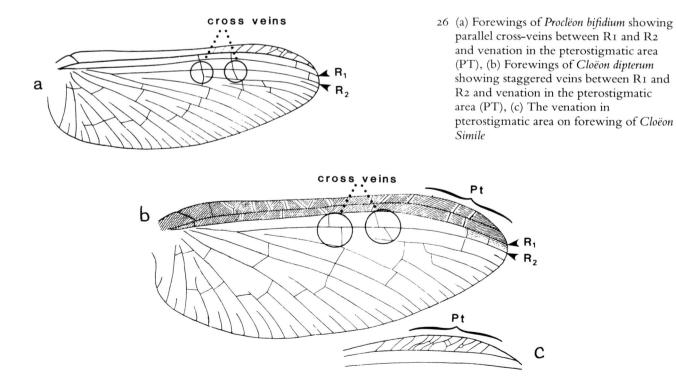

26 (a) Forewings of *Proclëon bifidium* showing parallel cross–veins between R1 and R2 and venation in the pterostigmatic area (PT), (b) Forewings of *Cloëon dipterum* showing staggered veins between R1 and R2 and venation in the pterostigmatic area (PT), (c) The venation in pterostigmatic area on forewing of *Cloëon Simile*

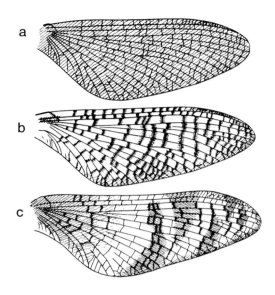

27 Forewings of (a) *Ecdyonurus dispar* (wing uniformly greyish-yellow), (b) *E. venosus* (cross veins strongly bordered blackish, giving the wing a mottled appearance, (c) *E. torrentis* (some cross veins strongly bordered blackish giving the wing a banded appearance)

28 Forewings and hindwings of (a) *Baëtis rhodani* (with small oval handwing), (b) *Centroptilum luteolum* (with small narrow spur-shaped hindwing). Note the double intercalary veins on all *Baëtis* Spp. single intercalary veins on *Centroptilum, luteolum, Pseudocentroptilom, pennulatium, Proclëon bifidum,* Cloëon dipterum and *Cloëon Simile*

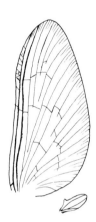

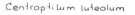

Baëtis rhodani   Centroptilum luteolum

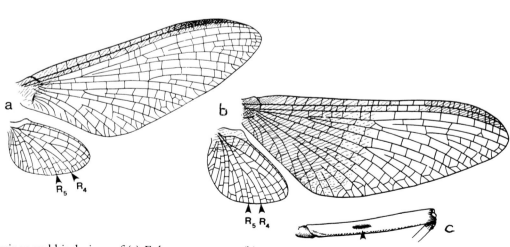

29 Forewings and hindwings of (a) *Ecdyonurus venosus*, (b) *Rhithrogena semicolorata*, (c) constant black mark on legs femur of *Rhithrogena* Spp. Occurs on nymphs, duns and spinners

19

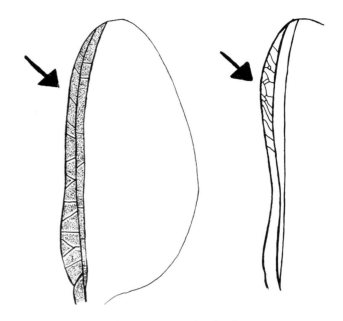

30 Constant black markings on ventral segments of the abdomen of *Ephemerall notata* and *Ecdyonurus insignis*

31 Difference in venation in the pterostigmatic area between *Cloëon dipterum* and *Cloëon Simile*

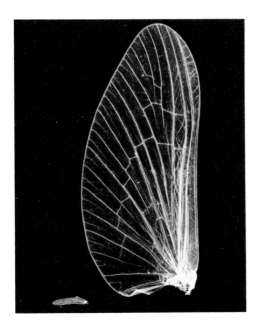

32 *P. pennulatum* × 10. Forewing and small narrow hindwing of subimago female. Note single intercalary veins

33 *C. luteolum* × 10. Forewing and small narrow hindwing of subimago female. Note single intercalary veins

34 *P. bifidum* × 5. Forewing of
subimago female. Note six to eight
cross veins in Pterostigmatic area

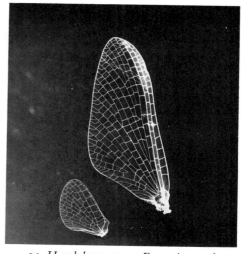

35 *H. sulphurea* × 5.5. Forewing and
upright hindwing of imago male

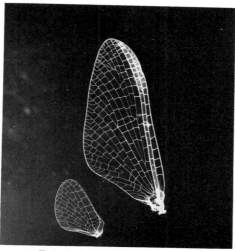

36 *E. insignis* × 5.5. Forewing and part
hindwing of subimago female

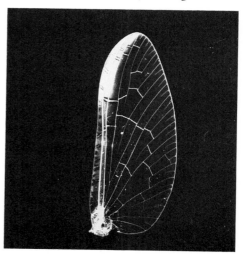

37 *C. dipterum* × 5.5. Forewing of
imago female. Note three to five
cross veins in pterostigmatic area.

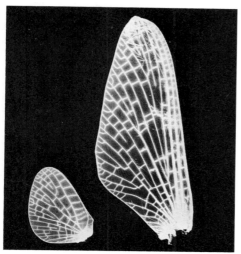

38 *R. Germanica* × 5. Forewing and
upright hindwing of subimago
male

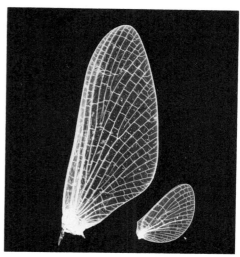

39 *R. semicolorata* × 7.5. Forewing and
upright hindwing of subimago
female

21

40 *E. ignita* × 5. Forewing and upright hindwing of imago female

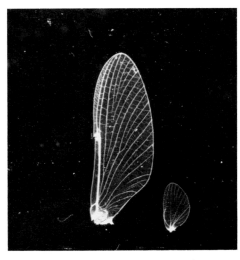

41 *L. vespertina* × 5. Forewing and upright hindwing of imago female

42 *L. marginata* × 5. Forewing and upright hindwing of subimago male

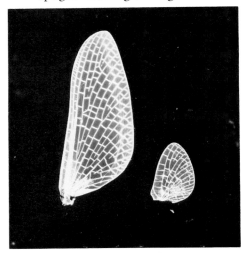

43 *E. dispar* × 5. Forewing and upright hindwing of subimago male

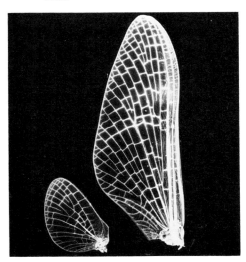

44 *E. torrentis* × 5. Forewing and upright hindwing of subimago male

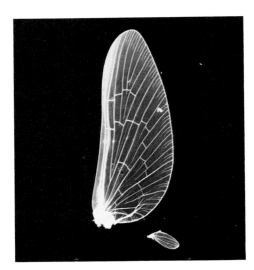

45 *B. rhodani* × 7.5. Forewing and small oval hindwing of subimago female. Note double intercalary veins

Some of the features mentioned in this chapter are tabulated below in a simple form which should assist in a quick identification of some species of both male and female dun and spinner (except where otherwise stated).

Constant feature	Species
Yellow streak each side of thorax in front of forewing root	H. lateralis
Brown streak in middle of each top leg section (femur)	All Rhithrogena Spp.
Mottled wings with clear area in centre	R. Germanica E. torrentis — duns E. insignis — only P. submarginata
Yellowish leading edge to wings	E. torrentis C. dipterum—female spinner only E. notata—male and female spinner only H. sulphurea—female spinner only
Blackish leading edge to wings	L. marginata—spinners only E. insignis—spinners only H. sulphurea—male spinner only
Upright hindwings without costal projection	L. marginata P. submarginata L. vespertina P. cincta
The femora (upper leg joint) have a dark reddish brown transverse band on the outer surface before junction with the tibia	Siphlonurus alternatus
Medium size duns and spinners with two parallel red lines transversing ventral segments	C. dipterum—females only
Small duns and spinners with distinct yellow eyes (turbinate)	P. bifidum — males B. fuscatus — only
Small duns and spinners with oval hindwings with spur	Baëtis Spp
Small duns and spinners with very small narrow spur shaped hindwing	C. luteolum P. pennulatum
Small duns and spinners with two tails and no hindwings	P. bifidum C. dipterum C. simile
Small duns and spinners with single intercallery veins along trailing edge of forewings	P. bifidum C. dipterum C. simile C. luteolum P. pennulatum
Small duns and spinners with double intercallery veins along trailing edge of forewings	B. rhodani B. vernus B. scambus B. fuscatus B. muticus
Very tiny duns and spinners with three tails, broad forewings and no hindwings.	Caënis Spp

APPENDIX TO CHAPTER 3 — *THE BAËTIDAE*

Before proceeding to the next chapter, it has been thought advisable to give some brief details and information on the Baëtidae family of Olives, as of all the Upwinged flies these are undoubtedly the most difficult to identify precisely. They are also dealt with in the following chapters, but as a rough guide the following points should be noted.

The *Baëtis* genus are a member of the Family Baëtidae, as are also the genera *Pseudocentroptilum, Centroptilum, Clöeon* and *Proclöeon*. As some of the generic species within this family differ only little from each other in size and colour, it is almost impossible to identify them positively by these characteristics alone. Therefore it is necessary to indicate certain physical differences in order to enable one to subdivide the Baëtidae family into their correct genera and species.

From the fishing viewpoint the importance of correct identification within these groups is in any case of dubious value. Apart maybe from the Large Dark Olive due to its size and the Iron Blue due to its very dark colour. A range of patterns from size 18 to 14 in a pale dressing to represent the Pale Watery, Pale Evening dun and Spurwings, and similar sizes tied with dark olive and medium olive dressings to represent the Olives will generally suffice.

However, in certain cases it can be helpful to identify the naturals, and as this is often a lot simpler than would at first appear, it is well worth a little time and trouble to master the processes of identification.

First of all let us look at the complete list of the Common and Widespread Upwinged duns that come in this group. It will be noted that some species in this group have been bracketed together, the difference between them being very slight so far as the angler is concerned. Rare or localised species are not included in this list.

Baëtis rhodani	The Large Dark Olive	*Baëtis fuscatus*	The Pale Watery
Baëtis atrebatinus	The Dark Olive	*Centroptilum luteolum*	The Small Spurwing
Baëtis vernus	The Medium Olive	*Pseudocentroptilum*	
Baëtis buceratus	,,	*pennulatum*	The Large Spurwing
Baëtis muticus	The Iron Blue	*Proclöeon bifidum*	The Pale Evening dun
Baëtis niger	,,	*Clöeon dipterum*	The Pond Olive
Baëtis scambus	The Small Dark Olive	*Clöeon simile*	The Lake Olive

The following table has been prepared giving the various physical characteristics of the flies in the above list. This should enable the reader to identify most of them correctly. All the flies in this group have *two tails*. Some of them have:

1.   Single or double marginal intercalary veins along the trailing edge of the forewings. See figs. 28 (p. 00).

2.   Narrow or oval hindwings. See figs. 28 (p. 19).

3.   No hindwings at all.

Finally it should be pointed out that in the male flies of all the above species, and indeed in all the male flies of the Ephemeroptera Order, identification is assisted by the shape and characteristics of the male genitalia. However, as these can only be studied with the aid of a microscope, they are not recommended as a means of identification in this book, except in a few isolated cases.

N.B. It should be noted that the true colour of the eyes of the male duns may not be apparent when freshly hatched. It is therefore advisable to let a short period elapse before examining freshly hatched males.

These form the basics of the following table.

IDENTIFICATION CHART FOR THE MOST COMMON
BAËTIDAE FAMILY OF DUNS

SPECIES	SIZE	COLOUR OF EYES OF MALE	SHAPE OF SMALL HINDWING	INTER-CALARY VEINS	REMARKS
Large Dark Olive (*B. rhodani*)	medium-large	dark brick-red	small oval with spur (Fig.)	double	These two are difficult to tell apart except for difference of hind-wing. Both have dark olive-brown bodies.
Dark Olive (*B. atrebatinus*)	medium	pale red-brown	small oval but no spur (Fig.)	double	
Medium Olive (*B. vernus,* or *buceratus*	medium	dull red-brown	small oval with spur (Figs. &)	double	Body colour ringed cream brownish olive.
Iron Blue (*B. muticus* or *niger*)	small	dull red-brown	small oval with spur (Figs. &)	double	Body very dark brown-olive with dull grey-blue wings.
Small Dark Olive (*B. scambus*)	small to very small	dull orange-red	small oval with spur (Fig.)	double	The females of these two species are anatomically almost identical. Body colour is grey-olive and pale grey-olive respectively.
Pale Watery (*B. fuscatus*)	small	bright yellow	small oval with spur (Fig.)	double	
Small Spurwing (*C. luteolum*)	medium to small	orange-red	very small narrow with apex pointed and prominent spur (Fig.)	single	Pale olive brown body.
Large Spurwing (*P. pennulatum*)	medium large	dull orange	very small narrow with apex rounded and prominent spur (Fig. 26)	single	Very pale olive-grey body with dark blue-grey wings.
Pale Evening Dun (*B. bifidum*)	medium	dull yellow	no hind-wings	single	Very pale straw body.
Pond Olive (*C. dipterum*)	medium to medium-large	dull orange-brown with two faint red lines across centre	no hind-wings	single	Dark brown-olive body. Female dun and spinner have two red lines running along under body.
Lake Olive (*C. simile*)	medium	pale orange	no hind-wings	single	Dark brown olive body.

CHAPTER 4

THE UPWINGED FLIES
(Continued)

WITH KEYS TO IDENTIFICATION OF NYMPHS AND ADULTS

In the preceding chapters the details given have been strictly factual, but in this and the following chapter every endeavour has been made to include hints and views that could be helpful to the angler.

All aquatic flies live the greater part of their lives under water, and in the course of evolution have adapted themselves to the environment most suited to the particular species. It will be appreciated therefore that the under-water forms of these flies (nymphs) vary considerably, both in actual physical shape and characteristic features evolved to suit their aquatic mode of life. Some nymphs have adapted themselves to rough stony streams, such as those of the North, and live the best part of their lives clinging with their flat bodies to stones. Others prefer slower water and live in little tunnels which they excavate in the bed of the stream. Various families of nymphs found in our chalk or limestone rivers live largely in the weed beds which abound in most of these waters. Some of them have a preference for alkaline water, others for slightly acid water. Some thrive in the highly oxygenated water of mountain streams, others in sluggish lowland rivers.

The study of insects in relation to the surroundings is known as the science of ecology, and from it we often can gather clues regarding the distribution of insects which can assist us to identify them when an element of doubt exists. To clarify this point further, let us imagine we are having a pleasant week's fishing holiday on an unfamiliar water. We may possibly rely on local information about the flies that are likely to be encountered, but this can sometimes prove misleading, and in any event if we have an inquiring mind we will probably want to identify the flies ourselves. Shortly after arrival at the water a few duns start to hatch out, and several trout and grayling move to them. We quickly catch one of the duns and, searching our memory (or perhaps even this volume), we come to the conclusion that our specimen is either a March Brown or a Turkey Brown. The latter has three tails and the former only two, so identification should normally be no problem, but in this case we will assume that the Turkey Brown has lost one of its tails, which occasionally happens. If so, we would probably conclude wrongly that our specimen is a March Brown, but a knowledge of their habits and distribution tells us that this is highly improbable: March Browns inhabit swift-flowing rivers with stony bottoms, and the river we are fishing is rather sluggish with a muddy bottom, much more suited to the Turkey Brown. Although this is an extreme case, it should help to illustrate the point being made, which relates to the preference of certain species for different habitats. Our study of ecology might even help us to decide where one may find different species of flies in a particular river, the more so when one happen to be fishing a stretch with varying water characteristics that support different insect species. A typical example is as follows.

The Blue Winged Olive, one of the most common chalk stream flies, often emerges at dusk, and an angler will gain an advantage if he can recognize in advance the most likely part of the river where this is likely to occur. Occasionally, especially on a bleak evening, spinners or indeed any other insects are in short supply and the best chance of some activity may be found in a rise to a hatch of the B.W.O. An angler knowing a little about the habitat of various species will be aware of the fact that such an event is most likely to take place below fast water where it runs over shallows, and will station himself accordingly. However let us first of all look at the nymphs of these Upwinged flies and the best way of classifying them.

NYMPHS OF THE UPWINGED FLIES

In general appearance the nymphs of these flies are somewhat similar to the adult winged fly without its wings or long tails. They have a rather humped-back shape caused by the wing cases, although these are not apparent in the immature nymphs. When these wing cases first develop they are of a pale shade of brown, and as the nymphs advance in maturity they become noticeably darker. In fully mature nymphs which are at the point of emergence, the wing cases are very prominent and very dark brown. These Ephemeropteran nymphs may be distinguished from small species of Stonefly nymphs by the single claw on each leg. Stonefly nymphs have two claws. They are supposed to feed mainly on detritus and minute organisms present in the water, but whether this is in fact the case is uncertain, as it is known that at least some species are strongly carnivorous, and will attack and devour other nymphs as large as themselves. The various types have adapted themselves to live under widely different conditions, and this is probably why we find certain species of Upwinged flies in some localities but not in others. For instance, the nymphs of Mayflies are adapted to live in the fine silt or fine gravel on the river bottom and are therefore found only in waters that offer this type of environment. They would find it impossible to survive in the fast-flowing, stone-bedded rivers that are common in some parts of the country. Yet flat, stone-clinging nymphs of the March Brown or Autumn Dun species are very much at home in this type of river, but would find it equally impossible to live in the type of river favoured by the Mayflies. Nymphs have to absorb oxygen from the water to live. Clear pure water has a high oxygen content whereas dirty or polluted water has a low content. For this reason both trout and grayling and most nymphs are found only in our cleaner swift-flowing rivers, as they all require a fairly high oxygen content to live. All nymphs have tracheal gills along the abdomen that can, if necessary, assist the oxygenated water to flow over the body, through the walls of which the oxygen is absorbed. In the case of the various species which have adapted themselves to live in fast flowing water, these gills are not entirely essential as the water is constantly flowing past the nymph and supplying all the oxygen required. The nymphs of species that have adapted themselves to life in still or sluggish water, such as the Mayfly or Pond Olive, have overcome this problem by evolving gills (with filaments in some cases) which are capable of considerable muscular movements that provides a constant flow or circulation of water around the body, and this supplies all the oxygen required. It will doubtless be appreciated that the examples quoted here are from opposite ends of the scale, and there are many species between these two extremes that have adapted themselves to more average conditions. For this reason of course, many of the species that come in this "in between" category are widespread in their habitat and more common to many parts of the continent. One of the very remarkable features of these Ephemeroptera nymphs, is the large number of moults (instars) they undergo before reaching the winged form. While the nymphal life of some of the bottom burrowers may last as long as two years many of the smaller nymphs may complete their life cycle in a little over 40 days and during this period moult as many as 50 times.

Nymphs of many species move over quite large areas of habitat in the course of their life underwater. Some overwinter only in the egg stage, while others overwinter as nymphs, with those living in stillwater usually moving towards deeper water during the winter and only returning to the shallower margins in the summer prior to emerging. Most nymphs are adept at the art of camouflage and none more so than the various nymphs of the Caenis family who are capable of very rapid changes as they move around on the silt on the bottom. When the time arrives for the final moult into the subimago (dun) they fill their gut with air or possibly even some form of gas (it is not known how they accomplish this) and then when they are ready to emerge they release their grip and float or swim up to the surface to hatch. This rise of the nymph to the surface is seldom a random event as it is usually regulated by weather conditions or more likely barometric pressure and it is an established fact that certain species are capable of synchronising this event at different times of the day to other species or genera. A good example of this must have been experienced by most fly fishers on stillwater when one of those collosal hatches of Caenis better known as the anglers Curse commences. One minute there is not a fly to be seen and the next the whole surface of the water is covered with tiny hatching flies.

Upon reaching the surface the thorax splits along the top and the newly emerging dun literally pulls himself out of his old case and often uses it like a miniature raft while he pumps up his wings preparatory to flight. In some cases part of his legs or tail may become trapped in the old case, a wing damaged or even after successfuly hatching the wind may topple him on his side and trap his wing in the surface film. Such flies that are trapped are often referred to by the fly fisher as stillborn, and there are special patters that have been developed to imitate this quite common event. Of course not all genera emerge on the surface as many species will seek out weeds reeds stones posts or any other projections on which they will crawl up until they emerge above the surface where they will hatch in complete safety at their leisure.

Oliver Kite in his standard work *Nymph Fishing in Practice* sub-divided Ephemeropteran nymphs into various groups according to their habitat, and as this seems a very sensible and practical arrangement, the same pattern will be followed in this book. The six main groups into which all the nymphs we are about to discuss can be placed are as follows:

BOTTOM BURROWERS	STONE CLINGERS
SILT CRAWLERS	LABOURED SWIMMERS
MOSS CREEPERS	AGILE DARTERS

A brief description of the various types of nymphs comprising the above groups will now be given before we proceed to the individuals of the various species.

Bottom Burrowers Plate 3 (21-3)
The only nymphs found in this country which come under this heading are Potamanthus luteus which is rather rare and the nymphs of the Mayflies (Ephemera Spp). They are comparatively large and have specially shaped gills with filaments along the body. They burrow into the river bed, and live in the tunnels so formed. The head is narrow and pointed, and is provided with a large pair of mandibles which are used for excavating. The gill plates, which are very active, provide a constant flow of water past the body of the nymph, thus supplying the necessary oxygen, and perhaps this flow of water also carries minute particles of food to the nymph in its burrow. There are several European species which also come within this group.

The Silt Crawlers Plate 3 (23)
The very tiny nymphs of the family Caënidae or Broadwings compose this group. So far as the Fly fisher is concerned no particular species is of any great importance, and it is not therefore proposed to name here the various species. They are all somewhat similar in appearance and habitat, living on the surface of the mud or silt in the slower sections of rivers or lakes. They are inactive creatures, move slowly, and are often well camouflaged.

The Moss Creeper Plate 1 (8)
This group embraces several species of the genus *Ephemerella*, including the nymphs of the Blue Winged Olive and the Yellow Evening dun. They are quite sturdy but rather inactive creatures which live mainly in the mosses or stones on the river bed. They also seem to favour decaying vegetation or old leaves which are trapped either in pockets on the river bed, or against obstructions such as large stones, pillars or posts in the water.

The Stone Clingers Plate 1 (1-6)
Nymphs in this group include many *Rhithrogena, Ecdyonurus* and *Heptagenia* species, and also in Europe only *Uligoneura, Epeorus* and *Nixie* species. The nymphs have a flattened appearance, and are wider than most of the other nymphs. They are heavily built with strong sturdy legs, specially adapted for clinging to stones in the fast-flowing waters which form their habitat. If these nymphs are observed on stones in fast currents it will be seen that they always face the flow of water, and will continue to do so even when they move, which often necessitates moving sideways or backwards. The pressure of water flowing on to the sloping flat head and thorax of this species of nymph helps them to retain their position by pressing them on to the rock or stone. They seem to favour the underside of stones during strong sunlight, and they feed on the algae (which forms on the exposed sides) when the sun is off the water.

Laboured Swimmers Plate 2 (11)
Nymphs in this group, which includes *Paraleptophlebia, Leptophlebia* and *Habrophlebia*, are somewhat similar in appearance and habitat to the Moss Creepers. They have gills or plates which are long and slender, although their

bodies are wide and heavily built. Their legs are as sturdy as the Moss Creepers, but they can often be observed swimming rather than crawling from place to place in a slow and leisurely manner. A European species *Choroterpes Picteti* also comes within this group.

The Agile Darters Plate 7 (7)

The nymphs of this group, which is by far the largest, include all species of *Baëtis, Centroptilum, Cloënm, Siphlonurus, Potamanthus, Ameletus* and *Procloëon*. As the name implies, they are strong and agile swimmers, slim and streamlined in appearance with long tails, the latter fringed with hairs to provide efficient propulsion. The favourite habitat of most species is undoubtedly in clumps or beds of weed and they are to be found in all depths of water, but seem to prefer the middle or top of the weed growth. Nevertheless, they will also often be found on the moss or weed debris, and if disturbed will dart away with a good turn of speed.

EPHEMEROPTERA – KEY TO THE FAMILIES, GENERA AND SOME OF THE MORE COMMON SPECIES OF NYMPHS AND ADULTS

The following keys to the nymphs and adults of the Ephemeroptera have been provided for those fly fishers that may wish to take the study of angling entomology to a greater depth than the average fly fisher. These keys cover many of the more common species and the collection and identification of these for those sufficiently interested will enable them to establish which species of Ephemeroptera are present in any given body of water in which they are particularly interested.

These keys are based on the physical structures of these insects as it is impossible to correctly identify the many species by colour and size alone. In most cases the salient points of identification are too small to see with the naked eye. However a microscope is not necessary as a hand held 10 power magnifying glass should be adequate.

General Characters of a Nymph

The basic external structure of the nymph is illustrated in fig. 46

Head

The shape varies between genera but there are always large compound eyes situated laterally or dorsally, and usually one median and two lateral *ocelli* situated between the eyes. The slender tapering *antennae* vary in length between genera. The mouth parts vary according to feeding habits but consist of four main elements. A *labrum* is the most anterior mouthpart and is a flap that can move slightly backwards and forwards. A pair of jaw-like *mandibles,* each with outer incisors and an inner molar region, lie posterior to the labrum and move laterally to provide a chewing action. In the genus *Baëtis*, the mandibles have an unusual appendage known as a *prostheca*. Posterior to the mandibles is another pair of chewing organs, the *maxillae*, each of which carries a segmented *palp* (usually three segments, sometimes two to four), The *labium* is the most posterior mouthpart and bears a pair of palps and two pairs of lobes, the inner pair being the *glossae* and the outer pair the *paraglossae*.

Thorax and legs.
There are three thoracic segments: anterior *prothorax* with the fore legs, *mesothorax* with the middle pair of legs and the developing fore wings in older larvae, posterior *metathorax* with the hind-legs and developing hind wings, except in those species whose adults lack hind wings. The dorsal surfaces of the three segments are known as the *pronotum, mesonotum* and *metanotum,* the largest always being the mesonotum which usually covers the metanotum. Each leg has six parts: a stout basal *coxa,* a small *trochanter,* a broad *femur,* a slender cylindrical or subtriangular *tibia,* a cylindrical unsegmented *tarsus,* and a single *claw* often with small 'teeth' (denticles).

Abdomen and gills
There are ten abdominal segments, some of which may be hidden beneath the mesonotum. Each segment has a dorsal *tergum* (or *tergite*) and a ventral *sternum* (or *sternite*). To determine the number of a segment, always count forward from the tenth posterior segment. The so-called 'gills' occur on up to seven abdominal segments (numbers 1–7) but are less numerous in some species. At the posterior end of the abdomen, two *cerci* and a median *terrminal filament* form the three *caudal filaments* or *'tails'* (all the British species have three tails but some species outside the British Isles do not have the median filament). Unlike that of the adults, the body shape of the nymph often varies considerably between families.

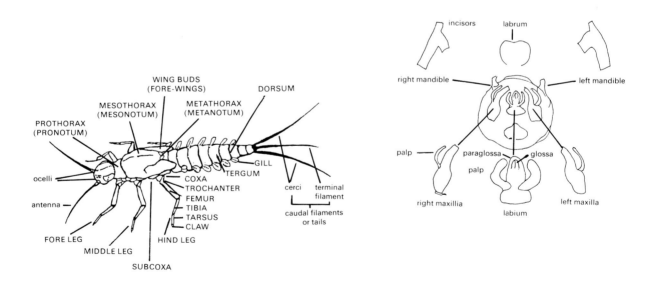

46 (a) Basic structure of a nymph, (b) ventral view of mouthparts.

1. *Ameletus inopinatus*
   Nymph

2. *Siphlonurus lacustris*
   Nymph

3. *Procloeon bifidum*
   Nymph

4. *Centroptilum luteolum*
   Nymph

5. *Ephemerella ignita*
   Nymph

6. *Baetis rhodani*
   Nymph

7. *Ephemera danica*
   Nymph

8. *Cloeon dipterum*
   Nymph

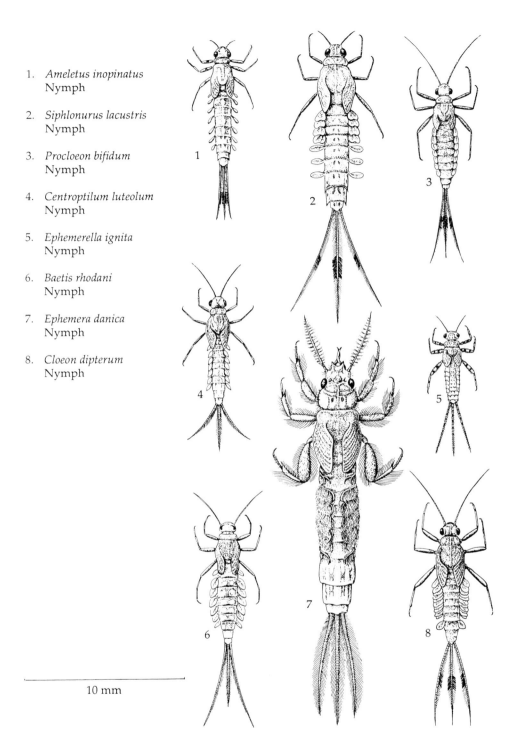

10 mm

47 Silhouettes of the more common genera of nymphs

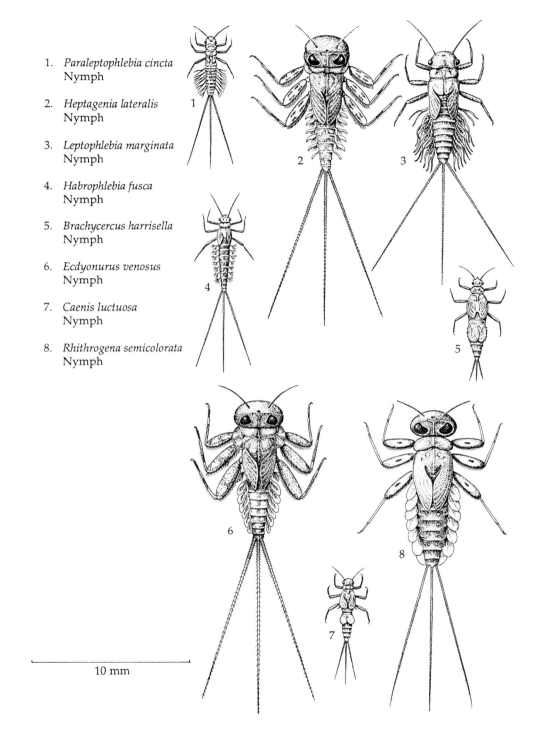

1. *Paraleptophlebia cincta*
   Nymph

2. *Heptagenia lateralis*
   Nymph

3. *Leptophlebia marginata*
   Nymph

4. *Habrophlebia fusca*
   Nymph

5. *Brachycercus harrisella*
   Nymph

6. *Ecdyonurus venosus*
   Nymph

7. *Caenis luctuosa*
   Nymph

8. *Rhithrogena semicolorata*
   Nymph

10 mm

48 Silhouettes of the more common genera of nymphs

Key I. Nymphs: starter key to genera

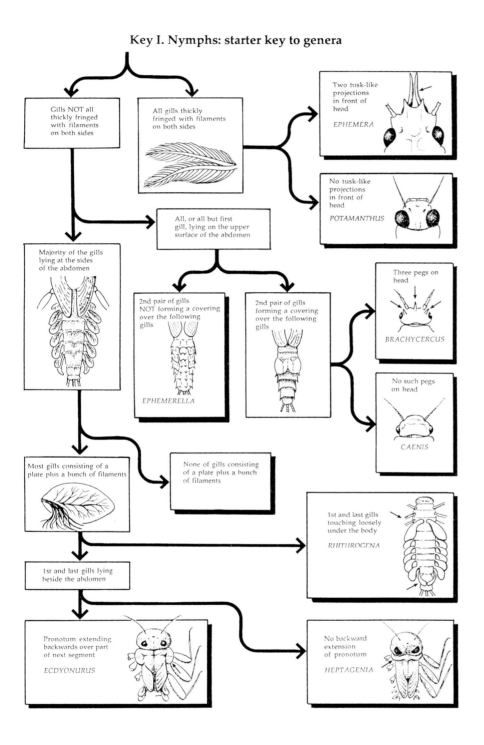

49 Key I – Nymphs: starter key to genera (common species)

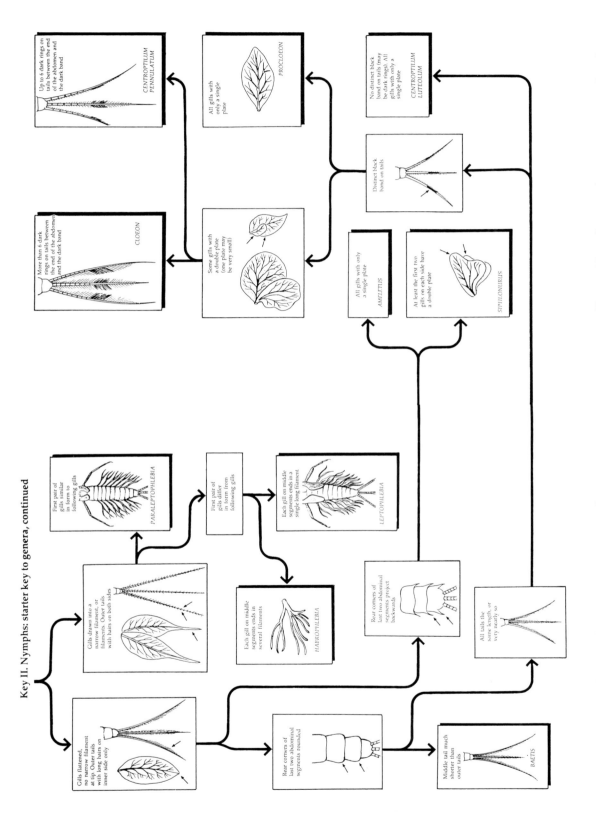

Key II. Nymphs: starter key to genera, continued

51 Key 2 – Nymphs starter key to genera – continued.

50 Key 2 – Nymphs starter key to genera – continued.

Key III. Nymphs: key to species of *Baetis*

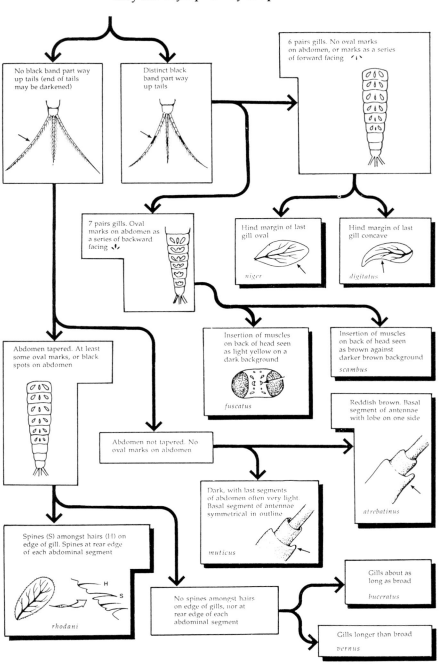

52 Key 3 – Nymphs: key to common species of *Baëtis*

EPHEMEROPTERA: KEY TO THE FAMILIES (NYMPHS)

1	Body and head flat; eyes positioned dorsally on head; gills consisting of plates and bunch of filaments (Fig 53A)	2
–	Body and head cylindrical; eyes laterally on head; gills of other shape (Fig 53C)	3
2	Gills on abdominal segments small; shorter than length of segments; head triangular (Fig 53A)	*Oligoneuriidae*
–	Gills longer than abdominal segments; head rounded or rectangular (Fig 53B)	*Heptageniidae*
3	Inner border of case of fore wings fused with mesonotum: not more than 4 pairs of gills visible (Fig 55K)	4
–	Case of forewings not fused with mesonotum; 6–7 pairs of gills visible (Fig 54G)	5
4	Four pairs of gills visible (Fig 55K)	*Ephemerellidae*
–	except for small 1st gill pair, gills are under cover (Fig 53C)	*Caenidae*
5	All gills feathery: branched and borders covered thickly with hairs (Fig 54G)	6
–	Gills not covered with hairs at their circumference (Fig 55L)	9
6	Manibular tusks are elongated and well visible: gills carried dorsally (Fig 54H)	7
–	no elongated manibular tusks: gills laterally (Fig 54G)	*Potamanthidae*
7	Manibular tusks with 6–8 teeth, curved upwards and flat in cross section (Fig 54H)	*–Palingeniidae*
–	Manibular tusks without teeth; not curved upwards; cylindrical in cross section (Fig 54E)	8
8	Manibular tusks curved inwards (Fig 54F)	*–Polymitarcydae*
–	Manibular tusks curved outwards (Fig 54E)	*Ephemeridae*
9	Gills filamentous, branched; caudal filaments longer than body; hairs on both sides at caudal filaments (Fig 55L)	*Leptophlebiidae*
–	Gills plate like, not branched; caudal filaments subequal or shorter; hairs only on the inner side of cerci (tails) (Fig 55J)	10
10	Antenna more than twice as long as width of head capsule; hind corners of abdominal segments blunt (Fig 55J)	*Baëtidae*
–	Antenna less than twice as long as width of head capsule; hind corners of abdominal segments form sharp points (Fig 53D)	11
11	Gill plates all single; lateral elongation of 9th abdominal segment; shorter than half of 10th segment	*Metamoniidae*
–	At least first two pairs of gills consisting of 2 plates; lateral elongation of 9th abdominal segment longer than half of 10th segment (Fig 53D)	*Siphlonuridae*

EPHEMEROPTERA: KEY TO THE FAMILIES (ADULTS)

Imagines (Spinners)

1	Wings transparent	2
–	Wings milky, turbid	9
2	Three equally long caudal filaments (tails)	3
–	Terminal (centre) filament missing or shorter than cerci (outer tails)	6
3	Short, free intercalary veins between most of the longitudinal veins on fore wings (Fig 56A)	*Ephemerellidae* *(See key to species)*
–	no such intercalaries	4
4	Eyes compound with two distinct lobes (large upper-small lower)	*Leptophlebiidae* *(See key to genera)*
–	Eyes compound with a single lobe	5
5	Fore wings with dark spots and veins: fore wings without any bright colour	*Ephemeridae* *(Ephemera* Spp:*)*
–	No such spots in forewings; venation yellow; costal area of fore wing yellow	*Potamanthidae* *(Potamanthus Luteus)*
6	Hind wings missing or of elongated (oval) shape, at least six times shorter than fore wings (Fig 56E)	*Baetidae* *(See key to genera)*
–	Hindwings triangular with rounded corners, not shorter than one fourth of the fore wing	7
7	For wings with two pairs of cubital intercalaries (Fig 56C)	*Heptageniidae* *(See key to genera)*
–	Cubital intercalaries in fore wing, forked or sinute (Fig 56B)	8
8	Tarsi (legs) with 2 identical sharply pointed claws	*Metamoniidae* *(Ameletus inopinatus)*
–	Tarsi with two claws, one pointed, one rounded	*Siphlonuridae* *(Siphlonurus* spp:*)*
9	Wings dark greyish brown, body bright yellow; length of body 35–40mm	*Palingeniidae* *(Palingenia Longicauda)*
–	Wings milky; body shorter than 30mm	10
10	Hind wings missing; all legs functional; length of body 3–8mm	*Caenidae)* *(Caënis* Spp:*)*
–	Hind wings present; most of the legs non-functional; length of body 15–25mm	11
11	Wing venation greatly reduced; apparantly only five longitudinal veins and no cross veins in the hind part of the fore wings (Fig 56D)	*Oligoneuriidae* *(Oligoneuria rhevana)*
–	Wing venation complete with numerous longitudinal and cross veins	*Polymitarcyidae* *(Ephoron virgo)*

HEPTAGINIIDAE: KEY TO THE GENERA

Nymphs

1	Two caudal filaments (tails)	*Epeorus*
–	Three caudal filaments (tails)	2
2	First and last pair of gills in contact ventrally (Fig 57A)	*Rhithrogena*
–	All gills laterally arranged (Fig 57B)	3
3	Pronotum laterally extended to a plate with pointed apical extension (Fig 57C)	*Ecdyonurus*
–	Pronotum not extended (Fig 57B)	4
4	On the maxilla (mouthparts) a single row of hairs (Fig 58.4)	*Heptagenia*
–	The surface of maxilla with scattered hairs (Fig 58.6)	5
5	Caudal filaments with short spines and long hairs (Fig 59B)	*Nixe*
–	Caudal filaments only with short spines (Fig 59A)	*Electrogena*

Imagines (Spinners)

1	Penis lobes outspread and boot shaped (Fig 60A and B)	2
–	Penis-lobes not so	3
2	Between head and thorax a neck is easily recognisable	*Epeorus*
–	Head and thorax in close contact at the outer surface	*Ecdyonurus*
3	Fore tarsus of male imago different from mid and hind tarsi	*Rhithrogena*
–	All tarsi similar in male	4
4	Penis lobes divergent, dorso–apically with pointed corners (Fig 60D)	*Heptagenia*
–	Penis lobes with rounded edges	5
5	Penis lobes contiguous, egg-shaped (Fig 60F)	*Electrogena*
–	Penis lobes latero apically with concave borders (Fig 60E)	*Nixe*

BAETIDAE: KEY TO THE GENERA

Imagines

1	Hind wing absent	2
–	Hind wing present	3
2	Body shorter than 6mm, 1st segment of hind tarsus twice the length of second segment	*Procloeon*
–	Body longer than 8mm, 1st segment of hind tarsus three times the length of second segment	*Cloeon*
3	Fore wings with paired intercalaries (See Fig 28A)	*Baëtis*
–	Fore wings with single intercalaries (See Fig 28B)	4
4	Apex of hind wing rounded (See Fig 13)	*Pseudocentroptilum pennulatum*
–	Apex of hind wing pointed (See Fig 14)	*Centroptilum luteolum*

Nymph

1	Gills simple	2
–	Gills of two platelets	4
2	Abdominal segment 8 with 4–9 teeth laterally; caudal filaments (tails) with black broad band	*Procloeon*
–	Without these characters	3
3	Gills apically rounded	*Baëtis*
–	Gills apically pointed	*Centroptilum luteolum*
4	Caudal filaments with hairs much longer than the individual segments of cerci	*Pseudocentroptilum pennulatum*
–	Caudal filaments with short hairs	*Cloeon*

EPHEMERELLIDAE: KEY TO THE SPECIES

Nymphs

1	Abdomen shorter than head and thorax; legs heavily covered with hairs (Fig 61D)	*E. major*
–	none of these characters present	2
2	Sternites (lower abdomen) with four black stripes and 2 points (Fig 62)	*E. notata*
–	sternites without this pattern	3
3	Hind margin of tergites (upper abdomen) with 2 proturberances; caudal filaments with dark and light striation; hind margin of last tergite triangular (Fig 61B)	*E. ignita*
–	Proturberances and stripes lacking; hind margin of last tergite round (Fig 61C)	*E. mucronata*

Imagines (Spinners)

1	Sternites with four black stripes and 2 points; (Fig 62D) and penis lobes with big V (Fig 63B)	*E. notata*
–	without this pattern	2
2	Caudal (tails) filaments uniformly coloured and penis lobes closed (Fig 63D)	*E. major*
–	Caudal filaments with dark and light segments	3
3	Thorax and abdomen sherry to dark orange penis lobes with small V (Fig 63A)	*E. ignita*
4	Thorax and abdomen dark brown to black and penis lobes long pointed and curved (Fig 63C)	*E. mucronata*

LEPTOPHLEBIIDAE: KEY TO THE GENERA

Imagines (Spinners)

1	Hind wing with costal process (Fig 64B)	2
–	Hind wing without costal process (Fig 64C)	4
2	Veins on wings black. Hind wing with large costal process (Fig 64D)	
	[2nd and 3rd segments of claspers under developed; penes apically pointed, tubulaire] (Fig 65A)	*Choroterpes*
–	Veins lighter. Hind wing with stepped costal process (Fig 64E)	
	[2nd and 3rd segments of claspers well developed; penes apically with finger like process] (Fig 65B)	3
3	Abdominal segments 2–7 translucent white;[the first of claspers on the inner side smooth]	*Habrophlebia*
–	All abdominal segments black or dark brown; [basal segment of claspers with finger like process (Fig 65C) and hind wing with costal process in centre (Fig 64A)	*Habroleptoides*
4	Cu^2 in fore wing at base lies mid-way between Cu^1 and A^1 (Fig 23)	*Leptophlebia*
–	Cu^2 in fore wing at base nearer to A^1 then to Cu^2 (Fig 23)	*Paraleptophlebia*

Nymphs

1	Tracheal gills form a tuft with several branches (Fig 66E)	*Habrophlebia*
–	Tracheal gills different	2
2	Gills 2–7 with 2 platelet like branches (Fig 66A)	3
–	Gills 2–7 with 2 filaments (Fig 66D)	4
3	Gills develop apically into 1 thin branch; first gill bifid (Fig 66 A or B)	*Leptophlebia*
–	Gills develop apically in 3 branches; the medial long and thin, the lateral ones broad and short; first gill simple (Fig 66C)	*Choroterpes*
4	Head hypognath; the hypopharinx laterally rounded process (Fig 67H)	*Paraleptophlebia*
–	Head prognath; hypopharynx laterally with pointed process (Fig 67G)	*Habroleptoides*

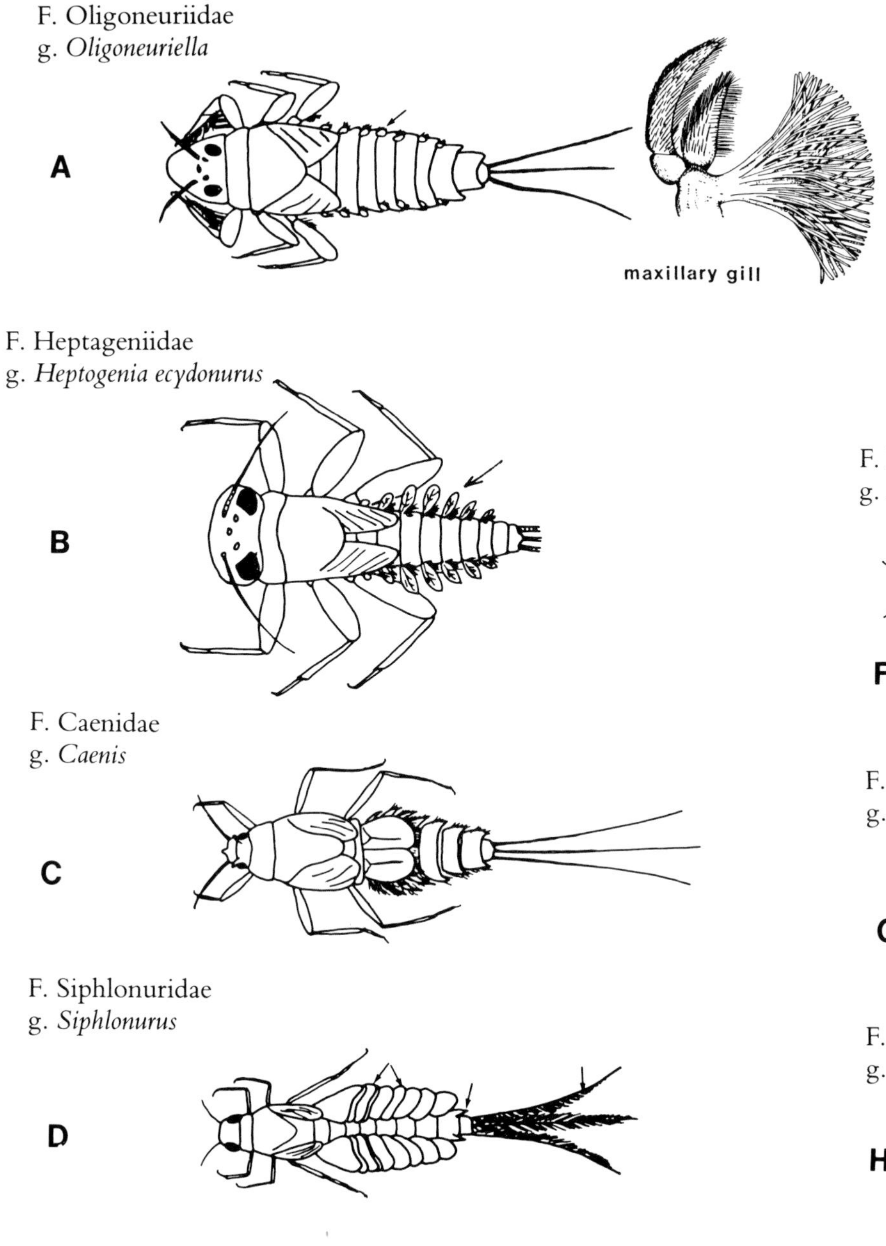

Manibular tusks

F. Ephemeridae
g. Ephemera

E

Gills

F. Polymitarcidae
g. *Ephoron*

F

gills

F. Potamanthidae
g. *Potamanthus*

G

F. Palingeniidae
g. *Palingenia*

H

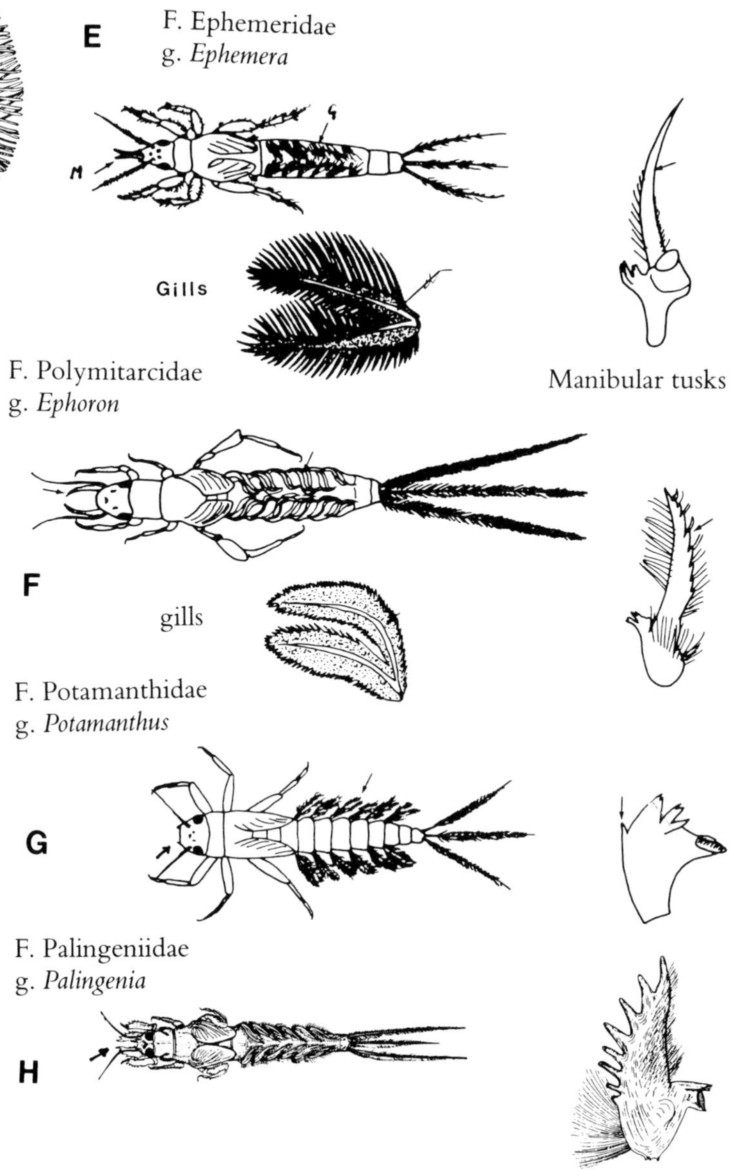

54 Key for the families of the Ephemeroptera (nymphs)

maxillary gill

F. Oligoneuriidae
g. *Oligoneuriella*

A

F. Heptagenidae
g. *Heptogenia eydonurus*

B

F. Caenidae
g. *Caenis*

C

F. Siphlonuridae
g. *Siphlonurus*

D

53 Key for the families of the Ephemeroptera (nymphs)

F. Baetidae
g. *Baetis*

J

F. Ephemerellidae
g. *Ephemerella*

K

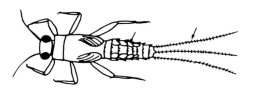

gills

F. Leptophlebiidae
g. *Leptophlebia*

L

55 Key for the families of the Ephemeroptera (nymphs)

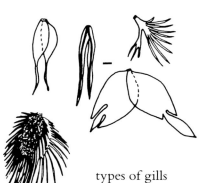

types of gills

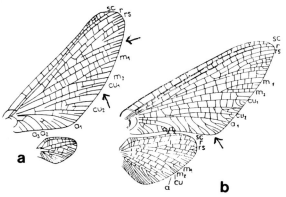

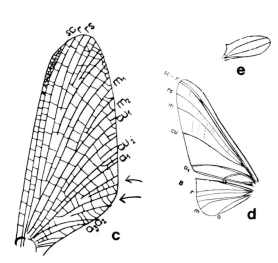

56 Key for the families of the Ephemeroptera (imagines), (a)
Ephemerella ignita, (b) *Siphlonurus croaticus*, (c) *Heptageniidae*
Spp., (d) *Oligonenriidae rhenana*, (e) *Baëtis* Spp. (hindwing)

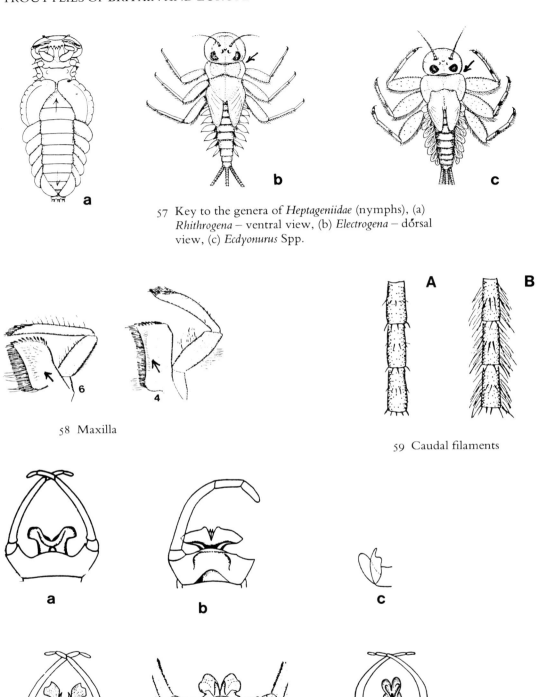

57 Key to the genera of *Heptageniidae* (nymphs), (a) *Rhithrogena* – ventral view, (b) *Electrogena* – dorsal view, (c) *Ecdyonurus* Spp.

58 Maxilla

59 Caudal filaments

60 Key to the genera of Heptageniidae (imagines), (a) *Epeorus* Sp., (b) *Ecdyonurus* Sp., (c) *Rhithrogena* claws. (d) *Heptagenia* Sp., (e) *Nixe* Sp., (f) *Electrogena*

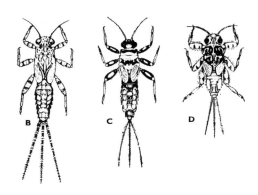

62 *Sternites,* (d) *abdomen E. notato* ventral, (c) abdomen
   E. notata lateral

d **c**

a **b**

61 Key to the species of *Ephemerellidae* (nymphs),
   (b) *E. ignita,* (c) *E. mucronata,* (d) *E. major*

c **d**

63 Key to the species of *Ephemerellidae* (imagines)
   Penes (a) *E. ignita,* (b) *E. notata,* (c) *E. mucronata,*
   (d) *E. major*

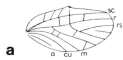

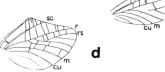

64 Key to the genera of *Leptophlebidae* (imagines)
   Hindwings (a) *Habroleptoides* Spp., (b)
   Paraleptophlebia Spp., (c) *Leptophlebia* Spp., (d)
   Chorotherpes picteti, (c) *Habrophlebia fusca*

65 Penes (a) *Chorotherpes picteti,* (b) Habrophlebia Spp.,
   (c) *Habroleptoides* Spp.

a **b** **c**

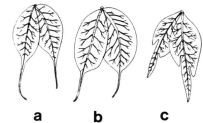

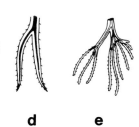

a **b** **c** **d** **e**

66 Key to the genera of *Leptophlebidae*
   Gills (a) *Leptophlebia marginata* (b) *Leptophlebia
   vespertina* (c) *Chorotherpes picteti* (d) *Paraleptophlebia* or
   Habroleptoides Spp., (e) *Habrophlebia* Spp.

67 Hypopharynx (g) *Habroleptoides* Spp., (h)
   Paraleptphlebia Spp.

g **h**

45

CHAPTER 5

THE UPWINGED FLIES NYMPHS AND ADULTS
(Continued)

DETAILED DESCRIPTIONS – DISTRIBUTION – FISHING INFORMATION – AND ARTIFICIALS TO REPRESENT THEM

The following detailed descriptions of the Upwinged flies include most of the common and widespread species as well as some rather localised species to be found in the British Isles and Europe. This list will enable the budding angler/entomoligist to identify most of the Upwinged flies to be observed while at the waterside. However, it must be pointed out that some of these species are of little value to the fly fisher, while others are so similar to each other that the same artificial will suffice. At the start of each description, the number of tails and type of hindwing is listed as this information will at least narrow the field down to the genera. These I have also grouped in sections to help in quick identification.

When referring to these descriptions the following points should be taken into account. The body colour of these Upwinged flies varies between the top (dorsum) and the underbody (venter) which tends to be of a paler colouration, but for identification purposes the colours given are in most cases those as seen from a side view as in the majority of the photographs. It must be emphasised that most colours given are those as seen on specimens that I have myself examined. Apart from the fact that the colours of these flies vary quite considerably even among the individual species, many of us describe colours as we see them in different ways, and therefore my interpretation of these colours may not be in strict accordance with other authorities. In some cases the colour of the eyes of the males can assist in identification, but as the true colour may not be apparent immediately after hatching or transposition it is advisable to allow a little time to elapse before your examination. It should also be noted that in many cases the rear edge of the body (abdomen) segments are of a lighter shade or even a different colour, so on those species where this is particularly apparent they will be referred to in the text as 'ringing' or 'joinings'. Also note the following symbols to be seen in the descriptions ♂ denotes male, ♀ denotes female.

Finally it should also be noted that while the size of these Upwinged flies can assist in identification this factor should not be taken too literally as some species particularly some of the smaller species do tend to vary quite considerably. The following size key should be helpful and these illustrations in the appropriate size will also be found in the margins to denote the approximate size of each species described in the detailed descriptions. The size of these upwinged flies is determined by the body length measured from the front of the head to the last segment of the body where the tails commence.

46

Group 1. Very large

Group 2. Large

Group 3. Medium large

Group 4. Medium

Group 5. Small

Group 6. Very small

68 Size key. The size of these upwinged flies is determined by the body length measured from the front of the head to the last segment of the body where the tails commence

In this chapter underneath the description of each dun and spinner will be found a sub-heading titled artificials. Here in order to assist the fly fisher as much as possible I have recommended an artificial or artificials as close as possible to match the natural. In a few cases there are no known specific artificials so I have suggested the closest general pattern I think should be applicable. In other cases particularly with the more common and widespread species there are often a plethora of patterns to represent them and it would be all but impossible or certainly impractical to list all of them. In most cases therefore I have restricted the list of suggested artificials to four or five and at least one of these is a general old established pattern which may be purchased from most large tackle shops that stock fly fishing equipment and materials. It will be noted that all the patterns recommended are dry flies, as wet patterns to represent these Upwinged flies do not come within the scope of this volume.

Artificial Patterns to Represent the Nymphs
It will also be apparent that I have not included any recommendations for artificials to represent all the different species of nymphs listed as from a practical fishing view point there is little to be achieved from having an exact copy of any of the nymphs, apart possibly from the Mayfly. Most nymphs have a similar silhouette and tend to be either a transluscent olive colour or dark brown and only vary from species to species in size. It is therefore usually only necessary to carry a selection in these two colours in different sizes. I would suggest my own P.V.C. nymph to represent the lighter coloured nymphs, or the Blue Darter an excellent New Zealand pattern by Norman Marsh, and Sawyer's Pheasant Tail nymph to represent the darker one. All these are weighted patterns. For trout feeding on the ascending or hatching nymph in the surface a Gold Ribbed Hare's Ear (G.R.H.E.) lightly weighted or unweighted is an excellent pattern, while my own Suspender Hatching nymph is a good alternative. To represent the large nymphs of the Ephemera species (Mayflies) Richard Walker's Mayfly nymph pattern is the best I know. While all the above patterns may be used with equal confidence both in rivers and stillwaters, three good patterns for stillwater only are as follows. For general lake or reservoir fishing the two patterns the Green or Brown nymphs perfected by the late David Collyer are highly recommended while to ambush those trout patrolling the margins of many stillwaters an excellent choice would be Conrad Voss Bark's nymph as this is a very slow sinker.

DETAILED DESCRIPTIONS OF SPECIES TO BE FOUND IN THE BRITISH ISLES AND ALSO IN EUROPE.

SECTION 1:
UPWINGED FLIES WITH 3 TAILS AND LARGE HINDWINGS
THE MAYFLY (GREENDRAKE)

Length of body: ♂ 15–20mm, ♀ 17–25mm
Tails of imago: ♂ 35–40mm, ♀ 18–27mm

The Mayfly Nymph. (Ephemera danica. E.vulgata. E.lineata & E.Glaucops.) (Plate 3, 20)

The nymphs of the four different species of Mayflies listed above are all bottom burrowers, adult specimens being over an inch long, having specially shaped gill filaments along the body. The head is narrow and pointed, and is provided with a pair of long mandibles which are used for excavating. They usually burrow into the silt or gravel of the river or lake bed. Their gill plates, which are very active, provide a constant flow of water past the body of the nymph in its burrow, thus supplying the necessary oxygen; perhaps this flow also carries minute particles of food. The nymphs emerge on the surface in open water and hatches are concentrated over a two to three week period during May or early June. A common and widespread genera, hatches are often on a colossal scale, but unfortunately both in Britain and Europe they have all but disappeared from some waters in recent years due to various forms of pollution. E.danica the most common of the four species is found in fairly fast flowing rivers and streams and also occasionally in stillwater. Plate 22 (169 & 170). E.vulgata which is less common than danica seems to have a preference for slower flowing rivers and small ponds. Plate 23, (181 & 182). E.lineata is now extremely rare in the U.K. although still quite common throughout Europe mainly in small rivers and streams. Plate 9 & 10, (72 & 73), E.glaucops is probably the least common of the four species and has not been recorded from the U.K. It is found in both rivers and lakes but only in a few areas in Europe, and tends to be a little smaller than the other three species. It has always been generally believed that Mayflies take two years to mature, but fairly recent evidence seems to throw some doubt on this as in 1958 Pleskot undertook research on E.danica and published a statement to the effect that there was a generation each year. Peart (1916–19) appears to be alone among British authorities in believing in a one-year cycle. All other authorities still seem convinced it is a two year cycle. From my own research I strongly favour one generation every two years, but I do believe under certain circumstances that they may be capable of reproducing in one year.

The Mayfly Dun. (Plate 22, 169 & 170)

While this is the largest British Upwinged fly there is one other species that is larger but this only occures in one area in Europe. Probably more has been written on this particular fly than all the other Upwinged species put together, so even the merest novice fly fisherman must be familiar with this most handsome and distinctive looking insect. They have three tails and large upright hindwings with a costal projection, their bodies are cream coloured with brownish markings and their mainwings are heavily veined and a blue grey colour with black markings and a distinct greenish tinge. When the newly hatched duns are floating along on

1. *E. danica*
2. *E. vulgata*
3. *E. lineata*
4. *E. glaucops*

69 Showing difference between constant black
    markings on dorsal segments of abdomens of
    Mayflies

the surface on sunny days these wings seem to give off a golden glow, which no doubt accounts for the extraordinary success of my Poly May Dun pattern with its pale golden wings. The difference between the four species is very slight although E. vulgata is a little darker than the others.

For positive identification of these species the only certain way is to refer to the sketches above (Fig. 69) of the markings of the body segments. Mayflies are abundant and common in many rivers on the continent, the British Isles and also Ireland, and while they are quite common on many continental stillwaters, only occur in comparatively few lakes in England and Scotland, although they are very prolific of many Irish loughs. They have a comparatively short season, usually lasting about two weeks, in either late May or early June. Hatches tend to build up to a crescendo during this period, culminating usually in two or three days of really prolific hatches at the end of the fourteen days, after which they rapidly thin out, during this time the emergence normally commences about midday, often continuing till early evening. However, on some occasions I have experienced a delay in the main hatch until four or five o'clock.

ARTIFICIALS: Grey Wulff – Hackle Point (Collyer) – Mayfly (Walker) – Poly May Dun (Goddard) and Assassine.

The Mayfly Spinner or Spent gnat. (Plate 22, 171 & 172)
These are the popular names given to the female spinner of the Mayfly as she lies dying on the surface after layer her eggs. The body of this spinner is a pale cream colour, and the wings, although transparent, have a distinct bluish tint. While ovipositing, the female spinner will often alight on the water for short periods and at this stage she is referred to as a Grey Drake, the artificial pattern of which is reputed to be particularly good at this period. The male spinners of the Mayfly are also worthy of mention as they often fall on to the water after mating. In appearance they have dark legs and thorax, with a transluscent creamy-white body, and the three rear segments of the body are brown. The transparent wings

49

are tinged quite distinctly with dark patches. A fall of Mayfly spinners is always eagerly awaited by fly-fishermen, as the trout seem to prefer the spinner to the dun and take them readily. Also, of course, it is much easier to deceive the fish with an artificial pattern representing the spinner. A useful indication of whether or not there is likely to be a fall of spinners in the evening can often be determined by looking for swarms of the male spinners. These normally form in the vicinity of trees or bushes along the banks in the late afternoon or early evening, and if the swarms are absent or sparse by mid-evening it is doubtful whether any appreciable fall will occur. It is interesting that at times even when there are huge swarms of males present no fall occurs and they gradually disperse. The reason for this is due to the fact that the males are polygamous and will mate with fresh females over several days before they die. The females on the other hand only mate once and die. Therefore, if hatches are sparce or absent for two or three days, there are few, if any females available for the swarms of males to mate with. The males of all four species are often considerably smaller than the females.

ARTIFICIALS: Deerstalker (Patterson) – Poly-May (Goddard) or Hackle Point Mayfly (Collyer).

DISTRIBUTION: E.Danical – all areas, E.vulgata – all areas except No's 4, 17, 19 and probably 5 and 6, E.Lineata – all areas except No's 1, 2, 3, 4, 17, 18, 19, 20 and 22, E.Glaucops – found in areas 1, 3, 7, 8, 9, 10 and 13.

THE PURPLE DUN (3 Tails & Large Hindwings)
Length of body: ♂ & ♀ 6–8mm
Tails of imago: ♂ 10–12mm, ♀ 6–8mm

Purple Nymph (Paraleptophlebia cincta)
This nymph which is very similar in appearance to the Turkey Brown has a preference for small fast-flowing streams or larger medium-paced rivers of an alkaline nature, and is a laboured swimmer with a liking for the more abundant weed. It is not a common species, being rather localised, and hatches are usually sparse. Although recorded from southern England, it is comparatively rare. However, it is often seen in Wales and the West Country and also parts of northern England, as well as in many European countries where sometimes hatches of a more prolific nature do occur. The adults emerge from May to August, mostly during the day.

The Purple Dun
This is a medium-sized dun. The body is dark brown with a purple tinge, and the wings are blackish grey. Many anglers undoubtedly mistake the Purple dun for a large Iron Blue, as superficially they are very similar, but careful examination will show that the former has three tails and large narrow upright hindwings without costal projection (Fig. 22) as opposed to the two tails and small oval spurred hindwings of the latter. The Purple dun seems to have a preference for fast flowing, highly oxygenated water, and is localised in distribution. They are to be seen on the wing during most of the summer.

ARTIFICIALS: No known pattern but an Iron Blue on a size 14 hook should suffice.

The Purple Spinner

This female spinner closely resembles that of the Turkey Brown, and although it is somewhat smaller, the only sure means of identification is by the venation of the clear wings. The colour of the body is brownish with a purple tinge. The male has clear wings and a translucent white body and is like a large Jenny spinner, but with three tails. These spinners swarm during the day.

ARTIFICIALS: None known. Would suggest a Pheasant Tail spinner. Paraleptophlebia Werneri is a very similar species but chiefly found in calcerous streams in heavy weed. The wings of the duns are pale grey.

DISTRIBUTION: P.Cincta – areas 3, 8, 9, 10, 11, 13, 14, 15, 16, 17, 18, 19, 20, 22 and 23. P.Werneri – areas 4, 9, 10, 11, 13, 14, 15, 16, 18 and 23.

THE TURKEY BROWN (3 Tails & Large Hingwings)
Length of body: ♂ & ♀ 9–12mm
Tails of imago: ♂ 12–15mm, ♀ 9–12mm

Turkey Brown Nymph (Paraleptophlebia submarginata)

A rather uncommon species of nymph, confined to rather local areas in Europe and in southern and northern England. Found mainly in slow-paced rivers and streams, the nymph is a laboured swimmer, generally frequenting the thicker weed beds or debris on the bottom. The adults appear fairly early in the year, in May and June. They hatch during the day very sparsely, and it is rare to see more than one or two on the water at any time.

The Turkey Brown Dun. Plate 24 (189)

This medium large species with its fawn-coloured mottled wings, with a distinct pale area in the centre, dark brown body and three tails, narrow upright hindwings without a costal projection (see Fig 21), it is quite a distinctive dun of a similar size or even slightly larger than the B.W.O. Its season is from mid May to mid June. Hatches are very sparse, and it is unusual to see more than one or two of these duns on the water at the same time. The Turkey Brown is believed to be disliked by the fish, but it seems more likely that this is due to its scarcity rather than to its taste. In any case it is of little importance as an angling fly.

ARTIFICIALS: No specific patterns but an August Dun should suffice.

The Turkey Brown Spinner. Plate 24 (190)

Like the dun, the scarcity of this spinner makes it of little importance to the fisherman, and in any case it is so similar to the Sherry spinner that there is difficulty in distinguishing one from the other. The body colour of the female usually has more brown in it than that of the Sherry, but apart from this the only sure way of identification is by checking the hindwings and the venation of the forewings. The male spinner is a very beautiful port wine colour. Swarming tends to occur in the morning in very small groups.

ARTIFICIALS: No known imitation. Would suggest a Sherry or Pheasant Tail spinner.

DISTRIBUTION: All areas except No's 1, 17, 20, 22 and 23.

THE CLARET DUN (3 Tails & Large Hindwings)

Length of Body: ♂ & ♀ 8–12mm
Tails of imago: ♂ 12–16mm, ♀ 10–12mm

The Claret Nymp (Leptophlebia vespertina)

The nymph of this fly which is very similar to P. Cincta and P. Submarginata is not very common and is of far more interest to the lake fisherman than to the river angler. It is found in stillwater as well as in small stony streams or rivers of a peaty or acid nature, and tends to be rather localised. This nymph is one of the laboured swimmers and lives in the stones or moss on the lake or river bed. The adult appears in May and June, although more in the latter than in the former. It is fairly widely distributed throughout the British Isles as well as Europe.

Ttake nymph is reddish brown in colour, and J.R. Harris suggests that in Ireland, where this species is common, its colour may be influenced by its location, which is usually confined to the peaty areas of many of the limestone lakes. The nymph is nearly invisible against wet peat, whereas its dark body would show up clearly against the grey-green limestone and would be easy prey for any predator. They are most likely to be found in the silt, mud or stones on the bottom and usually in shallower water. A Pheasant Tail nymph, either weighted or unweighted, depending on whether it is fished near the bottom to copy the nymph in its natural environment or in the surface film to imitate the transformation from nymph to adult, is a good representation. The nymphs emerge at the surface or via stones or water weeds.

The Claret Dun. Plate 20 (157)

I first encountered these medium large duns several years ago on a small lake, when they were hatching out in fair quantities, and I must admit that to start with I was a little puzzled as to their identity. On the wing they had the appearance of a Large Iron Blue, but as I realised these had never been reported from stillwater I was doubtful. The mystery was solved as soon as I had caught one, when I recognised it as a Claret from descriptions I had read of it. Despite its common name the colour of the dun can hardly be described as claret, for the body is a very dark brown, although in certain light conditions it does have a slight claret tinge.

Identification of this dun is fairly simple, as the combination of three tails and upright hindwings, without a costal projection (spur) (see Fig 17), only occurs in a few other species. Apart from the above physical features the Claret dun can be recognised by its dark grey forewings and the contrasting colour of the hindwings which are of a much paler buff colour. Hatches of the adult winged fly are often spasmodic and usually take place during the middle part of the day. They are to be seen from mid May until early July. It is known that they prefer water of an acid or peaty nature, which probably accounts for their abundance in Ireland. They are also to be found on many peaty tarns in the North. I have also encountered them on several waters in Europe, the Southern Counties and West Country. I was recently fortunate to visit a small water in the south-west where these duns are regularly observed, and on this occasion at least the trout seemed to prefer them to Pond Olive duns that were hatching at the same time.

ARTIFICIALS: Claret Dun (Harris), Kite's Imperial or a Mallard and Claret on stillwater.

The Claret Spinner. Plate 20 (158 & 159).

The female spinners will often be in evidence in considerable numbers usually in the early evening. Both sexes have a reddish-brown body with a distinct claret tinge, their wings (see Fig 41) are transparent with light brown venation, and their three tails are pale brown lightly ringed with black. These spinners often swarm in quite large numbers close to water up to 9ft in height usually in the late afternoons or evenings. The females dip over the water surface and release their eggs in batches.

ARTIFICIALS: Claret spinner (Harris) or a Pheasant Tail spinner.
DISTRIBUTION: All areas except Nos 3–7, 12 and 13.

THE SEPIA DUN (3 Tails & Large Hindwings)
Length of body: ♂ & ♀ 9–12mm
Tails of imago: ♂ 12–16mm, ♀ 10–12mm

The Sepia Nymph (Leptophlebia Marginata). Plate 25 (193)

Probably the easiest nymph of all to recognise. They are deep sepia brown, have very prominent gill filaments down either side of their bodies and three long tails and these like the tails of the adults are spread very wide apart. They are also included in the group designated laboured swimmers; they are heavily built and slightly flattened in appearance. As far as I have been able to ascertain they are seldom to be found in the shallower margins of lakes in any quantity until the first winged adults are seen in early April. As the period of peak emergence approaches, many of the nymphs move into very shallow water, and most of them change to the winged stage via emergent vegetation or in some cases by crawling up the bank. However, as I have also observed quite good hatches in open water, often in the deeper areas, it would seem that the location and method of emergence varies. They are very similar in shape and colour to the Claret nymph but a little larger and for those anglers who may be interested in identification, the leaf-shaped gill filaments along each size of their bodies are pointed in the Claret and rounded in the Sepia. They are fairly common and widespread throughout Europe and are most likely to be observed in ponds, lakes and slow flowing rivers.

The Sepia Dun. Plate 21 (165 & 166).

This is very similar in appearance though slightly larger than the Claret dun and is probably a little less common. It is an important fly to the stillwater fisherman in areas where it is found. This is throughout Europe and mainly in the south of England, the middle North and parts of Scotland. So far as I am aware it has not been reported from Ireland. It is a most handsome fly and with its very dark sepia body and dark wings (see Fig 42), is fairly easy to identify. The male is usually much darker than the female and in common with the Claret dun, the upright hindwings lack a costal projection, but in this species the hindwings are the same colour as the forewings. A further interesting feature of this species are the three tails which are spread very wide apart. As far as the stillwater angler is concerned they are the first of the Upwinged flies to appear, and the adults are on the wing from early April until May. Hatches are usually confined to the middle of the day and are seldom on a large scale.

ARTIFICIALS: The Sepia Dun (Kite)

The Sepia Spinner. Plate 21 (167 & 168)

Both male and female spinners are very similar in appearance and also similar to the Claret Spinner. As with most spinners of interest to the angler, only the females are of importance as the males are seldom found on the water. The female spinner of this species can be distinguished from the Claret fairly easily as its tails are very dark brown and it has a distinct smoky black patch along the leading edge of its semi-transparent wings. They form swarms in groups of 20 to 100 individual males at a height of 3 to 10 metres above ground up to about 50 metres from the waters edge.

ARTIFICIALS: No known pattern. A Pheasant Tail Spinner should suffice.
DISTRIBUTION: All areas except No's 1, 3, 5, 6, 7, 12, 17 and probably 23

THE BLUE WINGED OLIVE (3 Tails & Large Hindwings)

Length of body: ♂ & ♀ 7–11mm
Tails of imago: ♂ 8–12mm, ♀ 7–9mm

Blue Winged Olive Nymph (Ephemerella ignita). Plate 1 (8)

This is probably our most common species, and it occurs in abundance in nearly all parts of these islands, including Ireland and Scotland and most of Europe. The nymph is one of the Moss Creepers and lives below the faster stretches of water in the mass of debris on the bottom. It is found in small brooks as well as large rivers, in the lowlands as well as the highlands, and in many big lakes. It has also been recorded in rivers at altitudes of over 1000 metres but in these lower temperatures emergence is often as late as August. It seems equally at home in both acid and alkaline water. The adult fly is on record as having been seen in every month of the year, but first appears *en masse* about mid June, and in some summers hatches occur daily until October, and even later in a mild autumn on some waters. Hatches may be mainly confined to late evening, just as dusk approaches. It is interesting to note that E.ignita spends some months in the egg, and grows rapidly after hatching in the middle of the summer. According to Dr Macan the time spent in the egg is about ten months; other sources of information suggest a little less than this. The nymphs hatch in open water on the surface.

The Blue Winged Olive Dun. Plate 23 (177 & 178)

Without a doubt this medium large dun is one of the most common, widespread and well known of all our Upwinged duns. With its large bluish wings, three tails, upright hindwings with a costal projection (see Fig 16) and olive-coloured body, it is probably the easiest of all our flies to recognise. The male which has dark red eyes is considerably darker than the female and often has a very brownish-olive body. In the late autumn the body colour of both is often more of a rusty-brown colour than olive. This species is found all over the British Isles in nearly all types of flowing water and also in many big lakes, although until recently this was not generally recognised as a lake fly. In latter years it has been positively identified by qualified observers on several bodies of stillwater. In the summer of 1965 I personally observed large hatches of this fly on two widely separated lochs in Scotland. I therefore suspect that it may be present in many stillwaters where it has not been identified. In the early part of its season, hatches are frequently confined to the evenings only, often just as dusk approaches. Later on in August, when the days begin to shorten, hatches will often begin in the late afternoon or early evening, and on several occasions in recent years I have observed quite good hatches of this fly shortly after midday. It is a large and robust fly and with experience the angler can soon learn to identify it from a fair distance, as it hatches and floats on the surface. The reason for this is that the large forewings of this fly slope back slightly over the body, much more so than the wings of any other Upwinged flies.

ARTIFICIALS: B.W.O. Dun (Jacques), B.W.O. Dun (Nice), B.W.O. Dun (Walker), Orange Quill or Cul de Canard (Petitjean) in the dark brown colour.

The Sherry Spinner. Plate 23 (179 & 180)

Although the colour range of these female spinners, even of individuals within the same swarm, varies from olive-brown to sherry-red to a distinct lobster-red, the most common shade is the sherry-colour, hence the popular name. They have clear transparent wings (see Fig 40), with pale brown veins and small green brown eyes. The females are often to be seen in vast swarms flying upstream in the centre of the river in the late evening, preparatory to egg-laying. As a matter of interest, it should be mentioned here that several leading authorities have always maintained that the female spinner carried her egg ball cupped under her tails, which she curls under for this purpose. David Jacques, the late well-known angler/entomolist, recently carried out a study on this subject, and his findings confirmed the opinion made several years earlier by the late Martin E. Mosely, whose views were not entirely accepted. The function of the tail in the extrusion process is as follows. When the egg ball is extruded from the vent of the female, the tail presses the egg ball into the abdomen at a position between the ultimate and penultimate segments, after which they return to their original position – i.e. in a straight line to the rear – and the insect flies on her way with the egg ball held in position by the sticky nature of the egg mass. Retention is probably assisted by a pair of lobes which appear to be grasping, somewhat inadequately, the sides of the ball. The insect uses considerable force when she presses the egg ball into her abdomen, making a permanent dent in the body, which remains a prominent feature of her anatomy for the rest of her short life, even after the eggs are released on the surface. A photograph of a Sherry spinner with the egg ball in position and tails normally outstretched appears on Plate 26 (202) which proves the point beyond reasonable doubt. It is worth mentioning that male spinners of the B.W.O. are almost unique in that when they fall on the water in sufficient quantities, as they sometimes do, they arouse as much interest in the fish as do the females. On those occasions when I have observed this happen they have fallen prior to the spent females, and I must confess that I am uncertain if this phenomenon is frequent or infrequent; nor, indeed, is it certain why it happens. Nevertheless when it does, it is of no little importance to the angler, and being similar to the spent female, the same artificial pattern will do for both. The male spinner has a dark to rich red brown body, clear transparent wings with pale brown veins and bright red eyes. As dusk approaches an orange quill is often very effective as the trout seem to accept it well when both duns and spinners are on the surface.

ARTIFICIALS: Sherry Spinner (Lunn), Pheasant Tail Spinner or Orange Quill.

DISTRIBUTION: Very common and widespread likely to be found in all areas.

THE YELLOW EVENING DUN (3 Tails & Large Hindwings)
Length of Body: ♂ & ♀ 9–11mm
Tails of imago: ♂ 8–12mm, ♀ 7–9mm

Yellow Evening Nymph (Ephemerella notata)
This is a rather lethargic type of nymph of the group termed moss creepers, and lives in the mosses, stones or debris on the bottom of the river with a distinct preference for water below the more swift-flowing stretches. It is one of the less common species and is confined to localised areas. It occurs in parts of Ireland, Central Wales, NW England and the southern parts of Devon and some areas in central Europe. Specimens were taken occasionally in the Home Counties before the second World War, but it now seems practically non-existent in these areas. The adult emerges in May and June, and hatches generally occur late in the evening.

The Yellow Evening Dun. Plate 23 (183)
This medium large species is very similar in appearance and colour to the Yellow May dun; however, it can be readily identified as it has three tails and large upright hindwings with a costal projection, and is also smaller. Hatches usually occur in the late evening, and the adult winged fly is most commonly seen during May and June. It is a rather uncommon species, and is somewhat local in its distribution. According to recent reports, it is more scarce now than it was a few years ago. The female dun has pale green eyes pale yellowish grey wings with yellow veining and an orange yellow body. The male dun has amber-orange eyes with wings of pale grey with yellow veins and the body is orange yellow except for last three segments which are light amber. Both dun and spinner of both sexes have a clearly defined pattern of dots and dashes on the ventral (under) segments of their bodies (see Fig 30), and their tails are ringed dark brown.
ARTIFICIALS: A large Pale Watery or Yellow May Dun

The Yellow Evening Spinner. Plate 23 (184)
Both male and female spinner are very similar in appearance to the dun except for the wings which are transparent except for a strong yellowish tinge made by the veins along the leading edges. The spinners swarm in the evenings and lay their eggs by dipping onto the water surface.
ARTIFICIALS: Lunn's Yellow Boy, Hook 12–14
DISTRIBUTION: Uncommon and localised. Found in areas 6, 7, 9, 10, 14, 15, 17 and 19.

THE DITCH DUN (3 Tails & Large Hindwings)
Length of body: ♂ & ♀ 6–8mm
Tails of imago: ♂ 8–10mm, ♀ 8mm

The Ditch Dun Nymph (Habrophlebia fusca) Plate 2 (11)
As the name implies, this nymph is found mainly in small streams, ditches or silted up carriers with often only a slight flow of water. It is one of the laboured swimmers and appears quite at home in aquatic vegetation which is often so dense it all but chokes these small waters. The nymphs emerge via emergent vegetation from May to August but hatches are often sparse. They tend to be rather localised

in their distribution and although found in parts of England are not an important angling fly. On the Continent they may be of more importance as in some European countries they are sometimes to be encountered on the larger rivers. The tails of this nymph are spread well apart in a similar manner to that of the Sepia nymph.

The Ditch Dun. Plate 24 (185 & 186)

A rather uncommon species. The females have very dark greyish brown bodies ringed in a lighter colour greyish wings and three dark coloured tails, the males are similar except that their bodies are watery white with last three segments brown and they have dark red eyes. They are very similar in appearance to the more common Iron Blue but generally larger, they should not be confused as the Ditch dun has three tails whereas the Iron Blue has only two. Apart from this the Habrophlebia genera can always be positively identified by the unique shape of their hindwings (see Fig 15). In addition the forewings entirely lack the small intercalary veins which are a feature of all similar species.

ARTIFICIALS: Super Grizzly or a large Iron Blue.

The Ditch Spinner

The spinners of this genera are of very doubtful value to the fly fisherman as the females tend to oviposit their eggs on partially submerged stones or weeds close to the banks, and are therefore rarely available to trout feeding in the more open stretches of rivers. In both sexes the wings are fairly clear and lightly veined brown, their bodies are very dark brown ringed creamy brown and the eyes of the males vary from dark to orange red. Little is known about the swarming habits of these flies.

ARTIFICIALS: A Pheasant Tail Spinner in the appropriate size.

DISTRIBUTION: H.fusca found in all areas except No's 6, 12, 17, 18, 20, 22 and 23.

THE CAËNIS (3 Tails & No Hindwings)

Length of body: ♂ & ♀ 3–5mm
Tails of imago: ♂ 12–15mm, ♀ 3–4mm

Caënis Nymphs. Plate 3 (23)

There are six different species grouped under this common name, one Brachycercus species and five Caënis species, they are C.rivulorum, C.robusta, C.horaria, C.luctuosa, C.macrura and B.harrisella. Some species are only found in streams or rivers while others are also found in ponds and lakes. The tiny nymphs are adept at the art of camouflage and they are all so similar in appearance that it is pointless trying to identify the individual species. Some species prefer a habitat of mud rich in organic matter while others found in stony rivers will be found in the silt between the stones or pebbles. The various species are likely to be seen throughout the summer, but the peak hatches of most species seem to occur during warm weather between mid June and mid August. The nymphs hatch on the surface in open water. They are a very common, widespread and abundant species and are found in all areas of Europe and the U.K.

The Caënis Duns. Plate 24 (187) and 26 (203)

The smallest of the upwinged flies, these very tiny duns are very easily identified as they have very broad forewings nearly as wide as their bodies, no hindwings and three rather short tails. The various species vary slightly in size and also in body colour from a creamy brown colour to an almost transluscent whitish olive. On rivers, hatches are often fairly prolific and usually seem to occur in the very early mornings often commencing just after dawn. On stillwater hatches are often on an enormous scale and usually occur on warm or sultry calm days in the afternoons or early evenings. Both males and females are very similar in appearance and colour.

ARTIFICIALS: A small Last Hope (light) or Pale Watery

The Caënis Spinner. Plate 24 (188)

Often referred to in old angling literature as the 'White Curse' a name of course still justified the tiny duns often transpose into spinners within minutes of hatching, unlike their larger cousins which take many hours. For this reason the water surface will often be so thick with hatching duns and at the same time returning spinners that the chance of a trout feeding upon these taking your tiny artificial as opposed to the hundreds available is pretty remote. In any case the trout will often be very selective at this time either feeding exclusively upon the emerging nymphs, hatching duns or the returning spinners, so the fly fisher is faced with a difficult choice anyway as to which artificial to use. When feeding upon these the trout will often sip these down very rapidly taking several at a time, so your best chance is to cast accurately to the rising fish and stick with one pattern. Alternatively success can often be achieved by fishing a large completely different pattern. Both male and female duns and spinners are all very similar apart from the longer tails of the latter.

ARTIFICIALS: My choice would be the Caenis Spinner by Canham.

DISTRIBUTION: Very common and abundant at least some species will be found in all areas.

SECTION 2:
UPWINGED FLIES WITH 2 TAILS AND LARGE HINDWINGS

THE LARGE SUMMER DUN (2 Tails & Large Hindwings)
Length of body: ♂ 13–17mm, ♀ 14–18mm
Tails of imago: ♂ 25mm, ♀ 20mm

The Large Summer Nymph (Siphlonurus lacustris)

Apart from the above species which is probably the most widespread there are four other species which are all referred to under the same common name. These are S.alternatus, S.armatus, S.croaticus and S.aestevalis the latter two species are not found in the U.K. They are all large species although lacustris may be a little smaller than the other four species. The nymphs belong to the group Agile Darters and they are to be found in larger slower flowing rivers and also big lakes. Hatches are seldom on a large scale and are likely to occur any time during the summer between May and early September. The nymphs are reputed to crawl ashore or emerge via stones or emergent vegetation, but I have observed at least one species (armatus) hatching in open water. The various species are common and widespread throughout Europe and the U.K. but as hatches are often very localised they may be considered from the fly fishers viewpoint a fairly scarce species.

The Large Summer Dun. Plate 24 (191)

All five species in this genera are referred to by the above common name and apart from the Large Mayfly (Greendrake) are the second largest of our upwinged flies. They all have two tails and large upright hindwings with a costal projection (see Fig 25B), and most of them have dark grey mainwings and light olive bodies heavily banded dark brown. Both males and females are very similar.

One should have little difficulty in identifying the various species in this genera due to their large size. They are not an important angling fly in Great Britain but may be of more importance in some areas of Europe.

ARTIFICIALS: The Large Summer Dun (Price), a Verano Amarillo or a Grey Wulff.

The Large Summer Spinner. Plate 24 (192)

The female spinners may sometimes be referred to as Great Red Spinners. There is little difference between male and female, they have transparent wings with a dark venation (see Fig 25B), and the bodies are olive brown often heavily banded in darker brown while the bodies of the females tend to darken to a more reddish brown colour with age. The males swarm usually over water but sometimes inland though never in large numbers and the females lay their eggs on the water surface in one mass.

ARTIFICIALS: The Large Summer Spinner (Price), Large Red Spinner or a large Pheasant Tail Spinner.

DISTRIBUTION: Individual species are likely to be found in most areas of Great Britain and Europe.

THE LATE MARCH BROWN (2 Tails & Large Hindwings)
Length of body: ♂ 12–16mm, ♀ 14–18mm
Tails of imago: ♂ 30–35mm, ♀ 16–20mm

The Late March Brown Nymph (Ecdyonurus venosus). Plate 1 (1)

This is also one of the large mottled and flattened Stone Clinger nymphs, found mainly in stony or boulder strewn rivers and streams. They emerge at the surface in open water although they may occasionally emerge via sticks, stones or emergent vegetation. Hatches tend to be sparse and while they may be encountered throughout the summer the main emergence period is during August and September. They are to be seen in many European countries and in the U.K. they may be encountered in parts of Wales, the West country, Northern England and also in a few isolated areas of Scotland and Ireland. They tend to be very localised in their distribution.

The Late March Brown Dun. Plate 19 (145 & 146)

This is one of the largest of the Ecdyonuridae genera, and should not be confused with the other very similar species which are unlikely to be seen in any numbers this late in the season. Both male and female have two brownish tails and large upright hindwings with a costal projection (see Fig 19). The mainwings are bluish grey with distinct dark brown veins giving a faintly mottled appearance (see Fig 27B) and their bodies are olive with diagonal brown bands.

ARTIFICIALS: No known pattern. Would suggest a March Brown.

The Late March Brown Spinner. Plate 19 (147)
In common with other similar species these females are usually referred to as Great Red Spinners. Both male and female have transparent wings heavily veined black which give them a greyish appearance their bodies are dark olive with deep mahogany red diagonal bands and they have deep brown eyes. The bands on the body of the male are sometimes a dark brown colour. The male spinners form small groups over water or larger groups close to the water. The female lays her eggs in batches by dipping onto the water surface.

ARTIFICIALS: No known pattern. A large U.S.D. Spinner with a red body or a large Pheasant Tail Spinner.

DISTRIBUTION: Not a particularly common species, they occur in all areas except 12, 13, 14, 19, 20, 22 and 23

THE MARCH BROWN (2 Tails & Large Hindwings)
Length of body: ♂ 11–14mm, ♀ 12–16mm
Tails of imago: ♂ 27–30mm. ♀ 17–20mm

The March Brown Nymph (Rhithrogena germanica)
This large mottled brown and flattened nymph is also one of the Stone Clingers and is most likely to be found in larger faster flowing stony or boulder strewn rivers. Hatches in the surface in open water are usually to be observed in very considerable numbers during March and early April. The trout seem to have a preference for the hatching nymph, and are seldom to be seen feeding upon the freshly hatched Dun on the surface. For this reason emerger patterns are usually more effective than the traditional dry fly patterns. They are a common and abundant species in those areas where they occur. In the U.K. they are found in most areas except the Midlands and the Southern Counties, and in Europe although found in some countries are less widespread.

The March Brown Dun. Plate 18 (137 & 138)
There must be but few fly fishers that are not familiar with this species, in fact references to this fly are to be found in the earliest of fishing books. It is a large handsome fly and with its large mottled wings, two tails and its large spurred hindwing (see Fig 38), is unlikely to be confused with any other species that hatches this early in the year. While it is very similar in appearance to many of the Ecdyonuridae species a clue to its identity will be found in the large clear patch in the centre of its mottled wings. Both male and female have this feature and are very similar in appearance. Their bodies are dark mahogany brown ringed in a distinctive straw colour, their tales are dark brown and the eyes in both sexes are dark green with a horizontal black bar across the centre. A further useful identification features on both the Dun and Spinner and also the Nymph of this species is a very distinct dark oval spot to be seen on the femur joints of the legs this incidently is a hallmark of the Rhithrogena genus (see Fig 29C).

ARTIFICIALS: A March Brown or March Brown Spider fished in the surface film should prove effective, or any emerger patterns or a large brown Suspender nymph.

The March Brown Spinner. Plate 18 (139 & 140)
The female spinner of this species in common with many spinners of the

Ecdyonuridae species is usually referred to as a Large Red Spinner. However these particular spinners are of very doubtful value to the fly fisher as they are seldom seen on the water in any quantity. Both male and female are very similar, they have transparent wings with a light brown venation and their bodies are dark to red brown with a distinctive straw coloured ringing. Small swarms will very occasionally be observed over the water and the females oviposit their eggs by dipping.

ARTIFICIALS: No known pattern, but a Large Pheasant Tail or a Large Red Spinner may be tried.

DISTRIBUTION: Found in areas 1, 2, 4, 9, 10, 14, 17, 18 and 19.

THE LARGE BROOK DUN (2 Tails & Large Hindwings)
Length of body: ♂ 10–14mm, ♀ 12–16mm
Tails of imago: ♂ 30–32mm, ♀ 18–20mm

The Large Brook Nymph (Ecdyonurus torrentis). Plate 1 (5)
This nymph is one of the Stone Clingers, and while the common name implies that its main habitat is that of the smaller brooks, I have on many occasions observed it on quite substantial streams usually of a boulder strewn or stony nature in hilly or mountainous country. Emergence of the nymph usually takes place out of the water via sticks, stones or the stems of water plants and hatches are often sparse. They are to be observed from April to July with peak hatches during May although on the continent it is often later. They are a relatively scarce species and common to but few countries in Europe. In the U.K. they are confined to Northern England, Wales, Scotland and parts of Ireland.

The Large Brook Dun. Plates 20 & 21 (160 & 161)
This is a large and particularly handsome fly and once observed and identified is unlikely to be confused with any other species. They have two tails and large upright hindwings with a prominent costal projection (see Fig 44). Although the dun may be of doubtful value to the fly fisher as it does not hatch on the water surface, it will often under windy conditions be blown onto the surface where it makes a juicy mouthful for any trout. In France it is highly thought of in those rivers where it occurs. While it is very similar in size and appearance to the March Brown and the Late March Brown it should not be confused with either of these as neither of these species are likely to be seen during the main emergence period of this fly. Apart from this the wings of this species have several dark bands of horizontal shading (see Figs 27C), which should help towards a positive identification. The females are usually much larger than the males and have olive brown bodies heavily banded red brown, giving the fly a distinctly reddish appearance. The wings are fawn heavily mottled dark brown and have a strong yellowish tinge along the leading edges. The eyes are brown and the tails are distinctly ringed brown. The males are very similar except that the compound eyes are of a dark brown colour.

ARTIFICIALS: So far as I know there are no known specific artificials to represent this species but an Autumn Dun or any of the many March Brown patterns should suffice.

The Large Brook Spinner. Plate 21 (162)

The female spinners of this species oviposit their eggs on the water surface by dipping, these can quickly be picked out from other species as apart from their size they often glow a brilliant red in the setting sun. Again they are of rather doubtful value to the fly fisher due to their sparsity. The female is often referred to as a Great Red Spinner as are several other Ecdyonuridae species. The females have purple red bodies, while those of the males are bright reddish brown with tinges of olive. Both have transparent wings with a dark brown venation and the leading edges are often yellowish. Both males and females may be observed swarming over the water surface in the early evenings.

ARTIFICIALS: No known patterns, would suggest a Large Pheasant Tail Spinner or a Large Red U.S.D. Spinner

DISTRIBUTION: Area No's 1, 2, 4, 5, 8, 9, 13, 14, 17, 18 and 19.

THE AUTUMN DUN (2 Tails & Large Hingwings)

Length of body: ♂ 10–13mm, ♀ 12–14mm
Tails of imago: ♂ 20–24mm, ♀ 18–22mm

The Autumn Nymph (Ecdyonurus dispar)

This distinctive nymph with a very large head is one of the Stone Clingers and as the name implies is only found in stony or boulder strewn rivers usually in hilly or mountainous country. They are also found in stony lakes. The nymphs hatch in open water, although they may also hatch via emergent sticks or stones. While it is a common species in areas where it occurs, hatches are rarely prolific and as the name implies the main emergence period of this species takes place during August and September. In the U.K. they are common in Scotland, Wales, Northern England and parts of Ireland. They are less widespread in Europe although quite common in some areas.

The Autumn Dun. Plate 19 (148)

This is quite a large fly and in some areas is also referred to as the August Dun. Although similar to many of the other Ecdyonuridae species it should not be confused as it is a little smaller and the wings are not mottled but an overall greyish fawn colour (see Fig 27A) with a yellowish tinge veined darkish brown. This applies to both sexes. The body of the female is olive with diagonal chestnut brown patches or bands, while these are more reddish brown on the body of the male. The eyes of the female are dark brown while the compound eyes of the male are more prominent and greenish brown. They have two tails and large upright hind wings with a prominent costal projection (see Fig 43).

ARTIFICIALS: The August Dun or a March Brown pattern should suffice.

The Autumn Spinner. Plate 19 (149 & 150)

The female is usually referred to by fly fishers as a Large Red Spinner as are the spinners of many of the Ecdyonuridae family. Quite frankly they are all so similar in appearance there seems little point in segregating them. However for the record both male and females have transparent wings with dark brown veining (see Fig 43). The body of the female is a dull reddish brown, while that of the male is often a very bright reddish brown. The female lays her eggs underwater on the substratum of stones projecting above water. Males form small swarms over water.

ARTIFICIALS: No known artificial but a large Pheasant Tail Spinner or a Large Red Spinner should suffice.

DISTRIBUTION: Found in areas 2, 3, 4, 7, 8, 9, 14, 16, 17, 18 and 19.

THE LARGE GREEN DUN (2 Tails & Large Hindwings)
Length of body: ♂ 10–12mm, ♀ 12–14mm
Tails of imago: ♂ 23–26mm, ♀ 20–22mm

The Large Green Nymph (Ecdyonurus insignis)
The nymph of this species is one of the flattened Stone Clingers and emerges by crawling up sticks, stones or any projections above the water surface. Hatches tend to be on the sparse side and peak emergence of this species is during July or August. They inhabit large rivers and streams of a stony or rocky nature. They are fairly widely distributed throughout Europe but tend to be rather localised. In the U.K. they are only likely to be encountered in parts of Wales, the West Country and the North of England.

The Large Green Dun. Plate 19 (151)
A fairly large species the dun is of very doubtful value to fly fishers as they are seldom to be seen on the water surface except possibly under windy conditions. Both male and female may be quickly identified by the pattern of dots and dashes on the underbody segments (see Fig 30). They have two tails and large upright hindwings with a costal projection (see Fig 36). In both sexes the main wings are mottled and they have olive green bodies with very distinctive diagonal brown lines running across each segment, which is a further aid to quick identification.

ARTIFICIALS: No known patterns. I would suggest a Large Greenwell's Glory.

The Large Green Spinner. Plate 19 (152)
Both male and female are very similar. They have transparent wings heavily veined black and they have a smoky-olive patch along the top leading edge, their bodies are olive brown with distinct diagonal lines along each of the body segments and the female has greenish eyes while the compound eyes of the male are very dark brown. These spinners are seldom on the water in sufficient quantities to interest the trout. The spinners release their eggs in batches by dipping onto the water surface.

ARTIFICIALS: No known patterns. Try a Pheasant Tail Spinner.

DISTRIBUTION: An uncommon species. To be seen in most areas except No's 3, 5, 11, 12, 14, 15, 17, 20, 22 and 23.

THE YELLOW MAY DUN (2 Tails & Large Hindwings)
Length of body: ♂ 8–11mm, ♀ 9–12mm
Tails of imago: ♂ 20–22mm, ♀ 15–20mm

The Yellow May Dun (Heptagenia sulphurea). Plate 1 (2)
This nymph is a Stone Clinger but unlike many other nymphs of this type it emerges at the surface in open water. Found in smaller rivers often with gravelly reaches and sometimes in calcareous lakes. It is regularly seen on many of the chalk streams in the South of England. It is a very common and widespread

species and is to be observed throughout Europe as well as in many areas in the U.K. but hatches are usually very sparse and it is unusual to see more than one or two hatching at any one time. It is likely to be seen throughout the summer but June and July are its peak months.

The Yellow May Dun. Plate 18 (141 & 142)

Neither the dun or the spinner are of much importance as an angling fly in the U.K. as the trout are reputed to dislike them, but whether this is due to the sparsity of the hatches or some other reason is unknown. This is a medium large species and they have two tails and large upright hindwings with a costal projection (see Fig 18). They are unlikely to be confused with any other species as they are the only upwinged fly (apart maybe from the Yellow Evening Dun which is much paler yellow) with a very bright overall sulphur yellow colouration. Both male and female also has transparent wings (see Fig 35), but the leading edge is yellowish the brown venation, they both have bright blue eyes while those of the male are large and very distinctive.

ARTIFICIALS: Would suggest you try Taff Price's Yellow May Dun.

The Yellow May Spinner. Plate 18 (143 & 144)

The male spinner is a particularly handsome fly, it has a golden brown body transparent wings with a smoky leading edge and large brilliant blue eyes. The female also has transparent wings (see Fig 35), but the leading edge is yellowish and their bodies are yellow olive ringed pale brown. The females lay their eggs on the water surface by dipping, and I have on odd occasions observed these spinners being taken by the trout.

ARTIFICIALS: I believe there are some Yellow May Spinner patterns but a Lunn's Yellow Boy dressed on a 12 or 14 hook should suffice.

DISTRIBUTION: Found in most areas except No's 5, 6 and 7.

THE OLIVE UPRIGHT (2 Tails & Large Hindwings)

Length of body: ♂ 9–10mm, ♀ 10–12mm
Tails of imago: ♂ 22–25mm, ♀ 12–14mm

The Olive Upright Nymph (Rhithrogena semicolorata). Plate 1 (4)

The nymph of this species is slightly flattened and is classified as one of the Stone Clingers. They are to be encountered in stony streams and rivers and hatches are often on quite a large scale. It may be seen throughout the summer but peak hatches usually occur from mid May to mid July. They emerge in open water and hatch on the surface. They are a common and abundant species in many European countries and are to be seen in many areas of the U.K. apart from the Midlands and most of Southern England. However, it is worth recording that several years ago I personally observed big hatches of this species over a two week period at Abbott's Barton on the River Itchen in Southern England.

The Olive Upright Dun. Plate 17 (133 & 134)

This medium large species is very similar indeed in appearance to the Blue Winged Olive except that it has two tails as opposed to the three tails of the latter. However, apart from this it should not be confused as like all the Rhithrogena species they have a distinct dark oval mark in the middle of each top leg (femora) section (see Fig 29C). They have two tails and large upright hindwings with a costal projection (see Figs 39). The mainwings of both sexes are dark blue grey, while the hindwings often have a buff coloured trailing edge, and the thorax on each side at the wing roots is a distinct orange colour. The body of the female is grey olive brown ringed olive, while that of the male is a little darker.

ARTIFICIALS: The only imitative pattern I know is the H.P.B. (Evans). Failing this try a B.W.O. (Jacques) or even a Greenwell's Glory.

The Yellow Upright Spinner. Plate 17 (135 & 136)

This is the popular name that has been given to this spinner in areas where it is common. There is little difference between the sexes, they both have transparent wings with black venation and are tinted pale golden brown or smoky bronze in their basal half. Their bodies are brown olive ringed pale olive, while that of the female darkens to a reddish brown with age. They have olive yellow eyes with a dark bar across the centre. The spinners swarm in small groups sometimes over or near the water but on occasions very high above the trees. The females alight on stones or other projections above the water and then lay their eggs by extruding them on the substratum underwater.

ARTIFICIALS: No known pattern. Would suggest a Lunn's Yellow Boy, a Sunk Spinner, a Partridge and Orange or large Pale Watery Spinner. Fished in or below the surface.

DISTRIBUTION: Found in areas No's 1–4, 6–11 and 17, 18 and 19.

THE DUSKY YELLOWSTREAK (2 Tails & Large Hindwings)
Length of body: ♂ 7–10mm, ♀ 8–11mm
Tails of imago: ♂ 20–25mm, ♀ 12–15mm

The Dusky Yellowstreak Nymph (Electrogena lateralis). Plate 2 (9)

This medium size flattened nymph belongs to the group of Stone Clingers, it is found in stony streams, rivers and sometimes on the stony shores of lakes, usually at higher altitudes. The nymph of this species is unique among the upwinged flies as it has been observed hatching into the adult on stones underwater and then swimming to the surface. However it may also hatch on the surface in different habitats as the nymph has been found in considerable numbers in small wooded brooks full of detritus. Hatches are likely to occur throughout the summer months but it is not a particularly common species, as it tends to be rather localised in its distribution. Where it is found though hatches are often on a fair scale. It is found in many European countries and also in localised areas throughout the U.K. apart from the Midlands and Southern England.

The Dusky Yellowstreak Dun. Plate 20 (153 & 154)

This medium to medium large species can usually be identified fairly readily by the prominent triangular shaped yellow streak from which it derives its common name along each side of its thorax below the wing roots. This feature is more prominent on the spinner than on the dun. In most areas the main emergence is during June. Both sexes have two greyish brown tails, large upright hindwings with barely a costal projection. The mainwings are dark greyish brown heavily veined, and they have grey-olive brown bodies and dark brown eyes.

ARTIFICIALS: There are no specific patterns. Would suggest an Imperial,

Snipe & Purple or a Dark Watchett on size 14 hooks.

The Dusky Yellowstreak Spinner. Plate 20 (155 & 156)
Both male and female spinners have transparent wings veined light brown and dark olive brown bodies ringed reddish, the males have grey tails while those of the female are of a lighter reddish brown colour and their wings have a strong red brown venation along the leading edges. The yellow streak on each side of the thorax is more prominent on the spinner which should assist in a positive identification. The male spinners swarm near the banks in the evening and the females lay their eggs by dipping onto the water surface.

ARTIFICIALS: No known pattern, would suggest a Pheasant Tail Spinner size 12 or 14

DISTRIBUTION: Found in most areas except No's 3, 5, 6, 7, 12, 20, 22 and 23.

THE OLIVE DUNS

The various species of olives are among the most common and widespread of all the species of upwinged flies, and are most important to the fly fisher particularly on many rivers in the U.K. While detailed descriptions are given for each species, for those wishing to make a positive identification, so far as the fly fisher is concerned and also probably the trout at least four species the Medium Olive, Small Dark Olive, Pale Watery Olive and the Small Spurwing are so similar, apart from a slight variation in size, that they could for all practical purposes be referred to as Small Olives. In the following detailed descriptions, various artificials are recommended for individual species, and the only reason for doing this is really traditional as in some cases the artificials were originally dressed by their authors to represent one or two of these Olives and not the others. On clear, fairly slow moving rivers and streams, the fly fisher will be well advised to choose one of the recommended patterns listed to fish with, but on fast streams or big rivers the following patterns dressed on suitable sized hooks will probably prove to be more effective. The John Storey, a famous North Country artificial is very killing on this type of water, while the equally famous and traditional Greenwell's Glory will often prove effective. The Humpy or an Adams are both excellent American patterns, while the Palm Ailes or a Tricolore are both tried and tested French patterns. Finally do try a suitable size and colour Cal-du-Canard which also originated in France. This latter pattern is often very killing as it floats like thistledown and when dressed by Marc Petitjean the brilliant Swiss fly tier it is also pretty durable.

On some waters that are subjected to very hard fishing pressure, the trout often become very wary and will completely ignore the freshly hatched Olives floating on the surface, and will only feed upon the emerging fly. When they are so occupied it is extremely difficult to spot, as the rise form is so similar. In this situation, if during a good hatch of Olives the trout ignores several dry fly offerings, I then stop fishing and watch the freshly hatched Olives drifting over the Trout, if he continues to rise and none of these are taken I then know he is feeding on the hatching nymph or emerging dun. There are several excellent emerging patterns as follows. A Suspender Hatching Nymph, a G.R.H.E. unweighted nymph or an Ephemera emerger perfected by Piero Lumini the talented Italian fly dresser.

SECTION 3:
UPWINGED FLIES WITH 2 TAILS AND SMALL HINDWINGS

THE LARGE DARK OLIVE (2 Tails & Small Oval Hindwings)
Length of body: ♂ & ♀ 7–10mm
Tails of imago: ♂ 18mm, ♀ 16mm

The Large Dark Olive Nymph (Baëtis rhodani). Plate 1 (7)
The nymph of this species is one of the Agile Darters. It is a common and abundant species and is found in small streams and rivers both acid and alkaline at low altitudes as well as in the mountains, it is an important species on the chalk streams of Southern England. Hatches are often on a large scale and it is most likely to be observed during March, April or early May and again in late September and October. For the record their is another very similar species Baetis atrebatinus and the only means of seperating the two species is the lack of a spur on the small oval hindwings of atrebatinus (see Fig 8). This species is relatively scarce and is only to be found in some areas in Ireland and on the Continent. The nymphs of both species hatch in open water on the surface. R.rhodani is to be encountered throughout the U.K. and is also a very common species in most European countries.

The Large Dark Olive Dun. Plate 14 (109 & 110)
This is an important angling fly as it is one of the few species apart from the March Brown that hatches in quantity very early in the season. In fact it is fairly safe to state that any large Olive duns observed hatching in numbers during March or early April are likely to be this species. They are a medium large species and have two tails small oval hindwings with a distinct spur (see Fig 7), and double intercallery veins along the trailing edges of the mainwings (see Figs 28A and 45). The males have dark brick red turbinate eyes, while those of the female are small and greenish. Both sexes have pale grey wings with pale brown veins and their bodies are dark olive green to olive brown.

In March and April when hatches of this species are at their peak emergence usually starts about 12.30 and continues till about 2.30.

ARTIFICIALS: I strongly recommend an Imperial or Super Grizzly or good general patterns are a Beacon Beige or a Greenwell's.

The Large Dark Olive Spinner. Plate 14 (111 & 112)
This spinner is of doubtful value to the fly fisher as in my experience they are seldom observed on the water in sufficient numbers to interest the trout. Both male and female have transparent wings very lightly veined pale brown. The females body is red brown ringed pale olive, while the male has a pale olive body tinged brown and the last three segments are orange-brown. The turbinate eyes of the male are a dark red-brown. The female spinners tend to lay their eggs underwater by crawling down any handy projections sticking above the water surface. Males swarm usually over water at a height of 1-5m.

ARTIFICIALS: Try a Pheasant Tail Spinner ungreased in the surface film or a Sunk Spinner.

DISTRIBUTION: Very common and widespread, found in nearly all areas.

THE MEDIUM OLIVE (2 Tails & Small Oval Hindwings)
Length of body: ♂ & ♀ 6–8mm
Tails of imago: ♂ 14–16mm, ♀ 11–13mm

The Medium Olive Nymph (Baëtis Vernus)
This rather small nymph like all the Baëtis species is of a transluscent olive colouration and belongs to the group termed Agile Darters. Not quite so common and widespread as the previous species it is nevertheless found in most areas in small streams as well as quite large rivers, but seems to have a preference for alkaline or chalky streams, while it is also common in streams of a peaty nature. The nymphs emerge in open water at the surface, and it is an important species on many of the chalk streams of Southern England. Hatches are often quite substantial throughout the day and occur during most of the summer months with a peak in May and June. They are an abundant species and are found all over Europe and the U.K. but are unlikely to be found in rivers in hilly or mountainous country. For the record there is a very closely related species B. buceratus but this is a relatively rare species in the U.K. so can be more or less discounted, although it may be fairly common in parts of Europe. It can be identified by the venation of the hindwings (see Fig 12).

The Medium Olive Dun. Plate 14 (105 & 106)
This medium sized dun is probably the sheet achor of the chalk stream fisherman, but is so similar to the many other small species of olives it is difficult (many consider unnecessary) to positively identify. Like most of the Baëtis species they have a small spurred oval shaped hindwing (see Fig 9). Two tails and the trailing edges of the mainwings show small double intercallery veins (see Fig 28A). The females have dull to pale grey wings, small greenish yellow eyes and bodies that are distinctly brownish olive with paler ringing. The males have dull grey wings, large dull red brown turbinate eyes and bodies of an olive grey hue.
  ARTIFICIALS: An Imperial, Super Grizzly, G.R.H.E. (winged), Funnel Dun or a good general pattern would be a Beacon Beige. All on size 16 hooks.

The Medium Olive Spinner. Plate 14 (107 & 108)
The female spinner of this species is often referred to as the Red Spinner, and when these dead and dying spinners drift along on the current in the evenings during May and early June they are of considerable importance to the fly fisher. Most females lay their eggs underwater by crawling down any posts, stones or weeds projecting above the surface. The piers and walls of bridges are always favourites. Few of these females ever break back through the surface, so these dead and dying females drift along just beneath the surface film. It is therefore important to fish any spinner patterns used to represent them ungreased so they ideally sink just below the surface. Both sexes have transparent wings lightly veined pale brown. The females have small brown eyes and yellow brown bodies which with age take on a deep reddish brown colour. The bodies of the males are olive-grey with the last three segments red brown and they have large turbinate red eyes, and they tend to swarm along the bank.
  ARTIFICIALS: A Lunn's Particular, Pheasant Tail, Red Spinner, U.S.D. Spinner or a Sunk Spinner. All on size 16 hooks.
  DISTRIBUTION: A common and in some areas abundant species mainly in the lowlands. Found in most areas except No's 20, 22 and 23.

THE IRON BLUE (2 Tails & Small Oval Hindwings)
Length of body: ♂ & ♀ 6–8mm
Tails of imago: ♂ 9–12mm, ♀ 6–9mm

The Iron Blue Nymph (Baëtis muticus and B.niger). Plate 3 (18)
These two species are so similar that they may be treated as one although muticus is the more common and widespread. The rather small nymphs belong to the group termed Agile Darters. B.niger is found in streams and rivers with a good weed growth, while B.muticus is more likely to be found in streams and rivers with some weed but of a stony or gravelly nature. They emerge at the surface in open water and are likely to be seen at any time during the summer. Hatches are often quite prolific but seldom last for more than a few days, when they may not be seen again for several weeks. They are reputed to have a preference for hatching during wet, cold and windy weather which in my experience does seem to be the norm. On the other hand I have also experienced some hatches on lovely warm days. They are widespread and one species or the other is likely to be found in most European countries, while in the U.K. they are likely to be found in most areas except Eastern England.

The Iron Blue Dun. Plate 15 (113 & 114)
These small species of duns are unlikely to be confused with any other species of upwinged fly due to their very dark overall colouration, in fact at times when these are hatching they are quite difficult to see as they appear almost black on the water surface. They have two tails, small oval hindwings with a spur (see Figs 5 and 6 and mainwings with small double intercallery veins along the trailing edges (see Fig 28A). Both male and female are very similar in appearance, they have very dark grey wings, and very dark brown bodies sometimes flecked with olive. The eyes of the males are large turbinate and dull brownish red in colour.
ARTIFICIALS: An Iron Blue, Iron Blue Quill, Otter Ruby or on rough water try a Dark Watchett or a Snipe & Purple, all on small hooks sizes 18 or 16.

The Iron Blue Spinner. Plate 15 (115 & 116)
The common name for the female is the Little Claret, while the male spinner which is sometimes blown onto the water surface is often referred to as the Jenny Spinner. They both have transparent wings and the body of the female is dark claret brown. The male has reddish brown turbinate eyes and the body is transluscent white with the last three segments dark orange-brown. Like most other Baëtis species the female spinners are reputed to lay their eggs underwater by crawling down any projections above the water surface. However I have never personally observed this. The male spinners form swarms over the water.
ARTIFICIALS: A Houghton Ruby or a small Pheasant Tail Spinner.
DISTRIBUTION: A very widespread species found in most areas of the U.K. and also in most European countries.

THE PALE WATERY (2 Tails & Small Oval Hindwings)
Length of body: ♂ & ♀ 5–8mm
Tails of imago: ♂ 12–14mm, ♀ 9–11mm

The Pale Watery Olive Nymph (Baëtis fuscatus)
This small translucent olive nymph also belongs to the group referred to as Agile

Darters. Found in weedy sandy or gravelly streams and rivers it probably has a preference for water of a calcereous nature. The nymphs emerge in open water at the surface and hatches are often prolongued and quite heavy. It may be observed throughout the summer but is most common in May early June and again in September and October. It is a very common and widespread species and is to be found throughout Europe, but in the U.K. its range seems to be more limited as it is only common in England mainly in Wales and Southern England where it is an important species on the chalk streams. It is rare in Scotland and has not been recorded from Ireland.

The Pale Watery Olive Dun. Plate 13 (97 & 98)

This species seems to vary greatly in size more so than any of the other Olives, I have observed some specimens as large as the Medium Olive and others that have been as small as some of the very tiny Small Dark Olives. Both male and female duns have two tails, small spur shaped hindwings (see Fig 11), and mainwings with small double intercallery veins along the trailing edges (see Fig 28A). The female has pale to medium grey wings, small yellow green eyes and the body is pale watery olive with the last two segments yellowish. It is all but impossible for the layman to distinguish this female from other similar Olive species and in any case would serve no useful purpose. The wings and bodies of the male are very similar to the female but the males of this species are instantly recognisable as they have large bright yellow turbinate eyes. This feature only occurs in one other similar species the male of the Pale Evening Dun which has no hindwings.

ARTIFICIALS: A Last Hope (light), Little Marryatt, Moustique, Pale Watery, Funnel Dun or my new Super Grizzly emerger pattern. All on size 16 or 18 Roman Moser hooks.

Pale Watery Olive Spinner. Plate 13 (99 & 100)

The female spinner of this species is often referred to as the Golden Spinner which is quite an appropriate name as the bodies of these females vary from golden olive to a pale golden brown with the last three segments slightly darker. They have transparent wings and tails that are almost white. The male has a transluscent white tinged olive body with the last three segments orange brown, and like the male dun have large turbinate yellow eyes. The female spinners lay their eggs underwater by crawling down any projections above the water surface. Therefore as with the female spinners of most other Baëtis species any artificials should be fished either in or just below the surface film. The spinners of this species seem to be less commonly seen in the surface than other members of this genera. This could be accounted for due to the spinners of this species mating and ovipositing much earlier in the evening, so that the numbers at any given time are less as they are spread out over a longer period of time. Male spinners swarm along the banks.

ARTIFICIALS: A Lunn's Yellow Boy or a sunk spinner.

DISTRIBUTION: A common and abundant species found in all areas except No's 17 & 18.

THE SMALL DARK OLIVE (2 Tails & Small Oval Hindwing)

Length of body: ♂ & ♀ 4–6mm
Tails of imago: ♂ 8–10mm, ♀ 8mm

The Small Dark Olive Nymph (Baëtis Scambus). Plate 2 (14)

This very tiny nymph also belongs to the group referred to as Agile Darters. It is to be found both in small and large rivers of a calcereous or peaty nature and is also often to be seen in rivers at a considerable altitude.

The nymphs hatch in open water at the surface and while they are likely to be seen throughout the summer months the main emergence period is during the latter half of the summer with a peak in July and August. They are a common and abundant species in those areas where they occur and are widely distributed over the U.K. but are scarcer in Scotland and parts of Ireland, they are a very important species on the Chalkstreams of Southern England. They are also common in many European countries.

The Small Dark Olive Dun. Plate 13 (101 & 102)

Apart from some of the smaller species of Caenis this is the smallest of our upwinged flies. It is an important species to the fly fisher wherever it occurs as hatches are often on a fairly lavish scale and particularly later in the summer are likely to start emerging about midday and often continue until it is almost dusk. The trout seem to be inordinately fond of this tiny dun and in the evenings I have often observed them feeding on these to the exclusion of other larger species including many of the caddis flies that hatch at this time of the year in the evenings. They are a small to very small species with two tails, small oval shaped hindwings with a small spur (see Fig 10), and the trailing edges of the mainwings show small double intercallery veins (see Fig 28A). The males have large dull orange red turbinate eyes, their wings are pale to dark grey and their bodies are grey-olive with the last two segments yellowish. The females have small black eyes and also have pale to dark grey wings and their bodies vary from a pale transluscent olive to grey olive with the last two segments yellowish. I like most other authorities used to think that the paler bodied flies hatched in July while the darker ones were a product of the late summer. I am now inclined to think as a result of a more recent observations that the body colour varies with the water and air temperature, the hotter the day the paler the body colour.

ARTIFICIALS: A July Dun, a Funnel Dun, a Last Hope (dark) or a Super Grizzly Emerger (this is dressed with a tag of pearly or pale yellow Krystal Flash in place of the normal long tails and I now use no other pattern when this species is hatching). All dressed on size 18 Roman moser hooks.

The Small Dark Olive Spinner. Plate 13 (103 & 104)

The tiny female spinner of this species is commonly referred to as a Small Red Spinner. Like most of the Baetis species this female spinner lays her eggs underwater via any projections above the surface, therefore any spinner patterns used should be fished in or beneath the surface film. Both males and females have transparent wings. The males have large orange red turbinate eyes with translucent cream bodies with the last three segments orange-brown. The females have small black eyes and their bodies are dark brown to deep red brown ringed in a paler colour. The swarms of males usually form well away from the water.

ARTIFICIALS: A small Pheasant Tail, Lunn's Particular, Red Spinner or a Sunk Spinner. All on size 18 hooks. Fished ungreased.

DISTRIBUTION: Found in most areas except No's 6, 7, 10, 12, 15, 16, 20, 22 and 23.

THE LARGE SPURWING (2 Tails & Tiny Spur Shaped Hindwings)

Length of body: ♂ & ♀ 8–10mm
Tails of imago: ♂ 15mm, ♀ 10mm

The Large Spurwing Nymph (Pseudocentroptilum pennulatum). Plate 3 (19)

The nymph of this species also belongs in the group referred to as the Agile Darters. The nymphs are usually found in the slower flowing sections of streams and rivers amongst weed or sandy or gravelly bottoms and occasionally on the shores of lakes. They hatch in open water on the surface and are most likely to be seen during June or early July although small hatches may be observed throughout the summer. Hatches are usually rather sparce and it tends to be very localised in its distribution and is scarce in many areas. It is found in some European countries and in certain areas in the U.K. but not in Ireland.

The Large Spurwing Dun. Plate 16 (121 & 122)

This dun used to be referred to as the Blue Winged Pale Watery which I feel is more apt than its present common name. Both sexes have dark blue grey wings and single intercallery veins along the trailing edges (see Figs 28B and 32) and small spur shaped hindwings (see Fig 13). The male has large dull orange turbinate eyes and the body is pale greyish olive with the last three segments amber coloured. The body of the female is a dark straw colour. This is one of the easiest of the Baetids to identify, as it is the only medium large species that has a very pale body and dark grey wings. The only other species of a similar size with whom it may be confused is the Blue Winged Olive but this species has three tails and a much darker olive green body. A rather strange feature of this fly is the way it spreads its wings well apart after hatching or when at rest.

ARTIFICIALS: A Pale Watery, Moustique or a Funnel Dun.

The Large Spurwing Spinner. Plate 16 (123 & 124)

The common name for the female spinner is the Large Amber, a rather appropriate name due to the lovely and distinct amber-brown colour on the dorsum of the body of this species. Once identified it will never be confused with any other species. Both sexes have transparent wings. The male has large bright orange turbinate eyes and the body is translucent white with pale red ringing and the last three segments are dark amber. The female body varies from pale amber-flecked olive to a deep very rich brown amber with greyish ringing. It has been suggested that the female spinner oviposits her eggs on the surface in one batch, but I have never personally observed this. This species used to be quite common on many of our chalk streams but is now seldom seen.

ARTIFICIALS: A Yellow Boy or Pale Watery spinner.

DISTRIBUTION: A very localised species reported from areas No's 3, 4, 5, 7, 8, 9, 10, 11, 13, 15, 16 and 18.

THE SMALL SPURWING (2 Tails & Tiny Spur Shaped Hindwings)

Length of Body: ♂ & ♀ 6–8mm
Tails of imago: ♂ 12–14mm, ♀ 8–10mm

The Small Spurwing Nymph (Centroptilum luteolum)

This relatively small nymph also belongs to the group referred to as Agile Darters. They are to be found in small streams, rivers and also occasionally on the stony shores of lakes. They seem to have a preference for the slower flowing sections of rivers that are weedy or have sandy or gravelly bottoms. The nymphs hatch in open water on the surface and hatches at times can be fairly prolific particularly from late May through June although they may be seen throughout the summer months. It is common and widespread in most European countries and is found in most areas of the U.K. apart from Wales where it appears to be rather scarce.

The Small Spurwing Dun. Plate 15 (117 & 118)

This medium to small species of Olive was originally placed in the group of Olives referred to as Pale Wateries and in fact at one time was known as the Little Sky Blue Pale Watery. This is seems to me made good sense as the females of most of these small Olives are all but impossible to tell apart except with the assistance of a magnifying glass. However, in the early sixties I believe it was my good friend the late Major Oliver Kite first referred to this species and also C.Pennulatum as the Small and Large Spurwings due to their very tiny spur shaped hindwings. This name caught on and is now in common use. The wings of both sexes are very pale grey often tinged blueish white towards the basal section. The male has large orange-red turbinate eyes and the body is pale olive brown with the last two segments orange-brown. The body of the female is pale watery olive-brown. If one is so inclined this species can be positively identified by the small single intercallery veins along the trailing edges of the mainwings (see Figs 28B and 33) and the very tiny spur shaped hindwing (see Fig 14). However, a low powered glass will be required to see these.

ARTIFICIALS: A Last Hope (light), Little Marryat, Moustique or a small winged G.R.H.E. or my Super Grizzly Emerger.

The Small Spurwing Spinner. Plate 15 (119 & 120)

The female of this species is commonly referred to as the Little Amber Spinner due no doubt to its overall amber colouration. The wings of both species are transparent faintly veined olive. The male has large turbinate bright orange-red eyes and the body is translucent watery white olive with the last three segments orange-brown. The body of the female varies from a pale yellow-brown to a most beautiful brownish amber colour when fully spent. The female flies down to the water surface and the eggs are released in one mass. Swarms of these spinners may be observed over the edge of the water in the early evenings.

ARTIFICIALS: A Lunn's Yellow Boy, Pale Watery Spinner or a Tup's.

DISTRIBUTION: Common and widespread, found in all areas of Europe and the U.K.

SECTION 4:
UPWINGED FLIES WITH 2 TAILS AND NO HINDWINGS

THE POND OLIVE (2 Tails No Hindwings)
Length of body: ♂ & ♀ 7–10mm
Tails of imago: ♂10–16mm, ♀12–14mm

The Pond Olive Nymph (Cloëon dipterum)

The nymph of this species is also one of the Agile Darters. They are most commonly found in small ponds or shallow and weedy lakes, although they may also be found in the slower flowing sections of some rivers. They hatch in open water at the surface, the main emergence period is June and July often with a second and usually smaller generation later in the summer. They are a very common and widespread species and are likely to be found in all areas both in the U.K. and in Europe.

The Pond Olive Dun. Plate 16 (125 & 126)

This dun like the Lake Olive is of great interest to the stillwater fisherman as it is one of the few species of upwinged flies that hatch in numbers on lakes and reservoirs. The Pond Olive has several features which will quickly seperate it from other species of Olives. The mainwings have small single intercallery veins along the trailing edges (see Fig 37) and neither this species or the Lake Olive have any hindwings. To distinguish it from the Lake Olive look for the following four features. First the two tails of the Pond Olive are heavily ringed dark brown, the eyes of both sexes have two faint horizontal red lines across the centre and the females of both dun and spinner have two parallel red lines running along the underbody (venter). The top leading edge of the mainwings have three to five small cross-veins, while the Lake Olive has nine to eleven (see Fig 26b and 31). The wings of both sexes are pale to darkish grey. The eyes of the female are dark green and the body is olive brown sometimes with red patches. The large turbinate eyes of the male are orange-brown and the body is dull grey-olive with the last three segments a dull grey brown. They are a medium to medium large species.

ARTIFICIALS: A Pond Olive, Olive Quill or a Greenwell's Glory.

The Pond Olive Spinner. Plate 16 (127 & 128)

The popular name for the female is the Apricot Spinner and once identified is unlikely to be confused with any other spinners due to its startling colouration. The wings are transparent with pale reddish veining and the leading edges are a very distinctive and lovely smoky bronze colour. The eyes are dark green with two faint horizontal lines, the tails distinctly ringed dark brown and the body which is much bulkier than other similar species varies from a beautiful bronze apricot colour with red streaks to red–brown tinged dark yellow with two parallel red lines running along the underbody. The wings of the male are also transparent with brownish veins along the leading edges, the eyes are pale orange with two parallel red lines across the centre, and the body is dull translucent cream with the last three segments dark chestnut brown. The female spinner of this species is unique at least among the British species of upwinged flies as unlike all the other species which lay their eggs almost immediately after mating, this species retires to the bushes for 10 to 14 days where the eggs develop in the abdomen. Finally when the eggs are oviposited on the surface the nymphs hatch immediately. This final act often occurs during the hours of darkness so that the margins may be littered with dying spinners very early in the mornings.

ARTIFICIALS: A Pond Olive Spinner or a Lunn's Yellow Boy.

DISTRIBUTION: Recorded from all areas except No's 17, 20, 22 and 23.

THE LAKE OLIVE (2 Tails No Hindwings)
Length of body: ♂ & ♀ 7–9mm
Tails of imago: ♂ 12–14mm, ♀ 10–12mm

The Lake Olive Nymph (Cloëon simile)
Belongs to the group referred to as Agile Darters. The nymph is found amongst vegetation in the deeper areas of ponds and lakes. They hatch in open water at the surface during most of the summer months with peaks in May and June and again in August and September. A very common and very widespread species they are found in all areas in the U.K. and also Europe.

The Lake Olive Dun. Plate 17 (129 & 130)
Similar to the Pond Olive and found in the same type of habitat they can be quickly distinguished from each other. The Lake Olive is of a much drabber appearance and has tails that are but very faintly ringed as opposed to the heavily ringed tails of the former. Also if you examine the top leading edge of the mainwings carefully you will note that the Pond Olive has only three to five small cross-vein while the Lake Olive has nine to eleven (see Fig 31 and 26c). This is a medium sized species and both sexes are somewhat similar in appearance. They have pale smoky-grey wings with a yellowish venation along the leading edges, grey tails faintly ringed and their bodies are dark olive with red-brown patches. The eyes of the male are pale orange, while those of the female are olive with brown flecks. They lack hindwings and have small single intercallary veins along the trailing edges of the forewings.
    ARTIFICIALS: A Lake Olive, Olive Quill or a Greenwell's Glory.

The Lake Olive Spinner. Plate 17 (131 & 132)
The spinners of this species are more likely to be seen than those of the Pond Olive as during periods of good daytime hatches reasonable falls of spent females are likely to be encountered on warm summer evenings. The wings of both sexes are transparent with faint touches of yellow along the leading edges, and their tails are white faintly ringed red. The eyes of the male are large and pale orange and their bodies are pale olive brown with the last three segments deep red brown. The eyes of the female are small and olive green with reddish flecks and their bodies are deep chestnut brown with paler ringing. The female spinners lay their eggs in batches by dipping onto the water surface.
    ARTIFICIALS: A Lunn's Particular or a Pheasant Tail Spinner.
    DISTRIBUTION: Very common and widespread recorded from all countries in Europe and all areas of the U.K.

PALE EVENING DUN (2 Tails No Hindwings)
Length of body: ♂ & ♀ 5–8mm
Tails of imago: ♂ 12mm, ♀ 6–8mm

The Pale Evening Nymph (Procloeon bifidum). Plate 3 (17)
The nymph of this species is also an Agile Darter. It is found in the slower flowing sections of streams and rivers. The hatches tend to be sporadic over several weeks and rarely prolific and in some areas they seem to have a rather short season. They may be seen during any of the summer months. Emergence takes place on the

surface in open water. They are not a particularly common species but are found in localised areas over the whole of the U.K. and they are also to be seen in many European countries.

The Pale Evening Dun. Plate 21 (163)

It is only in recent years that this dun has been recognised as a seperate species by fly fishers as in the past it was undoubtedly looked upon as one of the Pale Wateries as it very closely resembles these. However this species like the Pond and Lake Olives have two tails and no hindwings and as it has a very much paler body little difficulty should be experienced in distinguishing it. For positive identification there are four cross veins in the top centre of the mainwings which run parallel (see Fig 26A). This is one of the few species of upwinged duns that only hatch during the evening hence its popular name. Both sexes are very similar they have light grey wings sometimes with a distinct green tinge along the leading edge of the mainwings. The bodies are a very pale straw colour often appearing almost yellow with brownish patches along the top (dorsum) and the last three segments of the males body are pale orange brown. The male is much easier to identify as apart from the Pale Watery it is the only other similar upwinged species that has large turbinate dull yellow eyes. They have small single intercallary veins along the trailing edges of the forewings, and six to eight small cross veins along the top leading edges of the mainwings (see Fig 26A).

ARTIFICIALS: A Last Hope (light), Pale Watery or a Little Marryat.

The Pale Evening Spinner. Plate 21 (164)

Little is known regarding the swarming or egg laying habits of this species although it has been suggested that the male swarms form along the edge of the water and that they may mate and oviposit either very late in the evening or even after dark. Whatever the reason these spinners are seldom to be observed on the water and are therefore of little interest to the fly fisher. The female spinners have transparent wings often with a green tinge along the leading edge and their bodies are pale golden olive with reddish blotches. This female is also often referred to as the Golden Spinner.

ARTIFICIALS: No known pattern. A Lunn's Yellow Boy would probably suffice.

DISTRIBUTION: Found in most areas except No's 5, 6, 10, 11 and 12.

THE UPWINGED FLIES (Ephemeroptera) FOUND IN EUROPE ONLY

The following detailed descriptions of species found only in European countries is presented in a different manner to the preceeding species that are also found in the British Isles which are listed under their common angling names. These common English names have evolved over the centuries and are now generally accepted and used by all the European countries where fly fishing is practised. During this same period artificial patterns have been perfected that are associated with these names so it is often possible to match an artificial fly to the common name of the natural fly. With the following European Species this is not possible as to the best of my knowledge none of them have been given common names that have been universally accepted by every European country and therefore no specific matching artificials have ever been listed to cover every country in Europe.

There are of course a legion of patterns that have been developed by individual fly tiers in most of the prominent fly fishing countries in Europe, to match naturals that may be known by a common name in that country alone, but very few of these would be known outside the country of their origin, so it would be pointless in covering these in this volume.

However where possible I have recommended commonly recognised artificials to match those species that are of the same genera as some of the preceeding British species. It will be noted that two species covered do occur in some areas of the British Isles but as they are both very rare in this country I decided not to include them in the British and European list.

It will also be noted that with these European species, I have where possible included certain specific fishing information which I hope may assist the reader to choose a relevant artificial of his own choice.

SECTION 5:
UPWINGED FLIES WITH 3 TAILS AND LARGE HINDWINGS

PALINGENIA LONGICAUDA (3 Tails & Large Hindwings)
Length of body: ♂ & ♀ 30–40mm
Tails of imago: ♂ 90–120mm

The Nymph. Plate 3 (22)
The very large nymphs of this species belong to the group termed Bottom Burrowers. The head is elongated forming 2 points, the forelegs are brown and their bodies are greyish or yellowish white. The life cycle of this species is the longest of all the upwinged flies as the nymphs take three years to develop. They are to be found in fairly large deep rivers with a sandy substrata, where the nymphs dig holes and feed on the detritus and bacteria in water depths between 6–10m. In the last century this species was present in many large rivers in central Europe and the Balkans but as these very large Ephemeropterans can only exist in very pure unpolluted water their territory has today shrunk and they are now only to be found in the river Tisza and its tributaries. The nymphs hatch in open water on the surface in late June or early July.

The Dun. Plate 10 (75)
This unique species is the largest of all the European Ephemeroptera and is very large indeed, nearly twice as large as our Greendrake the largest British species. The males have three tails and large upright hindwings. The mainwings are dull smoky brown, the head and eyes are dark brown, the thorax yellow and the body is darkish grey on top to dull yellow underneath. There is no female in the dun stage, as the females emerge at the surface direct from the nymph as sexually mature spinners.

ARTIFICIALS: No known patterns. Any very large Mayfly pattern would probably be effective.

The Spinner. Plate 10 (74)
Both sexes are very similar, the head and eyes are dark brown and the legs are yellow brown while the thorax is yellow. Their bodies are dark grey on top and

bright yellow underneath, and their wings are smoky brown. Hatches which are often heavy usually start in the late afternoon or early evenings but rarely last for longer than about two hours. The male duns as soon as they hatch fly to the closest vegetation and within a minute or so ecdysis takes place and the newly emerged spinners immediately fly back over the water within inches of the surface looking for the emerging female spinners. As soon as these females cast off their nymphal skins they are likely to be attacked by up to four or five males seeking copulation. Due to the large size of these insects this causes much disturbance on the surface attracting bottom species of fish up to feed upon them — even in the deepest of water. There are unfortunately no trout in these rivers, but their are some very large bottom feeding fish such as Huchen a type of salmon as well as many species of catfish and also chub, some of which grow to a very large size. This can result in some very interesting and exciting fly fishing. To see a really big fish of many, many pounds in weight suddenly break the surface and take your fly sometimes with an explosion of spray is a heart stopping moment indeed. After copulation those females that have escaped the depredations of the fish, and are ready to lay their eggs (after an hour or so) form into huge swarms. These swarms often composed of thousands sometimes millions of insects fly upstream 5–10 metres above the surface in the centre of the river following the bends and curves irrespective of the position of the sun or changing wind direction. In the setting sun this mass of spinners flying upstream looks like a huge golden airborn snake and can be an awsome sight — the locals refer to this phenominum as the flowering of the Tisza.

This upstream migration is important as the eggs when laid must settle on the bottom in water at least 5–10 metres deep. After the female spinners have laid their eggs the surface is again covered with masses of dead and dying flies which heralds the commencement of another hearty feeding period by most fish in the river. The annual emergence of this species seldom lasts more than about 14 days and within this period there may be between two to five days of heavy hatches, with a similar period of moderate hatches and in between these periods will be days when none hatch at all. Therefore if it is your wish to drop back into the stone ages for at least one afternoon in ones fly fishing life to enjoy the miraculous 'Blossoming of the Tisza' you should book accommodation in the area for at least three weeks commencing in the middle of June.

ARTIFICIALS: Any very large Mayfly Spinner patterns should suffice.

DISTRIBUTION: Found only in parts of areas No's 10 and 11.

OLIGONEURIA RHENANA (3 Tails & Large Hindwings)

Length of body: ♂ & ♀ 13–17mm
Tails of imago: ♂ 12–14mm, ♀ 3–5mm

The Nymph

These nymphs belong to the group termed Stone Clingers and are fairly easy to recognise as they are one of the but few species to have their eyes close together on the top of their heads, which is rounded and not as wide as most of the other Stone Clinging species. They also have long hairs on the insides of their forelegs. They are of a dark brown coloration with three rather short tails and are found at lower altitudes between 100–600m in rather shallow rapid rivers between stones and smooth pebbles. The nymphs hatch in open water at the surface, and hatches are usually confined to a two or three week period any time between mid April and mid August.

The Dun

The duns are of a large size and have three very short whitish tails the middle one being shorter than the others and large hindwings. Both sexes have grey white wings with a complete lack of any cross veins, their bodies and thorax are dark grey and the legs are small grey white and not functional. The wings of the female are very broad and almost as wide as the length of their rather short stubby bodies. Once you have seen one of them you are unlikely to confuse them with any other species. These duns do not hatch until it is almost dark and are seldom on a very large scale.

ARTIFICIALS: No known pattern, can only suggest you try a pattern such as an Ermine Moth.

The Spinner. Plate 12 (92)

The spinners are very similar to the duns both in colouration and also in physical appearance. Both sexes of spinners are also very similar except that their bodies are more translucent and often have a greenish tinge.

This facinating species is quite unique among the Upwinged flies due not only to its many different physical features but also due to its very strange method of transposition from dun into spinner. Unlike all the other upwinged flies which transpose when at rest usually within about 14 to 36 hours after hatching (apart from P. Longicauda and Caenis spp) this species probably due to their very weak legs which seem unable to support the weight of their bodies actually transpose while in flight shortly after hatching. Once the subimaginal skin has been cast off, this always takes place over the water surface the spinners male and female pair up and again copulation takes place in flight over the surface. After mating both males and females drop onto the water surface, the females to lay their eggs in the rapid water and the males from exhaustion.

While few fly fishers may be tempted out at night to fish for the trout taking these, it can be a very exciting and rewarding experience and those anglers that have fly fished for sea trout at night will have a distinct advantage.

On a dark night these large whitish insects look like ping pong balls scattered on invisible walls. The spinners prefer very fast water or rapids on which to lay their eggs and it is here that the trout and grayling congregate at night to feed upon them. However in this type of water it is impossible to observe the rises so one has to fish by instinct. Good spots are to be found on the submountainous tributaries of the Rhone (FR. CH) the Rhine (CH. BRD) and the Ticino (CH. I).

ARTIFICIALS: Try a Grey Wulff with white wings or a Large Royal Wulff.

DISTRIBUTION: A rather rare and localised species found only in areas No's 1, 3 and 16.

POTAMANTHUS LUTEUS (3 Tails & Large Hindwings)

Length of body: ♂ 10–13mm, ♀ 12–14mm
Tails of imago: ♂ 16–18mm, ♀ 12mm

The Nymph. Plate 2 (12)

These relatively large nymphs would probably be included in the group known as

Agile Darters. They are to be found mainly in the larger slower flowing rivers, and never in rapids. Their preferred habitat is under flat stones or in weed beds preferably Potamogeton sp: and often in side pools of a sandy or stony nature. The nymphs hatch in open water probably on the surface in the early or late evening during June and July.

The Spinner. Plate 22 (175 & 176)
This rather large species has large upright hindwings with a costal projection and three tails. They are fairly easy to identify due to their rather unusual colouring and also to two identifying features as follows. The males have dull yellow bodies with an orange tinge and they have a broad yellow brown stripe running along the dorsal segments which narrows towards the tails. Each dorsal segment also has a pair of pale short divergent lines and dots. Each tergite (body segment) from 2–9 also has a distinct black dot on the lateral sides (see Fig 69A). The large compound eyes are olive-yellow and the tails are ringed black, and the wings are veined greyish yellow to a distinct dull yellow along the leading edges (see Fig 24C). The females are very similar but are of an overall brighter colour but with dark brown eyes.

ARTIFICIALS: I would suggest a large Lunn's Yellow Boy.

The Dun. Plate 22 (173 & 174)
The body colour of the duns is very similar to that of the spinners and they also have the same broad yellowish brown stripes running along the top of the abdomen as well as the dark lines and dots on each tergite. The tails are brownish becoming whitish distally and both males and females have greenish eyes. The wings are dull yellow with dark reddish cross veins darkening towards the leading edges while those of the females also often have greenish grey patches. Hatches of these duns are often quite substantial in the areas where they occur. They are not a particularly common species and tend to be rather localised in their distribution.

ARTIFICIALS: Would suggest a large Yellow Sally

DISTRIBUTION: To be found in areas No's 1, 16 and 23. Also in parts of Wales and Northern England but rarely.

69a Showing constant marks on body of *Potamanthus luteus* abdomen

CHOROTHERPES PICTETI (3 Tails & Large Hindwings)
Length of body: ♂ & ♀ 10–11mm
Tails of imago: ♂ & ♀ 12mm

The Nymph
The nymph of this species is very dark brown with three tails spread well apart and belongs to the group termed laboured swimmers. Found in smaller rivers at higher altitudes the nymphs avoid fast water and are to be seen in the calmer areas of shallower water in vegetation or between pebbles. There is one generation a year and the adults hatch in late August through to October.

The Spinner. Plate 9 (69)
This is a medium large species with three tails and large rather wide hindwings with a pointed apex (see Fig 64D). Due to these rather odd shaped hindwings and its very dark overall colouration this species is fairly easy to identify. Both sexes are very similar. They have glassy clear wings, dark veins with dark brown leading edges which are tinged blackish in places, their legs and thorax are very dark

brown to black as are their bodies, except for the whitish joinings of the body segments which show up even at a distance.

ARTIFICIALS: This really requires a special pattern such as an all black spinner, failing this try a Dark Watchett.

The Dun

Also a very dark almost black fly both sexes are very similar and the only difference between the spinners and the duns are the purplish black wings and the reddish tinge on the upper legs of the latter. This species is reputed to be particularly attractive to grayling. In October on many rivers in France the grayling fisher prayed for hatches of this fly, but it has now lost a lot of its former importance in this country since the French brought the grayling season to a close at the end of September.

ARTIFICIALS: Try an all black fly like an adult midge or even a large Black Gnat.

DISTRIBUTION: Found in areas No's 1–3, 6–10, 12 and 16.

EPHEMERELLA MUCRONATA (3 Tails & Large Hindwings)
Length of body: ♂ & ♀ 10mm
Tails of imago: ♂ 8–12mm, ♀ 7–10mm

The Nymph. Plate 2 (10)

These dark olive green nymphs are slightly flattened and belong to the group termed Moss Creepers. They are to be found on the bottom of small stony rivulets or small streams. Fairly common throughout Europe, tend to be localised and where they occur hatches are less abundant than other members of the genus. An early season species hatches have usually finished by the end of May.

The Spinner. Plate 10 (79 & 80)

This medium large species is very similar to the Blue Winged Olive. They have three tails and upright hindwings with a costal projection and both sexes are very similar. They have clear wings but the longitudinal veins are pale brown, their tails are dark ringed and their thorax and bodies are dark brown fading to a lighter shade underneath. From a lateral view their bodies are pale brown. The female spinners are to be seen on the water during the afternoons.

ARTIFICIALS: A Sherry Spinner or a Red Spinner.

The Dun. Plate 10 (77 & 78)

Both sexes are similar, they have grey wings, ringed tails and their bodies are brownish olive on top fading to yellow olive underneath.

ARTIFICIALS: A B.W.O. (Nice) or a B.W.O. (Jacques)

DISTRIBUTION: Found in areas No's 5–11, 14–16 and 20–23.

EPHEMERELLA MAJOR (3 Tails & Large Hindwings)
Length of body: ♂ & ♀ 8mm
Tails of imago: ♂ 8–11mm, ♀ 7–9mm

The Nymph. Plate 3 (24)

These dark olive green nymphs are slightly flattened and belong to the group termed Moss Creepers. The nymph of this particular species is extremely broad much more so than any other members of the genus. They are to be found on the sandy bottoms of small rivers and large brooks in mountainous country at altitudes between 200–600m. Fairly common in South Eastern Europe tend to be localised but where they occur hatches are often abundant usually starting in the middle of the day during warmer spring weather from mid May to early June.

The Spinner. Plate 11 (82 & 83)
This medium size species is very similar but a little smaller than the Blue Winged Olive. They have three tails and upright hindwings with a costal projection and both sexes are very similar. They have clear wings but the longitudinal veins are pale brown, their tails are dark ringed and their rather stout bodies are dark to red brown fading to a lighter shade underneath. The female spinners are to be seen on the water in the early evenings. The males have bright red compound eyes.
    ARTIFICIALS: A Sherry Spinner or a Red Spinner but the bodies require to be well dressed to give a thick silhouette.

The Dun. Plate 11 (81)
Both sexes are similar, they have dark grey wings, ringed tails and their bodies are brownish olive on top fading to yellow olive underneath. The males have reddish compound eyes.
    ARTIFICIALS: A B.W.O. (Nice) or a B.W.O. (Jacques) but dressed on small hooks.
    DISTRIBUTION: Found in areas No's 4, 5, 6, 7, 9 and 11.

HABROLEPTOIDES 'MODESTA' (3 Tails & Large Hindwings)
Length of body: ♂ 6–8mm, ♀ 9mm
Tails of imago: ♂ 9–10mm, ♀ 10mm

The Nymph
This species has been incorrectly described as covering the whole of central and southern Europe, whereas in actual fact it is only endemic in Corsica. The probable reason for this confusion is due to the fact that there are several other very similar species. These are H.auberti, H.carpathica, H.confusa. So far as the fly fisherman is concerned it is impossible to tell them apart so we shall describe here the genus. The nymphs are quite small and rather lethargic and are usually referred to as laboured swimmers. They are to be found in the slower sections of large brooks or small rivers in the calm places between large stones or debris that has collected on the bottom, and they show a distinct preference for forested areas. The adults are to be seen on the water in May in the early afternoons.

The Spinner. Plate 9 (67 & 68)
They are a medium to small species with three tails and upright hindwings which due to their unique shape (see Fig 64A) makes it impossible to confuse these species with any of the other upwinged flies apart from the Ditch Dun, which is much lighter in overall colour anyway. Both sexes are similar, they are very dark looking flies, as their bodies, legs and even tails are a very dark brown almost black, as are their eyes which are dark chestnut brown. Their wings are clear with

a light purple brown venation, and the trailing edges lack any smaller intercallery veins. The central body segments of the males are slightly translucent.

ARTIFICIALS: Can only suggest a very dark coloured Pheasant Tail Spinner.

The Dun. Plate 9 (65 & 66)

The opaque wings of the duns are sepia grey with a purple brown venation giving a touch of colour along the leading edges. Both sexes are similar with dark brown legs and tails while their bodies are dark grey brown faintly ringed in a lighter shade of brown. The bodies of the females are often lighter in colour than those of the male. They are not particularly common or widespread but in areas where they are found hatches can sometimes be of quite an abundant nature when they are of interest to the fly fisher.

ARTIFICIALS: Would suggest any of the many Iron Blue patterns or even a Super Grizzly.

DISTRIBUTION: At least some of the species mentioned above will be found in most European countries apart from Scandinavia.

EPHORON VIRGO (3 Tails or 2 Tails)
Length of body: ♂ 10–11mm, ♀ 12–14mm
Tails of imago: ♂ 30–33mm, ♀ 16–17mm

The Nymph. Plate 3 (21)

The large nymphs of this species belong to the group termed Bottom Burrowers. The whole nymph is cream coloured and the fore and hindlegs are strong with stout femora. They are found in medium sized rivers where they burrow into the bottom forming U shaped tubes where they live and feed upon detritus and bacteria. There is one generation every three years and the nymphs hatch late in the evenings in August. The biggest hatches are to be encountered before thunderstorms. They are common and widespread in central and southern Europe.

The Dun. Plate 9 (70)

This is a large species and is again unique among the Ephemeroptera as in both duns and spinners the male has two tails while the females have three. Both sexes are very similar, the wings are white with a grey venation, the thorax is yellow brown while the top of their bodies are greenish the underbodies are yellowish white and the legs which are small and non-functional are white. Due to their non-functional legs these subimagines cannot rest to change into the imago, so ecdysis takes place in flight.

ARTIFICIALS: No known pattern but would suggest a Royal Wulff or my own Poly May Spinner dressed on a size 12 hook.

The Spinner. Plate 9 (71)

Apart from the fact that the male has only two tails and the female three, there is very little difference between the sexes. These spinners are also very similar to the duns except that the wings are milky white with numerous longitudinal and cross veins which are grey. Both ecdysis and mating takes place in the air with the male spinners swarming 1 to 2 metres above the surface and flying horizontally. From the time they hatch until the female lays her eggs seldom takes more than about an hour. After this the water surface is covered with the creamy white bodies of these spinners.

ARTIFICIAL: Suggest you try a Poly May Spinner or a Deerstalker on small hooks.

DISTRIBUTION: Found in areas No's 1, 3, and 5 to 16.

SECTION 6:
UPWINGED FLIES WITH 3 TAILS AND LARGE HINDWINGS

SIPHLONURUS CROATICUS (2 Tails & Large Hindwings)
Length of body: ♂ & ♀ 13–15mm
Tails of imago: ♂ 20mm, ♀ 25mm

The Nymph. Plate 2 (13)
The general colouration of this quite large nymph is greenish brown and it belongs to the group of Agile Darters. They are to be found in the smaller rivers or brooks in water with an optimum temperature of 11–12°C between aquatic vegetation or large stones avoiding strong currents. There is one generation a year with hatches usually confined to two weeks or so in early May. The nymphs usually emerge via stones or emergent vegetation.

The Dun. Plate 4 (25 & 26)
This large species belongs to the same genera as the Large Summer Duns, but as it only hatches in the very early summer a better common name could be the Large Spring Dun. They have two tails and large upright hindwings with a costal projection (see Fig 25B). In general appearance and colour they are very similar to the various species of Large Summer Duns. Both sexes are much alike and have dark grey wings (see Fig 24B) and light yellow olive bodies heavily banded in dark brown. These duns are of doubtful value to the fly fisher as they are seldom to be observed on the water unless blown on to it.

ARTIFICIALS: No known patterns. Try a Large Summer Dun.

The Spinner. Plate 4 (27 & 28)
The spinner is also very similar in appearance and colour to the various species of Large Summer Spinners often referred to as the Great Red Spinners. This spinner may be a little lighter in colour. Both sexes are similar they have opaque bluish wings lightly veined pale brown, greenish yellow bodies with dark brown markings on both dorsal and ventral segments and brownish tails (see Fig 69B). The spinners unlike the duns are a very important species to the fly fisher in those areas where they occur. While they are not a particularly common species and tend to be rather localised, hatches in these favoured areas can be very heavy indeed. When the female spinners return to lay their eggs in one mass on the water and the spent flies lay dying on the surface often in very large numbers the fly fisher can reap good rewards. The males always swarm in shaded areas carefully avoiding the sunshine, and when the females join them they are probably unique among the upwinged flies because the copulating pairs more often than not fall onto the surface together. These make a juicy mouthful for any trout but do of course require a special pattern to represent them at this time. At times this fall of spinners is so heavy that it becomes almost impossible to catch trout as they

69b *Siphlonurus* pattern on body

quickly become overfed. At this time it will pay the fly fisher to seek out areas in the sunshine where the fall is likely to be much lighter.

ARTIFICIAL: A Great Red Spinner or a Large Summer Spinner (Price).

DISTRIBUTION: Found in areas No's 4, 5 and 9.

EPEORUS SYLVICOLA (= syn E.assimilis) (2 Tails & Large Hindwings)

Length of body: ♂ & ♀ 14–17mm

Tails of imago: ♂ 35–40mm, ♀ 30–35mm

The Nymph. Plate 1 (3)

The dark brown nymph with two tails is wide and flattened as are the upper joints of the legs and belongs to the group referred to as Stone Clingers.

This is a species that is probably unique among the Upwinged flies as ecdysis takes place beneath the surface and the winged insect then floats up to the surface. They are to be found in fast turbulent rivers or rapids among the large stones or boulders and there is one generation a year with hatches in April, May or early June.

The Spinner. Plate 6 (47 & 48)

This is a large species and fairly abundant in areas where they occur, they have two tails and large upright hindwings with a costal projection. To assist in their identification the following points should be noted. The ventral and dorsal segments of the body have a broad dark patch containing light spots, and the lateral sides of these segments have dark brown diagonal bands, similar to those appearing on the Large Green Spinners but fainter (see Fig 70), they also have a distinct yellowish neck. Both sexes are similar with olive green bodies and transparent bluish tinged wings veined black. The wings of the males are tinged yellow green towards the base and in some cases also along the leading edges.

ARTIFICIAL: No known patterns, would suggest a large Lunn's Yellow Boy, or Large Summer Spinner.

The Dun. Plate 6 (45 & 46)

Both sexes of duns are also similar with dark green olive bodies and brown diagonal stripes. Their wings are light bistre grey with brown veins and darker patches and the wing roots are often yellowish, particularly in the males. The ventral segments like the spinners have dark patches containing light spots. Because these duns hatch below the surface usually in very turbulent water a large percentage never get airborne and drift along beneath the surface, so a wet artificial pattern is often more effective than a dry.

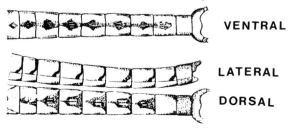

70 Abdominal markings on *Epeorus sylvicola*

85

ARTIFICIALS: Would suggest a Large Summer Dun (Price), a Partride and Orange, or a March Brown Spider fished well below the surface.

DISTRIBUTION: Found in areas No's 1 to 13 and 16.

ECDYONURUS HELVETICUS (2 Tails & Large Hindwings)

Length of body: ♂ & ♀ 10–14mm
Tails of imago: ♂ 25–35mm, ♀ 21mm

The Nymph

These also belong to the group referred to as Stone Clingers, they are a flattened type nymph with three tails and an olive brown body. They are to be found among loose stones in fast brooks or streams in both mountainous and sub-mountainous areas between 500–1200m. There is one generation a year and hatches commence in June at the lower altitudes until early September at the higher altitudes in the early afternoons. The nymphs hatch via emergent stones or boulders but the winged duns often drop onto the water surface during the first few seconds of flight.

The Spinner. Plate 5 (39 & 40)

A large species with two tails and large hindwings with a costal projection. Both sexes are rather similar with transparent wings veined brown tinged towards base with greenish-yellow, and their bodies are dark sepia brown to yellow brown underneath. The female spinners are to be observed in the early evenings dipping onto the water surface to lay their eggs. This is usually in fast turbulent sections of the stream where it is extremely difficult to see the trout rising to them.

ARTIFICIALS: No known pattern, can only suggest a Pheasant Tail Spinner.

The Dun. Plate 5 (37 & 38)

Both sexes are similar with wings of a dusky grey brown colour sometimes with darker stripes at the bases. The costal areas often have a sulphur yellow or greenish tint. Their bodies are dark brown to olive brown underneath. They have dark brown legs and black tails and the eyes of the female are dull yellow green.

ARTIFICIALS: Choose a pattern that floats well and is easily seen in rough water such as a Humpy or a Tricolore.

DISTRIBUTION: Found in areas No's 2, 3, 8 and 9.

ECDYONURUS PICTETI. Plate 11 (84 & 85)

Very similar to E.helveticus except for the wing colour of the duns which have cross stripes with a pronounced contrast. Similar distribution but at somewhat higher altitudes 800–1600m.

ECDYONURUS KRUEPERI. Plate 11 (86–88)

This species is also very similar to E.helveticus and E.picteti except for the wing colouration of both spinner and dun as there are black zones towards the leading edges and in the centre there is a yellow area. The hindwings are also distinctly yellow. E.krueperi is found at similar altitudes to E.helveticus, but replaces this species in the South West Balkans (Greece, Albania and Macedonia). Areas 6–7, 10 and 12. To assist identification of all these Ecdyonurus species refer to venation of forewings (see Fig 24A).

HEPTAGENIA FLAVA (2 Tails & Large Hindwings)
Length of body: ♂ & ♀ 9–12mm
Tails of imago: ♂ 24mm, ♀ 25mm

The Nymph
This is another of the Stone Clingers it has three tails a brownish body with light yellow spots dorsally on the body and their is also a dark red-brown line running down the centre of the dorsal body segments. There is one generation a year and the nymphs have a preference for the warmer rivers at lower altitudes. They are to be found in the more rapid rivers between large stones or boulders, and hatch during the middle of the day in open water in June or early July.

The Spinner. Plate 8 (63 & 64)
This is a medium large to large species which like many other insects used to be very common and abundant throughout Central Europe until agricultural pollutants reduced their habitat. They have two tails and large upright hindwings with a costal projection. Both sexes are similar the wings are opaque with black veins but have an overall yellowish colour this more pronounced along the leading edges of the mainwings, they are also tinged red-purple along the top leading edges. Their bodies and thorax are yellow-orange, and on the dorsal segments of the abdomen there is a dark purple stripe and point.
    ARTIFICIALS: Would suggest a Lunn's Yellow Boy.

The Dun. Plate 8 (61 & 62)
This particularly handsome fly is very similar to H. Sulphurea and should be easily recognised first by its overall yellow colouration and secondly by a distinct tinge of purple red along the top leading edges of the mainwings. Both sexes are similar with dull yellow wings and hindwings broadly bordered along the trailing edges with a greyish cloud. The bodies and thorax are dull yellow-orange with touches of purple.
ARTIFICIALS: Try a Large Yellow Sally.
DISTRIBUTION: Found in areas No's 7 to 16

RHITHROGENA HYBRIDA (2 Tails & Large Hindwings)
Length of body: ♂ & ♀ 9–10mm
Tails of imago: ♂ & ♀ 12–15mm

The Nymph
Very similar to the other species of Rhithrogena the brownish flattened three tailed nymph is also a Stone Clinger. These nymphs have no femoral markings as in the other species. They are to be found in large brooks and small streams at fairly low temperatures at altitudes between 800–2000m. They prefer the mid currents or the shallow outflow from pools in stony or gravelly streams and there is one generation a year which hatch in August in the afternoons.

The Spinner. Plate 7 (51 & 52)
A medium large species with two tails and large upright hindwings with a costal projection. In overall colour this is the darkest of all the Rhithrogena species and it is also one of the only species to have no dark oval patches on the top leg joints. Both sexes have transparent wings lightly veined black with a yellowish tinge

along the leading edges, and their body segments are dark greyish brown with lighter ringing. The small eyes of the females are pale olive with a transverse bar across the centre, while the large compound eyes of the males are almost black.

ARTIFICIALS: Try a Sunk Spinner or a Pheasant Tail Spinner.

The Dun. Plate 7 (49 & 50)

The whole insect is of a dark grey colouration. Both sexes have wings that vary from a very dull grey to a lighter blue grey which seems to be more common in the males. The thorax and body segments are dark grey brown with lighter joinings and the legs are of a similar colour. The compound eyes of the males are almost black while the smaller eyes of the females are dark olive with a transverse bar across the centre.

ARTIFICIAL: Would suggest an Iron Blue pattern on a size 14 hook.

DISTRIBUTION: Common and fairly abundant where it occurs which is only in area no 4.

RHITHROGENA BRAASCHI. Plate 7 (53–56) (2 Tails & Large Hindwings)

This species is so similar in appearance to Rhithrogena semicolorata (the Yellow Upright see Page No 64), in every stage of its life cycle, history and habitat that there is some doubt in listing it seperately. The only difference between the two species is a blue-brown tinge at the borders of the conspicuous cross veins on the mainwings of R.braaschi. This common and abundant species replaces R.semicolorata in the Balkans where hatches may be observed as early as April.

Like R.semicolorata the spinners of this species crawl underwater to lay their eggs and the dead and dying spinners are then carried downstream below the surface. This species is to be found at fairly low altitudes in fast turbulent streams and rivers and the best time for fishing when these naturals are about is in the late evenings when the spinners are returning to lay their eggs. However fishing can be very difficult at this time as the trout are feeding upon these spinners below the surface and in the turbulent water that they like it is difficult to see either the trout or their rises. In the magnificent white rock rivers of Macedonia in the south-west of the Balkans the spinners of this species provide the earliest evening rises of the year.

ARTIFICIALS: patterns as suggested for the Yellow and Olive Upright.

RHITHROGENA LOYOLAEA. Plate 8 (57–60) (2 Tails & Large Hindwings)

This species is also very similar in its life cycle, history and appearance to R.semicolorata but generally much darker in both body and wings, and replaces this species in the mountainous regions of areas No's 1, 4, 7, and 10 at altitudes between 800–2000m. The nymphs hatch in the afternoons in late July, August and sometimes in early September. Sometimes hatches are abundant but never to the same degree as other species in the genus. Fishing techniques and artificial patterns similar to those that apply for the Yellow or Olive Upright (see page 64).

AMELETUS INOPINATUS (2 Tails & Large Hindwings)

Length of body: ♂ & ♀ 9–11mm
Tails of imago: ♂ 16mm, ♀ 13mm

The Nymph. Plate 2 (16)

These medium sized nymphs belong to the group of Agile Darters and are to be found in the calmer reaches of small rivers or brooks between stones or boulders. Have also been recorded from stony lakes. Usually confined to the higher altitudes between 400–1800 metres. They have also been recorded from mountainous areas in Scotland and Scandinavia. Their is one generation a year with hatches commencing in late May and continuing through to August, by which time specimens are usually smaller. The nymphs usually but not necessarily always hatch out via emergent stones or vegetation.

The Spinner. Plate 4 (31 & 32)

This is a medium large species and belongs to the same family as the Large Summer Duns but cannot be included with them as it is much smaller. Both sexes are very similar indeed. The bodies are a pitch-brown colour inclining to burnt amber with the last three segments a dark red brown. The wings are glassy clear and tinted uniformly but very faintly with rusty brown, the cross veins are weak and opaque except in the upper leading edges (see Fig 25A). The tails are light brown with paler ringing. They have two tails and large upright hindwings with a costal projection.

ARTIFICIALS: Would suggest a Large Summer Spinner (Price) dressed on size 12 or 14 hooks, or a Pheasant Tail Spinner.

The Dun. Plate 4 (29 & 30)

The dun may be of doubtful value to the fly fisherman as it is unlikely to be seen on the water in sufficient numbers to interest the trout due to its method of emergence. Both male and female duns are very similar to the Spinners except that their wings are dark grey with yellowish brown veins.

ARTIFICIALS: Suggest a Grey Wulff if Duns should be observed.
DISTRIBUTION: Found in area No's 5 to 10, 14, 16, and 20 to 23.

RHITHROGENA SAVOYENSIS (2 Tails & Large Hindwings)

Length of body: ♂ & ♀ 7–9mm
Tails of imago: ♂ 11–15mm, ♀ 9–10mm

The Nymph

The reddish brown flattened nymph of this species has three tails and comes in the group of Stone Clingers. To be found in large brooks or small rivers of a stony nature, in warm water below 600m. Not a particularly common species hatches tend to be on the sparse side and there is one generation a year the nymphs emerging at the surface in open water during July. This species is very similar and often confused with R.diaphana, which is now very rare indeed and only occurs in the Southern foothills of the Pyrenees.

The Spinner. Plate 6 (43 & 44)

This is a medium to medium large species with two tails and large upright hindwings with a costal projection. Like most of the Rhithrogena genera this species has a dark oval shaped mark in the middle of each top leg (femora) joint (see Fig 29C). Both sexes have transparent wings brownish grey tails, yellow brown bodies with a faint diagonal stripe down the lateral sides of the body segments (see Fig 71). The females bodies are a lighter shade of olive, and their olive brown eyes are divided by a black transverse line.

   ARTIFICIALS: No known patterns, would suggest Lunn's Yellow Boy, fished in or just below the surface.

71 Abdomen lateral – *Rhithrogena savoyensis*

The Dun. Plate 6 (41 & 42)

Also has the same dark mark in the middle of each top leg joint. Both sexes have grey brown wings and yellow brown bodies and like the spinners have faint diagonal lines running down each lateral body segment. The tails are grey.

   ARTIFICIALS: Would suggest a July Dun, Greenwell's Glory or a Tricolore.

   DISTRIBUTION: Found in area No's 3 to 14 and 16.

NIXE JOERNENSIS (2 Tails & Large Hindwings)

Length of body: 8mm,   7.5mm
Tails of imago: 12mm,   10mm

The Nymph. Plate 1 (6)

These also belong to the group referred to as Stone Clingers, they are a flattened type nymph with three tails and have a dark olive body with no perceptable pattern. These nymphs are very restricted in their habitat and are only found in parts of Scandinavia. Found in small rivers and warm stony brooks at lower altitudes, there is one generation a year and hatches of the adult can be expected during August in the middle of the day.

The Spinner. Plate 12 (91)

This medium size species is one of the smallest in the Heptaginiidae family. They have two tails and large upright hindwings with a costal projection. Both sexes are very similar they have colourless wings with a grey-white nervation, greyish tails, dark green olive bodies fading to yellow olive ventrally, and the females have dark blue grey eyes. The spinners return to the water in the early afternoons.

   ARTIFICIAL: Would suggest Lunn's Yellow Boy or Dark Green Poly Spinner.

The Dun. Plate 12 (89 & 90)

Both sexes are similar they have medium grey wings turning yellowish towards the base with a brown olive body and yellow olive legs, and are very similar in appearance to the Olive Upright but a little smaller and darker. Although they are an uncommon species in those areas where they occur they could be important to the fly fisherman as most of the waters in these areas are of an acid nature and do not support large numbers of upwinged flies.

ARTIFICIALS: Try an H.P.B. or a Greenwells Glory/
DISTRIBUTION: Found only in area No's 20, 22 and 23.

SECTION 7:
UPWINGED FLIES WITH 2 TAILS AND SMALL HINDWINGS

BAËTIS ALPINUS (2 Tails & Small Oval Hindwings)
Length of body: ♂ & ♀ 7–10mm
Tails of imago: ♂ up to 23mm, ♀ 12–14mm

The Nymph. Plate 2 (15)

While the nymphs of most of the Baetis species belong to the group termed Agile Darters, the nymphs of this species although a little flatter and of a very similar appearance cannot be included as they are very weak swimmers and are more of a crawling type nymph. The tails all but lack swimming hairs and the centre tail is very short indeed. They are to be found in fairly fast rivers between stones and pebbles mainly in mountain areas at altitudes between 200–250m and in water temperatures ranging between 5–12°C. There are two generations a year and the adults are to be observed hatching in March and April and again in September and October. They are a common and abundant species in the area where they occur.

The Spinner. Plate 5 (35 & 36)

A medium large species with two tails and small oval spur shaped hindwings with double intercallery veins on the mainwings (see Fig 28A), they are very similar indeed to the Large Dark Olive (Baetis rhodani). The female spinners have a dark thorax, chestnut brown bodies fading to yellow brown ventrally and their transparent wings appear slightly brownish due to brown venation. The wings of the male are similar but their bodies are translucent white with the last three segments orange brown, and their turbinate eyes are pale brown on top with the lower part yellow to orange. Like most of the other Baetis species it is probable that they deposit their eggs underwater by crawling down projecting stones or boulders. These spinners are often to be observed on the water in the early mornings.

ARTIFICIALS: A Red Spinner (Harris), a U.S.D. Poly Spinner (Brown) or a Pheasant Tail Spinner.

The Dun. Plate 5 (33 & 34)

Both sexes have pale grey wings with a dark venation and their bodies are olive brown with a dark brown to blackish thorax. The male has red brown turbinate eyes. Emergence of these duns is usually confined to the middle of the day.

ARTIFICIALS: An Imperial, a Super Grizzly or a Beacon Beige.
DISTRIBUTION: Found in areas No's 4 to 10 12 and 16.

CHAPTER 6

FLIES WITH ROOF-SHAPED WINGS

SEDGE OR CADDIS FLIES (TRICHOPTERA)

The sedge, or caddis-flies, as they are known in some areas, make up a fairly large group containing over 700 different species throughout Europe, while in the British Isles alone there are nearly 200 species. It therefore may appear to be a daunting task for the average fly fisher to identify any of these. In practice it is not so difficult though as the majority of flies in this order are either rarely seen or are very localised in their distribution. They are related to certain families of moths, but differ mainly in the structure of the wings. Each has four wings, but those of the moth are covered with tiny flattened scales, while those of the sedge-flies are covered with tiny hairs. A brief account of the life cycle of the latter is given in Chapter 4.

Like moths, many of the sedges are nocturnal, hatching out either after dark or just as the light is beginning to fade. Fortunately for the angler, some species do hatch out during the day or late afternoon. To generalise, the nocturnal species of Trichoptera seem to be larger, paler and less hairy than the diurnal species. Several are well known to fly-fishermen, and while the most distinctive of all of the day-time sedges is the Grouse Wing, the sedges which are probably the most common of all seen at the waterside are the Silverhorns. These small to medium sized flies can be seen on most days in the late afternoon right through the summer, and are generally found flying in clouds just above the surface of the water. Unfortunately, although they are so prolific these adults seldom seem to interest the trout, and in hundreds of autopsies on trout I have seldom come across one.

The Larvae
Most species of sedge-flies make cases in which they live, but there are a few families that are either non-case making or free swimming. The case-making or eruciform larvae are to be found in all types of water while the free swimming or non case-making families referred to as Campodeiform larvae are mainly confined to running water, although they may occasionally be observed in bodies of stillwater that have flowing inlets or outlets or even on large lakes where wave action along the shoreline creates currents. The Campodeiform larvae are very much in the minority, these non-case making species build rough shelters and construct at the entrance funnels or purse-like webs with which to trap food,

while other species form tunnels or silken tubes which are attached to stones or boulders. The other even less common species in this group generally referred to as free-swimming are mainly carnivorous constantly moving on the lookout for food.

The larvae are often referred to as caddis grubs and they are somewhat similar in appearance to a caterpillar, except that they have a clearly defined head and six legs. The body colour varies and the head is usually of a darker colour, often brown, although in many species this is marked with dark patterning on a lighter ground.

Shortly after hatching the young case-making larvae commence to build their future home or caddis case, and although this may appear far from luxurious, it is in fact a masterpiece of insect ingenuity. Apart from being roomy and comfortable, being lined on the interior with a smooth secretion provided by the larva to seal the gaps between the sections of material holding the case together, the outside is well camouflaged as a protection against predators, and the whole complex structure can be increased in size when required. Most caddis cases are tapered from front to back, and when the larvae grows it builds on to the front or wider end. The cases are formed from a wide variety of materials, and although most species have their particular preferences, not only in this respect but also for the actual shape of their dwelling, it would be a mistake to rely on these characteristics alone for identification of the species. Among the materials used are small discarded shells, gravel, sand, pieces of stick, vegetable matter or cut sections of leaves. Whatever the substances, the artistry with which they are applied is quite incredible. As far as is known all larvae live in their cases for up to a year, and during this period they are in constant danger from predators. When on the move in search of food, their heads and legs are extended from the case, which is held in position by small hooks on their bodies, but when danger threatens they quickly retreat into the comparative safety of their cases. Most species are omnivorous, while a few are herbivorous, feeding on vegetable matter only, while many are carnivorous, feeding on other small aquatic creatures or at times even on their own kind. In the following descriptions of the more common species of adults, I have, where possible, also given a description of the larval case which can sometimes be helpful in identifying the species. This method is far from infallible, as previously mentioned, and is well illustrated by the following.

Some years ago I procured from Two Lakes, for rearing in my tanks, some specimens of caddis that had formed their purse-shaped cases from several large sections of fallen beech leaves. Apparently this particular species, apart from building its case from these leaves, also feeds on them, and before I became aware of it several of them had partially eaten their own homes. At the time I was unable to procure a further supply of these leaves, and, anticipating incorrectly that they would fail to survive in their incomplete cases, I left them to their fate. To my surprise, a few days later I discovered they had made completely new domains for themselves from various small shells, and they now bore little resemblance to their former appearance.

The larvae in their cases are usually to be found in the shallower waters in the vicinity of weeds or stones, although certain species that enjoy a measure of immunity from predators by attaching long pieces of stick to the outside of their cases will often be found in profusion on the bed of the lake in full view. Trout will feed on some species avidly when available, but as far as I am aware until comparatively recently few fly-fishermen have attempted to imitate them at this stage of their existence. In any case, even though this has been accomplished, it may appear to many anglers to be far removed from fly-fishing in the accepted sense. On the other hand, the very essence of fly-fishing is to deceive a trout with an imitation of fur, feather or silk to represent some particular form of food on which it may be feeding, so apart from the fact that here we are dealing largely with an inanimate object, as opposed to an animate one such as a nymph or a fly, there is basically little difference. While I am sure it is relatively easy to tie a lifelike artificial to represent some of these larvae in their cases, and indeed I give some later, it has certainly proved rather difficult to present them to the trout in an attractive or successful manner. Undoubtedly there is considerable scope for experiment in this direction for those fishermen who feel inclined to do so.

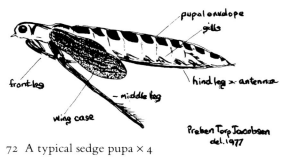

72 A typical sedge pupa × 4

The Pupae

When the time for pupation arrives, the larva anchors its case to weed, stones, etc., and then seals or plugs it at each end. This is accomplished in diverse ways, using tufts of algae or moss, cut pieces of weed, small stones or gravel or, in some cases, it is sealed with a web of its own chitinous substance. Whatever the material used, minute gaps are left to allow the passage of water, presumably for respiratory purposes, and the pupa constantly undulates its body within the case to assist the flow.

In the early stages of pupation certain changes take place until, shortly before pupation is complete, the main characteristics of the adult are noticeable. The wing cases are fully formed and the legs developed, and while these are bunched under the body, at least two of these usually the median legs are capable of independent movement to help its final journey to the surface (Plate 27, No. 216). The antennae, which are a characteristic of the adult, can also be observed lying down either side of the body, and with species that have antennae longer than their bodies the excess length is either folded at the tail end or, in some instances, actually wound spirally round the rear segments of the body (Plate 28, No. 219). The pupa is also equipped with a powerful pair of mandibles well adapted to their function of sawing through the sealed end of the case, to release the pupa for its journey to the surface, where transformation into the winged adult takes place (Plate 28, No. 217). The duration of pupation varies from days to weeks, according to species or conditions.

As previously mentioned, at least one pair of legs, although still enveloped in the pupal skin, are functional. These, as far as I have been able to ascertain, are always the median legs and generally are fringed with extensive hairs on each side, and so, well adapted for their purpose of providing the pupa with a pair of paddle-like instruments to enable it to swim to the surface (Plate 28, No. 224).

Certain species transform into the adult as soon as the surface is reached, while others apparently swim considerable distances until they find, projecting above the surface, some object or weed up which they climb, and where metamorphosis is completed. At this stage the pupal skin loosely enveloping the formed imago expands as internal pressure which eventually bursts it is built up. The skin usually splits at the top of the head behind the mandibles, and except that the wings are not yet fully inflated the fully developed adult emerges (Plate 28, No. 218).

It is during their final journey to the surface that the pupae are most vulnerable to predators such as trout, thereby providing the angler with an excellent opportunity of imitating them at this stage.

FURTHER INFORMATION ON THE SEDGE PUPA
(reproduced from an article provided for *The Fly Fisher's Journal* by the author.)

In recent years it has been established that on both rivers and particularly on lakes the pupa of the sedge, next to the pupa of the midge, provides the main diet of trout throughout the latter half of the season. Until comparatively recently apart from my own sedge pupa patterns and the longhorn patterns of Dick Walker, little progress has been made in this direction to develop specific pupa patterns to represent the many different species. To some extent this is now being rectified, as during the past two years several excellent new tyings have appeared from the United States where sedge pupa patterns are used extensively on rivers.

As a result of this I have been taking an increasing interest in this particular stage of the insect, and I have subsequently come to realise that there are many misconceptions about the anatomy of the average pupa. I am sure most amateur fly dressers will appreciate that it is essential to have a clear picture in one's mind of the precise appearance of the anatomical structure of an insect before one can attempt to dress a lifelike pattern. Despite a diligent search I have been unable to find full and accurate information in this respect as, unlike the larva and the adult, most books seem to skate over specific details on the pupa. The following information on the pupa has been gleaned from various statements in scientific papers and books, plus a certain amount of information which I have collected from my own research, which I hope will in the course of time prove to be accurate.

As the behaviour of the pupa prior to and after hatching into the adult is of direct interest to the fisherman, I will commence by giving some brief information on its life cycle. When the larvae are ready to pupate, case making species construct a cocoon by partially sealing the ends of their cases, while most non-case making species construct their cocoon from various materials such as tiny stones or gravel fastened together with silk on the side of a stone which is then sealed upon completion. Pupation can take from several days to two or three weeks according to conditions and species. When pupation is complete they cut their way out of their cocoon utilising powerful mandibles with which the pupa is equipped. They then swim either to the surface or towards the shore, depending whether they are species that hatch out on the surface or via emergent vegetation along the shoreline, where ecdysis into the adult takes place (Plate 28, No. 220 to 224). I would add that some authorities suggest they may swim around for some time before emerging. The pupa is quite a powerful swimmer as the middle pair of legs are fringed with dense hairs and are used like paddles for propulsion. Those species which transform into the adult on emergent vegetation seem to be provided with extra strong tarsal claws on their front legs probably as an aid to climbing, and once they have attained a safe position well clear of the water appear to take their time before the transformation into the adult is completed. On the other hand those species that hatch on the surface in open water usually do so quickly, which is probably nature's way of ensuring survival of at least a percentage. On most of the occasions when I have been able to observe closely the pupa hatching on the surface, it would appear that the emerging adult is able to inflate the pupal case from within until it bursts along the top of the thorax, whence the adult emerges (Plate 28, No. 218). This is usually within seconds rather than minutes. Whether the inflation of the case is peculiar to certain species or not I have been unable to ascertain. It should also be noted that certain structural features of the pupa such as the fringe of hairs along the legs, the powerful biting mandibles and abdominal hooks, are part of the pupal envelope which is eventually discarded.

I am indebted to my very good friend the Danish angling entomologist Preben Torp Jacobsen for the following description of the actual transformation, as he observed it many times recently during very dense hatches on a Norwegian river. 'We saw at close range how the caddis pupae swim up to the surface, using their middle legs like paddles, many hatched out on the surface which was the most usual way, but others – probably different species – upon reaching the surface moved rapidly over it like skaters using both middle and also the front legs as paddles creating a V-shaped wake, many being taken by the trout with a savage sort of rise. Those that reached emergent vegetation or in many cases our waders, crawled quickly out of the water, and within a short period ecdysis commenced. They appeared to arch their backs, then the front of the thorax would split and out would come the head followed by the thorax and then the wings. The antennae appear to lie alongside the body under the wing cases, as do the rear legs which seem to lie in such a position that they are used to actually withdraw the wings from the pupal envelope. Many trout, whitefish and grayling we caught were crammed full of sedge pupae, many of them still alive.'

The Pupa The pupal integument is transparent and loosely envelopes the fully formed imago lying underneath. The general shape and colour of the pupa therefore closely follows the shape and colour of the adult sedge. The abdomen of the pupa, composed of nine segments, is generally rather larger than the body of the adult, and in many species a pronounced fringe of dark hairs may be observed on each side along the lateral line. The dorsal or upper surface of the pupa also has a series of dark coloured plates surmounted by hooks. These vary in size and shape according to species, and are used for gripping the sides of the cocoon when emerging. The pupal envelope at the end of the body covering the genitalia is darker and in some species is elongated and equipped with distinct bristles. The antennae closely follow the colour and shape of the underlying adult and lie along the body but under the wing cases. In those with exceptionally long antennae they are wrapped spirally around the body many times, and it is worth noting that these often become unwrapped and trail behind the pupa as it swims along, while the spiral shape at the end often persists (Plate 28 No 219). Each of the four wings are separately housed in the integument, but as they are folded within these wing cases their length is considerably reduced and they only extend about half- to two-thirds along the length of the body. The larger fore wing cases are positioned over the shorter anterior ones so that they both cling closely along the sides of the body with the tips projecting slightly downwards. The colour of the wing cases of the pupa closely follow the colour of the wings of the adult. The legs, six in all, are free although they are covered closely by pouches of the pupal envelope. The middle legs used for swimming and lined with dense hairs are entirely free (as are the fore legs in some species), while the fore and rear legs are partly adherent to the body. Finally, the eyes of the mature pupa are usually black and very prominent.

It will, I hope, be appreciated that the above is a general description of an average pupa. There are of course minor features besides the size that differ according to the specific species. I have also excluded many taxonomical features as these are only of importance to the entomologist.

The Adult or Imago

Most sedges have wings confined to shades ranging from a pale yellow-fawn to a dark red-brown through to a dark grey-brown or almost black. The life cycle is similar to the previous Dipteran group, the insects passing through three stages before emerging as adult winged flies: egg, larva and pupa. The adult fly has four wings, the front wings being slightly longer than the hindwings, and when at rest these wings cover the abdomen rather like a roof. In general structure they are similar to the Ephemeroptera, though certainly not in appearance. The abdomen, or body, which is tailless, is composed of nine segments, and the thorax of the usual three. They have a fairly large pair of compound eyes and a pair of antennae of varying length. It is interesting to note that while all species of sedge-flies are equipped with a pair of these large, many-faceted compound eyes called oculi, some species are also equipped with very small simple eyes mounted on top of the head, and these are called ocelli. Protruding from the mouth parts are two pairs of palps called the maxillary and labial respectively (these were mentioned in Chapter 1). The legs are long, slender and many jointed. The middle joints often carry several slender spurs, and the number of these spurs on each leg can often assist the entomologist to identify the species. The sedge in the adult winged form is unable to partake of solid food but is able to consume liquid. It is rather difficult to distinguish between the sexes, and from the angler's point of view, unnecessary.

To generalise, adult sedge-flies may be divided into two groups as follows: day-hatching species and night-hatching species; each may be further sub-divided into those that hatch from open water and those that hatch via emergent vegetation, etc. The species that hatch out during the daylight hours are generally smaller, darker and more hairy than the night-hatchers, and although the former are very much in ther minority there are many species in this category classified amongst the fisherman's sedges. Fortunately for the angler, many of the night-hatching species hatch in the late evening as dusk approaches, so coming within the scope of the fly-fisherman. Several of the larger species that hatch from open water are of particular value to the fly-fisherman due to the disturbance they create while endeavouring to become airborne after emerging on the surface from the pupal case. Depending on species and conditions, some become airborne comparatively quickly, while others remain on the surface for a considerable length of time drying their wings preparatory to flight. Some species travel along the surface for comparatively long distances, flapping their wings occasionally in their efforts to take off, and this behaviour attracts the trout to them in no uncertain manner. At least one species, notably the Large Cinnamon Sedge, *Potamophylax latipennis*, usually after hatching, proceeds rapidly along the surface towards the shore, creating a V-shaped wake like a small speedboat. This usually occurs in the late afternoon or early evening, and on calm days they can be spotted from a long distance. If the hatch is a good one it is surprising how few escape the depredations of the trout on their shoreward journey. Some adults that hatch via emergent vegetation are of little interest to the fly-fisherman except for the females that return eventually to the water to lay their eggs.

As previously mentioned, there are nearly 700 different species of sedge-flies, and with such a large number of species anglers may well be excused for thinking that identification of any would be virtually impossible except by a trained entomologist. Nevertheless, while positive identification is often difficult, it is usually possible with practice to classify the family or genus of a specimen, and this will usually suffice. In any case, the problem is minimised to a certain extent as, despite the number of species involved, many are scarce and only occasionally encountered, whereas most of the fisherman's sedges listed are extremely common and widely distributed.

To illustrate this point my late colleague, Mr David Jacques, the noted angler/ entomologist, several years ago carried out a survey of the Trichoptera population of Two Lakes in Hampshire. This extended over four seasons, and during this period over 56 different species were identified. During the course of this research literally hundreds of specimens were caught and classified, but out of the resulting number that were identified 30 were restricted to less than half a dozen specimens each over the period. Furthermore, of the remaining 16 species only eight could really be considered common. However, it must be pointed out that this research was not necessarily conclusive, due to restrictions of time. Many fly-fishermen may rightly query the need for identification of any of the sedge-flies, and in defence I can only state that on occasions it can be of value if anticipating hatches of particular species in locations or at expected times, according to their known behaviour. Also, correct identification of the adult can in most cases give a clue to the colour and behaviour of the corresponding pupae, although much research is still required in this direction.

Despite the large numbers of species in this group, only relatively few have been identified by the angler with vernacular names, and of these many are common to both lake and river. In Chapter 2, which deals fairly extensively with the Ephemeroptera, it was possible to give considerable detail for positive identification of the various species and families for the angler with an entomological leaning. Due to the fact that there are many more species of sedge-flies, in a book of this nature it is just not possible to do this and, in any case, identification is so much more complex that it is not certain that even the keenest angler would want to identify precisely all the sedges in view of the doubtful value of such knowledge.

Unfortunately, much less detailed study has been made of the sedges than of the Ephemeroptera, possibly because nearly all the great fly-fishing writers of the past have been habitués of the chalk streams. Consequently most of the species of significance to the angler are lumped together under the headings of 'Large', 'Medium', or 'Small' permutated with 'Red', 'Brown', 'Grey', etc., and artificial patterns are dressed accordingly. The fact that these general patterns are usually effective leaves the average fly-fisher disinclined to investigate the natural insect any further. This is a great pity as, on many waters, the sedge-flies are a very important group.

It is possible to pick out certain species that are fairly regularly seen, and without too much technical detail to describe them.

These are listed here.

CHECK LIST OF COMMON AND WIDESPREAD SPECIES
THE SEDGE OR CADDIS FLIES

Anglers or Common Name	Entomological name	Approximate Length of Anterior wing
Great Red Sedge or Murragh	Phrygania grandis or P.striata	20–27mm
Caperer	Halesus radiatus H.digitatus or Stenophylax permistus	20–23mm
Large Cinnamon Sedge	Potamophylax latipennis P.cingulatus or P.rotundipennis	18–19mm
Mottled Sedge	Glyphotalius pellicidus	17mm
Speckled Peter	Phrygania varia	15–19mm
Silver or Grey Sedge	Odontocerum albicorne	13–18mm
Brown Sedge	Anabolia nervosa Hydropsyche angustipennis H.fulvipes or H.saxonica	12–16mm
Cinnamon Sedge	Limnephilus lunatus or L.centralis	14–15mm
The Peter	Phrygania obsoleta	12–15mm
Welshman's Button	Sericosotoma personatum	12–15mm
Yellow Sedge	Rhyacophila obliterata or Oecetis testacea	12–15mm
Longhorns	Oecetis ochracea O.lacustris, O.furva, O.notata	11–13mm
Grey Flag	Hydropsyche instablis H.pellucidula or Molanna angustata	11–12mm
Marbled Sedge	Hydropsyche contubernalis or H.gutatta	11–12mm
Medium Sedge	Goera pilosa	10–12mm
Sandfly	Rhyacophila dorsalis or R.fasciata	Variable
Yellow Spotted	Philopotamus montanus	11mm
Grannom	Brachycentrus subnubilus	9–11mm
Dark Spotted Sedge	Polycentropus flavomaculatus or Cyrnus trimaculatus	7–12mm
Black Sedge	Silo nigricornis S.pallipes, or Notidobia cilaris	8–10mm

Brown Silverhorns	Athripsodes cinereus	8–10mm
	A.annulicornis or	
	A.albifrons	
Small Silver Sedge	Lepidostoma hirtum or	9mm
	Lasiocephala basaliis	
Black Silverhorns	Mystacides azurea.	8–9mm
	M.nigra Athripsodes	
	atterimus A.bilineatus	
	or A.nigronervosus	
Grouse Wing	Mystacides longicornis	8–9mm
Small Red Sedge	Tinodes waeneri	8mm
Small Yellow sedge	Psychomia pusilla	5–6mm
Micro Grey Sedge	Agapetus fuscipes or	5mm
	A.ochripes	
Micro Black Sedge	Lype phaeopa or L.reducta	4–5mm

In the above list angler's common names have been attributed to specific species which are identified by their scientific names. It is more than likely, however, that fishermen have used, and still use, these common names not only for those identified in the list, but for any other species (and there are many) that superficially resemble them.

DETAILED DESCRIPTIONS OF THE MOST COMMON SEDGE OR CADDIS FLIES

The sedge-flies are particularly subject to variations in colour and size. Therefore the following detailed descriptions should be used only as a rough guide. The only sure way to achieve positive identification of any particular species is by a close study of the anatomical structure. This is the method used by trained entomologists, but it is unfortunately beyond the capacity of the average angler. It is interesting to note that the colour of the body of the hatching pupa is invariably similar to that of the subsequent emerging adult.

Common Name.	**The Great Red Sedge. Plate 29 (225)**
Species.	Phrygania grandis or P.striata.
General Description.	The largest sedge or caddis flies in the order, both species are very similar but P.grandis has a continuous black bar running along the centre of the anterior wing, while in P.striata this bar has a gap in the centre.
Wings. (Anterior)	20–27mm. Reddish brown with grey or black marks. The wings of P.striata are often a little darker and in size vary between 23–26mm.
Body.	Dark grey.
Antennae.	Stout and as long or slightly shorter than wings.
Flight Period.	May to July.
Habitat.	Lakes and slow flowing rivers while P.striata is also found in stillwater at considerable altitude.
Emergence.	In open water during late afternoon or early evening.

Type of Larva.

Distribution.

Case making. The cases usually made from cut sections of leaf are often up to 50mm long and are spiralled tapering towards the rear. Plate 27 (212)

Widely distributed. P.grandis found in all areas except No's 3 to 7. P.striata all areas except No's 1,2, 6, 7, 12, 22 and 23.

Another very similar species which is very widespread is Stenophylax permistus. The wings are paler in colour and have some speckles, and they are found in all areas.

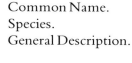

Common Name.
Species.
General Description.

The Caperer. Plate 29 (226)

Halesus radiatus or H.digitatus.

Both are very large species with broad wings. It is very common on the chalk streams of southern England and are also widely distributed throughout Europe. Can only be confused with the large Cinnamon Sedge which has a dark striate mark running down centre of anterior wings.

Wings. (Anterior)

Both males and females of radiatus are 20mm while those of digitatus are 23mm. The wings are broad and rounded at apex and are uniformly brown to brownish yellow with several pale areas with one in centre usually large. Digitatus has a slightly more pointed wing.

Body.
Antennae.
Flight Period.
Habitat.
Emergence.
Type of Larva.

Orange to greenish brown.

Stout and about same length as wings.

Late August to October.

Rivers and lakes.

In open water during late afternoon or evening.

Case making. The case often up to 32mm long and 6mm wide. Formed from pieces of bark stems and leaves of water plants. Usually have two or three sticks or pieces of bark attached considerably longer than case. Plate 27 (215)

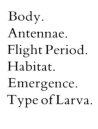

Distribution.

All species are common and widely distributed. H.radiatus is found in all areas except No's 6–7 and 12 while H.digitatus is likely to be found in all areas.

Common Name.
Species.
General Description.

Large Cinnamon Sedge. Plate 29 (227)

Potamophylax latipennis.

Large species with broad cinnamon/brown wings. Similar in appearance to the Caperer but a little smaller. P.cingulatus Plate 29 (228) and P.rotundipennis are two similar species also very widely distributed. The latter is a little smaller with wings 15/16mm.

Wings. (Anterior)

18–19mm. Broad with the apexes rounded. Cinnamon to brownish yellow with dark markings

101

usually with a large pale area in centre. A dark brown striate marking down the wings towards the apex distinguishes these species from the Caperer which is very similar but slightly larger.

Body.	Greyish green.
Antennae.	Stout and a little shorter than wings.
Flight Period.	Late June to September.
Habitat.	Small streams and rivers. P.cingulatus is also found in large rivers and lakes.
Emergence.	In open water during evening.
Type of Larva.	Eruciform – case making length about 20–22mm. The case is cylindrical and slightly curved. Composed of small flattened pebbles fragments of stone and large sand grains.
Distribution.	The three species between them cover all areas. P.latipennis found in all areas except No's 1–2–6–12 and 20. P.cingulatus found in all areas except No's 6 and 12. P.rotundipennis found in all areas except No's 3–5–7–20–22–23.

Common Name.	**The Mottled Sedge. Plate 29 (229)**
Species.	Glyphotaelius pellucidus.
General Description.	A handsome and distinctive species easily recognised at a glance due to its strongly mottled wings excised (scalloped) at the top end (apex).
Wings. (Anterior)	Males and females 17mm. These wings are elongate, widening slightly towards the apex the margin of which is strongly excised at the top. They have dark brown patches on a pale greyish background and the pattern is usually more prominent on the male.
Body.	Usually dull green.
Antennae.	Fairly stout and a little shorter than the wings.
Flight Period.	May to October.
Habitat.	Stillwater, Most likely to be found in tree lined ponds and lakes than in large bodies of water.
Emergence.	Late afternoon or evening.
Type of Larva.	The most distinctive case is formed from the leaves of trees cut in almost perfect circles. These are cemented on the outside of a central tube formed from vegetable debris.
Distribution.	Widely distributed in all areas except 1 and 2.

Common Name.	**The Speckled Peter. Plate 29 (230)**
Species.	Phrygania varia.
General Description.	This is quite a large species and comes from the same genera as the two species referred to as the Great Red Sedges. However this species apart from being smaller has a quite different appearance as it is much darker in colour and presents a slimmer silhouette.

Wings. (Anterior)	15–19mm. The wings are rather narrow and elongate greyish brown speckled and heavily marked in black. They also have several distinctive pale areas.
Body.	Very dark ochraceous.
Antennae.	Stout same length as body.
Flight Period.	July to October.
Habitat.	Ponds and lakes.
Emergence.	During afternoon or early evening.
Type of Larva.	Case making. Long spirally constructed from cut leaves and tapered.
Distribution.	Widely distributed recorded from all areas.

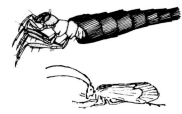

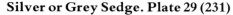

Common Name.	**Silver or Grey Sedge. Plate 29 (231)**
Species.	Odontocerum albicorne.
General Description.	A fairly large species that can be easily identified from its long rather narrow wings and overall silvery grey appearance.
Wings. (Anterior)	13–18mm. Long rather narrow and coloured grey with a few black markings and covered with silvery grey pubescence. They tend to become darker and yellowish with age.
Body.	Black covered with silver grey hairs.
Antennae.	Long and toothed. Each segment has a small but distinct spur like tooth.
Flight Period.	June to October.
Habitat.	Fast running water with a preference for stony or rocky bottoms.
Emergence.	Hatches often sparse during day.
Type of Larva.	Case making. Constructed from large smooth grains of sand it is cylindrical curved and tapers sharply. Up to 20mm in length.
Distribution.	Widely distributed and common. Found in all areas except No's 12, 16 and 22.

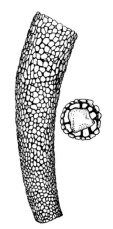

Common Name.	**The Brown Sedge. Plate 29 (232)**
Species.	Anabolia nervosa.
General Description.	A medium species which varies greatly in size and colour. Abundant and can often be observed swarming over water in great clouds. There are three other slightly smaller species with distinctive brownish wings all members of the Hydropsyche genus. These are H. angustipennis, H. fulvipes and H. saxonica. They are often seen during the day swarming over low trees and bushes.
Wings. (Anterior)	Males 11–14mm. Females 12–16mm. Varies from pale to chocolate brown with a large pale spot at the Thyridium (centre). Fairly broad with the apex rounded and slightly pointed. All the Hydropsyche are a little smaller with a wing length of 10–11mm.

103

Body.	Dark to reddish brown.
Antennae.	Stout and about same length as wings. In the other three species each segment of the antennae bears a distinct blackened spiral ridge.
Flight Period.	July, September and October. H.angustipennis all summer, H.fulvipes June to September and H.saxonica June and July only.
Habitat.	All types of water. The Hydropsyche species are only found in running water.
Emergence.	During early evening via emergent vegetation, stones or boulders. The Hydropsyche usually emerge in the afternoon.
Type of Larva.	Case making. Length of case 26mm by 6mm wide. Straight cylindrical but slightly conical formed from sand grains. One or more long sticks cemented to outside of case. The Hydropsyche species are net makers living in shelters that they construct.
Distribution.	A common and fairly widely distributed species found in most areas except in No's 1–5–6 12 and 15. H.angustipennis all areas except No's 1 and 2. H.fulvipes very widely distributed in all areas. H.saxonica all areas except No's 1–212.

Common Name.	**The Cinnamon Sedge. Plate 30 (234)**
Species.	Limnephilus lunatus.
General Description.	This species is but one in this very large Limnephilus genera. There are over 50 European species, most of which may be loosely termed Cinnamon Sedges. Viewed from the side when at rest the long usually rather narrow anterior wings provide a distinctive silhouette. In most species these anterior wings bear some resemblance to thin yellowish parchment covered with very variable brownish markings. One other common species, L.centralis, also has a distinct pale lunate patch at the apex of the anterior wings. Other very similar common and widespread species in this genera without the lunar patch are as follows: L.affinis – L.decipiens – L.extricatus – L.griseus – L.hirsutus – L.ignavus – L.rhombicus see Plate 30 (235) – L.sparsus – L.vittatus – L.bipunctatus and L.marmoratus.

Wings. (Anterior)	14 to 15mm long. Narrow, a rich yellow to cinnamon colour with variable dark patches and a distinctive pale lunate shaped patch at the apexes. While the average wing length of species within this genera is 14 to 16mm the smallest L.centralis has wings barely 12mm in length while the largest species in the genera L.rhombicus has wings almost 19mm long.
Body.	The body of L.lunatus is usually green but in some

Antennae.	other species may vary from green to orange grey. About same length as wings.
Flight Period.	Late May to September. Most other species are also to be seen throughout the summer months.
Habitat.	Many species in this genera are to be found only in stillwater, but all the species mentioned here by name are to be found in all types of water.
Emergence.	During hours of daylight close to emergent vegetation. This applies to many species in this genera.
Type of Larva.	Case making. The case is straight cylindrical 20–23mm long by 4mm wide and is made from vegetable debris, sometimes broken snail shells, twigs or sand grains are added. Plate 27 (213)
Distribution.	A very common and widespread species likely to be found in all areas. This also applies to all the other species mentioned.

The Peter or Dark Peter.

Common Name.	**The Peter or Dark Peter.**
Species.	Phrygania obsoleta.
General Description.	A medium sized species with rather broad dark wings. This species and also the Speckled Peter are very common and well known on many of the big loughs of Ireland. The two Peters are now included as Taff Price considers they are important and widely distributed throughout Europe.
Wings. (Anterior)	12–15mm. The wings of this species are quite broad for its size and they are dark brownish grey with blackish markings.
Body.	Black with grey segmentation.
Antennae.	Fairly stout and same length as the anterior wings.
Flight Period.	July to early September.
Habitat.	Pond and lakes only usually at higher altitudes.
Emergence.	Afternoons and early evenings in open water.
Type of Larva.	Case making made from cut sections of vegetable matter and formed spirally. The case is up to 35mm long and tapers at one end.
Distribution:	A common species in Ireland, Scotland and many countries in Northern Europe.

Common Name.	**The Welshman's Button. Plate 30 (236)**
Species.	Sericostoma personatum.
General Description.	A medium sized species rather slim in appearance and rather hairy. A common species on the English chalk streams, it was given this very odd name by F.M. Halford in the early 1880's. The palpi are also very hairy and often mask the face.
Wings. (Anterior)	12–15mm. Dark to golden chestnut brown and clothed with rather dense golden hairs. A triangular

white patch can often be observed on the centre top edge of these wings when at rest.

Body.	Dark grey sometimes tinged greenish.
Antennae.	Stout pale cream with brown annulations a little shorter than wings.
Flight Period.	June to early September.
Habitat.	Only found in fairly fast running water.
Emergence.	During the day and early evening.
Type of Larva.	Case making. The case up to 12mm in length is cylindrical and slightly curved and strongly tapered. Formed from large sand grains it has a very smooth mosaic surface.
Distribution.	Common and widespread found in all areas except No's 6 – 8 and 12.

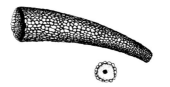

Common Name.	**The Yellow Sedge.**
Species.	Rhyacophila obliterata.
General Description.	This species can be quickly identified as it is one of the very few sedges with bright yellow wings. Another common species with yellow wings is Oecetis testacea. These are a little smaller and have much narrower elongate wings. I have now included these two species under this new common name as they are common in many European countries.
Wings. (Anterior)	12–13mm fairly broad and bright yellow in colour sometimes with faint grey markings.
Body.	Greyish to black. In O.testacea it is green.
Antennae.	Slender and shorter than wings. In O.testacea they are very long, over twice the length of the wings.
Flight Period.	June and again in August and September. O.testacea is only to be seen in June.
Habitat.	Both species are to be found in fairly fast flowing streams or rivers and O.testacea is also to be found in stillwater.
Emergence.	Afternoon and early evening.
Type of Larva.	R.obliitrata is non-case making, free swimming. O.testacea makes a case up to 14mm in length out of sand grains and vegetable matter and is conical but only slightly curved.
Distribution.	Widespread throughout Europe. Found in all areas except No's 16–17–18 and 19. Mainly to be found in alpine or sub-alpine districts. O.testacea tends to be more local and may be found in areas No 1–2–3–4–8–9–13–14–15–19–20 and 22.

Common Name.	**The Longhorns. Plate 30 (237)**
Species.	Oecetis Ochracea.
General Description.	This and the other species in the genera should be easily recognised due to their slim appearance and the

extraordinary length of their antennae. They are very common on many large lakes and reservoirs. The other species in the genera are all smaller. They are O.lacustris, O.furva and O.notata. The latter species is also to be found on slow or deep streams.

Wings. (Anterior)	11–13mm. The very slim wings vary from very pale brown to nearly colourless with a yellowish tinge and densely covered with a greyish brown pubescence. The wings of the other species are a little darker with a more distinct brown or greyish yellow colour.
Body.	Green to greyish green.
Antennae.	Very long pale grey without annulations often over two and a half times the body length.
Flight Period.	May to September. O.lacusris June to September. The other two species have a very short emergence in the middle of summer.
Habitat.	Ponds lakes and reservoirs.
Emergence.	Late afternoon and early evenings.
Type of Larva.	Case making. Up to 14mm in length. It is cylindrical slightly curved and tapered and formed from sand grains and vegetable matter. The cases of the other species are similar but smaller.
Distribution.	All species occur in all areas except No's 1–2–5 and 6.

Common Name.	**The Grey Flag. Plate 30 (233 and 238, 239)**
Species.	Hydropsyche instabilis.
General Description.	This is a common species on many rivers in Ireland where the common name evolved. Flag is a generic term for sedges in this country. H.pellucidula is similar and equally abundant. These Hydropsyche genera may be identified by the rather pointed wings and the blackened spiral ridge round most segments of the antennae. Molanna angustata is also very similar indeed but slightly larger and with much narrower wings.
Wings. (Anterior)	11–12mm. These are grey with dark well defined markings, but in H.pellucidula the colour is much more variable. In both species the apex of the wings are more pointed than in many other common species. In M.angustata the wings are very narrow and often partially wrapped around its body.
Body.	Pale green.
Antennae.	These are about the same length as the wings and both species have a blackened ridge running spirally round each segment.
Flight Period.	June to September. H.pellucidula May to August.
Habitat.	Fast flowing water.
Emergence.	Mostly during the day.
Type of Larva.	Net making. The larva form shelters on the bottom or

on stones or rocks with a net at the entrance to trap particles of food. M.angustata forms a unique shield shaped case from sand grains.

Distribution.	H.instabilis and H.pellucidula. Both species are widespread and very abundant. Found in all areas. M.angustata is very common and widely distributed and is found in all areas except No's 1–2–3–5–12 and 18 but in stillwater only.

Common Name.	**The Marbled Sedge. Plate 30 (240)**
Species.	Hydropsyche contubernalis.
General Description.	The marbled appearance of the wings make this species stand out from moth others. H.gutatta is very similar and both species like all those in this genera have rather pointed wings and a distinctive blackened ridge running spirally round most segments of the antennae.
Wings. (Anterior)	11–12mm. The wings are pale brownish grey with a well defined black pattern giving them a distinctly marbled look.
Body.	Distinctly greenish.
Antennae.	About the same length as the wings with a distinct blackened ridge running spirally round most segments.
Flight Period.	June to August.
Habitat.	Fast flowing water.
Emergence.	During the hours of daylight. Often to be observed on sunny days swarming around low trees or over bushes.
Type of Larva.	Net making. Makes a shelter with net formed at entrance. Plate 27 (209)
Distribution.	Both species are found in all areas except possibly 3 and 5. H.gutatta is the most common species of the two in Europe.

Common Name.	**The Medium Sedge. Plate 31 (241)**
Species.	Goera pilosa.
General Description.	A medium sized species which has an overall hairy appearance. There is a dark irregular shaped patch in the centre of the wings free from hairs which may assist to identify it.
Wings. (Anterior)	10–12mm. These are short and broad and of an overall greyish yellow colour clothed in dense pubescence apart from a irregular shaped patch in the centre.
Body.	Yellow grey.
Antennae	Short and fairly stout.
Flight Period	May to August.
Habitat.	All types of water.
Emergence.	During day and early evening.

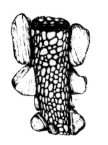

Type of Larva.

Distribution.

Case making. The straight and slightly tapered case up to 8mm in length is formed from sand grains with small pebbles cemented along each side. Plate 27 (214)
Widely distributed and very abundant. Found in all areas except Nos. 3–5–6 and 12.

Common Name.
Species.
General Description.

The Sand Fly. Plate 31 (242)
Rhyacophila dorsalis.
The common name for this sedge was first established by Ronalds in his *Flyfishers' Entomology*. A rather distinctive medium size species that vary greatly in size and colour. R.fasciata is another very similar species which although rather uncommon in England is more widespread on the Continent.

Wings. (Anterior)

Body.
Antennae.
Flight Period.
Habitat.
Emergence.
Type of Larva.

Distribution.

Very variable. Between 9–15mm. In my experience the most common colour is best described as sandy brown with darker markings or speckles, a colour which doubtless led to its original common name.
Green to greenish grey.
Slender and a little shorter than wings.
April to October.
Streams and rivers.
Late afternoon and evening.
One of the relatively few free swimming larva. Plate 27 (210)
Abundant in those areas in which it occurs which are No's 2–3–4–5–8–9–10–11–13–17 and 18. R.fasciate is widespread and occurs in all areas except No's 3–5–6–12 and 17.

Common Name.
Species.
General Description.

Yellow Spotted Sedge. Plate 31 (243)
Philopotamus montanus.
This is a species I am unfamiliar with however I have decided to include this in the list out of deference to Taff Price who considers it an important species particularly on the Continent. He calls this the Dark Spotted although he originally intended to call it the Yellow Spotted. I think he was right so I have altered it accordingly.

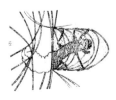

Wings. (Anterior)

Body.
Antennae.
Habitat.
Emergence.
Type of Larva.

Distribution.

11mm. These are variegated with brown and gold spots or blotches.
Dark clothed with yellow hairs.
Shorter than body.
Found at altitude on fast flowing streams.
Daytime and evening.
Non-case making. The larva construct a small purse like net under stones.
Widespread and abundant in all areas except No 12.

Common Name.	**The Grannom. Plate 31 (244)**
Species.	Brachycentrus subnubilus.
General Description.	This is one of the first sedges to be seen at the start of the season and with its broad strongly marked wings unlikely to be confused with any other species at this time of year. Hatches are often very dense over but few days. It is now seldom seen in some locations where it was once prolific.

Wings. (Anterior)	9–11mm. Smoky grey brown with dense yellow pubescence in patches giving wing a strongly marked appearance.
Body.	Pale brown to greenish.
Antennae.	Short and slender.
Flight Period.	April over a very short period. This species has been observed laying its eggs underwater.
Habitat.	Slow to fairly fast flowing rivers.
Emergence.	During day from mid morning onwards.
Type of Larva.	Case making. About 12mm long, square in section and tapered. Made from cut vegetable matter.
Distribution.	Widely distributed and very abundant in areas where it occurs. All areas except No's 5 and 6.

Common Name.	**The Dark Spotted Sedge. Plate 3 (245)**
Species.	Polycentropus flavomaculatus.
General Description.	There are several other very similar species to the above. Two of the most common but smaller are Cyrnus trimaculatus and Holocentropus picicornis. In my waterside guide I originally referred to all these as Yellow Spotted Sedges but I now think in line with Taff Price that this common name should now apply to P.montanus. I will therefore in future refer to the species discussed here as Dark Spotted.

Wings. (Anterior)	Very variable in size. 7–12mm. They are brown very closely irrorated with golden/brown spots.
Body.	Dark reddish brown.
Antennae.	Dark brown with narrow yellow annulations, barely half the length of the wings.
Flight Period.	June to September.
Habitat.	Lakes, ponds and slow flowing rivers.
Emergence.	Late afternoon or early evening.
Type of Larva.	Non-case making. These larva construct a purselike net underneath stones.
Distribution.	Widely distributed and very abundant. Found in all areas except No's 6 and 12. H.picicornis found in all areas except No's 1–2–3 and 6. C.trimaculatus found in all areas.

Common Name.	**The Black Sedge. Plate 31 (246)**
Species.	Silo nigricornis.

General Description.

The above species and also S.pallipes (Plate 31 No 247) have very broad wings, giving a rather triangular appearance when at rest. The wings of the males are jet black while those of the female are dark brown. It therefore seems to me that another species Notidobia cilaris, which is all black in both male and female has a better claim to this common name. Particularly as this latter species is found in all types of water.

Wings. (Anterior)

8–10mm. These wings are broad and black in the male and brown in the female. The wings in all species are heavily pubescent.

Body.

Greyish black.

Antennae.

About the same length as wings and fairly stout.

Flight Period.

All three species have a very short emergence period. S.nigricornis May and again in July. S.pallipes May and again in July and August. N.cilaris May only.

Habitat.

S.nigricornis and S.pallipes are found only in running water while N.cilaris is found mainly in large rivers.

Emergence.

During afternoon or evening.

Type of Larva.

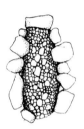

Case making. In the two Silo species the case is about 8mm long and 4.5mm wide made from sand grains with small pebbles cemented along the sides. The case of N.cilaris is up to 15mm long, curved and tapered, made from large sand grains giving a very smooth almost polished finish.

Distribution.

S.nigricornis all areas except No's 12–20–22–23. S.pallipes all areas except No's 1–5 and 12. N.cilaris all areas except No's 5–6 and 7. All are widely distributed and fairly abundant.

Common Name.

The Brown Silverhorns. Plate 31 (248)

Species.

Athripsodes cinereus.

General Description.

One of the most common and abundant species, these slim brown sedge flies with their very long antennae and are often observed flying in huge clouds close to the surface of the water. There are two other very similar species in this genus. They are A.annulicornis and A.albifrons. Both are equally common, similar in size and colour and are difficult to identify apart except for the latter species which has snowy white vertical bars on the wings. These may not always be apparent in the females. Plate 32 (249)

Wings. (Anterior)

8–10mm. They are long slim brown in colour and densely pubescent.

Body.

Dark brownish grey to black.

Antennae.

Very long up to two and a half times the wing length, slender pale brown with black annulations.

Flight Period.

June to August. A.annulicornis mid June to mid August. A.albifrons mid June to August.

111

Habitat.	Both A.cinereus and A.annulicornis are to be observed on fairly large rivers or lakes while A.albifrons seems to have a preference for smaller rivers.
Emergence.	Late afternoon and early evening.
Type of Larva.	Case making. The rather slim case strongly tapered and curved is formed from sand grains.
Distribution.	Very widely distributed and very abundant, found in all areas. A.annulicornis is found in most areas except No's 1–2–3–5–6–7 and 12. A.albifrons is found in all areas except No's 7 and 12.

Common Name.	**The Small Silver Sedge. Plate 32 (250)**
Species.	Lepidostoma hirtum.
General Description.	This is a very common species in many European countries. A fairly small species with silver grey wings. It is rather local and of doubtful importance in the British Isles. Another very similar sedge that could be mistaken for this species is Lasiocephala basalis. This is even more local in its distribution but both species are abundant where they occur. Plate 32 (251)
Wings. (Anterior)	9mm. These wings are smoke grey and sprinkled with black scales.
Body.	Dark to pale grey.
Antennae.	Fairly slim and slightly longer than wings.
Flight Period.	April to early September.
Habitat.	Fast flowing rivers and some lakes. L.basalis is found only in rivers.
Type of Larva.	Case making. Up to 17mm in length, square in section and slightly tapered, formed from cut sections of vegetable matter. The case of L.basalis is circular in section with a fairly abrupt curve at the posterior end and is formed from sand grains.
Distribution.	Rather local but abundant where it occurs. Found in all areas. L.basalis found in most areas except No's 12–22 and 24.

Common Name.	**The Black Silverhorns. Plate 32 (252)**
Species.	Mystacides azurea.
General Description.	Abundant where they occur. This and the following very similar species are often to be seen flying in the company of the Brown Silverhorns. All the species are of a similar size and appearance. They are very slim black flies with very long strongly ringed antennae. The other species are M.nigra, Arthripsodes atterimus, A.nigronervosus and A.bilineatus. The latter species has snowy white vertical bars on the wings similar to those on L.albinfrons.
Wings. (Anterior)	8–9mm. All species apart from A.atterimus have

black to blue black wings which are very narrow, giving the fly a slim appearance when at rest. The wings of A.atterimus may vary from black to dark brown. Both species of Mystacides have conspicuous reddish eyes.

Body.	Dark brownish grey to black.
Antennae.	Long and slim and black, over twice the length of the wings and strongly annulated in all species in white.
Flight Period.	June to September for M.azurea, A.atterimus and A.nigronoversus June to mid July and A.bileanatus mid May to July.
Habitat.	Most species are found in all types of water.
Emergence.	Afternoon or early evening.
Type of Larva.	Case making. Round narrow, straight or sometimes curved, formed from sand and or vegetable matter.
Distribution.	Widely distributed and abundant and some species found in most areas.

Common Name.	**The Grouse Wing. Plate 32 (253)**
Species.	Mystacides longicornis.
General Description.	Very common on many big lakes and reservoirs, this must surely be one of the easiest species to identify. Rather small with very long antennae white ringed brown, they have rather large reddish eyes, a slim appearance and as the common name implies they have wings often strongly marked like a grouse wing feather.
Wings. (Anterior)	8–9mm. Long and slim greyish, and clothed with dense golden yellow pubescence, generally with three broad dark transverse bands although these may appear faint in some specimens.
Body.	Grey brown or almost black.
Antennae.	These are long and slim over twice the length of the wings – white annulated brown.
Flight Period.	June to September.
Habitat.	All types of stillwater.
Emergence.	Late afternoon to early evening.
Type of Larva.	Case making. The case up to about 15mm long is very slightly curved, tapered and is formed from small sand grains and some vegetable matter.
Distribution.	Widely distributed and very abundant, it is to be found in all areas except No's 1–2 and 5.

Common Name.	**The Small Red Sedge. Plate 32 (254)**
Species.	Tinodes waeneri.
General Description.	This is the species often referred to by that great fly fisher of the English chalk streams, G. E. M. Skues as the Little Red Sedge. This is the only small common and abundant species with rather broad brownish

113

wings. Two other very similar species in the same genus are T.aureola and T.assimilis but both are very local in their distribution.

Body.	Dark greyish brown.
Antennae.	Stout and shorter than the wings.
Flight Period.	May to October.
Habitat.	Rather fast streams and rivers. May also be found in some larger lakes.
Emergence.	During day or early evening.
Type of Larva.	Campodeiform. They neither construct transportable cases nor construct nets but live in fixed tunnels made of silk like material and attached to stones or rocks.
Distribution.	Widespread and very abundant in all areas.

The Small Yellow Sedge. Plate 32 (255)

Common Name.	
Species.	Psychomia pusilla.
General Description.	One of the most common and widely distributed of all the caddis flies, its small size and yellowish overall colour should quickly identify it. A feature for positive identification is a strong spur like projection halfway along the top of the posterior wings.
Wings. (Anterior)	5–6mm. These are golden yellow and covered in dense golden pubescence.
Body.	Brownish yellow.
Antennae.	Stout and shorter than the wings they are pale yellowish white, annulated with brown.
Flight Period.	Late May to early September. May be observed on some large rivers swarming in hundreds of thousands.
Habitat.	All types of water.
Emergence.	Early to late evening.
Type of Larva.	Campodeiform. They live in silken tubes constructed on the sides of stones and boulders.
Distribution.	Very widely distributed and very abundant. Found in all areas.

The Micro Grey Sedge.

Common Name.	
Species.	Agapetus fuscipes.
General Description.	This and the following species has been given this common name by Taff Price which I think is very appropriate. Like the Micro Black I think these and some of the even smaller species as found in the Hydroptila genus could become of increasing interest to fly fishers. Another very similar and equally abundant species is A.ochripes.
Wings. (Anterior)	5mm. These wings are a very dark smoky grey colour and covered in dense golden brown pubescence giving the wings a soft grey tinge.
Body.	Greyish.
Antennae.	Rather short and stout.

114

Flight Period.	May to November. A.ochripes May to August.
Habitat.	Running water. Sometimes also found in large lakes.
Emergence.	Evenings.
Type of Larva.	Campodeiform. The larva inhabit elliptical cases made from sand grains and these cases are not transportable.
Distribution.	Fairly widely distributed and very abundant. A.fuscipes found in all areas except No's 5–6–7–15–16. A.ochripes found in all areas except No's 3 and 16.

Common Name.	**The Micro Black Sedge.**
Species.	Lype Phaeopa.
General Description.	These very tiny Black Sedges belong to the same family as the Small Red and Small Yellow Sedges and I have now decided to include these in this new list as like Taff Price I think these and the preceding species could be of more importance to fly fishers than they may have up to now realised. Another species L.reducta in the same genus is very similar, widespread but not so abundant.
Wings. (Anterior)	4–5mm. These wings are black and densely clothed with blackish pubescence. Another even smaller black species is Hydroptila sparsa and these can be identified by the very narrow and pointed wings.
Body.	Dark grey to black with often a greenish tinge, particularly in sparsa.
Antennae.	Short, no longer than wings.
Flight Period.	May to September.
Habitat.	Smaller streams and rivers and lakes.
Emergence.	Mainly evenings.
Type of Larva.	Non-case making. Larva form silken tunnels on sticks or submerged branches of trees.
Distribution.	Widely distributed, very abundant and all species found in all areas.

FISHING INFORMATION ON THE SEDGE-FLIES AND SUGGESTED ARTIFICIALS

The Larvae

The importance of caddis larvae has been known to fishermen for over 300 years and in the formative years the natural larva was a much favoured bait with coarse fishermen. It is only in the last two decades or so that fly dressers have evolved patterns to imitate the cased caddis, and so far as I know these up to quite recently have only been developed for use in stillwater. These patterns are usually most effective when fished either with no movement or very slowly along or close to the lake bed on a sinking line. However, for some unaccountable reason, they will often prove very effective when fished as a point fly in a team of three from a drifting boat.

Three good general patterns are the Stick Fly, a Woolly Worm or Brian Clarke's Ombudsman. A few popular more recent and specific patterns are the

Cased Caddis by Bob Carnhill, the Sand Caddis by the late Dick Walker and the Caddis Larva by an American fly dresser, Raleigh Boaze, or a well known French pattern called the Pallaretta.

The Pupae

Although pupae artificials are often successful when used indiscriminately throughout the fishing season, the most productive period is usually from late June onwards. Apart from this it will be apparent that maximum success will be assured during the actual emergence period of the natural. Unfortunately, the natural swimming to the surface is rarely observed, so one has to look for other clues to the event. Of these, undoubtedly the most reliable are the sudden appearance of adult winged sedges over open water, the appearance of empty pupal shucks floating in the surface film where previously none had been observed, or finally, the discovery of live pupae in the stomach content of a freshly caught trout.

The artificial pupa should, of course, imitate as closely as possible the natural in both size and colour. The size of the natural varies greatly according to species, and while the colour of the hatching pupa is usually the same as the subsequent adult, the colour range is rather limited, and therefore artificials dressed with bodies of cream, green, orange or very dark brown will cover most eventualities. At times I feel the colour aspect is of considerable importance and it should be noted that, as the pupal case of the natural is virtually transparent, the colour of the developed imago underneath is always apparent. On those rivers not restricted to dry fly fishing artificial pupae may be successfully fished at any depth from just off the bottom to just below the surface with either floating or slow sink lines. They seem to be most effective on fast, free stone rivers when fished downstream like a wet fly. A more recent method now becoming popular is to fish them either upstream or downstream on a floating line with a braided weighted leader and a bright wool indicator to denote a strike. On stillwater the artificial may be successfully fished from either boat or bank but it is undoubtedly most effective from the latter. It is suggested that a floating line be used with, depending on personal preference, either a single artificial on the point or additional artificials on each dropper. There are two methods of retrieve which are, sink-and-draw to represent the natural swimming from the bottom to the surface, or a slow, steady retrieve in the sub-surface to simulate the natural swimming along under the surface. The latter is, of course, the more suitable method of the two for the boat fisherman. To the best of my knowledge there are only a few patterns available to represent the pupae, and of them the best known is probably the Amber nymph perfected by Dr Bell of Blagdon to represent, I believe, these particular creatures. While it is an excellent pattern when naturals of a brown or orange colouration are in evidence, it has its limitations. Other patterns which have been popular for many years are the famous old Irish pattern called the Green Peter which can be fished wet or semi-dry according to the position of the hen hackle and another quite old pattern is called Sharp's Favourite.

More modern patterns which I can personally recommend are my own range of Sedge Pupa dressed in different colours and sizes of hook, and the late Dick Walker's Longhorn and Shorthorn pupa patterns. To represent the pupa hatching in or just under the surface film I would suggest either the Hatching Sedge Pupa by myself and Brian Clarke or a similar pattern of the same name by John Roberts.

The Winged Adult

On rivers the methods of fishing artificials to represent the adults are rather restricted. The traditional and time honoured way is to cast your artificial upstream to a rising fish, first of all of course ascertaining the size and colour of the natural on which the trout may be feeding. On large, fast, roily or mountainous rivers where the rise of a trout can not always be seen, large buoyant patterns are usually favoured as attractors and fished in likely runs or holding areas. On very fast ripply or boulder strewn rivers a very effective method is to fish a well greased artificial and leader downstream and across the top of the surface. This will often provoke slashing rises to the fly, but if you strike too quickly you will not set the hook in many fish.

On stillwater the fishing methods are less well known and far more complex so I have decided to provide as much information as possible.

Fishing the artificial sedge to represent the winged adult on stillwater is essentially dry fly fishing, and as such is probably one of the most exciting experiences of all. There are several methods of presenting the floating artificial and, broadly speaking, most of these may be practised equally well from boat or bank. These varying methods should be related to the particular type of species of sedge-fly that may be on the water at the time and that one is endeavouring to copy. A floating line should be used and it is the normal practice to fish only one artificial on the point, and this should be lightly greased with a floatant in calm conditions, but on rough, windy days I find a light application of a heavy grease such as mucillin most helpful.

The first method to be discussed is meant to represent the action of those species of sedge-flies which, hatching out in open water, run or flutter along the surface in their efforts to become airborne; it also proves effective in imitating those naturals blown on to the water which are endeavouring to take off. For this fishing I prefer an artificial with a hackle tied along the body Palmer fashion but in reverse, so that the hackle points face forward. This seems to provide the maximum animation and disturbance, and this is highly desirable. The artificial should be cast as far as possible and recovered at speed with frequent pauses along the surface. In some situations a medium fast recovery will prove effective, while at others it is impossible to retrieve too fast. An effective technique seems to be to retrieve the line in one hand with a long fast pull and at the same time accelerating the action by lifting the rod from the horizontal to the vertical. With this method the artificial moves so fast that on a rough day it will literally skip along the tops of the waves, and from the way the trout jump out of the water in their eagerness to intercept it, it seems they love it fished in this manner. Another successful plan is to loop the point of the leader in a half-hitch round the eye of the hook of the artificial; this has the effect of keeping the artificials head elevated so that it skips along when retrieved in a most attractive manner. Although the open water may be fished, this method seems particularly productive when practised in the vicinity of trees, reeds or other vegetation either in the water or lining the banks. When fishing in this way it is not always necessary to strike, as the trout invariably hook themselves, and for this reason it is prudent to use fairly heavy monofilament on the point, as the 'take' is often quite savage. Fished from a boat it is surprising how often a trout that has probably been following the artificial for some distance will suddenly decide to rise to the fly close to the boat just as the artificial is being lifted in preparation for the next cast. On some days this happens time and time again, and I find it is always a good plan to anticipate a rise to the artificial at this juncture and if it occurs try to set the hook with a forward roll cast. Another very similar and well-known technique from a boat that can be practised when sedge-flies are about is to fish a hackled Palmer or Sedge artificial on the top dropper. This is also most effective when fished fast so that it is dribbled along the surface, and again the trout will often take extremely close to the boat.

It will doubtless be appreciated that there are several ways in which an artificial may be fished to represent the natural adult in its various phases before it dies. The first stage of the adult life of those species that hatch out in open water, when the insect is struggling on the surface to free itself from its pupal case, is particularly vulnerable to the attentions of the trout. At this period the most successful method seems to be to use a normal standard sedge pattern on a floating line and to fish it ungreased so that it sinks into or even slightly below the surface film. The artificial should then be retrieved either very slowly or in small jerks. It is interesting to note that two well-known general patterns, namely the Invicta and the Silver March Brown, often prove effective when the natural sedges are on the water, and it therefore seems quite probable that these are taken by the trout for hatching sedges.

The final method to be discussed is probably the best known and is the normally accepted dry fly method of fishing the artificial. This to my mind is undoubtedly the most exciting and satisfactory of all forms of stillwater fishing; the joy of covering a rising fish and see it turn and sip down your fly makes most other fishing pleasures pale into insignificance. Unfortunately, opportunities to practise this style do not occur every day, but it is often one of the best methods to adopt during July and August, although there are probably many stillwater anglers who have never considered trying it.

Many species of sedge-flies return to the water to oviposit by dipping or releasing their eggs on to the surface, and at least a proportion of these eventually finish up lying spent and struggling on the water surface. Apart from this many are accidentally, in windy conditions, blown on to the water. It is at this time when the naturals are observed that dry fly fishing should be most effective. Although this method may be practised either from boat or bank, under very windy conditions, owing to the fast drift of a boat in the wind it is better from the bank. A floating line should be used, and the artificial should be well greased to give maximum floatability, particularly if one is fishing the water rather than to rising fish. When trout are rising, the artificial can be placed either in the estimated path of the fish or, alternatively, if one can cast quickly and accurately, within the actual rise ring. But either method will often be successful. The artificial can be retrieved either very slowly, or it can be left motionless but for an occasional twitch to imitate the struggle of the natural trapped in the surface film. This is best achieved with a sharp jerk or lift of the rod top. This latter method is my personal favourite and will often bring a slashing rise to the fly.

Some lakes have heavy screens of rushes or similar aquatic vegetation extending from the shore, usually at the shallower end, forming interesting little bays and points. Most fishermen tend to ignore these areas due to this very shallow water, but with a stealthy approach from either boat or bank they often prove to be most productive. Providing they are not alarmed, trout during the warmer weather frequently lie close to these reeds or rushes, in spite of the shallow water, waiting for any unwary insects that may venture forth or be blown off the vegetation. An artificial sedge presented therefore in the manner described above will often take a heavy toll.

Finally, it should be pointed out that when choosing the colour of the artificial to match the colour of the natural on the wing, the following fact should be taken into consideration. The colouration of the freshly hatched sedge-fly is usually a lot weaker or paler than specimens that have been hatched out for several hours. This applies in particular to the wings. As most authorities seem to indicate that trout can discern the difference between colours, this is a point worthy of consideration. Both those eminent authors, Col Jocelyn Lane and Courtney Williams, mention this factor. The former also emphasises the desirability of using a sparse amount of hackle on artificial sedge patterns, and while I am inclined to agree when using these patterns as a dry fly, I cannot agree with the assertion he makes in his book that over-hackling is also a mistake on patterns to represent the adult sedge moving rapidly over the surface. In this case I am of the opinion that the more disturbance one can create the better, and a heavy hackle is a definite advantage.

ARTIFICIALS TO REPRESENT THE ADULT SEDGE

Patterns to represent these adults have now been around for a very long time and can be traced back to the earliest days of fly fishing. Consequently over this very long period of time many, many hundreds of dressings have been devised. It is obviously impossible and also impractical to list all of these, so I have made a small selection of both old and time tested patterns as well as more modern ones which in recent years have proved to be very popular and also very effective. Some patterns have been developed to represent specific naturals, while the majority have been developed as general patterns and all of those listed here unless otherwise stated should be fished as dry flies on the surface.

Green Peter A traditional Irish pattern. Fished dry to represent any of the large cinnamon coloured sedges.

Caperer (Lunn) Well known and popular pattern on the English chalkstreams, where it is meant to represent the natural of the same name, or a more realistic pattern is Dr Voljc's Caperer.

Grannom (Pat Russell) An excellent pattern to match the natural with the same name.

Brown Sedge (Terry Thomas), tied to represent the natural Brown Sedge.

Black Silverhorns (Alfred Ronalds), a good copy of the naturals of the same name.

Cinnamon Sedge, of which several patterns represent the naturals of the same name.

The Grouse Wing Sedge, a very realistic pattern by Dr Voljc.

Little brown Sedge (Courtney Williams), an excellent pattern to represent the Brown Sedge when it is on the water.

Mottled Sedge (Jocelyn Lane), a particularly good pattern when the natural is hatching.

Silver Sedge, representing any of the light-coloured sedges.

Little Red Sedge (Skues), perfected to represent the Small Red Sedge and one of the best all-round patterns.

There are many excellent general patterns, a few of which are:

The Universal Sedge. A Swiss pattern.

The Elkhair Caddis. A very popular U.S. pattern.

The Preska Caddis Fly. A well known French pattern.

G&H Sedge, my own pattern, dressed by the late Cliff Henry and an excellent floating pattern for use on large lakes or large, fast rivers and, under the name **Goddard Caddis**, now one of the most popular sedge patterns in the United States.

Poly-caddis, a pattern I have recently devised and which has proved exceptionally killing and is easy to tie. It is dressed with either a normal hackle or a fully-palmered hackle and in two colours and different sizes. Two other patterns worth trying are Trichoptera 1 and 2 by the Italian fly dresser Piero Lumini.

It is essential to have some wet sedge patterns for big lakes and reservoirs, but while there are many from which to choose, the best are without doubt **Wickham's Fancy**, or **Invicta**, or, a more recent pattern, the **Shredge** (Tony Knight). An excellent general stillwater pattern is the **Red Palmer** (which should always be fished well oiled on the top dropper) and so is the **Terry's Terror**. Finally, on large stillwaters, a **Muddler Minnow** fished fast at the surface in a big wave is always worth a try in late summer.

To complete this chapter on fishing methods I feel I must bring to the attention of the reader some new and exciting ways of fishing various artificial sedge-patterns in rivers that have recently been perfected by one of Austria's top fly fishers. The famous Traun river in Austria probably has heavier hatches of sedges throughout the season than any other river I know and without doubt Roman Moser is the unquestioned master of this river which he has fished all his life. A superb caster he has developed four relatively new methods which rely on a combination of special casting techniques and some unique new patterns.

Method 1

The Free Swimming Larva. This weighted pattern is fished with a lead or copper cored braided leader to a 3 or 4lb point, in conjunction with a wool indicator attached to the end of the fly line. The fly is cast upstream and across the current

73 Casting – method 1

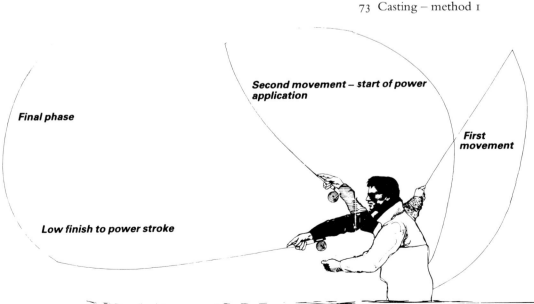

utilising Roman's parachute roll cast. When the roll cast is made the rod is not stopped at the usual 10 o'clock position but continued until it is almost horizontal to the water, this creates a very large loop which causes the fly to drop vertically into the water near the end of the fly line and allows the fly to reach the bottom quickly even in quite a fast current. The fly is fished downstream on the dead drift and the fly line should be mended downstream to allow the larva pattern to fish close to the bottom where it imitates the free swimming natural larvae which are often dislodged by the current and carried downstream. With this method one fishes the water searching the bottom in any likely fish holding areas or runs during the day. Later on in the day or early evening when the first few adult sedges start hatching Roman suggests that you exchange the larva pattern for another of his masterpieces the Gold Head Pupa. This is also a weighted pattern and fished in exactly the same method as described above for the larva, but instead of using a weighted braided leader you use a standard monofilament leader made up of 7ft of 5lb test and 10ft of 3lb test. This allows the artificial to swim freely a little way off the bottom where the fish are expecting to see the naturals as they swim upwards to the surface.

Method 2

This is a very useful technique for fishing fairly deep white water or fast flowing torrents during the day when free swimming larva are likely to be present or in the latter half of the day when natural pupa are likely to be hatching. Either of the above patterns may be utilised but they should be fished with an extra fast sinking braided leader to help get the fly down deep. This is essential in this type of water, as a heavily weighted leader alone will not accomplish this, so Roman has developed a special casting technique to solve the problem. This he refers to as his

74 Casting – method 2

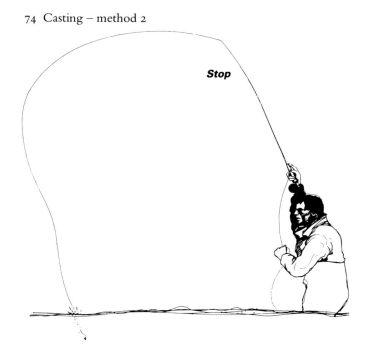

deep water Tuck cast. When fishing this type of water long casting is not necessary as the fish have an extremely limited vision in this fast very rough water, so one can wade out to the head of such a run and fish it down with little chance of disturbing the fish. Aerialising about ten yards of line or even less, the rod and arm should be held as high as possible and the forward cast should be stopped prematurely at 11 o'clock. If stopped sharply enough the weighted fly will be flipped back under the end of the fly line and will drop vertically into the water followed by the weighted leader where it will sink reasonably close to the bottom even in the fastest of water. Still holding the rod as high as possible the artificial is fished downstream as far as the short length of line will allow and it is often surprising how close to you the takes will come, often resulting in some very big trout or grayling. In such fast water takes will often be quite savage and it is all too easy to break off fish after fish on the strike. To overcome this problem use a heavier point on your leader 5 or 6lb (the fish will not be aware of this in this heavy water) and better still also incorporate an 8 or 10 inch length of power or shock gum between the end of your braided leader and the point. In very rough water it is also often necessary to use a cork indicator instead of wool for better visibility.

Method 3

The Wet Fly Swing cast. This is used for fishing Roman's unweighted Caddis Pupa pattern just below the surface. This method is best practised in the early evening when the heavy hatches of sedge-flies commence. Depending upon the size and body colour of the adults hatching mount an appropriate Hatching Pupa on a long leader down to a 3lb point. This should then be cast as far as possible across and downstream mending the line downstream as soon as possible. Immediately this has been achieved take your hands away from both the line and the reel and allow the line to swing downstream naturally and straighten. Most of the takes will come as the line starts to straighten and they will often be very savage indeed and if at this time you are either holding the line or checking the reel

75 Casting – method 3

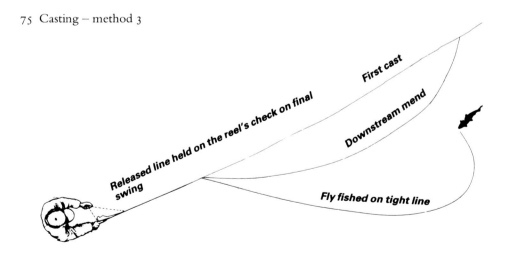

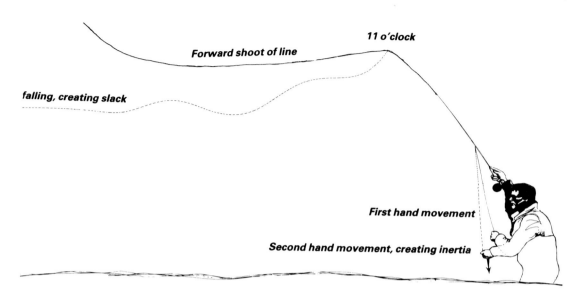

a break is almost guaranteed. In practice you will find that the check on the reel is quite adequate to set the hook when a trout takes the artificial.

Method 4

The Reach Cast. This should be practised on those magical summer evenings we sometimes encounter just as it is getting dark when every trout in the river seems to be rising either to freshly hatching sedges or those returning to lay their eggs on the surface. With this method Roman uses two super new dry fly patterns that he has perfected—the Balloon Caddis to represent the hatching adults or the Egg Laying Caddis to represent the ovipositing females. Accurate casting is essential as in a heavy rise of this nature the fish will not move to take your artificial, so position yourself upstream of a rising fish within easy casting distance. This reach cast is made with quite a short line and on the forward cast the rod is stopped at the 11 o'clock position allowing the line to almost straighten when the hand holding the fly line is pulled sharply back a yard or so. This allows the line to fall on the water in line with the rising fish but with plenty of slack which, when perfected eliminates drag completely. However do not try this method on any of the English chalk streams or other similar rivers where downstream fishing is all but a hanging offence.

The dressings for Roman Moser's new patterns are as follows. All of his patterns are dressed on Roman Moser Barbless Arrow Point hooks in sizes from nos 12 up to 18.

Roman's Free Swimming Larva. Lead wire is wound around the shank and then a 3mm wide strip is cut from a sheet of 'Bodygills' of the required colour (this is a new very lifelike hair bonded to a plastic backing) and wound round the shank two thirds of the way up to the eye. This is followed up to the eye with dubbed

Hare's ear to represent the head and thorax of the pupa.

Roman's Gold Head Pupa. First of all slip over the eye of the hook a gold metal or bright yellow coloured bead of an appropriate size to the hook used and cement into position immediately behind the eye. Then wind lead around the shank for weight. It is then only necessary to wind on a body behind the bead of another new material called Erezi-dub formed from poly antron fibres in an appropriate colour.

Roman's Unweighted Caddis Pupa. The body is formed from the appropriate colour of seal's fur or substitute and wound two thirds of the way up the shank. Next wind on two or three turns of a red game cock hackle fairly short in the flue and then form the head or thorax again from an appropriate colour of Erezi-dub.

The Balloon Caddis. First of all cut a 5mm strip of bright yellow plastizoat and tie in about 3/16 of an inch of this on top of the shank immediately behind the eye, leaving the balance of this strip pointing away from the eye not along the shank. Behind this wind on a body of light olive seal's fur or substitute and then tie in behind the plastizoat and over the body some brown deer hair sloping back over the body to represent the wings. Finally double the plastizoat strip back over itself and tie this in front of the wings and trim. If tied correctly this will look like a little plastic ball behind the eye. This provides both extra buoyancy and excellent visibility to the fly when it is fished. It is interesting to note that on more than one occasion Roman Moser has stated that if he was restricted to one artificial pattern for the rest of his life this Balloon Caddis would be his first choice.

The Egg Laying Caddis. Tie in a bunch of brown deer hair to represent the wings, these should be tied in immediately behind the eye sloping upwards and over the front. Next cut a strip of brown plastazoat 5mm wide and tie about 3/16 of an inch of this immediately behind the wings then double this strip back over the top of itself and trim. You will then have a ball of plastic on top of the shank behind the wings. Finally cut a 3mm wide strip from a Bodygills sheet in brown or grey and wind round the shank to form a body.

The new materials mentioned above are marketed under the name of Traun River Products of West Germany and may be obtained from Messrs Partridge of Redditch as well as the Roman Moser Arrow point hooks. Partridge are also marketing a new video made on the river Traun and featuring Roman Moser fishing and describing all the methods detailed above with a commentary by Bernard Cribbins. This is a really excellent production and the title is *New ways of fishing the Caddis*.

CHAPTER 7

THE FLAT-WINGED FLIES-
DIPTERA

This order of flies is far larger than all the other aquatic orders put together, and in all contains several thousand species, although by far the greater number are terrestrial and of little interest to the angler. They are commonly known as the true flies and, as the name Diptera indicates, have only two wings, which lie flat along the top of the body, often overlapping. These wings are usually transparent and colourless, although in some species small areas of colour are to be seen. Some of the more common flies in this group are House-flies, Mosquitoes, Crane-flies (Daddy-long-legs), Dung-flies, Gnats, Horse-flies, Smuts and various species of Chironomidae or Midges. We are concerned with only a very few of the many land-bred species, because it is only on windy or gusty days that they may be blown on to the surface of the water in sufficient numbers to arouse the fish. We will start with the midges as to the fly fishers they are by far the most important family in the order.

The Midges (Chironomidae spp)
This family sometimes referred to as buzzers is a relatively large one containing over 400 different species, and while a few of them are of terrestrial origin, most are aquatic in both larval and pupal stages. In size they vary tremendously, the adults of some of the largest species having a wing length of almost 8mm and the smallest having wings less than 1mm. Without doubt these insects provide a source of food of the utmost importance for trout particularly in stillwaters. Throughout the season hardly a day goes by without hatches of at least some species occurring between dawn and dusk.

For these reasons it is considered that they are probably the most important group of all insects to the stillwater fly-fisher. Up to comparatively recent times their value to anglers seems to have been overlooked and consequently little information on their life history and behaviour was known to them. Nor has this lack of detailed information in angling literature been supplemented from other sources, as entomologists have not paid as much attention to fisherman's Chironomids as they have to many other Families. In an effort to rectify this situation I was able over a period of several years to breed and study under laboratory and field conditions many of these species, and I have consequently been able to fill in at least a few gaps. However, much work still remains. In view of the importance of these insects to the fisherman an endeavour will be made to provide as much detail as possible on all facets of their life and behaviour.

So far as I have been able to ascertain, that famous fisherman, Dr Bell of Blagdon, was the first angler to foster a pattern to represent the pupa of one of the more common species. He called it the Black Buzzer, or Buzzer Nymph, and even today the pattern is still popular and widely used. Although their importance may not have been apparent before Dr Bell's research, individual anglers, long before, were probably aware of these insects, and I am indebted to Conrad Voss Bark for the following interesting snippet of information. In the early days of Blagdon, between 1904 and 1913, his grandfather, one William J. Cox, was a well-known local angler who used to tie many of his own flies. A pattern that he used to dress and thought very highly of, and probably devised himself, he referred to as a Midge pattern. I have personally handled one of his original tyings that has survived the years, and unquestionably it is meant to represent a Midge pupa.

It is also interesting to note that quite recently I discovered in a book written by J. C. Mottram entitled *Fly Fishing some new arts and mysteries*, a chapter headed 'Flies of the future'. In this chapter he gives the dressing for a pattern to represent a midge pupa which in appearance is very similar indeed to Geoffrey Bucknall's Footballer pattern which was initially introduced and became popular in the late sixties. Mottram even states in his book that while it is used as a wet fly, it should be cast to the fish like a dry fly. This book was published in 1915 so presumably he must have developed and been experimenting with this pattern at least a few years before this date. So I am now inclined to give him credit for the introduction of the original concept.

The following detailed descriptions and behaviour of the larva and pupa are actually based on observations of different specimens over long periods and therefore do not refer to any one particular species. Most of the artificially reared specimens, however, were of the most common types, and so should be reasonably representative of the various species that anglers are likely to encounter.

The Eggs
These are deposited by the adult females on the surface in a gelatinous mass, sometimes being laid in the shape of a string or rope, and at other times in the shape of a raft. The mass floats on the surface and within a matter of days the larvae that have developed within the eggs emerge and descend to the bottom.

The Larvae   Plate 35 (273)
These form a staple diet of many trout and will often be found among the stomach contents in considerable numbers.

In size they vary greatly, according to species, in a similar manner to the adults, with some of the larger species being in excess of 1 inch in length. The larvae, which generally feed on organic detritus, are most likely to be found in depths between 3 and 18ft; they are not confined to the deeper water as many anglers have been led to believe. They also vary their habitat a great deal, some living in tubes of mud which they build and locate in the bottom silt or which they attach to stones, shells or the leaves of plants. Others build tubes of sand, or make tunnels in the mud, while a few isolated species make cases, which they carry around similar to those made by caddis larvae. Many species are free swimming and will be found among the leaves of aquatic plants. The Tanypodinae, which is a sub-family of the Chironomidae, belong to this latter group, and a fuller description of these particular insects will be found at the end of this chapter under the heading 'Other Diptera'.

The larvae vary in colour, brown, green or red being predominant, although some are almost colourless. The red larvae are probably the best known and are often referred to as blood worms. Most of these belong to the Genus *Chironomus*, and this startling red colouration is due to the presence of haemoglobin. This substance, which is also found in the human body, is present in the blood of these particular larvae, and this substance assists the blood by storing oxygen and providing it when required, thus enabling them to live in water or situations of a low oxygen content. In many of the specimens that I have studied it has appeared that the more mature the larva, the brighter the red colouration, and therefore suspect that the density of the haemoglobin may increase as pupation approaches. Many of the red larvae in this group build a 'U'-shaped tube of mud and spin a net over one end to collect food, while others emerge from it to feed. As previously stated, some species are free swimming, but at times even those that live in fixed abodes leave them and move about. On numerous occasions I have found the red larvae in quantities amongst silkweed, presumably feeding. When swimming they all follow the same routine, and this vigorous means of locomotion can best be described as a figure-of-eight lashing movement.

In appearance these larvae are very worm-like, but under a low power magnifier the head section and body segments can clearly be defined. As pupation approaches the thorax or section behind the head becomes swollen and the legs and wings of the coming adult may be faintly seen through the skin. So far as I have been able to ascertain the larva goes through four moults or instars (Ford 1959) when it completely sheds its old skin or cuticle.

The Pupae Plate 35 (274)

In the latter stages of its larval life the developing insect undergoes a complete change within its case, and in a comparatively short time it is ready to cast the final larval cuticle or skin and emerge in its new pupal shape (see Plate 35, No 275). I understand that it often takes several hours to shed its old skin, and as a matter of interest I have observed quite a high mortality rate among pupae I have raised in captivity due to their inability at times to free themselves completely. Thus, when pupal maturity is reached, partly trapped in their old larval skin, they are unable to swim to the surface to transform into the adult insect. The new pupa develops very rapidly, and although in the early stages the wing cases and filaments on the head are not fully formed (see Plate 35, No 275), these take up the typical pupal appearance, as shown in many of the photographs, within a matter of hours.

So far as I have been able to observe, the pupal stage in captivity lasts between 36 and 72 hours, although this probably varies with different species. During much of this period they remain in their burrows, but as the time approaches for the final ecdysis the now mature pupae emerge partially from their burrows and commence a rhythmic swaying movement. This presumably creates a constant circulation of water, which assists the whitish bunches of filaments (tracheal gills) on their heads to abstract the maximum amount of oxygen. During this period they are particularly vulnerable to predators such as trout, who feed on them when the opportunity arises. In the final stages of pupation the body darkens considerably, or in some species changes colour completely, and the thorax and wing cases turn to light or dark brown.

When conditions are conducive for emergence, they swim slowly to the surface, where the final transformation takes place and the adult winged insect becomes airborne. This last stage in the life of the midge is of utmost importance to the fishermen, so it will be described in detail. Up to now observations in my aquaria and in the field lead me to believe that the pupae ascend directly to the surface and spend little time in midwater, as do pupae of many other insects. The majority of species in this family hatch into the adult in the surface film. On the other hand I have read reports in the angling press that many of these Chironomids hatch on the way to the surface and emerge very rapidly in a similar manner to Simulium or reed smuts. While I do not doubt the authenticity of these observations, I am somewhat dubious about them being identified as Chironomidae.

The Chironomid, or Midge pupae, as they are commonly called by anglers, vary greatly in size and colour, and as a general rule the resulting adults fairly closely follow the pupae in both respects. Most of the species in this Family that are of particular interest to the fisherman belong to the Genus *Chironomus*. They have a strongly segmented body, and caudal fins or appendages at the tail which facilitate swimming, and while these are mainly transparent they often have a distinct whitish tinge around the edge which under water gives the pupae the appearance of having white tails. The dark wing cases and thorax are very distinct, and on top of the head are four tufts of very white tracheal gills (respiratory filaments). After arrival in the surface film some species seem to transform immediately, but I have observed others that remain suspended in the film for as long as two or three hours. The density of the film on the surface may account for this delay, as under these conditions they appear to have great difficulty breaking through. Consequently, the heaviest rise of trout are most likely to be encountered on hot, calm evenings when these conditions are most likely to apply, and large numbers of the pupae are hanging in the surface film. Midges appear to favour reasonably calm water for emergence, for they certainly do not like cold windy weather with consequently rough water, and at such times hatches are likely to be sparse or absent.

The movement of the pupae in the surface prior to emergence is particularly interesting and is subject to considerable variation. Some remain hanging stationary with the head filaments just touching the film, and some swim spasmodically for short distances towards the bottom. Others spend most of the time swimming along horizontally just under the surface with a strong wriggling action, looking for a crack or weak area in the surface film, only occasionally stopping to take up the more typical vertical position. When a weak or clear area in the surface film has been located, the pupa, hanging vertically, slowly adopts a completely rigid posture and then floats upwards until it is horizontal in the surface, with the thorax just breaking the surface film. Finally, the thorax splits down the centre and the fully adult winged insect emerges on the surface, resting briefly near its now empty pupal case (Plate 35, No 276) before flying away. The time taken for this transformation varies a little according to conditions, but an average time would be about ten seconds. If a specimen in the surface film is observed closely just before the cuticle splits, it will be noticed that the pupa apparently contains air or gas, as the head and thorax can be seen to swell as pressure, which probably splits the skin, is built up. It is also interesting to note that in those species which possess it, the red haemoglobin seems to gather at the tail end *en masse* and slowly travels up the body as the thorax expands. Specks of this red pigment will often be found on freshly hatched adults. Also at least one of the very common species emerges with distinctly orange wings, but this colour disappears very rapidly and no trace of it remains by the time the insect is airborne. Whether this is due to the haemoglobin, or to some other reason peculiar to an individual species, I have been unable to ascertain.

It is generally accepted by many anglers that these pupae emerge only from the deeper water, and this up to a point is a fallacy, as some species actually prefer shallow areas, although many are found in deep water only. The heaviest hatches of the larger species nearly always take place in the late evening, after the sun has set, but quite often good hatches occur in the early morning shortly after dawn.

Some of these larger midges also hatch during the day, but they usually emerge rather sparsely and seldom in sufficient quantities to bring about a general rise. On the other hand some of the medium sized or smaller species do emerge in large numbers during the day or early evening, and this quite often results in a good rise. Apart from these, there are also some species which hatch out after dark, but they will not be dealt with as they are of no interest to the angler. Most species have an emergence period extending from two to three weeks, and some of these appear to have two or three generations during the summer. A few species appear to have a much longer emergence period. As far as the fly-fisher is concerned, the first midges appear in late March or early April, and different species are to be seen throughout the whole season until late October.

The Adult Midge

Despite the fact that there are many species in this family, they are all of a similar appearance but, as previously stated, they vary tremendously in size. The females have stout, strongly segmented cylindrical bodies, and the wings, which are usually colourless and strongly veined are almost always considerably shorter than the body. These are mounted well forward, giving the insects a rather humped-back appearance in profile. They have six long legs and two rather short antennae protruding from the head. When at rest the wings are folded down the body and barely overlap, and an interesting characteristic of these midges is their habit of often holding their front legs clear of the ground. The males are similar to the females except that their bodies are usually slimmer and a little longer, *pro rata*, and their antennae are also longer and heavily plumose. With a low power glass the male claspers can clearly be seen at the tail end of the body. The colours of these midges are very diverse and the more common species and colours are listed at the end of this section.

The male adult midges usually form large swarms early in the evenings, and while many of the smaller species may be found adjacent to the water, most of the larger seem to favour localities inland. Swarms are often on a very large scale, and can sometimes be observed in the vicinity of trees or buildings, while at other times they form high in the air, even on occasions over the tops of very high trees.

In this latter case, from a distance they give the appearance of a column of smoke. The females, after mating, return to the water to deposit their eggs, and in the case of the larger species this is usually in the very early morning, after sunset, as dusk approaches or possibly during the night. Most anglers will be familiar with the hook-shaped silhouette of these egg-bearing females flying around one's head while fishing; indeed, their colloquial name arises from the buzzing sound they emit. The appearance of these females is often the prelude to a buzzer rise and many fishermen seem to be under the mistaken impression that they are in fact the freshly emerging adults. I must again emphasise, however, that they are the returning females of a previous emergence, bearing at the tail end of their bodies the egg mass which appears to be held in position by the long trailing rear legs.

Up to the time of the publication of my book *Trout Flies of Stillwater* in 1969 no one had attempted to provide even a partial list of the more common midges for the angler, and in an effort to remedy this situation I suggested the following. A few species had already been given vernacular names by various authors and therefore, to save unnecessary confusion, I retained them.

It must be pointed out that the following list of midges is only a rough one, as due to the very large number of species within this family many are similar in size, colour and appearance. It should also be noted that the vernacular names suggested in this list are related to the colour of the natural as seen by the fisherman on the water surface, and not necessarily the specific colour as viewed under magnification out of water. I am deeply indebted to Mr A. M. Hutson, of the British Museum of Natural History who was largely responsible for identifying most of the species that appear below.

THE ADULT MIDGES (Chironomids)

Angler's name	Entomological name	Wing-length
Large Green Midge	*Chironomus plumosus* group	6.5–8mm
Large Red or Ginger Midge	*Chironomus plumosus* group	6.5–8mm
Grey Boy (previously the Orange and Silver)	*Chironomus plumosus* group	6.5–8mm
Golden Dun Midge	*Chironomus plumosus* group	6.5–8mm
Olive Midge (previously the Ribbed Midge)	*Chironomus plumosus* group	6.5–7mm
Blae and Black (previously the Black Midge)	*Chironomus anthracinus*	5–7.5mm
Blagdon Green Midge	*Endochironomus albipennis*	4–6mm
Small Brown Midge	*Glyptotendipes paripes*	4–6mm
Small Red Midge	*Microtendipes pedellus*	4–4.5mm
Small Black Midge	*Polypedilum nubeculosus*	3.5–4mm

It will doubtless be noticed that out of the three species of midges mentioned in most angling literature covering this particular subject only *C. plumosus* appears. The remaining two, namely *C. tentans* and *C. viridis*, do not appear in this list, as during my fairly extensive research on this group I found them to be less common than the species chosen for final inclusion. All the more common specimens of the larger midges collected were found to be of the *C. Plumosus* group despite differences in size and colour, and it therefore seems possible that this species may one day be sub-divided into a number of different sub-species.

DISTRIBUTION: As all the adult midges (or very similar species) are abundant and very widespread throughout all the countries in Europe and the British Isles, no attempt will be made to divide the various species into specific areas.

THE FLY FISHERS' ADULT MIDGES

The Large Green Midge   Plate 35 (277)

The dark green body of the adult has a pale brown thorax with darker patches and yellow-olive legs. These seem to be the largest of all the midges. The pupae have a similar body colour with a dark thorax and brown wing cases and as they are so large I would suggest an artificial tied on a size 10 hook to represent them. The adults hatch in the late evening, often in large numbers, usually during late July or August.

The Large Red or Ginger Midge   Plate 35 (278 & 279)

Very nearly as large as the species mentioned above, they are in my opinion the most handsome of all the Chironomids, having beautiful reddish-orange coloured bodies and legs. The pupae are dark red and some specimens have dark blotches on their bodies, and a hook size 10 or 12 is suggested for the corresponding artificial. These seem to be a mid- to late-summer species and hatches are usually rather sparse, often occurring in the late afternoon or early evening from June to September.

The Grey Boy   Plate 35 (280)

This would seem to be one of the most common and widespread species of all and I have personally encountered numbers of them on practically every stillwater that I have fished. The adult has a silver-grey body with reddish-orange ringing, and a greyish thorax with touches of bright orange; the legs are orange-brown. Hatches are usually prolific, and the insects have a very long season from April to early June, probably consisting of more than one generation, while odd localised hatches are likely to be encountered throughout the season. The main emergence period is in the late evening, although later in the season hatches may also occur in the early mornings at sunrise. The colour of this particular pupa is quite fascinating (see Plate 35, No. 274). It has a dark thorax, orange wing cases, and the body segments are bright silver ringed with dark red. A hook size 10 or 12 should be used for the artificial. I have also observed quite good hatches of a medium-sized species in the late morning or early afternoon during May and June. Whether or not they are a different species I have been unable to ascertain, but apart from size the colours of both adults and pupae are exactly the same.

The Golden Dun Midge   Plate 36 (281)

This is also a medium to large species, the adults having bodies of a distinct golden-olive colour with dark patches along the top of some of the body segments. Their legs are a similar colour to their bodies but often have touches of black at the joints. They are common and widely distributed and are likely to be encountered from time to time during most of the summer months. The main emergence is usually confined to the late evenings. The pupa has a pale buff thorax and wing cases and the body varies from olive to olive-brown; again a hook size 10 to 12 is recommended (Plate 36, No 281).

The Olive Midge   Plate 36 (282)

The adults of this species are of medium size and, as the name suggests, their bodies are olive-brown ribbed very distinctly with thick ivory coloured bands. They too are an extremely common and widespread species having quite a long season. They emerge during May and June and again in August and early September, the gap possibly dividing two distinct generations. The pupa has a body of a similar colour to the adult, with the bands of ivory still apparent although thinner, while its thorax and wing cases are often dark olive brown. The adults hatch either in the late evening or very early morning, and on occasions odd specimens will be found emerging during the day. A hook size 12 is suggested for the artificial to represent the pupa.

The Blae & Black Midge   Plate 36 (283)

There are many species of midges with dark or almost black bodies, but of all these *Chironomus anthracinus* seems to be the one most frequently encountered, and for this reason it was the species I decided to include in the list. *C. tentans*, which is so often classified as the Black Midge or Buzzer in fishing literature, is in fact quite dissimilar as this is a large and pale coloured species. The former has a grey–black body with black legs, and in some cases the transparent wings have a whitish tinge; they are of a medium size and the bodies of the males seem to be very much slimmer than the females, and although this difference between the sexes is apparent with all the species in this group, it seems to be particularly noticeable in this one. Unfortunately, I have been unable to discover much information on the life cycle of this midge, as they proliferate in parts of the country which I seldom visit. I think the pupae may be brownish-grey in colour but I am by no means certain. It seems likely that it is this species that is referred to in parts of Wales and Scotland as the Duck Fly or Harlequin Fly. They hatch out in the middle of the day and although they are seen throughout the summer the main emergence occurs during late March and early April; a well-known artificial tied to represent them is the Blae and Black.

The Blagdon Green Midge   Plate 36 (284)

This is a medium to small species, the adult having a vivid green body, a brownish thorax and faintly white wings. A closely allied but smaller species similar in colour with a wing length of 3.5mm is *Chironomus viridis*. Up to now it is this particular species that has been classified in angling literature under the above vernacular name. However, of the two, *Endochironmus albipennis* appears to be the more common and is therefore the species I have decided to include in the list. Although it is a very common and widespread species it tends to emerge in relatively small numbers. Hatches are usually spread over a period of two or three hours often during the middle part of the day, although on occasions a larger emergence over a shorter period sometimes takes place in the very early mornings. I have seen these midges during most of the summer months, and the trout seem inordinately fond of the pupae, which have pale green bodies with buff-coloured wing cases. These pupae are small, and on many occasions I have spooned out trout to find literally hundreds of the little creatures among the stomach contents. Despite this, when trout are feeding on them they seem to be very difficult to tempt with an artificial, which should be tied on a hook size 14 or 16. The common name originated on Blagdon Reservoir in Somerset where prolonged hatches often occur throughout the day.

The Small Brown Midge   Plate 36 (285)
This is a day-hatching species and is very common and occurs in most areas. The adults are medium to small with dark to chestnut-brown bodies and dark brown legs. The main emergence period seems to be between 11 a.m. and 5 p.m. and they are most likely to be seen during mid-summer. Hatches are often on a large scale, and trout seem extremely fond of them, feeding on the pupae or emerging adults in the surface film. The rise form of such trout is unmistakable, being quick and often repeated, usually in a circular direction during a flat calm, or in a straight line upwind in a ripple. Unfortunately, the fish are notoriously difficult to catch when so occupied. The very dark brown pupae which often have a distinct orange tinge are small and for the artificial a hook size 14 or even 16 is recommended.

The Small Red Midge   Plate 36 (286 & 287)
This is also a predominantly day-hatching species, the adults being small with dark legs and port wine red bodies. They are not quite as common as the species mentioned above, nor is the emergence always on a large scale. Apart from the above, the remarks applying to the Small Brown Midge also apply to these and other even smaller species, although the Small Red are often in evidence a little later in the season. The pupae are so similar to the Small Brown that it is virtually impossible to tell them apart.

The Small Black Midge   Plate 36 (288)
The adult is very small and has a black body and thorax and dark brown or black legs, with distinctly whitish wings. It is common and widespread, and hatches are often on an exceptionally large scale in the early evenings or occasionally mornings during the spring or late summer. During this period the winged adults form large swarms along the banks of lakes and reservoirs. When the trout commence feeding on these or other even smaller species (usually too small to imitate) they often become preoccupied and very selective, and are extremely difficult to catch. In some cases they seem to feed on the ascending pupae, while on other occasions they will only take them in the surface film or when the pupae are transforming into adults. The pupae are very small and dark in colour, and it is essential to use a very small hook to represent them, a 16 or even smaller. The rise form is similar to that described for the Small Brown Midge.

In conclusion, I should like to make it quite clear that there is still considerable scope left for further research on this particular family of insects. Up to the late sixties little was known by fishermen about their life cycle or behaviour, and although I have during past years been engaged in an extensive study of them, and I hope, resolved some of the problems, I feel I have barely scratched the surface. It is therefore possible that in the course of time my descriptions of the life cycles of some of the species mentioned may have to be modified and the numbers of species covered considerably extended as more information becomes available.

FISHING INFORMATION ON STILLWATER

The Adults

Due to the fact that, to the fisherman, the winged form of the adult fly is marginally the least important of the three stages of its life, I propose describing it first. Undoubtedly trout do occasionally accept on stillwaters the winged adults, and in fact since my original research into this family of flies there have been quite a few patterns developed to represent them. In recent years reports on trout feeding on the adults particularly during some of the heavier early morning or evening rises have been escalating. Many years ago I remembered reading a report in one of our fishing journals which I viewed with some scepticism about trout feeding regularly on adult winged Chironomids or buzzers as they are popularly referred to by many fishermen.

For a long time now I have made a special study of this fascinating family of insects and until 1974 it had only been on rare occasions that I had personally observed trout feeding upon these adults on the surface. However, I now feel I owe the writer of the article an apology for my doubts as during the early part of that season for a period of two or three weeks on our local reservoir the trout started feeding on these in the evenings and were not interested in any other form of food. This phenomenon was also observed at this time on other reservoirs in the area according to reliable reports I received.

First of all I should like to make it quite clear that the reason for this appeared to be an unusual behaviour pattern on the part of the buzzers not of the trout, after all it is a natural reaction of the fish to feed on the form of food that is most easily accessible and that is what was happening at this time. Let me explain! To start with the trout usually commence feeding on the ascending pupae as they slowly swim to the surface to transpose into the adult. On windy mornings or evenings when the surface is rough and broken, the pupae hatch at the surface very quickly indeed and almost immediately fly off. The trout being wise in the ways of nature find it easier to feed upon this ascending pupae at this time and only occasionally chase one and take it at the surface. However, on calm still days when there is a relatively thick film present on the surface of the water, the ascending pupae often have difficulty in breaking through this to hatch, and the trout quickly realise it requires much less effort to feed upon the pupae hanging in the surface which is more often than not the reason for those splendid evening rises we sometimes encounter on calm warm evenings. It is also under these conditions that I have sometimes seen the odd trout also taking the newly hatched winged adult, but in my experience until the 1974 season this had been very much the exception rather than the rule.

The season of 1974 started quite normally with some good evening rises to the buzzers and plenty of trout were taken on midge pupae artificials, but by about the third week of May the position altered dramatically. The evening rises were still as good if not better, but very few were being caught, and the normally highly successful midge pupa patterns were steadfastly refused. After a couple of evenings with very poor results my fishing companion the late Cliff Henry and I decided to make a closer study of the feeding pattern of the trout. First of all we noticed that the trout were feeding higher out of the water and furthermore instead of the normal rather slow head and tail rise associated with fish feeding on the pupae, the movement was more hurried and closer allied to trout feeding on sedges or similar surface flies. We were extremely puzzled by this as despite careful observation the only insects hatching in sufficient quantities were buzzers. The next calm evening we therefore concentrated on studying the surfaceof the water and it was only then that we noticed that there appeared to be considerable numbers of adult winged buzzers or midges actually flying low over the water surface.

They flew relatively slowly with their legs actually trailing in the water, and once we became used to spotting them their flight could easily be observed as they left a very faint V shaped trail on the surface, in most cases the wake would suddenly cease as the insect disappeared in the swirl of a rising trout.

We studied this phenomenon closely over the ensuing three weeks and after catching many of these adults we ascertained the following facts. To start with we have never previously seen adult midges flying for long periods over the surface in this manner since normally, as soon as they hatch, they fly to the nearest land and mating takes place at a later period. The egg bearing females then return to the water usually at dusk to drop their egg clusters over or onto the water. Most anglers will be familiar with the swarms of these females that gather round ones head just as it is getting dark emitting an audible buzzing sound from which of course they obtain their common name. We caught many dozens of these adults on the surface, and for the first week or ten days they were the familiar Grey Boy midge, but during the last few days of June and early July, the majority were a medium sized Green midge. These were very similar to the Common Green midge normally to be seen a little later in the season, except that they had a distinctly yellow thorax as opposed to the normal greenish colour. Finally and of particular interest in each and every case they proved to be females, but their gyrations over the surface seemingly had nothing to do with ovipositions as in no case were there any traces of eggs.

Now what can we deduce from these facts, and the answer I am afraid is very little. Our first reactions were that this peculiarity could be accredited to a species with which we were unfamiliar, but this theory was quickly dispelled when we found that many we caught were the common Grey Boy variety. Secondly we thought it may have something to do with distribution of the eggs onto the surface, but his idea was also quickly discarded as there was no traces of any eggs at all. Could it be due to weather conditions as in this particular year we had had one of the driest springs on record.

Apart from our very interesting study of the natural insects involved, we also tackled the problem of evolving a suitable pattern and technique to catch the trout that at this period were preoccupied in feeding exclusively on these adults. So far, sad to relate, we have only met with mediocre success. After some experimenting we perfected a dressing that floated well and in appearance closely approximated the natural in flight. The method of fishing this pattern however proved to be the most difficult problem. Fished without movement it brought negative results. Fished along the surface with either a slow or fast retrieve resulted in far too much wake which apparently scared the trout. A compromise of giving an occasional slow pull on the line did result in the capture of a few fish, but apart from this the only real success we attained was in the latter part of the evening when the light was fading and the odd trout rose extremely close. When this happened by dapping the artificial lightly on the water immediately in front of the trout, it was immediately accepted without hesitation.★ Taff Price has recently developed a pattern for this style of fishing which has proved to be very effective. He has given it the appropriate name of the Skating Midge.

★   The use of a 14ft dapping rod now appears to be at least a partial answer to this problem as with a light line you can virtually dap your artificial very lightly along the surface.

The Larvae.

As previously stated, these form a staple diet for the trout on many stillwaters and are often to be found in the stomach contents. Unfortunately, due to their appearance and mode of life, they are exceedingly difficult to imitate. The larvae spend most of their life in the mud, silt, weed or silkweed on the bottom, but they do move freely along the bed of the lake sometimes. It is therefore possible to impersonate them at this stage reasonably successfully with a special pattern. There are several dressings available, but the pattern with which I have experienced most satisfactory results is one I have devised myself (red and green larvae) and which is given in the appropriate section at the end of this chapter.

This pattern should be fished where possible in the deeper water on a sinking line. It is essential to let it sink to the bottom, and it is then retrieved very slowly indeed in a way which loosely simulates the lashing movement of the natural. I tie it in either of the two most common colours of the natural larvae, red or green. An excellent alternative pattern that I strongly recommend is called the Bloodworm by John Wilshaw.

The Pupae.

It is at this stage of their existence that the midges on stillwater are most accessible to the trout, thereby providing the angler with excellent opportunities to imitate them. When trout are feeding on these medium to large hatching Chironomid pupae the rise form is most distinctive and is best described as a slow head and tail rise, with the tip of the dorsal and tail fins just breaking the surface. As a general rule the only other time that trout rise in this manner is when they are feeding on rarer occasions, on Caenis or on floating snails. As mentioned previously, a pattern to represent the pupa as it hangs in the surface film preparatory to transposing into the adult is the Black Buzzer. This, and several other lesser-known artificials dressed in a similar manner have, over the years, been very successful, and the most popular method of fishing them was as follows. The leader would be lightly greased to within an inch of the two or more artificials being fished to keep them as near the surface as possible. They would then be retrieved very slowly with a long steady pull or, alternatively, very slowly with brief pauses. As with all pupa patterns a floating line was used. Buzzer rises, which usually take place either early in the morning or late in the evening on most summer days under calm, warm conditions, are often heavy, and there is considerable difference of opinion as to whether it is better to cast in the path of a rising trout or whether to fish the water. Personally, I prefer to fish the water during a heavy rise and only cover individual fish during a sparse rise.

So far as I am aware the above method, was in the early years the only one generally recognised, and I feel sure most anglers will agree that although it is successful on occasions it often proves of little avail. During the early sixties I carried out many experiments to try and find more effective methods of fishing these pupa patterns. Although I evolved several new styles of fishing these patterns with a certain amount of success, none in particular have proved to be the complete answer, and it therefore seems apparent that the trout vary in the way in which they feed on the natural. Consequently, it would seem that there is still considerable scope for further experimenting in this direction. Before proceeding with details of these methods, I should like to point out that I feel that close imitation of the artificial is of the utmost importance, more so than with any other stillwater pattern. The reason for this should be apparent. The natural pupa is a relatively slow-moving creature, and consequently an artificial representing it must be fished in a like manner with little or, on some occasions, no movement at all. The trout therefore have every opportunity of a close appraisal of the artificial. Following this line of thought many years ago I dressed a series of patterns which I called the Hatching Midge pupa. They were based on a close study of the naturals, and I believe that they are sufficiently lifelike to fool the trout. It should be noted that I dress my patterns with a bunch of white hackle fibres tied in sloping forward over the eye of the hook to represent the head filaments of the natural and a tag of the same material to represent the whitish tail or caudal fins of the natural. I felt at the time that these features were particularly important and were certainly not incorporated in commercially tied or older standard patterns of this period which were tied with white floss sloping back over the body to, I quote, 'represent wing cases', which is of course a fallacy. My tying has certainly proved very effective over the intervening years and they are included in the colour photographs of artificials under their popular name of the Hatching Midge Pupa. I still use these today when fishing methods 1 and 2.

Although trout sometimes sift the pupae from the bottom silt, the first real opportunity they have of feeding upon them is during their ascent to the surface. Of the following methods the first two are intended to simulate the natural at this particular stage.

Method 1

This can be used satisfactorily only from an anchored boat. When all the signs indicate that a buzzer rise is about to commence, two or three Hatching Midge patterns should be mounted on the leader, one on the point and one on each dropper, each about 3ft apart. The leader is left ungreased and as long a rod as possible is used, only enough fly line being pulled off the reel to sink the leader as far as the top dropper. It will be appreciated that a short length of line and leader will now be hanging straight from the rod tip into the water. If the angler is fishing on his own from a boat in a flat calm it will be necessary to slowly raise and lower the rod tip about 2ft at a time. If there is a slight wave or another angler is in the boat casting, it will only be necessary to hold the rod perfectly still, as the rocking of the boat will provide all the movement necessary to animate the artificials.

On the face of it this method may appear to be a little revolutionary, but it certainly seems to be very effective on occasions providing the angler has sufficient patience to persist and ignore the temptation to cast to any trout that may rise within casting distance. Fishing a team of three Hatching Midges in this style, the artificial on the top dropper, which will be moving slightly up and down just below the surface is likely to be taken by any trout feeding on or just under the surface. The other two artificials being fished deeper and moving in a like manner simulate the natural pupae on their journey to the surface and will account for trout feeding on them at a deeper level. It may be thought that fishing directly under the rod top in this manner will put fish down, but this does not seem to be so, probably due to the fact that this method is usually practised either during failing light, or with a minimum of movement.

Method 2
This presents the artificials in a similar manner but enables a larger area of water to be fished, and is equally suited to both boat and bank fishermen. In this case the Hatching Midge on the top dropper is replaced with a large Sedge pattern which is heavily greased to float. The team of artificials is then cast as far as is necessary, and the floating Sedge carefully watched; at the slightest sign of any movement it is usually necessary only to tighten and any trout that has taken the artificial pupa below the surface will be hooked. On several occasions when fishing in this manner I have had trout literally hook themselves, as they seem to accept the artificial fished in this way very confidently. It is best to use this technique when there is a ripple or wave on the water, as the bobbing sedge will provide the necessary animation to the artificials below. In a flat calm a slow sink and draw retrieve is suggested to provide the desired animation.

Method 3
Both this and the following method require the Hatching Midge or similar patterns to be tied on straight-eyed hooks. The first artificial is threaded direct on to the leader, and a 3ft length of about 5lb breaking strain monofil is then tied into the leader with a treble blood knot; the second artificial is then threaded on to this and a 2ft point of the same monofil is then tied in with a further blood knot. The third artificial is then tied direct on to the point. The two artificials tied direct into the cast are held in the requisite position by the blood knots. The leader should then be lightly greased along its complete length. This team of artificial pupae may be cast either in the path of a rising trout or the water may be fished. They can be fished without movement to represent the natural pupae hanging vertically in the surface film, or retrieved very slowly with short pulls and frequent pauses to simulate the swimming and resting action of the naturals. In practice it will be found that the artificial on the point tends to sink a little below the surface, thereby allowing the angler to represent the natural insect rising to the surface also. When I first thought of this idea of threading the artificial directly on to the leader in an effort to present the artificial in a natural manner hanging vertically with the head just breaking the surface where the natural is found, I was a little dubious as to the hooking qualities, but I am happy to relate that so far this has presented no problem.

Method 4
Basically this is very similar to the above method, and the straight-eyed pupae artificials again are mounted on the leader in the same manner and the leader lightly greased. The pattern on the point, however, is now replaced by a large heavily greased artificial sedge. When fishing this team it will be found it will float almost indefinitely, allowing the fisherman to cast and to leave the artificials hanging motionless in the film until taken by a trout. As in Method 3, the team may also be retrieved slowly if desired. Later in the summer, when the natural sedges are found on the water, the angler will often be presented with a bonus when the artificial sedge on the point is taken in no uncertain manner. I have found

during a heavy buzzer rise that it is best to cast the artificials in the vicinity of rising trout and allow them to lay there until one is accepted. I usually adopt the alternative of a little movement when the rise is less heavy, but the angler in time will be able to judge this best in the light of experience.

I would add that Methods 1 and 2 are best practised during the early part of the rise before the trout have settled to feeding on the surface. When the pupae first start ascending the trout tend to feed on them at this stage gradually working nearer to the surface. On warm, calm evenings, when there is a heavy surface film, the emerging pupae often have difficulty in breaking through and therefore hang in the film for longer than normal. This, of course, nearly always results in a heavy and extended rise of trout, as the pupae are then in large concentrations and provide rich pickings for the fish. During this period Method 3 or 4 is the best proposition. Cold and breezy evenings during summer are never conducive to a large emergence, and the rise on these occasions is seldom on a worthwhile scale, and under these conditions Methods 1 and 2 are well worth trying.

The above methods (3 and 4) were perfected many years ago and at the time it was the only way one could ensure that your artificial pupa patterns were fishing with their heads piercing the surface film in the position where the trout would expect to find them. Today the situation is different as during the last decade we have seen the introduction of several new pupa patterns that incorporate buoyant materials tied in just behind the eye of the hook. These new and revolutionary patterns have when available obviated the necessity of using straight-eyed patterns threaded directly on to the leader, as these new artificials float in the perfect position independently so can be tied direct on to the droppers. The first of this new breed of artificial midge pupa were developed in the late '70s by myself with the encouragement and assistance of my good friends Brian Clarke and Neil Patterson. We gave the pattern the name of Suspender Midge Pupa which we felt was very appropriate, as the little ball of foam tied in behind the eye suspends the pattern perfectly in a vertical position in the surface. The big advantage in using these buoyant artificials is that the leader need not be greased, and in practice we now actually degrease the leader so there are now no tell tale ripples from the links of leader between the droppers to alert or scare the trout when any movement is imparted to the fly line. We are also now experimenting by mounting three or even four suspenders on droppers very close together – between 12″ and 18″ apart. I am sure that most fly fishers have experienced those very heavy and frustrating rises of trout in the evenings on both lakes and reservoirs when the trout will not look at any artificial you offer them. For several years now I have carried out much research on trout vision, and I have recently come to the conclusion that under the above conditions when trout are rising and cruising virtually in the surface film, their vision is limited, and it is very doubtful whether they can see any flies in or on the surface much further than about 12″ in front or to either side. It is therefore hardly surprising that during these heavy evening surface rises your artificial is seldom taken as unless you cast it almost on the nose of a rising trout he is unlikely to see it. By mounting your artificials close together and casting into the path of a rising trout your chances as we have found out are much enhanced.

Method for Small Pupa on Stillwater
The information given up to now applies to the large and medium size pupae. For the smaller pupae a different technique is required, although as yet I have been

unable to discover a really satisfactory one. These small midges, of which the predominant colours are green, red, brown or black, usually hatch during the day or early evening. They often emerge in large numbers, and the trout usually become preoccupied in feeding upon them on the surface. For some reason the trout in calm conditions usually move in a circular direction, or in a straight line upwind in a ripple and sip down the hatching pupae extremely rapidly. My observations to date lead me to believe that the trout are in fact feeding on the pupae as they lie horizontally in the surface film in the act of emergence. When the trout are so engaged they are most difficult to tempt. Up to now I have enjoyed most success with my Suspender Hatching Midge pattern tied on a very tiny hook on a fine point. Under these conditions I have found the key to success appears to be very accurate casting. If you can place your fly about 18″ in front of a rising trout and then give it a slight tweak, this will often result in a positive take.

Midge Pupa on Rivers

In more recent years I have been carrying out research on trout feeding upon chironomids in rivers, this is an area that has largely been ignored by river fly fishers in the U.K. despite the fact that my research had shown me that in most rivers the population of these small members of the diptera order outnumber the ephemeroptera order by at least four to one. It would seem that on many continental rivers the percentage may be even higher as the well-known French author and fly fisher Raymond Rocher has over the past few years written on several occasions about a certain amount of success he has experienced with tiny emerger patterns to trout feeding upon these chironomids. During this period I have also experimented with various small emerger patterns but with very indifferent success.

Up to comparatively recently I had always associated trout feeding in slow flowing sections of rivers upon chironomids with a slow leisurely head and tail rise, but as this rise form is somewhat similar to the slow sipping rise of trout feeding upon smuts I idly wondered whether there may be some connection, particularly with trout feeding in this manner in faster water where the precise rise form is more difficult to establish. Now these two rise forms have two things in common, in both cases the trout is lying very close to the surface, I therefore wondered whether these two slightly different rise forms were in fact indicative of trout feeding upon both smuts or chironomids and even in some cases both at the same time. In an effort to establish whether this was so, towards the end of the season before last I kept a record of the stomach contents of all trout caught that seemed to be rising either to smuts or chironomids. The results confirmed that most trout were indeed feeding upon both species at the same time, as on many occasions I found their stomachs packed both with smuts and small brown or green chironomids and in some cases both brown and green. Only occasionally did I find one species to the exclusion of the other. Could this then be the missing section of the puzzle? To find out it was necessary to find a chironomid (midge) pattern that was acceptable to the trout. This appeared to pose a problem as for many years I had been experimenting with various emerger patterns with but little success. However I now had the advantage of knowing the type colour and size of midges that these river trout were feeding upon and it struck me that a Suspender Midge Pupa may be worth trying, dressed with either brown or green bodies on very small hooks. This subsequently proved to be astonishingly successful even on those rivers that had previously posed serious problems because of drag. On countless occasions now I have observed trout deviate and chase one of these tiny Suspender patterns that has been dragging yet still take it quite confidently.

The reason for this is that it probably appears quite natural to the trout, as when the natural pupa rise to the surface to hatch they initially hang vertically in the surface film, but when they are ready to emerge from the pupal case they nearly always adopt a horizontal posture and then swim along beneath the film looking for a weak area through which they can emerge from the pupal case. It is at this juncture that they simulate the dragging natural. During this past season this tiny Suspender pattern has also provided me with many bonus trout that I would not normally have caught. I am sure that many of you will have experienced the frustration of trying to cast a dry fly to trout you can barely see rising as darkness approaches. Most of the time you really have very little idea where your dry fly is in relation to the rising trout and consequently you are very unsure when to strike. I have found that in many cases trout tend to often feed on small midges at this period so they will often take a Suspender very confidently. The big advantage in using a Suspender at this time is because if you cast it hard down upon the surface it makes a very distinctive plop which can be seen quite clearly if you are looking into the dying light, so you then know exactly where your artificial is in relation to the next rise of the trout. When fishing the Suspender at this time of evening I find that the takes are very gentle indeed, so I have found in practice it is essential to keep the line and leader under tension. This is best accomplished by slowly raising the rod tip as the artificial drifts towards you in the current. Smutting or midging trout now no longer poses a problem for me as I know that if they will not take my smut pattern (see section on smuts) they will most certainly take a Suspender. The dressing is as follows:

Suspender Midge Pupa
Hook: Roman Moser arrow point size 16 or 18.
Silk: Fine nymph-brown.
Body: Green or brown seals fur or substitute.
Rib: Fine silver lurex.
Tail: White nylon or organza filaments.
Thorax: Brown dyed turkey herl.
Ball: White Ethafoam or similar enclosed in fine white nylon mesh (from a lady's nylon stocking – how you obtain this is up to you). This should be tied in first on top of hook over the eye.

Suggested Artificials to Represent the Midges on Stillwater
The larvae of the midges are difficult to imitate with fur and feather as they swim with a figure-of-eight lashing movement. I can suggest only three artificials: my own **Red** or **Green Larva**; the **Bloodworm** (John Wilshaw); and the **Marabou Bloodworm** (Taff Price).

Of the three stages of interest to the fly-fisher, the pupal stage is the most important, and here there are plenty of artificials from which to choose. My recommendation is that the following patterns should be carried in various colours and sizes to match the naturals most likely to be hatching. **Hatching Midge pupa** (Goddard); **Hatching Buzzer Pupa** (Collyer); **Marabou Buzzer**

(Price); and the **Footballer** (Bucknall). But while all these are excellent patterns, my own preference is my own **Suspender Hatching Midge Pupa** during a heavy surface rise, while at other times, when trout are taking just below the surface, my favourite is Bob Carnill's **Poly-Rib C Pupa**. These may not be to everybody's taste as they are time-consuming patterns to dress, but they are super-imitative patterns. An excellent general pattern is Dr Bell's **Grenadier** or Piero Lumini's **Chironomid Emerger**.

There is also a good choice of patterns to represent both the emerging or hatching adult and the fully-winged adult. These are, to my mind, less important, as the trout will take at least a dozen pupae for every adult taken. But these hatching and adult patterns should also be dressed in different colours and sizes. They are: **Adult Midge** (Richard Walker); **Emergent Midge** (Price); **Resting Midge** (Price); **Green Adult Midge** (Lumini); **Black Midge** (Henderson); **Duck Fly** (J. R. Harris); and that good wet pattern, the traditional **Blae and Black**. My own preference is for Bob Carnill's series of **Adult Buzzers**, which are fished as wet flies just in or even below the surface to represent dead, dying or drowned midges, or to simulate the freshly-hatched adults struggling to become airborne.

THE OTHER DIPTERA

The Hawthorn Fly (*Bibio marci*) Plate 37 (289), also known as St. Mark's Fly

This latter name is probably due to the fact that hatches usually start about St. Mark's Day (25th April). It is quite a large black fly with a hairy body, about 12mm long, an obvious characteristic of which is a pair of long, drooping hind legs. When this fly is on the wing it can usually be identified immediately by these long, trailing hind legs. It is normally found in the vicinity of Hawthorn trees, or even at some distance from water, often over open meadowland, flying in swarms about 6ft or higher above ground level. In a strong wind, numbers of insects from these large swarms are often blown on to the water. When this happens the trout take them greedily and the fly-fisherman usually has a day to remember. Unfortunately for the trout-fisher, these days are all too rare, as in most localities the season for this fly is comparatively short, lasting only about two or three weeks. Although this species is more frequently encountered by rivers during late April or May, it is also to be observed at times close to stillwaters when it is of considerable value to the fly-fisherman. On rivers it usually requires a fairly heavy fall before the trout will start feeding on them, but this is not always so on stillwater. Therefore, at this time of the year, even when only a few specimens may be observed on the water, an artificial pattern is usually worth a try and will often succeed. There are many artificial dressings available to represent this species, and while some are dressed to be fished wet or dry, others are essentially dry flies. My own preference is for a dry pattern fished on a floating line with a greased leader and, as with so many floating patterns particularly when stillwater fishing, I find that a slight twitch to the rod top every now and again to provide a little animation to the fly is most effective. For some reason a little difficult to understand, wet dressings are quite popular and will often kill when fished slowly a little below the surface, but this seems strange, as the natural fly will rarely, if ever, be encountered beneath the surface. Another effective artificial is a pattern called the Mating Hawthorn, which represents the mating pair locked together, and during prolific hatches these will sometimes land on the water still joined. These pairs naturally make a very juicy mouthful and the trout will often become selective, feeding on these in preference to single flies, hence the value of this particular pattern.

ARTIFICIALS: There are many dressings that have been perfected over the years and most of these are listed under the common name of Hawthorn Fly. A good alternative is a pattern developed by Brian Clarke and myself called the U.S.D. Hawthorn.

DISTRIBUTION: A very common and widespread species it is likely to be found in most areas throughout Europe except in areas No 20–22 and 23.

The Heather Fly (Bibio pomonae). Plate 37 (290)

This is also a terrestrial species of the same family as the Hawthorn Fly, and is in fact very similar in size and appearance. The Heather Fly, however, can be readily identified as the tops of the legs or tibiae are a distinct reddish colour. As the name suggests, this fly is found in the vicinity of heather and is therefore most likely to be met in parts of Wales or the North, including Scotland. It is a very prolific species, and in areas where it abounds it is undoubtedly of considerable value to the fly–fisherman, being often blown on to the water in large numbers, where the trout accept them readily. It is in season longer than the Hawthorn, and is on the wing during July, August and September. The local Scottish name for this fly is the Bloody Doctor. I do not know of any particular dressing for it, but any of the many dressings to represent the Hawthorn Fly should suffice, the black hackle being enhanced with a reddish one. Strange to relate several years ago I observed a good hatch of these along the banks of the Middle Test.

DISTRIBUTION: Most areas except No 20–22 and 23.

Black Gnats (Bibionidae Family) Plate 37 (291)

This is another similar but much smaller land-bred fly of importance to the fly-fisher. The scientific name is often given as *Bibio johannis*, but the name Black Gnat is in fact given to a number of different species, and *B. johannis* is but one of them. In some parts of Europe *Dilophus febrilis* is the Black Gnat, in others it is *Hilara maura* or *Ocydromia glabricula*. *Bibio* spp. can be positively identified by the venation of the wings and the curious long-pointed spur on the knee joints of the two front legs (see Fig. 78). In a similar manner *D. febrilis* can be recognised by the many-spurred projections on the knee joints of the two front legs (see Fig. 77). The males of *Hilara* can be similarly recognised by the enlarged 'Popeye' joints of the tibiae on the forelegs. These latter flies are a more important fly to the fisherman than is generally realised in areas where they abound. The late Dr Michael Wade made a study of this particular insect, and I am indebted to him for the following extract from one of his letters.

At Monkswood on the Usk in Wales, *Hilara* are the most important type of Black Gnats from the fisherman's point of view, and in May they are accepted eagerly by the trout. It should be pointed out however that they are not true Black Gnats because they belong to the very large Family of Empididae which contains over 300 species. Apart from *Hilara* mentioned here there are probably many other members of this family that are similar in size and appearance that are found in the vicinity of water. They can be seen flying in all directions in swarms very

77 Showing spurs on the knee joint on forelegs of *D. febrilis*

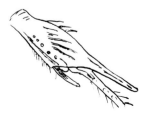

78 Showing long spur on knee joint of forelegs of *Bibio* Spp.

close to the water; these swarms I believe are associated with mating, during which the males often secure small midges or seeds or even bits of grit and wrap them up in a silk web for presentation to the female. Mating takes place while she unwraps the parcel. These mating couples often fall on the water and the trout do not hesitate to bring this hasty marriage to a speedy and tragic end.

Apart from the above, there are many other flies which could equally come under the general heading 'Black Gnats', including, of course, many of the Simulium spp. found in running water. Some of these species are seen only in spring, others only in the summer or autumn, so from the angler's point of view 'Black Gnats' are about at any time during the fishing season. Again, as with the Hawthorn Flies, they are usually on the water during windy conditions but, owing to their longer season, they are likely to be seen more frequently. They are all very small flies and vary between 5mm to 7mm. Most species have quite long legs. Their bodies are black to blackish brown and the wings are transparent, sometimes with a blue tinge and in other species with a brown tinge.

As far as artificial patterns are concerned there is a wealth of Black Gnat dressings from which to choose, and one of the most successful is the Knotted Midge, which is meant to copy the paired gnats as they fall on the water during mating, and it certainly seems to be good medicine during a heavy fall. Apart from dry patterns there are also many wet patterns, but which of these is most effective I have been unable to discover. The floating patterns should be fished as a normal dry fly on a lightly greased leader, on both rivers and also stillwater.

ARTIFICIALS: There are a host of Black Gnat patterns but I would suggest the following. The Black Gnat (Halford), the Altiere (Rochet), the Chochin (Antunez), a good rough water fly or a good general pattern is the Dogsbody.

DISTRIBUTION: As there are literally hundreds of different species of various genera that can all be loosely termed Black Gnats it seems pointless in giving information on distribution of a few species. Black Gnats of one species or another are very common and widespread and are likely to be found in the vicinity of lakes and rivers all over Europe.

The Blue Bottle

Familiar to most people this extra large house fly with its metallic blue or greenish body is equally common in the countryside and is occasionally blown onto the water where such a juicy mouthful is a bonus for any trout. An artificial pattern such as the Blue Bottle by Taff Price will often tempt a trout off the bottom in clear water.

DISTRIBUTION: Found in all countries throughout Europe.

The Dung-flies (Cordilurida)

This large family, containing over fifty different species, specimens of which are sometimes blown on to the water, is of doubtful value to the fisherman. Another fly which comes into this category is the Oak Fly, commonly known as the Downlooker. If one refers to many of the very old angling books you will find repeated references to both of these flies. There are also many old patterns to represent them. Despite this in all the years I have been fishing I have never even come across any in autopsies.

The Gravel Bed (Hexatoma fuscipennis) Plate 37 (296)

This is a dark brownish grey insect with black legs and two brownish heavily veined wings which looks very much like a miniature Crane Fly. It is a terrestrial insect, but as the pupa prefers damp ground, it is often found in abundance on the damp gravel or sandy banks of certain rivers. The Gravel Bed is very prolific, and when a hatch occurs they are often blown on to or swarm over water (which appears to attract them), dancing and dipping as the Silverhorns do. They are mostly to be encountered in late April, May or early June, and are great favourites with both fish and fishermen where they occur.

ARTIFICIALS: Despite the fact that the natural is common and well thought of by fly fishers in northern Britain I have only been able to locate one pattern to represent them and this is a wet pattern called a Blue Partridge. The dressing is given in Courtney Williams *A Dictionary of Trout Flies*.

DISTRIBUTION: Apart from being a common species in many northern areas of Great Britain I have been unable to trace their location in other areas, but suspect they may be common in some European countries.

The Crane Flies (Tipulidae etc.) Plate 37 (295)

The larger species of this family are a familiar sight at home or in the garden as well as by the waterside, and they are generally referred to as Daddy-long-legs. This is a very large family and anglers may be surprised to learn there are nearly 300 different British species alone which vary greatly in size, a large number being no larger than some of the mosquitos. The largest species is *Tipula maxima*, and with a body length of about 32mm has the distinction of being one of the largest of all the British flies, exceeded only by some of the Dragonflies. This is the species most likely to be seen on the water by the fly-fisherman as the larva is semi-aquatic, frequenting the damp margins of lakes or reservoirs, or in some cases actually living underwater. Gardeners refer to this larva as the leatherjacket where it is found in lawns that are well-watered. Pupation takes place ashore, the larva seeking a drier location in which to bury itself. Apart from this species there are many belonging to other genera of a similar appearance but smaller in size that are likely to be on or near water. One of the more common of them is a handsome yellow and black species, *Nephrotoma crocata*, usually found in bodies of water adjacent to woodland. Another very common species, *Ptychoptera contaminata* and other species of the Family Ptychopteridae, have larvae of a purely aquatic nature, which live in the mud or debris on the bottom in the shallow margins and these larvae are usually referred to as rat-tailed maggots in common with the larvae of some of the Drone flies. The long tail of this larva is in reality a breathing tube which reaches to the surface, thereby allowing the larva to breathe air. This tube or tail, consisting of three sections, is telescopic and this enables the tube to be adjusted to a water depth of up to about three inches.

From the above it will be apparent that there are very many species that are likely to be found in the vicinity of water. As they are all very similar in appearance although varying in size, they can all be classified by the angler as Crane flies and it is therefore only necessary to have two or three patterns in different sizes.

They are all poor fliers and if they fly or are blown out over the water they soon descend on to the surface, where their struggles soon attract any trout in the vicinity. The fish seem inordinately fond of these large ungainly insects and seem to accept them eagerly and, furthermore, they are reputed to attract the attentions of the larger fish, although I have not personally found this to be so.

They are probably better known on some of the Irish loughs, where the live insect is a great favourite for dapping. This is usually throughout the month of August when the naturals are at their maximum. However, they are likely to be effective throughout the summer, although July, August and September seem to be the best months to fish the artificial. During this period, when one is often faced with hot, bright windless days of flat calm, they can often provide the chance of a fish when all else has failed. Under these conditions providing a few of these flies are on the water a correctly tied and presented artificial will sometimes succeed in enticing an otherwise lethargic trout to the surface.

There are not many dressings to imitate these Crane flies but one I can personally recommend is the Daddy Long Legs by Dick Walker.

ARTIFICIALS: Should be fished on a floating line, as a dry fly, with a lightly greased leader. Due to the long, thin shape of the natural, artificial patterns, unless tied with a very buoyant body, are not good floaters and therefore they will have to be retrieved and re-cast regularly. It should be fished in jerks to simulate the struggle of the natural insect as closely as possible, although on other occasions it is very effective fished on the dead drift, particularly under rough conditions. Crane flies are seldom seen on rivers in any numbers and therefore artificial patterns to represent them are seldom used on this medium.

DISTRIBUTION: With so many very similar species all grouped together under the common name, Crane flies of one species or another will be found in most areas throughout Europe.

Drone Flies (Syrphidae) Plate 37 (292)

This family includes the Hover flies, and as far as the angler is concerned they can all be classified as Drone flies, for only an expert on entomology could classify the species correctly. In appearance and size they are somewhat similar to honey bees or common wasps, except of course they have only two wings like all Diptera. The larvae and in some cases the pupae of many species of this family are aquatic or semi-aquatic in origin and may therefore be of some interest though of little value to the fisherman.

One species of Drone fly in particular is quite common in stillwater and this is *Eristalis*, the larvae of which are colloquially known as Rat-tailed Maggots. These curious creatures are usually found in the black mud or silt in shallow water of small ponds or possibly larger bodies of stillwater rich in decaying matter. Their bodies are about half-an-inch long, greyish in colour, and their tails are extended into long breathing tubes which reach the surface of the water. It is supposed that these tubes, which are telescopic, can extend up to a length of nearly three inches, allowing the larvae to live and move freely about the bottom in water up to this depth, although they are also known to occur in water that is deep as they are fairly active and can swim. The pupae are very similar to the larvae except that near the heads they have two small breathing tubes which are used by those species that remain in the water to take in air while they are suspended passively near the surface. Usually they are located in shallower water, but at times they may be found in deeper water, where I have no doubt trout would take them, although I have not personally observed it.

The adults vary tremendously but the predominant body colours being dark

PLATE 1 BRITISH AND EUROPEAN SPECIES

1 *Ecdyonurus venosus*

2 *Heptagenia sulphurea*

3 *Epeorus sylvicola*

4 *Rhithrogena semicolorata*

5 *Ecdyonurus torrentis*

6 *Nixe joernensis*

7 *Baëtis rhodani*

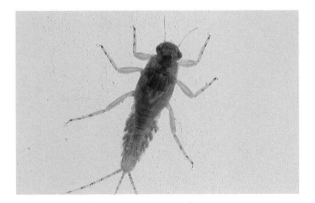

8 *Ephemerella ignita*

NYMPHS OF THE UPWINGED FLIES – EPHEMEROPTERA

♀ – Female species   ♂ – Male species

PLATE 2   BRITISH AND EUROPEAN SPECIES

9   *Electrogena lateralis*

10   *Ephemerlla mucronata*

11   *Habrophlebia fusca*

12   *Potamanthus luteus*

13   *Siphlonurus croaticus*

14   *Baëtis scambus*

15   *Baëtis alpinus*

16   *Ameletus inopinatus*

NYMPHS OF THE UPWINGED FLIES – EPHEMEROPTERA (cont.)

♀ – Female species   ♂ – Male species

PLATE 3   BRITISH AND EUROPEAN SPECIES

17   *Procloeon bifidum*

18   *Baëtis muticus*

19   *Pseudocentroptilum pennulatum*

20   *Ephemera danica*

21   *Ephoron virgo*

22   *Palingenia longicauda*

23   *Caënis luctuosa*

24   *Ephemerella major*

NYMPHS OF THE UPWINGED FLIES – EPHEMEROPTERA (cont.)

♀ – Female species   ♂ – Male species

PLATE 4   EUROPEAN SPECIES

25   *Siphlonurus croaticus* dun ♀

26   *Siphlonurus croaticus* dun ♂

27   *Siphlonurus croaticus* spinner ♀

28   *Siphlonurus croaticus* spinner ♂

29   *Ameletus inopinatus* dun ♀

30   *Ameletus inopinatus* dun ♂

31   *Ameletus inopinatus* spinner ♀

32   *Ameletus inopinatus* spinner ♂

THE UPWINGED FLIES – DUNS (SUB-IMAGO) AND SPINNERS (IMAGO) – EPHEMEROPTERA

♀ – Female species   ♂ – Male species

PLATE 5   EUROPEAN SPECIES

33   *Baëtis* alpinus dun ♀

34   *Baëtis* alpinus dun ♂

35   *Baëtis alpinus* spinner ♀

36   *Baëtis alpinus* spinner ♂

37   *Ecdyonurus helveticus* dun ♀

38   *Ecdyonurus helveticus* dun ♂

39   *Ecdyonurus helveticus* spinner ♀

40   *Ecdyonurus helveticus* spinner ♂

THE UPWINGED FLIES – DUNS (SUB-IMAGO) AND SPINNERS (IMAGO) – EPHEMEROPTERA

♀ – Female species   ♂ – Male species

PLATE 6 EUROPEAN SPECIES

41 *Rhithrogena savoyensis* dun ♀

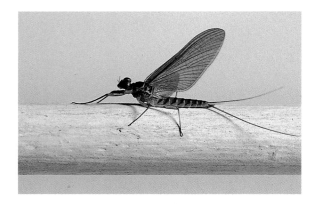

42 *Rhithrogena savoyensis* dun ♂

43 *Rhithrogena savoyensis* spinner ♀

44 *Rhithrogena savoyensis* spinner ♂

45 *Epeorus sylvicola* dun ♂

46 *Epeorus sylvicola* dun ♀

47 *Epeorus sylvicola* spinner ♀

48 *Epeorus sylvicola* spinner ♂

THE UPWINGED FLIES – DUNS (SUB-IMAGO) AND SPINNERS (IMAGO) – EPHEMEROPTERA

♀ – Female species   ♂ – Male species

PLATE 7   EUROPEAN SPECIES

49   *Rhithrogena hybrida* dun ♀

50   *Rhithrogena hybrida* dun ♂

51   *Rhithrogena hybrida* spinner ♀

52   *Rhithrogena hybrida* spinner ♂

53   *Rhithrogena braaschi* dun ♀

54   *Rhithrogena braaschi* dun ♂

55   *Rhithrogena braaschi* spinner ♀

56   *Rhithrogena braaschi* spinner ♂

THE UPWINGED FLIES – DUNS (SUB-IMAGO) – EPHEMEROPTERA

♀ – Female species   ♂ – Male species

PLATE 8   EUROPEAN SPECIES

57   *Rhithrogena loyolaea* dun ♀

58   *Rhithrogena loyolaea* dun ♂

59   *Rhithrogena loyolaea* spinner ♀

60   *Rhithrogena loyolaea* spinner ♂

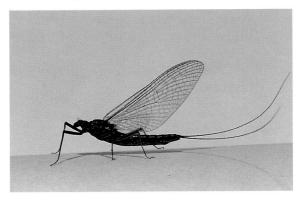

61   *Heptagenia flava* dun ♀

62   *Heptagenia flava* dun ♂

63   *Heptagenia flava* spinner ♀

64   *Heptagenia flava* spinner ♂

THE UPWINGED FLIES – DUNS (SUB-IMAGO) AND SPINNERS (IMAGO) – EPHEMEROPTER

♀ – Female species   ♂ – Male species

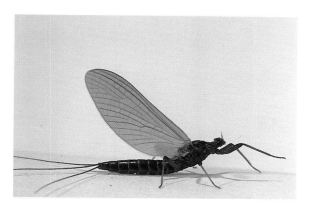

65   *Habroleptoides confusa* dun ♀

66   *Habroleptoides confusa* dun ♂

67   *Habroleptoides confusa* spinner ♀

68   *Habroleptoides confusa* spinner ♂

69   *Chorotherpes picteti* spinner ♂

70   *Ephoron virgo* dun ♀

71   *Ephoron virgo* spinner ♂

72   *Ephemera lineata* dun ♀

THE UPWINGED FLIES – DUNS (SUB-IMAGO) AND SPINNERS (IMAGO) – EPHEMEROPTERA

♀ – Female species   ♂ – Male species

PLATE 10   EUROPEAN SPECIES

73   *Ephemera lineata* spinner ♀

74   *Palingenia longicauda* spinner ♀

75   *Palingenia longicauda* dun ♂

76   *Palingenia longicauda* spinner ♂

77   *Ephemerella mucronata* dun ♀

78   *Ephemerella mucronata* dun ♂

79   *Ephemerella mucronata* spinner ♀

80   *Ephemerella mucronata* spinner ♂

THE UPWINGED FLIES – DUNS (SUB-IMAGO) AND SPINNERS (IMAGO) – EPHEMEROPTERA

♀ – Female species   ♂ – Male species

PLATE 11   EUROPEAN SPECIES

81   *Ephemerella major* dun ♂

82   *Ephemerella major* spinner ♀

83   *Ephemerella major* spinner ♂

84   *Ecdyonurus picteti* dun ♀

85   *Ecdyonurus picteti* dun ♂

86   *Ecdyonurus krueperi* dun ♂

87   *Ecdyonurus krueperi* spinner ♀

88   *Ecdyonurus krueperi* spinner ♂

THE UPWINGED FLIES – DUNS (SUB-IMAGO) AND SPINNERS (IMAGO) – EPHEMEROPTERA

♀ – Female species   ♂ – Male species

PLATE 12   EUROPEAN SPECIES

89   *Nixe joernensis* dun ♀

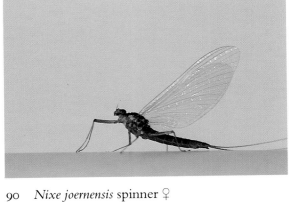

90   *Nixe joernensis* spinner ♀

91   *Nixe joernensis* spinner ♂

92   *Oligoneuria rhenana* spinner ♂

93   Transposition from dun to spinner – stage 1

94   Transposition – stage 2

95   Transposition – stage 3

96   Transposition – final stage

THE UPWINGED FLIES – DUNS (SUB-IMAGO) AND SPINNERS (IMAGO) – EPHEMEROPTER

♀ – Female species   ♂ – Male species

PLATE 13   BRITISH AND EUROPEAN SPECIES

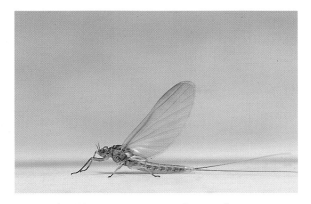

97   Pale Watery Dun *Baëtis fuscatus* ♀

98   Pale Watery Dun *Baëtis fuscatus* ♂

99   Pale Watery Spinner *Baëtis fuscatus* ♀

100   Pale Watery Spinner *Baëtis fuscatus* ♂

101   Small Dark Olive Dun *Baëtis scambus* ♀

102   Small Dark Olive Dun *Baëtis scambus* ♂

103   Small Dark Olive Spinner *Baëtis scambus* ♀

104   Small Dark Olive Spinner *Baëtis scambus* ♂

THE UPWINGED FLIES – DUNS (SUB-IMAGO) AND SPINNERS (IMAGO) – EPHEMEROPTERA

♀ – Female species   ♂ – Male species

PLATE 14 BRITISH AND EUROPEAN SPECIES

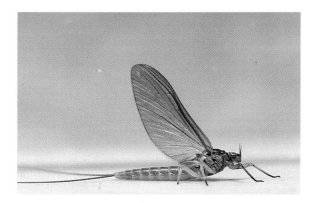

105 Medium Olive Dun *Baëtis vernus* ♀

106 Medium Olive Dun *Baëtis vernus* ♂

107 Medium Olive Spinner *Baëtis vernus* ♀

108 Medium Olive Spinner *Baëtis vernus* ♂

109 Large Dark Olive Dun *Baëtis rhodani* ♀

110 Large Dark Olive Dun *Baëtis rhodani* ♂

111 Large Dark Olive Spinner *Baëtis rhodani* ♀

112 Large Dark Olive Spinner *Baëtis rhodani* ♂

THE UPWINGED FLIES – DUNS (SUB-IMAGO) AND SPINNERS (IMAGO) – EPHEMEROPTER

♀ – Female species   ♂ – Male species

PLATE 15   BRITISH AND EUROPEAN SPECIES

113   Iron Blue Dun *Baëtis niger* ♀

114   Iron Blue Dun *Baëtis niger* ♂

115   Iron Blue Spinner *Baëtis niger* ♀

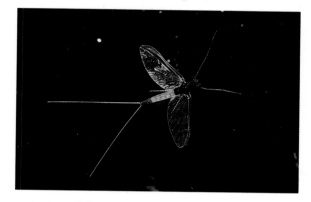

116   Iron Blue Spinner *Baëtis niger* ♂

117   Small Spurwing Dun *Centroptilum luteolum* ♀

118   Small Spurwing Dun *Centroptilum luteolum* ♂

119   Small Spurwing Spinner *Centroptilum luteolum* ♀

120   Small Spurwing Spinner *Centroptilum luteolum* ♂

THE UPWINGED FLIES – DUNS (SUB-IMAGO) AND SPINNERS (IMAGO) – EPHEMEROPTERA

♀ – Female species   ♂ – Male species

PLATE 16   BRITISH AND EUROPEAN SPECIES

121   Large Spurwing Dun
Pseudocentroptilum pennulatum ♀

122   Large Spurwing Dun
Pseudocentroptilum pennulatum ♂

123   Large Spurwing Spinner
Pseudocentroptilum pennulatum ♂

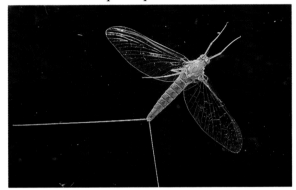

124   Large Spurwing Spinner
Pseudocentroptilum pennulatum ♀

125   Pond Olive Dun *Cloëon dipterum* ♀

126   Pond Olive Dun *Cloëon dipterum* ♂

127   Pond Olive Spinner *Cloëon dipterum* ♀

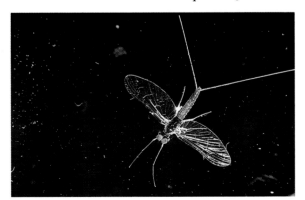

128   Pond Olive Spinner *Cloëon dipterum* ♂

THE UPWINGED FLIES – DUNS (SUB-IMAGO) AND SPINNERS (IMAGO) – EPHEMEROPTER.

♀ – Female species   ♂ – Male species

PLATE 17   BRITISH AND EUROPEAN SPECIES

129   Lake Olive Dun *Cloëon simile* ♀

130   Lake Olive Dun *Cloëon simile* ♂

131   Lake Olive Spinner *Cloëon simile* ♀

132   Lake Olive Spinner *Cloëon simile* ♂

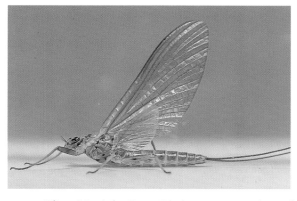

133   Olive Upright Dun *Rhithrogena semicolorata* ♀

134   Olive Upright Dun *Rhithrogena semicolorata* ♂

135   Yellow Upright Spinner
Rhithrogena semicolorata ♀

136   Yellow Upright Spinner
Rhithrogena semicolorata ♂

THE UPWINGED FLIES – DUNS (SUB-IMAGO) AND SPINNERS (IMAGO) – EPHEMEROPTERA

♀ – Female species   ♂ – Male species

PLATE 18   BRITISH AND EUROPEAN SPECIES

137   March Brown Dun *Rhithrogena germanica* ♀

138   March Brown Dun *Rhithrogena germanica* ♂

139   March Brown Spinner *Rhithrogena germanica* ♀

140   March Brown Spinner *Rhithrogena germanica* ♂

141   Yellow May Dun *Heptagenia sulphurea* ♀

142   Yellow May Dun *Heptagenia sulphurea* ♂

143   Yellow May Spinner *Heptagenia sulphurea* ♀

144   Yellow May Spinner *Heptagenia sulphurea* spinner ♂

THE UPWINGED FLIES – DUNS (SUB-IMAGO) AND SPINNERS (IMAGO) – EPHEMEROPTER

♀ – Female species   ♂ – Male species

PLATE 19 BRITISH AND EUROPEAN SPECIES

145 Late March Brown Dun *Ecdyonurus venosus* ♀

146 Late March Brown Dun *Ecdyonurus venosus* ♂

147 Large Red Spinner *Ecdyonurus venosus* ♀

148 Autumn Dun *Ecdyonurus dispar* ♀

149 Autumn Spinner *Ecdyonurus dispar* ♀

150 Autmn Spinner *Ecdyonurus dispar* ♂

151 Large Green Dun *Ecdyonurus insignis* ♂

152 Large Green Spinner *Ecdyonurus insignis* ♀

THE UPWINGED FLIES – DUNS (SUB-IMAGO) AND SPINNERS (IMAGO) – EPHEMEROPTERA

♀ – Female species   ♂ – Male species

PLATE 20   BRITISH AND EUROPEAN SPECIES

153   Dusky Yellowstreak Dun *Electrogena lateralis* ♀

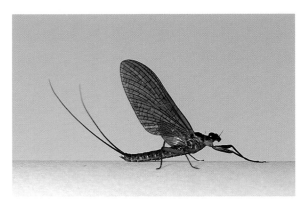

154   Dusky Yellowstreak Dun *Electrogena lateralis* ♂

155   Dusky Yellowstreak Spinner
Electrogena lateralis ♀

156   Dusky Yellowstreak Spinner
Electrogena lateralis ♂

157   Claret Dun *Leptophlebia vespertina* ♀

158   Claret Spinner *Leptophlebia vespertina* ♀

159   Claret Spinner *Leptophlebia vespertina* ♂

160   Large Brook Dun *Ecdyonurus torrentis* ♀

THE UPWINGED FLIES – DUNS (SUB-IMAGO) AND SPINNERS (IMAGO) – EPHEMEROPTERA

♀ – Female species   ♂ – Male species

PLATE 21 BRITISH AND EUROPEAN SPECIES

161 Large Brook Dun *Ecdyonurus torrentis* ♂

162 Large Brook Spinner *Ecdyonurus torrentis* ♀

163 Pale Evening Dun *Procloëon bifidum* ♀

164 Pale Evening Spinner *Procloëon bifidum* ♀

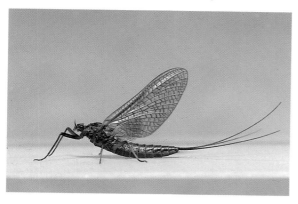

165 Sepia Dun *Leptophlebia marginata* ♀

166 Sepia Dun *Leptophlebia marginata* ♂

167 Sepia Spinner *Leptophlebia marginata* ♂

168 Sepia Spinner *Leptophlebia marginata* ♀

THE UPWINGED FLIES – DUNS (SUB-IMAGO) AND SPINNERS (IMAGO) – EPHEMEROPTERA

♀ – Female species   ♂ – Male species

PLATE 22   BRITISH AND EUROPEAN SPECIES

169   Mayfly (Greendrake) Dun *Ephemera danica* ♀

170   Mayfly (Greendrake) Dun *Ephemera danica* ♂

171   Mayfly Spinner *Ephemera danica* ♀

172   Mayfly Spinner *Ephemera danica* ♂

173   *Potamanthus luteus* dun ♀

174   *Potamanthus luteus* dun ♂

175   *Potamanthus luteus* spinner ♀

176   *Potamanthus luteus* spinner ♂

THE UPWINGED FLIES – DUNS (SUB-IMAGO) AND SPINNERS (IMAGO) – EPHEMEROPTERA

♀ – Female species   ♂ – Male species

PLATE 23   BRITISH AND EUROPEAN SPECIES

177   Blue-winged Olive Dun *Ephemerella ignita* ♀

178   Blue-winged Olive Dun *Ephemerella ignita* ♂

179   Sherry Spinner *Ephemerella ignita* ♀

180   Blue-winged Olive Spinner *Ephemerella ignita* ♂

181   Mayfly (Greendrake) Dun *Ephemera vulgata* ♀

182   Mayfly Spinner *Ephemera vulgata* ♂

183   Yellow Evening Dun *Ephemerella notata* ♀

184   Yellow Evening Spinner *Ephemerella notata* ♀

THE UPWINGED FLIES – DUNS (SUB-IMAGO) AND SPINNERS (IMAGO) – EPHEMEROPTERA

♀ – Female species   ♂ – Male species

PLATE 24 BRITISH AND EUROPEAN SPECIES

185 Ditch Dun *Habrophlebia fusca* ♀

186 Ditch Dun *Habrophlebia lauta* ♂

187 *Caënis luctuosa* dun ♂

188 *Caënis luctuosa* spinner ♂

189 Turkey Brown Dun
Paraleptophlebia submarginata ♀

190 Turkey Brown Spinner
Paraleptophlebia submarginata ♀

191 Large Summer Dun *Siphlonurus armatus* ♀

192 Great Red Spinner *Siphlonurus armatus* ♀

THE UPWINGED FLIES – DUNS (SUB-IMAGO) AND SPINNERS (IMAGO) – EPHEMEROPTERA

♀ – Female species   ♂ – Male species

PLATE 25 BRITISH AND EUROPEAN SPECIES

193 Nymph of Sepia dun – *L. marginata* (Note tails spread well apart)

194 Mature and immature mayfly nymph (captured close together in April)

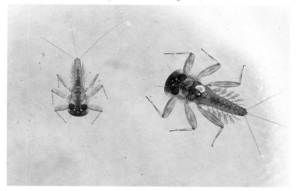

195 Two generations of stoneclinging nymphs

196 *Caënis* nymphs (top one camouflaged with specks of chalk)

197 Flies viewed from underwater on edge of trout's window

198 Flies in trout's window

199 Trout rises to artificial on the edge of his window

200 Trout's view of flies in mirror at sunset

UPWINGED FLIES – VARIOUS

♀ – Female species   ♂ – Male species

PLATE 26   BRITISH AND EUROPEAN SPECIES

201   *E. danica*: mating mayflies

202   *E. ignita* BWO female spinner with egg ball

203   *Caënis horaria* dun ♀

204   *P. longicaudia*: flight of males near water surface

205   A nymph breaks through water surface to transpose

206   *Baëtis* spinner crawls down post to lay eggs underwater

207   *Baëtis* spinners underwater egg-laying

UPWINGED FLIES – VARIOUS

208   A sad end for many riverside insects

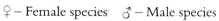

♀ – Female species   ♂ – Male species

PLATE 27   BRITISH AND EUROPEAN SPECIES

209   *Hydropsyche Spp:* larva of net-making caddis

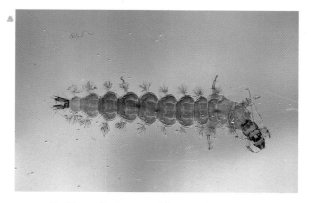

210   *R. Dorsalis:* larva of free-swimming caddis

211   Typical case-making larvae

212   *P. Grandis:* cased larva

213   Cased caddis larvae: *Limnephlus Spp.* and *L. Hirtum* (small)

214   Cased caddis: *G. Pilosa*

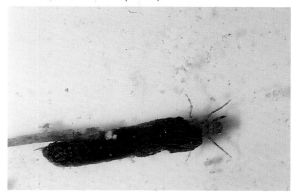

215   Cased caddis: *H. radiatus*

216   Typical sedge pupa ascending to surface

LARVAE AND PUPA OF SEDGE (CADDIS) FLIES – TRICHOPTERA

♀ – Female species   ♂ – Male species

PLATE 28   BRITISH AND EUROPEAN SPECIES

217   Sedge pupa on surface

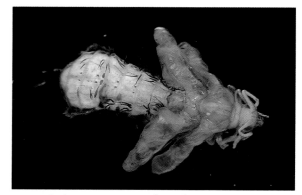

218   Sedge pupa on surface about to transpose.
Note inflated wing cases

219   Note length of antennae on this sedge pupa

220   Sedge pupa – transposing stage 1

221   Sedge pupa – transposing stage 2

222   Sedge pupa – transposing stage 3

223   Sedge pupa – transposing stage 4

224   Sedge pupa showing paddle-like medianlegs

PUPAE OF SEDGE (CADDIS) FLIES – VARIOUS TRICHOPTERA

♀ – Female species   ♂ – Male species

PLATE 29   BRITISH AND EUROPEAN SPECIES

225   Great Red Sedge: *Phrygania grandis*

226   The Caperer: *Halesus radiatus*

227   Large Cinnamon Sedge: *Potamophylax latipennis*

228   Large Cinnamon Sedge: *Potamophylax cingulatus*

229   Mottled Sedge: *Glyphotalius pellucidus*

230   Speckled Peter: *Phrygania varia*

231   Silver or Grey Sedge: *Odonticerum albicorne*

232   Brown Sedge: *Anabolia nervosa*

THE SEDGE (CADDIS) FLIES ADULTS – TRICHOPTERA

♀ – Female species   ♂ – Male species

PLATE 30 BRITISH AND EUROPEAN SPECIES

233   Grey Flag: *Hydropsyche pellucidula* ♂

234   Cinnamon Sedge: *Limnephilus lunatus*

235   Cinnamon Sedge: *Limnephilus rhombicus*

236   Welshman's Button: *Sericostoma personatum*

237   The Longhorns: *Oecetis Spp.*

238   Grey Flag: *Hydropsyche instabilis*

239   Grey Flag: *Hydropsyche pellucidula* ♀

240   Marbled Sedge: *Hydropsyche contubernalis*

THE SEDGE (CADDIS) FLIES ADULTS – TRICHOPTERA

♀ – Female species   ♂ – Male species

PLATE 31   BRITISH AND EUROPEAN SPECIES

241   Medium Sedge: *Goera pilosa*

242   Sand Fly Sedge: *Rhyacophila dorsalis*

243   Yellow Spotted Sedge: *Philopotamus montanus*

244   The Grannom: *Brachycentrus subnubilus*

245   Dark Spotted Sedge: *Polycentropus flavomaculatus*

246   Black Sedge: *Silo nigricornis*

247   Black Sedge: *Silo pallipes*

248   Brown Silverhorn: *Athripsodes cinereus*

THE SEDGE (CADDIS) FLIES ADULTS – TRICHOPTERA

♀ – Female species   ♂ – Male species

PLATE 32   BRITISH AND EUROPEAN SPECIES

249   Brown Silverhorn: *Athripsodes albifrons*

250   Small Silver Sedge: *Lepidostoma hirtum*

251   Small Silver Sedge: *Lasiocephala basalis*

252   Black Silverhorn: *Mystacides azurea*

253   Grouse Wing: *Mystacides longicornis*

254   Small Red Sedge: *Tinodes waeneri*

255   Small Yellow Sedge: *Psychomia pusilla*

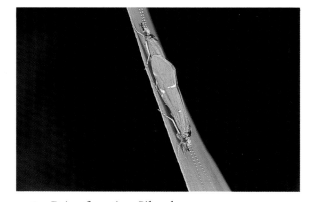

256   Pair of mating Silverhorns

THE SEDGE (CADDIS) FLIES ADULTS – TRICHOPTERA

♀ – Female species   ♂ – Male species

PLATE 33 BRITISH AND EUROPEAN SPECIES

257 Medium Stonefly Nymphs: *Diura bicaudata*

258 Yellow Sally Nymph: *Isoperla grammatica*

259 Large Stonefly Nymph: *Perlodes microcephala*

260 Large Stonefly Nymph: *Perla bipunctata*

261 Large Adult Stonefly ♀: *Perla marginata*

262 Large Adult Stonefly ♂: *Perlodes microcephala*

263 Large Adult Stonefly ♀: *Perlodes microcephala*

264 Medium Adult Stonefly: *Diura bicaudata*

THE STONEFLIES – PLECOPTERA – NYMPHS AND ADULTS

♀ – Female species   ♂ – Male species

PLATE 34 BRITISH AND EUROPEAN SPECIES

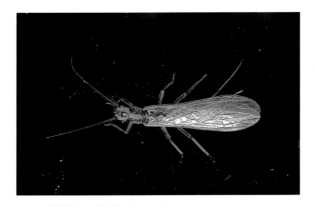

265 Yellow Sally: *Isoperla grammatica*

266 February Red: *Brachyptera risi*

267 February Red: *Taeniopteryx nebulosa*

268 Willow Fly: *Leuctra geniculata*

269 Early Brown: *Protonemura meyeri*

270 Small Brown: *Nemoura cinerea*

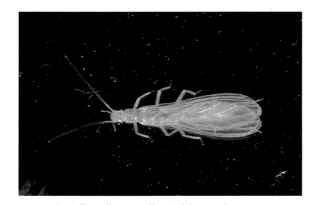

271 Small Yellow Sally: *Chloroperla torrentium*

272 Needle Fly: *Leuctra Spp.*

THE STONEFLIES – PLECOPTERA – ADULTS

♀ – Female species   ♂ – Male species

PLATE 35   BRITISH AND EUROPEAN SPECIES

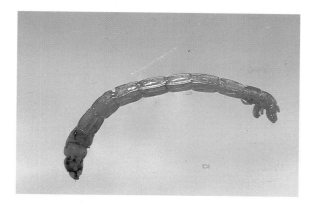

273   Midge Larva Red (Bloodworm)

274   Typical pupa hanging in surface film – Grey Boy

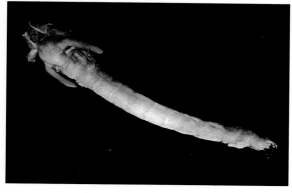

275   Chironomid pupa – immature stage

276   Pupa hatching into adult on surface

277   Large Green Midge ♀

278   Large Red Midge ♀

279   Large Red Midge ♂

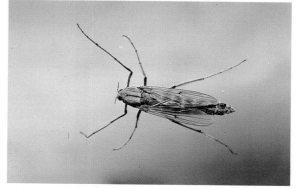

280   Grey Boy Midge ♀

THE FLAT-WINGED FLIES (DIPTERA) – CHIRONOMIDS (BUZZERS)
LARVA – PUPAE AND ADULTS
♀ – Female species   ♂ – Male species

PLATE 36   BRITISH AND EUROPEAN SPECIES

281   Golden Dun Midge ♀

282   Olive Midge ♂

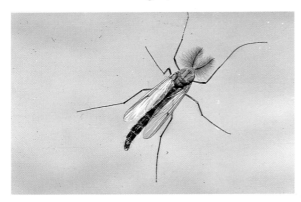

283   Black Midge ♂

284   Blagdon Green Midge ♂

285   Small Brown Midge ♀

286   Small Red Midge ♀

287   Small Red Midge ♂

288   Small Black Midge ♂

THE FLAT-WINGED FLIES (DIPTERA) – CHIRONOMIDS (BUZZERS) ADULTS

♀ – Female species   ♂ – Male species

PLATE 37   BRITISH AND EUROPEAN SPECIES

289   The Hawthorn Fly: *Bibio marci*

290   The Heather Fly: *Bibo pomonae*

291   Black Gnat ♀: *Bibio johannis*

292   Drone Fly: *Eristalis tenax*

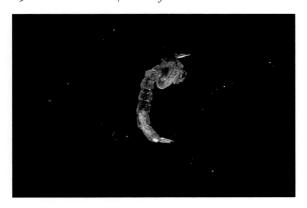

293   Pupa of Phantom Fly: *Chaoborus Spp.*

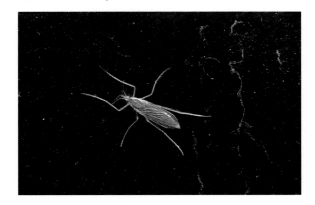

294   Adult Phantom Fly ♀: *Chaoborus Spp.*

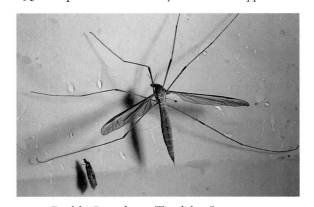

295   Daddy Longlegs: *Tipulidae Spp.*

296   Gravel Bed Fly: *Hexatoma fuscipennis*

THE FLAT-WINGED FLIES – VARIOUS DIPTERA

♀ – Female species   ♂ – Male species

PLATE 38   BRITISH AND EUROPEAN SPECIES

297   Alder Larva: *Sialis lutaria*

298   Alder Fly: *Sialis lutaria*

299   Coch-y-bonddu Beetle: *Phylopertha horticola*

300   Cockchafer Beetle: *Melolontha melolontha*

301   Soldier Beetle: *Cantharis rustica*

302   Sailor Beetle: *Cantharis lividia*

303   Larva of Water Beetle

FAUNA – VARIOUS

♀ – Female species   ♂ – Male species

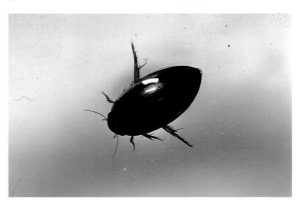

304   Great Diving Beetle M: *Dytiscus Spp.*

PLATE 39   BRITISH AND EUROPEAN SPECIES

305   Green Leaf Beetle

306   Semi-aquatic Beetle: *Donacia Spp.*

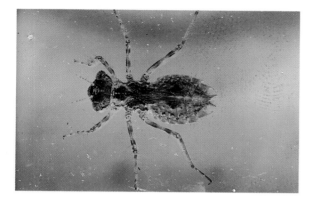

307   Dragonfly Nymph: *Sympetrum Spp.*

308   Damselfly Nymph

309   Green Damselfly ♀

310   Freshwater Louse: *Asellus aquaticus*

311   Freshwater Shrimp: *Gammarus Spp.*

FAUNA – VARIOUS

312   Corixa – *Corixa punctata*

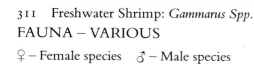

♀ – Female species   ♂ – Male species

PLATE 40   BRITISH AND EUROPEAN SPECIES

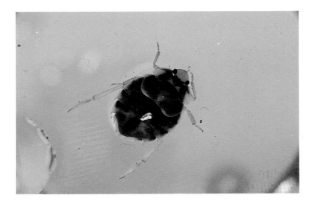

313   Water Bug: *A. montandoni*

314   Water measurer: *Hydrometra*

315   Green Lacewing: *Neuroptera Spp.*

316   Aquatic China Mark Moth

317   Aquatic Spider in its bubble nest

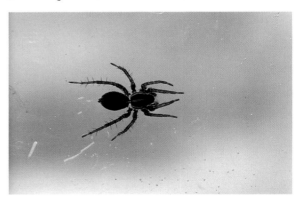

318   Aquatic Spider: *Argyroneta aquatica*

319   Large Red Water Mite

320   The Saw Fly

FAUNA – VARIOUS

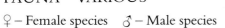

♀ – Female species   ♂ – Male species

PLATE 41   ARTIFICIAL FLIES (in alphabetical order)

ADAMS

ADULT BUZZERS (Carnhill)

ADULT MIDGE (R Walker)

ALDER FLY

ALDER LARVA (Canham)

ALTIERE

AMBER NYMPHS (Dr Bell)

ASSASSINE

AUGUST DUN (Wooley)

BALLOON CADDIS (Moser)

BEACON BEIGE

BLACK BEAR HAIR (Henry)

BLACK GNAT (Halford)

BLACK BEETLE (Price)

BLACK MIDGE (Henderson)

BLACK & PEACOCK (Ivens)

BLACK SILVERHORN (Ronalds)

BLACK STONEFLY (Lumini)

BLAE & BLACK

BLOODWORM (Wilshaw)

BLUEBOTTLE (Price)

BLUE DARTER (Marsh NZ)

BLUE UPRIGHT (Austin)

BOOBY

BROWN SEDGE (Thomas)

BWO (Jacques)

BWO (Nice)

BWO (C F Walker)

PLATE 42   ARTIFICIAL FLIES (in alphabetical order)

CADDIS LARVA (Boaze)

CAENIS SPINNER (Canham)

CAL-DU-CANARD BWO

CAL-DU-CANARD OLIVE (PETIT JEAN)

CAL-DU-CANARD SEDGE (PETIT JEAN)

CAPERER

CAPERER (Dr Voljc)

CASED CADDIS (Carnhill)

CHIRONOMID EMERGER (Lumini)

CHOCHIN

CHURCH FRY

CINNAMON SEDGE

CLARET DUN (Harris)

CLARET SPINNER (Harris)

COLLYER'S NYMPHS

COCH-Y-BONDDU

COCKCHAFER

CORIXA

DADDY LONGLEGS (R Walker)

DAMSEL FLY ADULT (Canham)

DAMSEL NYMPH (Henry)

DAMSEL WIGGLE (Goddard)

DARK SPANISH NEEDLE (Pritt)

DARK WATCHETT (Pritt)

CLOUSER DEEP MINNOW

CLOUSER DEEP MINNOW

DEERSTALKER (Patterson)

DOG NOBBLER

PLATE 43 ARTIFICIAL FLIES (in alphabetical order)

DOG'S BODY

DUCKFLY

DUSKY WOOD ANT

EGG-LAYING CADDIS (Moser)

ELK-HAIR CADDIS (Troth)

EMERGING PUPA (Moser)

EMERGENT MIDGE (Price)

EPHEMERA EMERGER (Lumini)

ERIC'S BEETLE

ERMINE MOTH

FLOATING SNAIL (Henry)

FOOTBALLER (Bucknall)

FRESHWATER LOUSE (Lapsley)

FUNNEL DUN (Patterson)

GERROFF (Goddard)

GHOST SWIFT MOTH (R Walker)

GODDARD CADDIS

GODDARD SMUT

GOLDHEAD PUPA (Moser)

GRAFHAM DRONE

GRANNOM (Russell)

GREEN ADULT MIDGE (Lumini)

GREENWELL'S GLORY

GREEN LACEWING (Price)

GREEN PETER

GRENADIER (Dr Bell)

GREY DUSTER

GREY WULFF

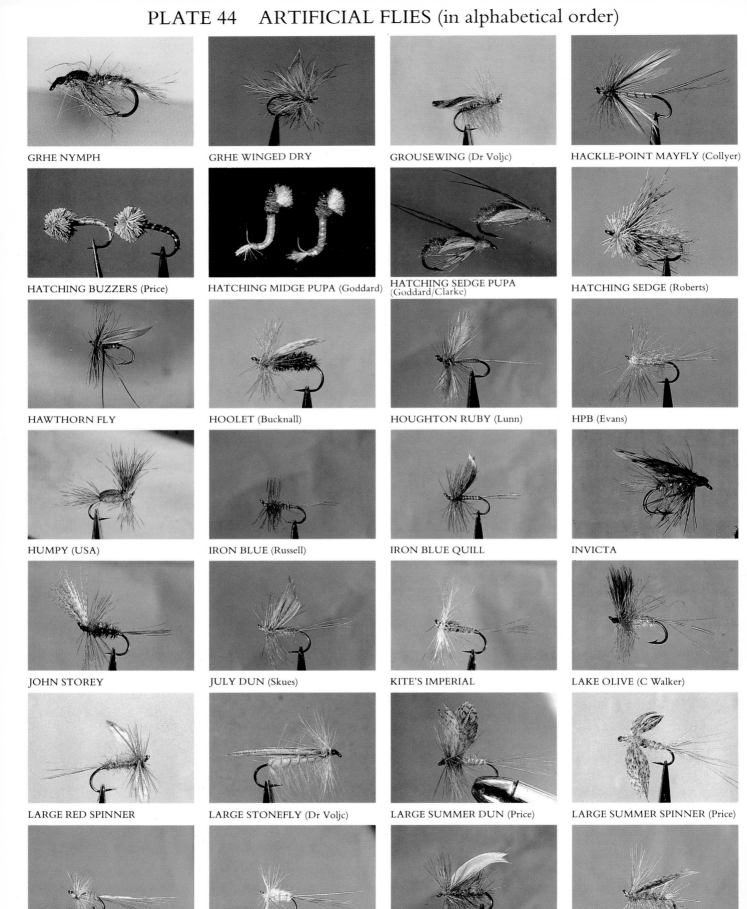

PLATE 44   ARTIFICIAL FLIES (in alphabetical order)

GRHE NYMPH

GRHE WINGED DRY

GROUSEWING (Dr Voljc)

HACKLE-POINT MAYFLY (Collyer)

HATCHING BUZZERS (Price)

HATCHING MIDGE PUPA (Goddard)

HATCHING SEDGE PUPA (Goddard/Clarke)

HATCHING SEDGE (Roberts)

HAWTHORN FLY

HOOLET (Bucknall)

HOUGHTON RUBY (Lunn)

HPB (Evans)

HUMPY (USA)

IRON BLUE (Russell)

IRON BLUE QUILL

INVICTA

JOHN STOREY

JULY DUN (Skues)

KITE'S IMPERIAL

LAKE OLIVE (C Walker)

LARGE RED SPINNER

LARGE STONEFLY (Dr Voljc)

LARGE SUMMER DUN (Price)

LARGE SUMMER SPINNER (Price)

LAST HOPE DARK (Goddard)

LAST HOPE LIGHT (Goddard)

LITTLE BROWN SEDGE

LITTLE RED SEDGE (Skues)

PLATE 45   ARTIFICIAL FLIES (in alphabetical order)

LITTLE MARRYATT	LONGHORNS (R Walker)	LUNN'S PARTICULAR	LUNN'S YELLOW BOY
MALLARD & CLARET	MATING SHRIMP (Goddard)	MARABOU BLOODWORM (Price)	MARABOU BUZZER (Price)
MARABOU LEECH (Price)	MARCH BROWN	MARCH BROWN SPIDER	MEDIUM STONEFLY (Price)
MOTTLED SEDGE (LANE)	MOUSTIQUE	MUDDLER MINNOW	MYLAR MINNOW (Brock)
NEEDLE FLY (Dr Voljc)	OLIVE QUILL	OMBUDSMAN (Clarke)	ORANGE QUILL
OTTER RUBY (Nice)	PALE WATERY (R Walker)	PALE WATERY SPINNER	PALLARETTA
PARTRIDGE & ORANGE	PALM ALLIES (Dr Vaux)	PETER ROSS	PHANTOM LARVA (Gathercole)

PLATE 46 ARTIFICIAL FLIES (in alphabetical order)

PHANTOM PURA (Gathercole)

PHEASANT-TAIL NYMPH (Sawyer)

PHEASANT-TAIL SPINNER

POLYCADDIS (Goddard)

POLYMAY DUN (Goddard)

POLYMAY SPINNER (Goddard)

PLLYRIB C PUPA (Carnhill)

POLYSTICKLE (R Walker)

POND OLIVE (Price)

POND OLIVE SPINNER (Goddard)

PRESKA CADDIS

PERSUADER (Goddard)

PVC NYMPH (Goddard)

RED MITE (R Walker)

RED OR GREEN LARVA (Goddard)

RED PALMER

RED SPINNER (Harris)

RED SPOT SHRIMP (Patterson)

RESTING MIDGE (Price)

SAILOR BEETLE (Price)

SAND CADDIS (R Walker)

SEDGE PUPAE (Goddard)

SEPIA DUN (Kite)

SHERRY SPINNER (Lunn)

SHARPE'S FAVOURITE

SHREDGE (Knight)

SINFOIL'S FRY

SNIPE & PURPLE

PLATE 47 ARTIFICIAL FLIES (in alphabetical order)

SOLDIER BEETLE (Price)

SPURWING DUN (Lumini)

STICK FLY

STONE FLY (Wooley)

SUNK SPINNER (Patterson)

SUPER GRIZZLY (Goddard)

SUPER GRIZZLY EMERGER(Goddard)

SUSPENDER HATCHING MIDGE (Goddard)

SUSPENDER HATCHING NYMPHS

TADPOLLY (Goddard)

TERRY'S TERROR

TUP'S INDISPENSABLE

TRICOLOUR

TRICHOPTERA 2 (Lumini)

TRICHOPTERA 3 (Lumini)

UNIVERSAL SEDGE

USD DUN

USD HAWTHORN

USD POLYSPINNERS

VERANO AMARILLO

VOSS BARK NYMPH

WALKER'S MAYFLY DUN

WALKER'S MAYFLY NYMPH

WICKHAM'S FANCY

WILLOW FLY (Ronalds)

WOOLEY WORM

YELLOW MAY DUN (Price)

YELLOW SALLY (Dr Voljc)

brown or blackish combined with yellow stripes and patches. When the females return to the water to deposit their eggs in small clusters on the surface, as they sometimes do, they may at this period be of interest to both fish and fisherman. Although I would not normally expect to find them on large lakes or reservoirs I am given to understand that they are native to Grafham Water and also Hanningfield reservoir in Essex, and that at this period a striped yellow and black artificial often does well. This is called the Grafham Drone Fly and is the only artificial I know. N.B. It should be noted that one of the Crane flies results from aquatic larvae of a very similar appearance to some of the species just mentioned and which is also referred to as a Rat-tailed Maggot.

DISTRIBUTION: Not known although common and widespread.

The Phantom Midges (Chaoburus spp.) Plate 37 (294)

There are a number of species in this family and one of the more common is *Chaoborus flavicans*, and it is this species that I have reared and studied. The adults hatch out during the warmer weather of summer, but as the emergence period seems to be between midnight and dawn they are of little interest at this stage to anglers. In appearance the winged fly is very similar to a medium sized Chironomid or midge. They average a little over a quarter of an inch in length and the body colour of the female is a very pale green, while that of the male is a dirty white on the underside turning greyish on top. The adult females return to the shallower margins of lakes in the late evenings in considerable numbers to oviposit, and at this period it may well prove worth while to fish a representative artificial floating pattern.

This particular family of insects, up to now largely ignored by the fisherman, is undoubtedly most prolific and many stillwaters support extremely large numbers. The phantom larvae and pupae are taken occasionally by the trout and therefore should be of interest to the fisherman. Unfortunately, the larvae which when fully grown are about 16mm long and for the most part lie horizontally in the water completely motionless, are quite transparent apart from two black eyes and four blackish air bladders, two in the thorax and two in the rear end of the abdomen. It will, therefore, be appreciated that it is virtually impossible to dress or fish an artificial to represent them in this stage of life. They do, of course, move at quite frequent intervals but this movement is very rapid and difficult to follow with the naked eye.

The pupae, on the other hand, have a little colour (Plate 37, No 293) and although they remain stationary for short periods, they frequently wriggle and occasionally move position. They are a little over quarter-of-an-inch long and have a creamy semi-transparent body with a large bulbous thorax. This turns a pale brown or orange colour as pupation progresses, and they hang in a vertical position resembling a comma in outline, similar to a Chironomid pupae but not quite so curved.

The pupae have a pair of appendages on top of the thorax shaped rather like a pair of donkey's ears, and many authorities state that the pupae regularly ascend to the surface to absorb air through them. As a result of the observations and experiments of David Jacques and myself, we are reasonably certain that these appendages play no part in respiratory action, but probably assist to maintain the pupae in an upright position and to control their depth in the water.

We have reared many dozens of these creatures to maturity and the average time in the pupal stage is approximately four days. During this period they hang in the water at various depths between the bed and the surface of the lake, and it is only immediately before transformation to the winged adult takes place that they actually ascend into the surface film. It will therefore be realised that as countless numbers of these pupae are present in many of our stillwaters at varying depths, mostly in the shallower areas, it may be possible to present an artificial in a manner to deceive a trout.

ARTIFICIAL: The main difficulty is to present the artificial in a natural manner and although I have developed a pattern which closely resembles the natural I have not yet succeeded consistently with the presentation, but feel there should be considerable scope for experiment in this direct. Two well known patterns that should prove effective are the phantom larva and the Phantom Pupa both by Peter Gathercole.

DISTRIBUTION: So far as I am aware these flies are only to be found in stillwater. They are common and widespread and are to be observed in most European countries.

Reed Smuts or Black flies (Simulium spp.)

These very tiny flies often hatch out in countless numbers and in many old angling books are referred to as the Black Curse. They are extremely small, the average size being less than an eighth of an inch. There are little more than a dozen species in this family, and some of the larger types closely resemble the terrestrial Black Gnats and are possibly mistaken for them by many anglers. The body is short and stout with the segments hard to discern. The wings are short, broad and transparent and are carried flat on top of the body when at rest. Resembling House flies in miniature and varying in colour from dark brown to black, they are found only in a reasonable current for the very good reason that the larvae require water with a fair amount of movement. Therefore, they are only found in rivers or bodies of stillwater that are fed by constant inflow and then only in the area immediately adjacent to it. Despite the small size of these insects, trout will often feed on them avidly to the exclusion of all else, and fish so engaged are extremely hard to catch, due partly to our difficulty in dressing an artificial small enough to deceive them. The larvae are often found at autopsy by anglers on rivers, the trout having browsed them off the weeds.

Ever since the inception of dry fly fishing in the middle of the last century the advice proffered by most angling authors in relation to smutting trout has been to ignore them, as they were considered all but impossible to catch. I am sure that all fly fishers that fish the dry fly on rivers either in the U.K. or on the continent will be only too aware that a percentage of trout in most rivers seem to spend a lot of time throughout the season feeding exclusively on smuts or other tiny insects. Trout so engaged are instantly recognisable as they will be observed lying very close to the surface sucking in the hatching flies in or just below the film. The ring of the rise is sometimes only faintly perceptible as the neb of the trout barely breaks the surface and they rarely deviate from side to side as they so often do when feeding upon other surface hatching flies. In addition the rise is often very regular and rapid, sometimes exceeding ten rises per minute. There is no doubt that smutting trout can be most infuriating as in most cases they will completely ignore normal or even small dry flies. To tempt them at all it is usually necessary to come down to a size 22 or even 24 and on such tiny irons even to hook a trout is an achievement while the odds on actually landing one are fairly remote. It is therefore little wonder that our forefathers often referred to smuts as the 'Curse' or 'Black Curse'. One of the earliest references to these minute flies was in *A Book on Angling* by Francis Francis published in 1867 where he refers to them briefly and also incorrectly under the heading of Black Gnats as the fisherman's curse. So far as I have been able to ascertain it was not until the end of the last century that anyone even suggested a suitable pattern to present to smutting trout. This was the great F.M. Halford the father of the dry fly. During the early 1880s he perfected a couple of patterns dressed on small size 00 hooks which he called his male and female Black Gnat.

While these patterns were undoubtably dressed to represent the various species of black gnats, he suggested in the many books he wrote that these were also very effective for smutting trout. In the late 80s two specific patterns appeared both dressed on size 000 hooks (size No 17) which were the smallest hooks obtainable in those days, these were the Fisherman's Curse by G.S. Marryat and the Hackle Curse by Sir M. Duff-Gordon but sad to relate neither proved to be very successful. In 1910 in the *Book of the Dry Fly* its author George A. B. Dewar obviously had but little regard for such patterns as he wrote 'The true smuts or curses cannot be properly imitated, partly because no hook is made small enough for the purpose'. This is of course no longer the case as it is now possible to obtain hooks as small as size No 28 but as previously explained even very tiny hooks do not solve the problem.

Like many other fly fishers before me I have in the past experimented with various patterns in an effort to solve this most vexing of all dry fly problems but with little or no success. Occasionally I would perfect a new pattern that would seem to show some potential but none of them provided consistently reasonable results. Four years ago I took some fishing on the river Test, the most famous of all our chalk streams, which included about a quarter of a mile on a rather slow flowing section of a carrier stream. During the summer of that season I found that most of the trout in this little stream spent nearly every day feeding on smuts so I was once again literally forced to review the situation. They say that necessity is often the mother of invention and in this case so it proved to be. The basic problem was without doubt directly linked to the extremely tiny size of the natural reed smuts that the trout were feeding upon, so the answer appeared to lie in an artificial small enough to deceive the trout but with a hook large enough to hold a fish once it had been hooked. Viewed in this way the answer when it occurred was so simple I was amazed that I had not thought of it before. What was required was a relatively small hook with a nice wide gape.

I eventually located a fine wire up eye size No 17 Partridge hook that filled the bill. I dressed this hook with several turns of very fine black ostrich herl for about a third of the length of the hook shank from the eye, and then immediately in front of this tiny body behind the eye I tied in two turns of a black Metz cock hackle that was very short in the flew. This provided me with a pattern giving a very small silhouette in keeping with the size of the natural reed smut but at the same time providing a hook large enough to hold even the biggest of trout. This consequently proved a very killing pattern and has since become established in the U.K. as the Goddard Smut. Up to comparatively recently I had always associated trout feeding in slow flowing sections of rivers upon chironomids with a slow leisurely head and tail rise, but as this rise form is somewhat similar to the slow sipping rise of trout feeding upon smuts I idly wondered whether there may be some connection particularly with trout feeding in this manner in faster water where the precise rise form is more difficult to establish. Now these two rise forms have two things in common. In both cases the trout is lying very close to the surface, I therefore wondered whether these two slightly different rise forms were in fact indicative of trout feeding upon both smuts or chironomids and even in some cases both at the same time. In an effort to establish whether this was so, towards the end of the season before last I kept a record of the stomach contents of all trout caught that seemed to be rising either to smuts or chironomids. The results confirmed that most trout were indeed feeding upon both species at the same time, as on many occasions I found their stomachs packed both with smuts and small brown or green chironomids and in some cases both brown and green. Only occasionally did I find one species to the exclusion of the other. Could this then be the missing section of the puzzle? To find out it was necessary to find a chironomid (midge) pattern that was acceptable to the trout. This appeared to pose a problem as for many years I had been experimenting with various emerger patterns with but little success. However I now had the advantage of knowing the type colour and size of midges that these river trout were feeding upon and it struck me that my Suspender Midge Pupa may be worth trying, dressed with either brown or green bodies on very small hooks. This subsequently proved to be astonishingly successful even on those rivers that had previously posed serious problems because of drag. These days smutting trout no longer poses a problem for me as I have now found out if they will not accept my new smut pattern they will almost certainly take a tiny Suspender Midge Pupa.

ARTIFICIALS: The dressings for my two patterns are as follows:
The Goddard Smut
Hook: U/E size No 17 or 18
Silk: fine nymph – black
Body: four or five turns fine black ostrich
Hackle: two turns of small black cock.
The Suspender Midge Pupa
Hook: Roman Moser Arrow Point size 16 or 18
Silk: fine nymph – brown
Body: green or brown seal's fur or substitute
Tail: white nylon or organza filaments
Rib: fine silver lurex
Thorax: brown dyed turkey herl
Ball: white ethafoam or similar, enclosed in fine white nylon mesh.
A small Wickham's Fancy a good general pattern will sometimes be successful when trout are smutting.
DISTRIBUTION: Reed Smuts which are also known in many areas as Black flies, are very abundant and very widespread and are likely to be found in all areas throughout Europe wherever there is running water.

FISHING TECHNIQUES FOR VERY TINY PATTERNS
While I find the above two patterns very killing indeed when trout are smutting and seldom if ever now have to resort to other patterns, there may be odd occasions when an alternative is desirable as apart from smuts there are many

other aquatic insects that are very tiny indeed. There are for example many species of caddis or sedge flies barely 3mm in length, while some species of upwinged flies are almost as small particularly some of the Caenis species and furthermore many species of Chironomids (midges) are even smaller, so as an alternative one may decide to try and match the hatch with correspondingly tiny patterns dressed on very tiny hooks from sizes 20 up to 26. From time to time over the years I have experimented with these very small patterns with lamentable lack of success. First of all I found that while it was often easy to persuade the trout to accept the fly it was all but impossible to set the hook. I tried striking quickly, I tried striking slowly, I even tried waiting until the leader started to draw but all to no avail. Secondly when I did succeed in hooking a trout if it was a big one I invariably lost it as the leader would break. When fishing such tiny patterns you have to mount them on a very fine point either 6x or even 7x. For many years I had been hearing of the successes enjoyed by American fly fishers fishing these tiny flies where midge fishing as they call it is extremely popular. Furthermore I had received many authenticated reports of double figure trout being taken on these very fine tippets. How could this be? Well last year I spent several weeks in the States and was privileged to fish with some of Americas top fly fishers and eventually discovered the secret of their successes. The answer to the problem of setting the hook consistently is really very simple, you either dress your patterns on a hook with an offset point or alternatively offset the point with a small pair of pliers before tying it on your line. The answer to landing big trout on a very fine point is a more recent innovation and came about with the introduction of a new material introduced into the tackle trade in the late 70s called 'Power Gum'. This is a synthetic, elasticised line that is almost colourless and although considerably thicker than monofilament can be tied into the leader successfully if a surgeon's knot is used. The position it is tied into the leader is rather critical and the following measurements should be closely followed. To the end of the fly line use a floating 4ft to 7ft braided and tapered leader and to this attach a 6 inch length of 1x nylon. Then with a surgeon's knot tie in an 8 inch length of power gum to the other end of this. Using the same knot tie in a further 6 ins of 1x. To this with normal knots tie in 6 ins of 3x and then 6 ins of 5x and then finally tie in a point of 6 or 7x to the desired length. In practice this is a little more difficult to cast than a normal leader particularly into a strongish wind but on the other hand it does allow you to play and land very large trout that would be impossible with a normal leader.

Other Diptera

As previously mentioned, Diptera are an extremely large Order of flies and, apart from individual species of particular interest already discussed in some detail, there are many others that are sometimes found in, on or near water, and some may be of interest to fishermen. Most of them are only encountered occasionally and are consequently of dubious value.

Culicidae

Of those that could be included in this category, the one of most interest to anglers is the Common Gnat, *Culex pipiens*, a Mosquito. They are very prolific insects and both larvae and pupae are aquatic, being found in all types of stagnant water such as wells, tanks, water butts and ponds. They are also on occasion to be found in numbers in larger bodies of water, and in fact those that I have reared were collected from Grafham Water.

The larvae are long and slender and spend most of their lives hanging head downwards from the surface film. They are more or less colourless and when disturbed sink slowly to the bottom. In the pupal form they seem to be short lived, as I have observed the pupae hanging in the surface film for only a matter of hours. They are considerably smaller than the common large species of midge pupae, while in shape they look like an inverted question mark with a large head equipped with two trumpet-like appendages or ears, which protruding through the surface film are apparently used for respiratory purposes. They spend most of their brief lives in the surface film, but at frequent intervals they make short journeys to the bottom, particularly when disturbed. This is accomplished by powerful strokes from their tail fins, and while they can move quite rapidly their movements are rather jerky.

The transformation from pupa to adult winged insect takes place on the surface, in a manner similar to a midge, usually as dusk approaches. Although it seems generally accepted that these gnats prefer a habitat of stagnant water, I wonder to what extent this is true, as I have found the larvae in quantities in at least two large bodies of stillwater. If, in fact, they are more common on lakes and reservoirs than is believed, these or other similar species dealt with next could account on at least some evenings for the late and widespread rise of trout that are apparently rising to nothing visible and are notoriously difficult to hook. Although I must make it clear, in my personal experience this typical rise is usually due to hatches of midges. However, in either case in the poor light of dusk it is almost impossible to see any of these adult insects actually emerging or even if one does, to identify them.

I think it would be possible to dress an artificial to represent these smaller species, but it would have to be on a very tiny hook, and the artificial would have to be fished actually in the surface film in a manner similar to the new method described for fishing the midge pupa. In any case I feel that there is considerable scope for further research and experiment in this direction.

There are many other similar species of Diptera worthy of further study and some of the more common types are as follows.

Tanypodinae

These are common in stillwater and while the larvae, which are almost colourless, are similar in appearance to the larvae of the midges although generally smaller, the brownish coloured pupae resemble in shape, size and habitat the gnat pupae described above. It is therefore likely that research in this direction may also one day prove to be of considerable value to the fisherman. The adults of Tanypus are very similar indeed to some of the smaller midges, the predominant colour being brown, while the wings of some species are also faintly mottled brown; they average 6 to 7mm in length. It is interesting to note that the pupae of this species prior to transformation into the adult are usually found in midwater, and when disturbed descends rapidly to the bottom or nearest cover.

Ceratopogonidae

These are extremely small biting midges and the adults are barely one-tenth of an inch in length. They are most commonly encountered during May or June and they are quite widespread on many bodies of stillwater. The larvae are slender worm-like creatures usually found on the surface in the shallow margins among floating or decaying vegetation, and are therefore unlikely to be readily available to the trout. The pupae which have slender segmented bodies with a large bulbous head may be found near the surface in open water and could be worthy of further investigation by the angler.

The Dixinae

This small sub-family contains several species, all somewhat similar in appearance and in the light of recent research they would now appear to be more widely distributed than was previously supposed, particularly in many small stillwaters in the Home Counties. They belong to the same family as the Chaoborus (Phantom Flies), and while the pupae are similar in size and shape, with a slender strongly segmented body and a very large elongated head on top of which are a pair of ear-like appendages, the larvae are dissimilar. The larvae usually found in the shallow margins on rocks or weed are inactive creatures and when at rest usually adopt a U-shape. They are smaller and stouter than the larvae of the chironomidae Many of the adults in this sub-family have dark brown or even black bodies, and they have two or three distinct thoracic stripes or patches on the head. The wings, some of which have a brownish tinge and vary in length according to species between 4 to 6mm, are similar in appearance to a medium sized chironomid but the males do not have the strongly plumose antennae which are characteristic of this family. Both the pupae and the adults of these Dixa-Midges could be important to the angler where they occur. There are about a dozen species and one of these, *Dixa Aestivalis*, is a particularly handsome insect, the adult having a stout black cylindrical body, contrasting strongly with its bright yellow legs and head on top of which are three distinct black stripes. I am indebted to the late Alec Pearlman who provided the specimens of this species from the stomach content of a trout he caught.

ARTIFICIALS: There are no known patterns to represent any of these other Diptera.

DISTRIBUTION: These other Diptera include so many hundreds of different species, it would be an impossible task to designate any of these to specific areas. However they are mostly very common and widespread.

CHAPTER 8

THE STONEFLIES OR HARDWINGED FLIES-PLECOPTERA

While the flies in this group can be extremely important to the flyfisher in some areas or types of water, in others they can be relatively unimportant. Generally speaking most low lying waters of a calcerous nature that are highly alkaline with good weed growth such as many limestone or chalkstreams have such high concentrations of other orders of insects that Stoneflies even when they are present create little interest either for the trout or the flyfisher. However on those waters often at some altitude of an acid nature where other orders of flies are less prolific even quite sparse hatches can be of importance.

Unlike flies in some other groups most species in this Order seem to favour waters with stable or slightly lower temperatures and are therefore more likely to be observed on the faster flowing streams or rivers at some altitude particularly in hilly or mountainous country. They are also likely to be found on many of the wilder lakes and reservoirs. They also seem to favour rocky, boulder strewn or stony waters which undoubtedly led to the origination of their common name. It may be worth mentioning that in the past in the northern areas of Great Britain where these Stoneflies are of more importance, the larger species would often be referred to as Mayflies in the absence of a true Ephemerid Mayfly.

Worldwide this is quite a large Order of insects containing between 2000 and 3000 different species, although in the British Isles it is considered quite small as there have been but 34 different species recorded. But when we take into account all the European species the number increases dramatically to well over 300 different species. This would seemingly create great problems for the fly fisher who may wish to identify them, but in practice fortunately it does not really arise as, like the sedge-flies, the vast majority of these are either very rare or very localised.

The Stoneflies vary a great deal in size, the larger specimens having a wing span of nearly two inches, and the smaller barely three-quarters of an inch. The anatomical structure is similar to that of the sedge and other flies, with the usual three-segmented thorax and the ten-segmented abdomen. The legs are of fairly uniform length but somewhat stouter than those of the sedges. On top of the head there are two prominent antennae which are usually about half the length of the body and thus relatively shorter than those of most sedges. Unlike the latter, which are tailless, all Stoneflies have two tails which vary considerably in length. Some are as long as or slightly longer than the body, while others have tails which are reduced to mere stumps and are difficult to see. When the fly is at rest the wings, which are hard and shiny, lie flat along the top of the body. They are often slightly convex and, particularly in some of the smaller species, appear to mould around the body. There are four wings, the hindwings always being broader than the forewings. In many cases, particularly in the larger species, the wings of the male fly are foreshortened and so atrophied as to be merely vestigial, and flight is impossible. A brief account of the life cycle of this group is given in Chapter 1.

Stonefly nymphs or creepers, as the larger ones are called in angling circles, are somewhat similar in appearance to the nymphs of many of the Upwinged flies, but are in most cases considerably larger. The latter, however, have three tails and the former only two. This is a point worth remembering. They are a very active and robust crawling type of nymph, and some of the larger species are carnivorous. As maturity approaches, the nymph crawls (or possibly in the case of some of the smaller species, swims) to dry land, usually after dark, and seeks shelter before transforming into the winged adult fly. Mating is said to take place on the ground, and usually two or three days later the female extrudes her eggs, which adhere to the underside of her abdomen prior to oviposition. Favourite resting-places for the adult Stoneflies are the bark and foliage of trees and shrubs, stones, rocks, posts and the walls of sheds and huts. It is believed that the Stonefly nymph, which during its aquatic existence crawls along the bed of the river or lake, is of doubtful interest to the fly-fisher because of the difficulty of simulating the crawling action of the natural, on which trout are by no means averse to feeding. The life-span of these nymphs is about twelve months, but species of at least two genera, namely Perla and Dinocras, I believe to have a life-span of three years. However I strongly suspect that one other species, *Perlodes microcephala*, has a span also of three years, as I personally have obtained specimen nymphs in one locality on the same day, each in a different stage of growth. The largest was about 23mm, the next about 13mm and the smallest barely 7mm, and as on this particular river hatches are limited to a maximum period of three weeks, I suspect that the two smaller specimens (of which there were many) would not be sufficiently mature for metamorphosis within the given period. Therefore, it appears to me likely that their change into the winged state must await the following year and perhaps, in the case of the smallest one, the year after that. The natural nymph or creeper is a very popular bait on many of the North County lakes and rivers. Stonefly imitation really comes into its own when the female returns to the water to lay its eggs, and what a tempting target it makes for a hungry trout as it flutters and flops about on the surface!

Stoneflies—Fishing Information

In the following detailed description of the Stoneflies I do not propose to give fishing information on each particular species as I have with some other Orders and groups of insects. In the first place, apart from size which varies tremendously from species to species there is very little difference in their appearance except that in some of the smaller species they are a little slimmer, so it is extremely unlikely that a trout would be able to differentiate between closely allied species. Secondly, apart from a few distinctly yellowish species the adults are all of a similar colouration, a greyish to yellow-brown body and brown or mottled brown wings. From this it will be apparent that a small, medium and large pattern in basically brown colours and ditto in yellow-green or yellow-brown should suffice.

It is interesting to note that as long ago as the thirteenth century Dame Juliana Berners gave a Stonefly dressing in her famous *Treatise*, and other great angling authors of the past such as Markham, Cotton and Ronalds also produced patterns. Since those early days literally scores of dressings have been devised but few have proved to be consistently successful. It is therefore difficult for me to recommend specific patterns. The following are good general patterns that have stood the test of time: the Grey Duster, Blue Upright, John Storey, Partridge & Orange and the Dark Spanish Needle. A few of the more popular specific patterns are as follows: the Stonefly (Roger Wooley), the Willow Fly (Alfred Ronalds), the Medium Stonefly and the Black Stonefly (Lumini). There are also three excellent patterns by Dr Voljc, the Yellow Sally, the Needle Fly and the Large Stonefly.

To the flyfisher the nymphs are usually of value only as a means of forecasting the presence of the adults at a later time because, as I explained earlier, due to their habitat and mode of life underwater they are extremely difficult to imitate.

However, that is not to say it is impossible to take a trout on an artificial to represent them and in the last decade some flyfishers have had a modicum of success both on rivers and lakes with a good representation. In his book *Stillwater Flies* Taff Price suggests three modern patterns which should prove effective. The first is a very life-like American pattern called a Stonefly Creeper and this is a good representation of the Yellow Sally Creeper. Next is a British pattern called a Dark Stonefly Creeper and this dressed in a variety of sizes will suffice for most of the other species of Creepers. Finally he recommends a New Zealand pattern by Keith Draper called a Perla Nymph designed to represent one of the larger New Zealand creepers which are very similar to some of our larger species.

The majority of flies in this Order are found in running water only, but a few of the more common species are found in both running and stillwater. The following list I hope includes all those species likely to be of use to the flyfisher. It covers only common and widely distributed species.

CHECK LIST OF COMMON AND WIDESPREAD SPECIES THE STONEFLIES (PLECOPTERA)

ANGLERS OR COMMON NAME	ENTOMOLOGICAL NAME	LENGTH OF FEMALE ADULT
Large Stonefly	Perla bipunctata P. marginata, Perlodes microcephala or Dinocras cephalotes	18–24mm
Medium Stonefly	Diura bicaudata	12–14mm
Yellow Sally	Isoperla grammatica, I. rivulorum or I. obscura	9–13mm
February Red	Taeniopteryx nebulosa, Brachyptera risi or B. seticornis	9–11mm

Willow Fly	Leuctra geniculata	8–11mm
Early Brown	Protonemura meyeri or P. intricata	7–9mm
Small Brown	Nemoura cinerea N. avicularis, Nemurella picteti, Amphinemura sulcicollis, A. triangularis or A. standfussi	6–9mm
Small Yellow Sally	Chloroperla torrentium, C. apicalis or C. tripunctata	6–8mm
Needle Fly	Leuctra fusca, L. hippopus, L. inermis or L. nigra	5–9mm

In this list, anglers' common names have been attributed to specific species which are identified by their scientific names. As with the sedge flies, it is more likely, however, that fishermen have used and still use these common names not only for those identified in the list, but for any other species (and there are several) that superficially resemble them.

INFORMATION ON THE VARIOUS SPECIES

The Large Stonefly (Perla bipunctata and P. marginata) Plate 33 (261)
These and the following species, all with wing spans often exceeding two inches, are the largest of our Stoneflies. The above two species are probably the more common, and are found in the fast-flowing rivers with rough beds, composed of large stones which are mainly free of silt or moss. As this type of river is subject to sudden spates, the nymphs (Plate 33 No 260) probably take shelter between the stones where they are in less danger of being swept away. It is common and widespread all over Europe and in the British Isles except Southern England and East Anglia, but most common in the North. The adults of these and the following species seldom travel far from the banks of the river and are likely to be found sheltering among stones, boulders or projections along the banks. The adults have chestnut brown wings and legs and yellow brown bodies and are most in evidence in May and June. The male fly is 16 to 23mm and the female 18 to 24mm.

DISTRIBUTION: Common and abundant. Found in most areas in flowing water only. *P. marginata* is not found in areas 12 to 23.

The Large Stonefly (Dinocras cephalotes)
This is very similar in size and appearance to the last species. However, it is possible to distinguish between them reasonably accurately as follows: on the preceding species (*P. bipunctata*) the pronotum—which is the top of the first segment of the thorax between the head and the forewings—is pale yellow with a black border and a black line down the centre, on each side of which lies a dark patch. On *D. cepholates* the pronotum is all black. They prefer rivers with a firm bottom, or where the bed contains a number of partly buried moss-covered stones. They occur in roughly the same areas as the preceding species, except in Ireland where they are not quite so prevalent. The adults are seen on the wing in May and June and are of a mottled brown appearance.

DISTRIBUTION: Very common and abundant. In flowing water only. Found in most areas except Nos 12, 15, 16 and 22.

The Large Stonefly (Perlodes microcephala) Plate 33 (262)

It is widely believed that this is the only large stonefly found in still as well as running water and it seems to be particularly common in parts of Scotland. The wings of the adult fly are chestnut brown; the underbody varies from cream to yellow, and the legs are frequently tinged with yellow. It is often a bright yellow overall colour when first hatched, but quickly darkens with age. It is usually found resting in the shelter of posts, large stones or on the bark of trees or fences several yards back from the banks. The wings of the adult male are often atrophied or mere stubs, (Plate 33 No 262) and the insects are incapable of flight, although active on their feet. Like many of the stoneflies, the female is a poor flier and, even when disturbed, seems reluctant to take to the air. The male is 13 to 18mm and the female 16 to 23mm. Like most of the other large species, it is unable to partake of solid food, but it can and does take liquid. The adults are seen from March to July, being most common in April and early May. The nymphs are very large varying between 18 and 28mm, and their basic colour is yellow with a dark brown pattern along the head, the thorax, and the dorsal segments (Plate 33 No 259). They are usually encountered in rivers, large lakes or tarns on high ground, but rarely above 1,200ft; they prefer an exposed shore composed of large boulders or loose stones, the underside of which they inhabit. When the fully grown nymph is ready to transform to the winged adult it migrates to the water edge and crawls out, and with this particular species this usually occurs at night. These larger Stonefly nymphs will often crawl several yards from the water's edge until they find a suitable rock or tree on which to transform. They will then fix themselves firmly to the substrate with their claws, and their skin splits down the thorax and the fully adult winged fly emerges.

The adult winged females when ready for ovipositing either crawl or fly to the water's edge and then swim along the surface to the deeper water. The three or four hundred eggs which have been previously extruded are then washed off as they swim. The eggs fall away a few at a time until finally the whole mass becomes detached and sinks to the bottom. It is supposed that the eggs take about 90 days to hatch out, and that the nymphs mature in one or possibly three years.

DISTRIBUTION: Widespread but hatches rather sparse. Likely to be found in all types of water with stony substrata. Found in most areas except Nos 5 and 15.

The Medium Stonefly (Diura bicaudata). Plate 33 (264)

On lakes this is more common than the previous species, but even so, although it is often abundant in areas where it occurs, which is mainly on high ground above 700ft in parts of Scotland, Ireland, the Lake District and Western Wales, it is not widespread. The adult winged flies tend to be more reddish brown and of a slimmer appearance and they are smaller, the males being 10 to 13mm, and the females 12 to 14mm. They are to be seen from April to July, and peak hatches occur during April and early May. According to Dr Hynes the adults, both male and female of this particular species, are incapable of flight, and consequently the female is forced to crawl to the water's edge, where it swims out to release its eggs in a manner similar to the Large Stonefly. The nymphs, as in most cases in this Order, are larger than their corresponding adults, the males varying between 9 to

17mm and the females 19 to 14mm; their general colour is grey-brown with yellow markings above, yellow below (Plate 33 No 257). They are also found in similar localities to the Large Stonefly, under large boulders or stones in rivers and on exposed shores of lakes, but at higher altitudes. They have a life cycle of approximately twelve months.

DISTRIBUTION: Common. Fairly abundant where they occur in small stony streams or stony lake shores. Found mostly in following areas: Nos 1, 2, 8, 9, 10, 17, 19, 20, 22 and 23.

The Yellow Sally (Isoperla grammatica, I. rivulorum or I. obscura). Plate 34 (265)

Of all the Stoneflies these species are probably the easiest to recognise, due to their conspicuous yellowish-green wings, yellow-brown legs and yellow body. They are medium-sized species and their name is often confused with one of the large yellow Upwinged flies known as the Yellow May dun, which is also referred to in some areas as a Yellow Sally. The male varies between 8 and 11mm and the female 9 and 13mm.

I. grammatica is the most common of the three species to be found on rivers in most parts of the British Isles, while specimens found in stillwater seem to be confined to the northern parts of the country. The adults are to be seen on the wing during most of the summer from April to August, but are probably most common in June and July. They seem to be stronger fliers than any other Stonefly species of their size, and the adult females are often to be observed ovipositing while on the wing by dipping on to the water surface. The nymphs vary greatly in colour, but average specimens seem to be a uniform dark grey-green to yellow with dark markings on the head, thorax and dorsal segments (Plate 33 No 258). They vary between 11 and 16mm and are seldom found at altitudes above 1,000ft. They seem to favour a sandy or gravelly bottom, interspersed with small stones, under which they can usually be found.

DISTRIBUTION: Very common and very abundant. Found in all areas mainly in larger rivers. *I. obscura* is also found in larger rivers but is not so common. Found in most areas except Nos 1, 2, 3, 4, 5, 6 and 7. *I. rivulorum* is only likely to be found in small streams in areas No 3, 4, 5, 8, 9, 10, 20, 22 and 23.

The February Red (Taeniopteryx nebulosa) Plate 34 (267)

T. nebulosa is a common fly in the areas in which it occurs, but it is rather localised and is confined mainly to the North of England, parts of Wales, Scotland, and the West Country. It is probably the only Stonefly which dislikes a stony environment, being more partial to slow-flowing rivers with much vegetation. It is an early season fly and is seen usually between February and April. It is medium to small, and has dark-brown legs and wings, marked with two dark bands, the last three body segments being of a reddish brown colour. The male is 7 to 9mm and the female 9–11mm. The wings of the male are often short, and it is usually the female of the species that is recognised by anglers as the February Red.

Brachyptera risi (Plate 34 No 266) and B. seticornis are two very similar species more common and widespread than the preceding species, and their season is longer, extending from March to July, and these in some areas may also be referred to as the February Red. They are similar in size to T. nebulosa, but often found in small stony streams as well as slower-paced rivers.

DISTRIBUTION: T. nebulosa; fairly widespread but rather localised, found in most areas, mainly in larger rivers. B. risi; common and fairly abundant, found in most areas except Nos 4, 11, 12 and 16, small rivers and streams. B. seticornis; fairly common and fairly abundant, found in many areas except Nos 3, 12, 15, 17, 18, 19, 20, 22 and 23, small rivers and streams.

The Willow Fly (Leuctra geniculata) Plate 34 (268)

This is also a medium to small fly, the male being 7 to 9mm and the female 8 to 11mm. It is very abundant and is widespread over the whole of the British Isles except East Anglia and Ireland. The nymph prefers the stony beds of large streams, although it is also found in the gravelly sections of deep rivers, and is one of the few stoneflies common to the English chalk streams. It is also to be seen in stony lakes. A late season fly, it is most in evidence from August to November. It is similar to the two following species, but has one distinct feature which should assist identification. The two long antennae have a whorl of outstanding hairs round the apex of each segment, which can be clearly seen with a magnifying glass. This Stonefly, like many of the smaller species, is often found on the limbs or bark of trees, posts or fences, where it feeds on the lichen or algae. It is a very slim fly with reddish brown coloured wings and legs, and the females lay their eggs by dipping onto the water.

DISTRIBUTION: Very local but abundant where it occurs. It has only been recorded in numbers in but few areas but may well occur in many other areas. Common in areas Nos 1, 2, 3, 8, 9, 18 and 19. Also recorded from Corsica and Sardinia.

The Early Brown (Protonemura meyeri). Plate 34 (269)

This is a little smaller than the previous species, the male being 5 to 8mm and the female 7 to 9mm. The wings and legs of this fly are also a reddish brown colour, but the head usually has a transverse pale bar across the top. Apart from this, however, it can hardly be mistaken as it is an early season fly, the adult first appearing in February and seldom seen later than May. It prefers fast water with a firm bed lined with moss–covered stones or boulders. It is prolific and widespread and is often found at high altitudes. P.intricata is very similar and is also to be found in the same habitat. Both species of females fly out over the surface where the eggs are oviposited.

DISTRIBUTION: P.meyeri is very common and very abundant and widespread. To be found in all areas except No 4. P.intricata is common and abundant in those areas where it occurs. Found in most areas except Nos 12, 17, 18, 19, 20, 22 and 23. Both species are found only in fast flowing water.

The Small Brown (Nemoura cinerea, N.avicularis & Nemourella picteti). Plate 34 (270)

These three species are so similar in appearance that they may be grouped together under the above anglers' vernacular name, and for the sake of brevity I intend to describe them as one species, as they can only be separately identified by microscopic examination which is, of course, of little consequence to the angler. Without doubt, these are the most prolific and widespread of all the stoneflies found in stillwater. The adults are fairly small, the male being 6 to 7mm and the female 6 to 9mm. They are of an overall dark brownish colour, and are to be observed on the wing throughout the fishing season. The active flying females oviposit in a similar manner to the previous species. The nymphs have very long tails and antennae and their general colours are either olive-grey, or light reddish-brown, with a paler under-abdomen. They vary in size between 5 and 9mm and they prefer both slow flowing rivers and stillwater where the bottom is composed of small stones, well silted and interspersed with weed. They are common and found in most countries in Europe as well as the British Isles. There are also three other very similar but slightly smaller species which may be referred to under the same common name. These are Amphinemura standfussi, A.sulcicollis and A.triangularis.

DISTRIBUTION: N.cinerea; very common, very abundant in all types of water, found in all areas. N.avicularis; fairly common and abundant in larger rivers only, found in all areas except No 6. N.picteti; common and abundant in most types of water, found in most areas except Nos 3 and 6. A.standfussi; not so common nor widespread as the other species and found only in small streams in most areas except Nos 1, 4, 5, 6 and 16 during June to September. A.sulcicollis; very common and very abundant April to August mostly in larger stony rivers, found in most areas except Nos 12 and 15. A.triangularis; fairly common and abundant in areas where they occur in small streams, found in areas Nos 1, 2, 3, 4, 5, 6, 7, 8, 9, 10, 11, 13 and 15.

The Small Yellow Sally (Chloroperla torrentium). Plate 34 (271)

This is also a very common and widespread species and is found in most areas of England, except perhaps East Anglia and parts of the Home Counties. It is not so common in Europe. The adults are quite small, the males between 5 and 7mm and the females 6 and 8mm; of a rather slim appearance; the general colouration is yellow to yellow-brown. They are on the wing from April to August, being most common in May. The females lay their eggs in a manner similar to some of the previously mentioned species, and the egg mass, which contains between 15 to 40 eggs, is carried under the abdomen near the tails. They usually fly out over the water slowly, losing height, until the egg mass comes into contact with the water, where it becomes detached from the abdomen. The members of this species, in common with several others of the smaller species, are fairly active fliers and will often be observed on the wing prior to ovipositing. All stoneflies can be readily identified in flight as they always fly in a more or less straight line, and their four large wings make them appear far larger than they actually are.

The nymphs are 7 to 9mm long, grey-brown with constant darker markings on top and yellow below. The tails and antennae are much shorter than in the previous species, and they are most likely to be found amongst the small stones or gravel in both rivers and some lakes. In some localities they will also be found on sandy lake shores, where they tend to burrow into the sand.

DISTRIBUTION: They are very common and abundant in areas where they occur, and are likely to be observed in all types of water with a stony substratum. Found in areas Nos 1, 2, 3, 4, 5, 8, 9, 10, 17, 18 and 19.

The Needle Fly (Leuctra fusca and L.hippopus). Plate 34 (272)

This is the smallest fly of this Order in this country and, as the name implies, it is extremely slim in appearance when at rest. The wings and legs are pale brown and whilst seen on many rivers it is only occasionally found on bodies of stillwater. The two species mentioned above are so similar in appearance it is impossible to tell them apart with the naked eye. However, *L. hippopus* is an early season species, on the wing from March to June; being most common in March and April, whereas *L. fusca* is seen from June to November, with main hatches occurring during July and August. They are exceptionally common flies on rivers in all parts of the country, but as far as the stillwater fisherman is concerned they seem to be rather localised. The adult males are between 5 and 7mm and the females 6 and 8mm. The nymphs seem to have a preference for small stones and gravel among decaying leaves. The general colour is grey-brown on top with pale wing pads and dark head, and underneath they vary from yellow to pale rose. They vary between 6 and 9mm in length, are very slim, with fairly short antennae about a third the length of their bodies, and their tails are of a similar length but densely clothed with bands of bristles. Another very similar and common species is L.inermis which is most likely to be observed between April and August.

DISTRIBUTION: L.fusca; very common and very abundant in all types of water with a stony substratum, found in all areas. L.hippopus; common and abundant in streams and larger rivers with a stony substratum, found in all areas except No's 20, 22 and 23. L.inermis, very common and very abundant in streams and larger rivers with a stony substratum, found in most areas except Nos 12 and possibly 20, 22 and 23.

CHAPTER 9

SUNDRY INSECTS AND OTHER FAUNA

All the flies that have so far been mentioned may be classified into definite Orders, all families in each Order having a similar life cycle. However, in other Orders such as many of those that are covered in this chapter there are a number of miscellaneous flies so diversified that it is impossible to deal with them in this manner. In addition, anglers are concerned with small creatures such as spiders and shrimps, which are not insects at all, but which, with the indulgence of the reader, I will refer to as flies or insects for the sake of simplicity. Each of these flies will therefore be dealt with separately, and where necessary a brief account of their life histories will be given. Under this heading there are many terrestrial insects whose life cycle is, to anglers, of little consequence, and it is only when they find their way on to or into the water that they become of significance to the flyfisher.

It is remarkable that many of the insects in this category are largely ignored by flyfishermen, and it is probable that the chance of an exceptional fish is sometimes missed because of it. A trout that has been born and bred in a river or in a lake, or a stock fish that time has made wild and wary, and which has learned from sad experience of the dangers to be met from painful encounters with a seemingly innocuous floating or aquatic insect, may live for many years and grow big and lusty. A fish of this type is usually very cautious and experienced in recognising the difference between the natural and the artificial of the more common flies. However, it is surprising how often, in an unguarded moment, it can be deceived with an artificial pattern, which, although of an unfamiliar nature, nevertheless represents some kind of natural insect of an unusual variety.

Most bodies of stillwater harbour a far larger variety of insects and other fauna than do rivers and consequently the trout have a greater choice of food, much of which is of an aquatic nature, present, in some cases, throughout the fishing season, while in other cases present only for comparatively short periods. They also, have a wide variety of surface food, much of it of a terrestrial nature. It has been shown that trout in certain circumstances become selective feeders, and will concentrate on one particular species to the exclusion of all others. This is particularly apparent with some species, notably fauna that often appear in large quantities for a short period, such as the Flying Ant or the Hawthorn fly. It will therefore be to the angler's advantage to take careful note of many of the species which are described in this chapter as many of them come in this category.

The Alder-fly, Order Neuroptera (Sialis spp.). Plate 38 (298)

There are two species, *Sialis lutaria* and *S.fuliginosa*, and so far as the angler is concerned they can be treated as one as they are so similar in appearance.

However, only the former is found in stillwater. The Alder has been known to the river angler for many many years and it has always had an extraordinary capacity for attracting antipathy or affection among flyfishers. Despite the fact that Halford made a detailed and complete study of the life history of this species, he finally denounced it as valueless to fly fishermen. On the other hand, Kingsley and other leading anglers of their day spoke very highly of it, and looked upon the artificial as a very killing pattern, as do many anglers of this day. So far as the stillwater fisherman is concerned, it is only in recent years that it has been recognised as a useful lake fly mainly in its larval form. It is very common and widely distributed and is to be found near all types of water, mostly in the early part of the season, about May and June. it is similar in appearance to some dark, medium-size sedge flies, having the same roof-shaped wings when at rest. The head and legs are very dark, being almost black, and the wings are hard and shiny like those of the stoneflies. Like other members of the Megalopteran sub-Order, its life cycle is partly aquatic and partly terrestrial. The adult winged female lays its eggs in masses of between 500 and 800 on the leaves of plants or on reeds overhanging the water. After about ten or twelve days the young larvae emerge and fall to the bed of the river or lake, where they live in the silt and mud on the bottom. The larvae, when fully grown, reach a length of approximately one inch and are of a dark, sepia-brown colour. They have six stout legs, seven prominent tracheal gills down either side of the body, a single tail, and are equipped with a powerful pair of mandibles. During their early life in this form they spend most of the daylight hours in a tunnel that they dig quite rapidly in the mud or silt on the bed of the river or lake. It can be observed, however, that they nearly always leave the tip of their tails protruding above the surface of the mud; the tail is periodically waved, no doubt to provide a fresh current of water over the tracheal gills.

The larvae (Plate 38, No 297) are carnivorous, and at night they leave their burrows and roam the bed of the lake or river in search of prey, which they seize with their powerful mandibles. Any small, slow-moving form of aquatic life is acceptable and they seem particularly partial to the various species of caddis grubs. During the latter part of their larval lives they become increasingly active and will often emerge from their retreat during the hours of daylight as well as at night. When they are ready to pupate they crawl ashore and burrow into the damp ground or debris along the margins, the pupae emerging within a few days, when transformation into the adult winged flies take place. Although most authorities accept that the larvae crawl ashore to pupate, there appears to be considerable doubt about it, but so far as my experiments in artificial conditions to date are concerned, in all cases pupation occurred out of water.

From the above it would seem to be quite likely that so far as the stillwater fisher is concerned an artificial tied to represent the larva and fished very slowly along the bottom during the early part of the season would prove effective. I have already had some success in this direction and I know of other anglers who find this is a killing method at the right time. Also, I now suspect that the success at times of the well-known Worm fly, when fished slowly and deep, could be attributed to the similarity of this pattern to the natural. C. F. Walker, in his book *Lake Flies and Their Imitation*, gives an effective dressing to represent the Alder larva.

When the adult flies emerge from their pupal cases they appear on the soil surface as fully winged flies. The adults seem to swarm mostly in the shelter of trees or bushes in the vicinity of water, and thus often over the water itself. Sometimes they may be blown on to the water by accident, but even when this happens trout only occasionally accept them, and on this evidence it would seem doubtful that a specific pattern to represent the adult would be of value, but strange to relate, the artificial alder, which is a fairly popular general pattern, does take trout fished during the season of the natural.

ARTIFICIALS: The Alder Fly. This is an old and traditional pattern and should be fished as a dry fly when the adults are observed on the wing. On stillwater or on rivers where a wet fly is allowed the best pattern that I know of to represent the larva is the Alder Larva (Stewart Canham). This should be fished on a sinking line as slowly and as near to the bottom as possible.

The Ant (Order Hymenoptera)

There are many creatures of a terrestrial origin which, when they fall or are blown on to the water in sufficient quantities, will often bring trout up to the surface to feed. The fish are sometimes a little slow on the uptake, but once they get the taste of whatever particular species it may be, they probably look upon them as manna from heaven and commence feeding on them avidly, usually to the exclusion of anything else. Among these, to mention just a few, are several fauna of a seasonal nature such as the June Bug and several other beetles, the Hawthorn fly, the Black Gnat and the Heather fly. However, the particular insect I am about to mention is certainly not seasonal in the accepted sense so far as the fisherman is concerned, as some years it may not be observed at all, while in others it may be encountered on several widely separated occasions in different localities. This is the ant, or rather I should say, the ant in its winged form. As most people are aware, at certain times of the year, usually on hot sultry or thundery days during July, August or early September, many species of ants develop wings for their annual nuptial flight. It seems that they are often attracted by water in this winged state, and should there be a breeze blowing to take them out over a river or lake because they are poor fliers they invariably finish up struggling in the surface film, thereby making a tempting target for any hungry trout. There are, of course, many species of ants throughout Europe, but the two most common and likely to be encountered are the small Black Ant (*Acanthomyops niger*) and the common Yellow Ant (*A. flavus*). The former is black and the latter usually brownish varying between red-brown and yellow-brown. An artificial pattern is fairly easy to tie and should be fished in the surface film with an occasional twitch to animate and represent the struggle of the natural as closely as possible. An angler is indeed fortunate to find himself at the waterside during a fall of ants, but when it does occur the fortunate angler present is likely to have a day to remember all his life, providing he is able to offer the requisite artificial in either brown or black, as the trout are unlikely to accept a substitute.

ARTIFICIALS: A big brown wood ant reminds me of some of the old photographs we see of Victorian women—large chests and hips and tiny waists—and unless an artificial is tied in this manner it is unlikely to attract many trout. Many ant dressings are available or if you are a fly tier they are a simple pattern to dress. An old but excellent pattern I can commend is the Dusky Wood (Skues). Ant patterns should be fished as a dry fly in the surface film and cast to rising fish.

Beetles (Order Coleoptera)

This is a very large Order of more than 3000 different species and it is therefore impossible to pick out many individual species of particular value to the fisherman. All sorts of different beetles find their way accidentally on to the water, and as they come in all sizes, shapes and colours, it is important to note whether any particular species is seen regularly on a water one fishes, and then endeavour either to buy or tie an artificial for future use. There are, however, several types that are known and recognised generally by anglers in certain areas; these are as follows.

The Coch-y-bonddu (Phyllopertha horticola) Plate 38 (299)

This is a beetle that appears in very large swarms in June, and is often blown on to the water. In some areas in Britain it is known as the June Bug or Bracken Clock, and is most common in certain localities in Wales and Scotland. It is a small beetle about half-an-inch long with a metallic bluish green head, thorax, and legs, and reddish-brown wings. Falls are most likely to be encountered during the middle part of warm days. It is likely to be found in hilly country in many areas throughout Europe.

ARTIFICIALS: Patterns should be fished as a dry fly, but in rather than on the surface film. Should a fall of these beetles be encountered an old yet excellent traditional pattern called the Coch-y-bonddu should suffice.

The Soldier-beetle (Cantharis rustica) Plate 38 (301)

Is a very prolific species, seen in thousands during June, July and August. It is about half-an-inch long, quite slim, with orange-red wings which have a distinct bluish colour at the tips, and a dull yellow body. Another closely allied beetle is the Sailor-beetle (*Cantharis livida*) Plate 38, (302), very similar in appearance but with dull blue wings and a more reddish body. Both are sometimes blown on to the water in sufficient quantities to merit the flyfisher's attention. It is common throughout the British Isles, and is likely to be observed in most European countries.

ARTIFICIALS: Various patterns representing the Soldier beetle under the name the Fern fly can be traced back over 300 years so there are many patterns to choose from, but the pattern that I prefer is the Soldier Beetle by that grand old master, G. E. M. Skues. To represent the Sailor Beetle I would suggest a pattern of the same name by Taff Price. Both should be fished as a dry fly on rivers as well as stillwater.

The Cockchafer (Melolontha melolontha) Plate 38 (300)

This species belongs to the same family as the Coch-y-bonddu and is very similar in appearance, having a black head and thorax and wing cases of reddish-brown, while the underpart of its body is banded with black and grey. It is, however, larger and is in fact one of our largest terrestrial beetles, being well over an inch long. It is common in May and June and fairly widespread in habitat, although it is seldom encountered by anglers in the southern parts of the country. It is a dusk-flying species and is therefore only likely to be encountered on the water on windy evenings. The only dressing that I know to represent this particular species is one given by Henderson in his booklet *Fly-fishing on Lakes and Reservoirs*. Unfortunately, I know nothing of its distribution in Europe.

Common Ground-beetles (Harpalus and Carabus spp.)

Rarely fly but will often fall into a river or lake from the banks. They are of medium size, about three-quarters of an inch long and shiny black in colour. Also, of course, there are many other similar terrestrial beetles found in the bankside vegetation that will find their way on to the water by crawling rather than flying.

Apart from the terrestrial species mentioned above, there are very many other species which may be blown on to the water from time to time; of these probably the most likely to be encountered are many of the relatively small beetles from the Staphylinidae family commonly referred to as Staphs. These beetles have long and slender bodies with rather short wing cases, and some of the smallest members of this extremely large family are barely 3mm long. They may be seen on the water in May and June and again in September, and many are shiny black in colour. A good artificial pattern to represent any of the above is the Rove Beetle by Taff Price.

Apart from beetles of a strictly terrestrial habitat there are also many of an aquatic nature, and in their larval forms are readily accepted by the fish. Most of these beetles spend both the larval and adult stages under water although, strangely enough, in most cases the pupal stage is passed in the earth. There are two main groups, the Adephaga and the Polyphaga. The former, carnivorous by nature, breathe by pushing the tip of their abdomen at intervals through the surface film, while the latter, mainly vegetarian, breathe by regularly ascending to the surface and absorbing a bubble of air which they hold on the underside of the thorax.

They vary in size, shape and colouration tremendously, and some species, including the great Diving beetle (*Dytiscus marginalis*) Plate 38 (304) attain a length of over 30mm. In most cases the larvae Plate 38, (303) are very much larger than the subsequent adults. Some of these larger species of larvae are vicious creatures and should be handled carefully. Apart from certain species such as the common Whirligig beetle, which tends to congregate in colonies, the majority are encountered in small numbers.

Occasionally adult aquatic beetles are found in the stomach contents of trout, but in my experience they are not of great importance. The larvae on the other hand are more commonly found in trout, particularly those of medium size. It is impossible, however, to quote specific species of larvae that are acceptable to trout, as a large number are involved and these vary on different waters and at different times of the year. It therefore behoves the angler to note those most common on the stillwaters he fishes or those most commonly found in autopsies and then endeavour to dress matching artificials. Patterns to represent the adult terrestrial beetles should of course always be fished on the surface, and it is often surprising how effective they are, particularly on rivers on hot and sunny days when the trout are dour and reluctant to rise. These floating patterns on stillwater should be fished very slowly; a particularly effective method is to present a well-greased fly on a greased leader and to fish dry, occasionally tweaking the line to provide animation. To illustrate the importance of beetles on some occasions, I should like to recount the following incident.

Some time ago I was discussing trout fishing with Brian Harris and he mentioned that he had recently spent a successful day on Darwell reservoir when most other rods had drawn a blank. The reason for his success on this occasion was due mainly to his power of observation. He described how most other anglers were fishing the deeper water at one end of the reservoir, which early in the year usually offers the best chances, when he observed what appeared to be a rise at the shallower far end of the water.

Deciding to investigate he walked towards it and settled down to watch. Within a few moments he noticed several more trout moving and so he proceeded to the water's edge in order to discover to what the trout were rising. At first he was unable to see any life in the water in sufficient quantities to account for the activity, but soon he noticed several small black beetles crawling in the marginal weeds. A light breeze was blowing offshore and numbers of these beetles were being blown out into the body of the reservoir on the surface film. Suspecting that it was these little creatures that the trout were feeding on, he followed one with his eye as it drifted out into the reservoir, and sure enough about twenty yards from the shore it disappeared in a swirl as a hungry trout rose to it. Mounting a small Black and Peacock Spider, heavily greased, so as to float high in the surface film, he commenced fishing. He subsequently netted several nice trout.

ARTIFICIALS: Despite the vast number of naturals there are relatively few patterns to represent them. A few general patterns worth carrying are Eric's Beetle, the Little Chap, Black and Peacock spider and the Black Ground Beetle by Taff Price. The Americans have recently perfected some rather effective looking patterns made from black foam (plastic) and shaped.

DISTRIBUTION: Common and widespread throughout Great Britain and Europe. There are so many hundreds of different species it is impossible to give precise locations.

The Rape Seed Beetle

These days particularly in Great Britain fields of Rape are a common sight in the countryside as this is now a very popular crop with farmers for cattle feed. The Rape beetle is a small black beetle which colonises the seed in very considerable numbers. On windy days where these fields of rape are ajacent to lakes or reservoirs the beetles are often blown onto the water surface in large numbers and are much appreciated by the trout. When this occurs fly fishers are now enjoying considerable success with a black 'Suspender Pattern'. This is dressed with a short black Ostritch herl body on a short shank wide gape hook size 12 or 14 and the white ethafoam ball is coloured with a black waterproof marker. This pattern is fished more or less on the dead drift in the surface in the vicinity of trout rising to these small terrestrials.

Dragonflies and Damselflies (Order Odonata)

Without a doubt the different species which make up these two groups of flies contain some of the best known of all insects frequenting fresh water. Their brilliantly coloured bodies, large size, and shining transparent wings makes it impossible to confuse them with any other Order of insects. Although both groups are very similar in appearance they can easily be distinguished, as the Dragonflies (sub-Order: Anisoptera) have unequal wings held open when the insect is at rest, while the Damselflies (sub-Order: Zygoptera) have equal wings which are held closed or nearly closed when at rest. The difference between Dragonfly and Damselfly nymphs, both of which, unlike most adults, are attractive to trout, seem to be as pronounced as the differences between the winged flies. The former are large, robust creatures with plump bodies, attaining a length in some cases of almost 50mm. They are generally sluggish creatures only found in stillwater and spend much of their lives among the stones or mud on the lake bed, although at times they are to be found in the weed, particularly when pursuing their prey, which are often small fish. When disturbed they, as do other dragonfly nymphs, escape by shooting water from the rectum—moving in fast jerky leaps. Their colouration blending with their environment provides the camouflage which helps to protect them from predators (Plate 39, No 307). They are of little interest to the flyfisher. The latter, with their long slender pale green or brownish bodies equipped with three large flat, leaf-shaped tracheal gills which look like tails at the extremity of their bodies, are quite dissimilar but they are of much more interest to the flyfisher particularly on stillwater – Plate 39 (308). They appear to prefer weed and can often be found clinging to the stems where their stick-like bodies and olive colouration blend into their background and make them very difficult to locate. The nymphs of both these sub-Orders are equipped with a so-called mask, formed from a fused third pair of jaws or labium, which is equipped with a powerful pair of strong claws and which can be rapidly extended from the head to grasp any unfortunate prey that comes within reach. Most species have an annual life cycle of a year, but it seems possible that some of the larger species may spend two years or more in the aquatic stage.

Most of the larger Dragonfly nymphs emerge at night to transform into the adult. This is accomplished by either crawling ashore or to the surface via emergent vegetation, and therefore at this stage they are of no interest to the flyfisherman, unlike the nymphs of the Damselfly which are of interest, as when the time for emergence arrives, usually during the hours of daylight, many of them ascend to the surface and swim ashore on to any handy emergent vegetation. They swim with a most distinctive wriggle, creating quite a disturbance which seems to attract the trout. At certain periods during the summer, between May and August, these Damsel nymphs hatch out in fair quantities usually between 8 a.m. and 2 p.m., and when their shoreward migration commences they attract the trout in no uncertain manner. The trout, when taking the nymphs, generally do so in a typical way, slashing at them in a manner similar to a rise to a Mayfly, sometimes leaping right out of the water as a result of their eagerness. A pattern to represent this Damselfly nymph is given later and although it is impossible to fish it in the exact manner of the natural, it nevertheless seems to be effective if fished with a lightly greased cast, in the surface film, and retrieved at a moderate speed. An artificial to represent these nymphs should always be fished towards the bank, and this is best accomplished by the bank angler. Although as previously mentioned, many of these nymphs swim ashore on the surface, some of them do swim along near the bottom or even crawl ashore, so therefore on occasions a sunk artificial fished slowly along the bottom will prove effective.

Two of the most common Damsels, very similar in appearance, are *Enallagma cyathogerum* and *Agrion splendens* (Plate 39, No 309). The adult males have a bright blue body, while the females are a grey-green colour. At certain periods during the summer they may be observed in considerable quantities and at this time it is always worth while fishing the Damsel nymph pattern, even though the main emergence period of the natural nymph may have already taken place.

There are many different species of Damsel flies throughout Europe with a wide variety of colours ranging from grey to brown through to bright red. They are to be observed on the wing, both alongside rivers as well as over stillwater but these adults are of very doubtful value to the flyfisher as the trout are unable to reach them, although on very odd occasions on both rivers and lakes I have observed trout leap clear of the water and take one on the wing. These large flies must make a juicy mouthful for a trout so there is little doubt that they will accept them if and when they become available as the following incident shows.

In the article I provided for the *Trout & Salmon* magazine some time ago I described how the adult egg laying female damsel climbs down emergent vegetation or other projections sticking out of the water, such as decaying tree branches or posts, in order to oviposit her eggs. She will sometimes remain underwater for upwards of half an hour existing on the oxygen trapped under her wings. During this time she will often travel along the bottom or over weed for a considerable distance to find suitable egg laying sites. When oviposition is completed she swims to the surface where the attendant male who has been quartering the surface all the time literally plucks her out of the water. I am satisfied that trout do feed on the female as she returns to the surface, as I have on several occasions found partly digested adults in the stomach contents of trout. I have since fished a pattern to represent these female adults with some success. It should be fished in the surface film and cast into the areas where the copulating flies are observed.

ARTIFICIALS: While there are artificial patterns to represent the dragonfly nymphs I have never found the necessity to carry one. On stillwater the nymph of the damselfly is important and although there are many patterns available, in my opinion the only one you need consider is that excellent original imitation the Damsel Nymph by the late Cliff Henry. As an alternative should you wish to try and imitate the wriggling motion of the natural as it swims towards shore, I suggest you try my own Damsel Wiggle Nymph. Many fly dressers have endeavoured to produce patterns to represent the winged adult, but the only patterns that I have had success with are two excellent floating patterns called the Damosel perfected by gifted fly dressers Stewart Canham, and American Gary Borger.

DISTRIBUTION: Both dragonflies and damsel flies are very common and widespread throughout Great Britain and Europe with some species even to be found as far north as the Arctic circle.

The Freshwater Louse (Asellus aquaticus or A.meridianus) Plate 39 (310)
This small crustacean is also known in some parts of the country as the Water Skater or Water Hog-Louse. Extremely common, it is found in nearly all types of stillwater and seems able to exist in water of a lower oxygen content than can the closely related shrimp. The fully grown adults average 15mm in length and in appearance they closely resemble the well-known terrestrial Wood Louse. Although sometimes found in the company of the shrimp and of a similar colour, unlike the latter they seem to prefer a habitat of detritus or decaying vegetable matter rather than weed itself. Usually found in shallow water in vast numbers, they crawl in a slow or deliberate manner.

The two species of this family mentioned above are the most common and likely to be encountered. Of the two, *A. aquaticus* is the larger and darker, and it is interesting to note that during the winter the male of this species has a habit of carrying the female under him. So far as the angler is concerned these crustaceans are rather difficult to imitate as they tend to remain on or near the bottom, and their movements are rather sluggish compared to many other fauna, but as they are often found in autopsies they are undoubtedly worth consideration. There are several dressings available to represent this creature, and the best of these seems to be Peter Lapsley's weighted pattern tied to represent the natural as closely as possible, which with these particular species is of prime importance. The natural is usually found in fairly shallow weedy water, and therefore the artificial is best fished individually on the ungreased point on a floating line. It should be allowed to sink and retrieved in short jerks along the bottom as slowly as possible.

DISTRIBUTION: Very common and widespread. They are to be found in all types of stillwater as well as slow flowing weedy rivers and streams where they tend to frequent the muddier areas.

The Freshwater Shrimp (Gammarus spp.) Plate 39 (311)

There are several species of these small freshwater crustaceans and probably the most common of them is *G.pulex* or *G.Lacustris*. The adults vary in size from about 12mm to a little over 18mm. In appearance they are arched from head to tail, and have many legs. The colour varies from a translucent grey olive to a distinct brownish orange during the mating season in mid–summer. Fairly strong swimmers when they are disturbed, most species swim on their sides. However, at least one species imported from Canada a number of years ago does swim on an even keel. The males are generally larger than the females, and they will often be found swimming together, the male carrying the female under his body.

This species of fauna is one of the most common found in fresh water and few rivers or bodies of stillwater are without large colonies, although it is believed that they dislike waters of an acid type, and it is certainly most unusual to find them in small ponds of a stagnant nature where the oxygen content is too low to enable them to survive.

Despite their abundance in most waters they are of doubtful value to the stillwater angler. Although these shrimps form a major part of the diet of trout, unfortunately for the fisherman this is mainly during the winter months when other forms of food are often in short supply. During the summer months the trout rarely seem to bother with them and it is only occasionally that I have come across them in autopsies. Nevertheless, a good artificial representation will often take trout, even though they may not be feeding on the naturals at the time. In stillwater the artificial is best fished in the vicinity of weed beds or large stones where the naturals abound, and I have recorded most success fishing it along the bottom, using a fairly slow retrieve with frequent pauses.

On rivers these crustaceans are far more important both to the trout and also to the flyfisher as they are a staple diet for the fish throughout the year. The freshwater shrimp like the louse seems to prefer weedy or gravel strewn rivers where they will be found either amongst the weed or among small stones, gravel or even in moss or detritus. They are seldom found in very fast rocky or boulder strewn rivers. For fishing shrimp patterns in rivers I advise a floating line with a long leader which will allow you with a heavily leaded pattern to get the fly down to the bottom even in the deepest of water. In rough water any likely looking runs, eddies or pools should be covered. In clearwater such as chalk or limestone streams one should only fish to trout that can be actually seen scooping shrimps off the river bed.

ARTIFICIALS: There are a host of shrimp patterns to choose from but my preference is for a pattern called the Mating Shrimp developed several years ago by Brian Clarke and myself. This has proved to be a very killing dressing due I think not only to the lifelike silhouette but to the correct mix of the body material which is dubbed seal's fur or substitute blended 55% olive, 35% brown and 10% fluorescent pink. Another excellent pattern is Neil Patterson's Red Spot Shrimp. For fishing to shrimping trout in shallow water I have found another pattern of my own to be most effective. This is an unweighted artificial I call The Gerroff.

DISTRIBUTION: Very common, abundant and widespread. Found in all areas throughout Great Britain and Europe in all types of water except fast flowing stony streams at altitude.

Grasshoppers

Despite the fact that there are quite a few artificial patterns available to imitate these creatures, I have personally never had cause to require one. According to tradition it is a useful pattern to fish and is reputed to have a particular appeal to really large trout. Certainly the meadows or grass land which form the banks of many of our rivers, lakes and reservoirs used to abound in these active insects, and under conditions of high wind one would in the past see many of these blown out on to the water. This, however, in my personal experience rarely happens today as it would seem that in most areas these relatively harmless insects have been all but wiped out due to the extensive use of pesticides on all agricultural land. I believe they are still to be found in the more remote areas in Ireland where on some of the big loughs they still dap with the natural insect.

ARTIFICIALS: In the past there have been patterns available, but today unless you are prepared to dress one yourself the only way to obtain any suitable artificials is via America where they are still an extremely popular fly.

DISTRIBUTION: Widespread throughout Great Britain and Europe but nowhere are they as common or abundant as they used to be.

The Lesser Water Boatman (Corixa spp.). Plate 39 (312)

The Corixidae Family is quite a large one, containing in all thirty-one different species. Many of them are scarce and rarely encountered, while others are very small and difficult for the angler to imitate. However, several of the more common species are quite large, many being in excess of 10mm and are encountered in nearly all types of stillwater. In appearance they are somewhat beetle-like with a hard and shiny keeled back with long oar-like hind legs heavily fringed with hairs, and as the popular name implies, they do have a resemblance to a tiny boat, the legs looking like a pair of oars. The colour of their backs varies from yellow-brown greenish-brown to dark brown with darker patterning, and in contrast their abdomens are distinctly whitish. Their backs are in fact wing cases, although in immature forms (nymphs) these wing cases are not fully developed and the abdomen shows through. It would seem that these wings do not develop sufficiently for flight until late summer, during which time the adults leave the water and are capable of flying a fair distance. This is usually during late June or July. It is a sight I look forward to every year and it is one that never fails to fascinate. The flight is very rapid and when the Corixae re-enter the water they immediately disappear from sight, rather like a cormorant diving from a height.

Although they are to be observed throughout the summer in varying densities, when odd trout will be found to be taking them, the best period to fish the artificial is during August and early September, a period when the trout seem to accept the natural most readily. This is probably due to the fact that at this particular time they are actively flying and usually in their thickest concentrations, and this also often coincides with a shortage of other forms of aquatic food. I would once again emphasise the large variation in size of these insects, depending on species and time of year. However, to generalise it would seem that concentrations of the larger varieties are usually to be observed throughout August.

Specimens are usually to be found in the weeds in water less than three feet deep. It is interesting to notice their frequent journeys to the surface to replenish their oxygen supply, which is absorbed as a bubble of air and held near the tail between the wings and body; this glistens a bright silver when they are under water. The supply of oxygen lasts only for a limited period and it is therefore necessary for them to return to the surface at regular intervals, and it is at this period they are most vulnerable to any patrolling trout.

Many artificial dressings are available, but my favourite method is to fish a well-weighted pattern on the point by the sink and draw style to simulate the naturals swimming to and from the surface. It should be cast in the vicinity of weed beds, where concentrations of Corixae are seen, and then allowed to sink to the bottom and retrieved in a series of quick jerks. Sometimes a non-weighted pattern fished on the dropper and retrieved fairly fast just under the surface proves to be very killing, particularly early mornings or late evenings during September.

As a matter of interest, a closely related species of the Family Notonectidae, referred to as the Greater Water Boatman, are often to be seen. In appearance they are very similar indeed to the Lesser Water Boatman but should not be confused as, apart from being very much larger, they swim upside down with their abdomens uppermost. These are of little interest to the fisherman as they are seldom taken by the trout.

ARTIFICIALS: Patterns sold or listed under the name Corixa are legion so the angler has a very wide choice, but should carry a selection of both weighted and unweighted patterns.

DISTRIBUTION: A very abundant common and widespread genera they are likely to be found in all areas in shallow water mainly in ponds, lakes and reservoirs. While they are reputed to inhabit all types of fresh or even brackish water, I have never observed them on any of the rivers I have fished.

Water Bugs (Order Hemiptera, sub-Order Heteroptera)

Although the Corixa should officially be included in this category, it was decided to treat them separately in view of their importance. Most of the creatures that come under this heading are of little interest to the fisherman, and it is therefore considered unnecessary to give detailed descriptions and information on all of them. A few that may possibly be of some interest are dealt with briefly.

The Pond Skater (Gerris spp.)

These are quite a common sight on most ponds or in the margins of larger lakes. They have slender bodies about 14 to 17mm in length, very long legs, and skate on the surface in short bursts, hence their colloquial name. In my experience they are seldom taken by the trout and as far as I am aware, there are no dressings available to represent them.

The Water Measurer (Hydrometra stagnorum). Plate 40 (314)

Is very similar in appearance, although a little smaller, about 9 to 10mm, and its body is very much more slender. They are also to be found on the water surface often in the company of the previous species.

The Water Cricket (Velia caprai)

Also a surface dweller with a slightly stouter body and shorter legs than the two preceding species. They are quite small, about 6mm long, and fairly common, usually in the quieter water close to the banks.

The Water Mites (Arachnids). Plate 40 (319)

Although of doubtful value to the fisherman, they are worthy of mention as there are over 200 different species and some of them are very common in all types of stillwater, and at least a brief description will enable the angler to recognise them. Of the same order as the spiders, but somewhat dissimilar in appearance, they also have four pairs of legs, and most of them have round or spherical bodies. In size they vary from the smallest species which is less than 2mm to the largest of over 8mm. The predominant colour is bright red, but some species are yellow, blue or green. Purely aquatic, they live in the weed or silt on the bottom and are often to be found in large colonies. One of the most common bright red types is *Hydrachna geographica*, and it is often to be found adhering to the underside of corixa which it apparently uses as a host. It is quite often found in trout at autopsies and it may therefore be worth while to fish a pattern to represent it. The late John Henderson, in an article, stated that he has had some success fishing a pattern that he devised, but unfortunately I have been unable to trace the dressing for this. The only dressing I know of is The Red Mite by Richard Walker.

Common Water Bugs

A few closely-allied species of round or oval shaped water bugs are often to be observed swimming in the weedy margins of ponds or lakes. They are mostly brownish in colour and may be taken by trout occasionally when they are seen. Most are fairly small and can be discounted but at least two species are fairly large. They are *Ilyocoris cimicoides* commonly called the Saucer Bug. This is oval in shape up to 15mm in length. *Aphelocheirus montandoni* (Plate 40, No 313) is almost round and about 10mm in length.

ARTIFICIALS: None of the above genera are of very much interest to the flyfisher and apart from the Red Mite I do not know of any patterns to represent them.

DISTRIBUTION: All of the above water bugs are common, widely distributed and likely to be found in most areas in the sheltered parts of lakes or ponds.

Leeches (Hirudinae)

There are many European species, while in Great Britain alone there are 16 different species which vary in size from about 10mm up to nearly 100mm.

While a few species are almost transparent, most are greenish to brown, while some are greyish to black. They can often be seen either looping their way along the bottom or on waterweed. Sometimes they may be seen in open water, as they are excellent swimmers. Although some species may be found in rivers, they are of little account to the river flyfisher. However, in stillwaters they are important, as the trout are rather partial to them and a free-swimming leech makes a tempting target. This is without doubt one of the reasons that lures are so effective on many of our large lakes and reservoirs.

The leech is a long, worm-like creature with a sucker at each end. The one at the head contains the mouth parts. Its free-swimming movement is undulating. Marabou is an excellent material for simulating this, so I thoroughly recommend an artificial called the **Marabou Leech** (Taff Price). Another pattern I would suggest is the **Black Bear's Hair Lure** (Cliff Henry). Tied correctly, this also swims with a distinctive undulating motion.

DISTRIBUTION: Common and widespread in most areas in all types of water.

Lacewings (Neuroptera)

These beautiful insects have wonderful golden eyes and transparent gauzy wings which reflect all the colours of the rainbow. They are closely related to the Alder Fly and are of a similar size and shape, often exceeding three-quarter of an inch in length.

Although more than 50 different species are known, they are of doubtful value to the fly-fisher as thjey are strictly terrestrial. However, they do seem to have an affinity for water and are sometimes blown on to the surface in considerable numbers. The trout can then often become very selective. Twice in recent years I have experienced a good evening fall of these flies, once on the Itchen and once on the Kennet, and on each occasion the trout picked out the lacewings in preference to other flies. The two most common species are the Green and the Brown Lacewing.

ARTIFICIALS: Try the Green (or Brown) Lacewing by Taff Price.

Moths, Aquatic (Order Lepidoptera). Plate 40 (315)

It may not generally be realised that there are in fact several species of moths that are aquatic by nature. They nearly all belong to one Family Pyralidae, and most of them spend their larval and, in some cases, pupal life under water. One of the most common is the brown China Mark Moth (Plate 40, No 316); as the name suggests the adults are dark brown in colour with a whitish patterning; they are quite large, being about 16mm in length, while the larvae or caterpillars are as much as 20mm long. During the early spring the larva bites oval sections out of leaves and from these forms its case, which will then often be found floating in the surface where there is floating vegetation in abundance. I also understand that in some localities the larvae cut these oval sections from the floating leaves of water lilies, and seal the resulting case to the underside of the lily leaves. Other smaller species make their cases in a similar fashion from duckweed fronds, and they look rather like the caddis cases of some sedge flies.

So far as the fisherman is concerned, moths in their aquatic mode of life are of little interest, but the adults may be of some value, particularly during the evening, when they will often be found on or near the water. Apart from these aquatic species there are also several other species of moths, not strictly aquatic, often to be found in the vicinity of water. Among them are the Ghost and Swift Moths, Family Hepialidae, and some of the Wainscott Moths. The male Ghost Moth, incidentally, is fairly large with narrow wings and has a distinctly white appearance, and it may possibly account for the White and Ermine Moth artificials. In all probability the well-known Windermere Moth pattern, called the Hoolet, represents the aquatic China Mark Moth. This latter pattern is a favourite of Geoffrey Bucknall, the well-known professional fly-tier, and he informs me it is a very popular and apparently successful pattern. **The Wainscott Moths**, Genus *Leucania* and *Nonagria*, previously mentioned, are often seen in the vicinity of water. They are variable in size, with a wingspan of about 16mm, very thickset and drab-coloured creatures usually a dull yellow-brown in colour. Both caterpillar and adult inhabit the reeds in the margins, and the former bores into the reed stems and feeds on the pith. The resultant hollow reed stem provides a residence for the creature when it pupates.

The Water Ermine (Spilosoma urticae)

Is a medium size terrestrial white moth and is seen mostly late at night usually in the vicinity of bankside vegetation. It has a wingspan of about 18mm and its soft white wings are often covered in small black spots. It is most likely to be seen in June.

The Small White Aquatic Moth (Acentroupus niveus)

Is a very tiny moth with a wingspan of barely 8mm, and was given this common name by Taff Price who on more than one occasion has observed trout feeding upon them. The adults are most likely to be seen during July and August. This insignificant little moth may be important to flyfishers on some stillwaters as it apparently hatches out in very large numbers and has a habit of flying very close over the water surface often leaving a V shaped wake. When the trout are feeding on these it would be easy to assume incorrectly that the fish are rising to a hatch of caenis.

According to the late well-known angler/entomologist John Henderson, one of the most common species of moths that are likely to be blown on to the water surface in sufficient quantities to interest the trout are a small light-coloured species commonly called Grass Moths. However, I have not personally encountered these and I am therefore unable to give any further information on them.

Apart from the artificials mentioned above, there are many patterns and dressings available, including several tried and tested imitations listed in Courtney Williams' book, a *Dictionary of Trout Flies*. In most cases, however, a pattern of each of the most predominant colours, brown, pale brown or white permutated on large, medium or small hooks will suffice.

Moth patterns should be fished on a floating line with a greased leader, and they should be cast to land on the water with a distinct plop, as this disturbance will help to attract any trout in the vicinity, and will simulate the natural falling on the surface accidentally. The artificial should be retrieved in short, sharp jerks in an effort to copy the struggle of the natural in the surface film. The most productive areas in rivers or stillwater to fish these patterns at dusk are the sheltered bays lined with sedges, reeds or other fairly heavy marginal vegetation.

ARTIFICIALS: Many patterns have been evolved some of which date back to the last century but few are available now commercially. Today the most popular patterns are the Ermine Moth, the Hoolet Moth (G. Bucknall) and the Ghost Swift Moth (R. Walker).

DISTRIBUTION: The Lepidoptera Order is a very large one and many of the above or very similar species are likely to be common in most areas in all types of water.

Spiders, Aquatic, the Arachnids (Order Araneae)

This Order, unlike the insects, have four pairs of legs instead of the three pairs of the latter. Although an extremely large group, there is, in fact, only one true aquatic species and this is *Argyroneta aquatica* Plate 40, (318). They are quite common and are to be found in all types of stillwater, usually in the vicinity of weed, where they construct what is best described as a diving bell. This is formed from silk Plate 40, (317) and in due course is filled with air by the spider, and in this it can live for a considerable period, thus obviating the necessity of repeatedly returning to the surface to replenish its air supply. On its underwater travels air is retained on the fine body hairs, and this air or bubble of air around the body gives the spider a distinct silvery appearance. In shape they are very similar to ordinary land spiders, and are commonly found in the weedy margins of lakes and ponds. It is interesting to note that the males of this particular species, the members of which average a little under half an inch in length, are usually a little larger than the females. This is unusual in spiders, as the reverse is most often the norm, and may well account for the fact that the female aquatic spider does not devour her spouse after mating, which so frequently happens in the spider world.

There are several other families of spiders, apart from the above mentioned truly aquatic species that are to be found in the vicinity of water, and they are as follows. The Wolf Spiders (Family Lycosidae) are not very large, growing to about 8mm. They are hunting spiders and are quite common along the shores of lakes, and usually spin a vertical white silken tube among weed of Sphagnum moss in which they live. The top of this tube is usually open above the water surface and through it the spider descends into the water encased in a silvery bubble of air when alarmed. When in search of prey it emerges from the top of its retreat and, like the pond skaters, is able to travel along the water surface without difficulty. Another genera found in similar areas that also builds a white silken tube below the surface are the Pirate Spiders (Pirata Piraticus and P. Piscatorius). They vary in size between 5 and 9mm and the body of the former is chocolate brown with two yellow lines running along the abdomen.

Another common species found in streams swamps and dykes, and occasionally in the shallow margins of lakes, is a species commonly referred to as the Raft Spider. These belong to the Genus *Dolomedes*, which consists of some of the largest of the British spiders. The females are dark brown with two broad white or yellow bands along their sides. There are also sometimes small white spots on the abdomen – particularly on those of the males. The males are about 14mm and the females 20mm and they are usually to be found residing on the floating leaves of water plants. Like the previous species, they are hunting spiders, and can also run along the surface of the water. When alarmed they often descend under water via any handy weed stem. The web spider, the last species worthy of mention, belongs to the Genus *Tetragnatha* and is of medium size, averaging 10mm. Very common in bogs and along the shoreline of lakes, it spins a web low over the water surface in marginal plants, and will occasionally be blown on to the water surface.

From the above it should be apparent that artificial patterns to represent some of these spiders should, on the appropriate occasion, be effective particularly on stillwaters. It therefore seems strange that up to the present time spiders as a whole have been largely ignored by the fisherman. It is worth noting that Courtney Williams mentions in his book that it is beyond dispute that when a spider gets on to the water in the vicinity of a trout, it never progresses very far before it is taken. With this I am inclined to agree, and therefore if any spiders are in evidence at all I think it well worth trying an artificial in an appropriate size or colour, fished either on or under the surface in the shallower water. I am sure there is also considerable scope here for the amateur fly dresser to evolve patterns to represent these spiders even those under water enveloped in their silvery sheath of air. To save confusion I feel I should point out that the many wet fly patterns popular for so long and referred to as spider patterns on the northern rivers of Great Britain were never intended to represent spiders but are merely the style of dressing.

DISTRIBUTION: This Order contains many thousands of species so doubtless at least some of the species or very similar species will be found in most areas throughout the British Isles and also Europe.

The Snail

Apart from terrestrial forms of life, there are also many aquatic insects or other fauna that at some stage in their life cycle provide food for the trout in or on the surface. It is probably not generally realised at certain times of the year some of the common aquatic snails may be included in this category. Most anglers are aware that snails, where they exist in quantities, form a major part of the diet of the stillwater trout. They are normally browsed off the weed or bed of the river or lake by the fish in their search for food, but it is unfortunately rather difficult to represent successfully the snail with an artificial in its natural aquatic abode. However, on occasions, usually during the hot weather of mid or late summer, there takes place on many stillwaters a mass migration of snails to the surface. This phenomenon is most interesting, and although I have personally observed it on many occasions, I have so far been unable to ascertain the reason for it. I have also discussed this with one or two people who have made a study of the life history of snails but with nil results. Therefore, one can only hazard a guess, and the most likely explanations seem to be that it is due either to a migratory instinct, coupled with mating, or alternatively to the slight de-oxygenation of the water resulting from high temperature which causes the snails to rise to the surface. This seems to be confirmed, as snails are very much more sensitive to the oxygen content of the water than many other forms of underwater life, including fish. To favour this theory it is interesting to note that snails introduced into a tank of water that has previously been boiled, thereby reducing the oxygen content, immediately rise to the surface.

When they rise to the surface in this manner the snails float with their shell below the surface, but their foot or pad adheres to the underside of the surface film. In this way they can move quite rapidly along the underside of the film or, alternatively, they can be carried along in the film by the current or the wind. When one of these mass rises occurs the snails will often remain in the surface for several days, and on at least one small lake I know the snails were to be found over a period of nearly three weeks, but this is probably unusual. From the fisherman's point of view this is a golden opportunity, even though it is probably not realised by the majority. When the snails are up the trout are most selective, as they are then presented with one of their favourite foods in a very accessible position on the surface, and are unlikely to be caught with anything other than an artificial pattern to simulate these floating snails. However, providing you have an imitation with you at the time this phenomenon occurs, wonderful sport is usually assured. The wandering snail is the species usually connected with this event.

Without doubt the most difficult aspect of the rise to the snail is to know when it is taking place, but it is worth remembering that it is a typical head and tail rise usually associated with trout feeding on midge pupae, nymphs or *Caënis* spinners, all of which are common during mid-summer. Apart from the difficulty of recognising the rise, one would assume that it would be an easy matter to spot the snails in the surface, but in fact this is extremely difficult, and it can only be done by looking directly down into the water.

Finally, I should like to recount a little story in connection with the snail that happened to a friend of mine on a day in August at Grafham. Having fished all morning from the south bank with the wind in his face, with little success, he decided to join the majority of anglers on the north bank, fishing with the wind behind them. Upon arrival there was little space left to fish, so he engaged one of two anglers in conversation. He was promptly informed that the fishing was terrible and, despite the fact that numerous trout were rising, none had been caught. His curiosity aroused, he walked down to the water's edge to try and discover what the fish were taking. There at his feet was the answer; snails in profusion floating along the margin. The wind was gradually blowing them out into the lake a few at a time and odd trout, being aware of this, were patrolling near the shore awaiting their arrival. Mounting the appropriate snail artificial my friend was able to attain his limit of trout in a very short time, much to the amazement of the many anglers in the vicinity. Questioned as to the successful fly, he was happy to furnish the information but, unfortunately, none of the fishermen had such a pattern.

It is also worth mentioning that cork-bodied snail patterns may be fished successfully near the bottom, which is the more common abode of the natural. The method is as follows. Mount the artificial snail on the point, and tie on a weighted nymph pattern on a dropper about twelve inches above it. In the water that you are fishing choose a location that has an area of silkweed or similar type of weed covering the bottom. Cast out and allow your flies to sink to the bottom. In practice it will be found that the weighted pattern on the dropper will sink into the weed, but the buoyant artificial snail will ride just above it. In this manner it will appear quite natural to any patrolling trout, and it is only necessary to give the line a slight twitch occasionally to attract any fish in the vicinity.

There are many species of Gastropods throughout Europe and in the British Isles alone there are at least 36 different species. The aquatic snails, those that are found either in water or close to it, such as boggy or marshy areas may be divided into two groups—the Operculate and the Pulmonate snails. The former have a hard plate on their foot which enables them to seal off the shell once they withdraw their body inside. They are also equipped with gills through which they obtain their oxygen. As most of the species within this group tend to be found in running water, they are of no interest to the flyfisher as it is all but impossible to fish snail patterns in this medium. Some species in the latter group however are of great interest as most of them are more common in stillwater. These Pulmonate snails can be immediately identified as they do not have the hard plate on the foot. It is also interesting to note that they have a dual method of breathing either taking air direct from the atmosphere or when underwater by absorbing it through the skin. Here are a few of the more common species to be found in this latter group. They have thin, mostly brownish coloured shells.

The Great Pond Snail (Limnaea stagnalis)

Somewhat similar to a whelk in shape, they often attain a length of almost 60mm and are by far the largest of the aquatic species.

The Wandering Snail (Limnaea Peregra)

Without doubt this is by far the most common species of pond snail and while it is most likely to be found in large numbers in stillwater it does frequent all types of fresh or even brackish water. Variable in size according to the type and size of water it is inhabiting, they often reach a length of over 20mm.

The Eared Pond Snail (Limnaea auricularia)

This is also quite a common species but mainly to be found in large lakes or slow flowing rivers and also seems to favour alkaline water, particularly those with a limestone or chalk content. It received its common name from the ear-like opening of the shell. In size and shape it is very similar to the previous species.

The other species of interest in this group are all Trumpet or Ramshorn snails as they are commonly referred to from the flat spiral shape of their shells. There are 14 species in the British Isles the largest having a shell diameter of over an inch, while the smallest has a diameter of barely one-eighth inch. A few of the more common species are as follows.

The Great Ramshorn (Planorbis corneus)

This is the largest of all the Ramshorn snails and its shell formed from 5 or 6 convex whorls, is over one inch in diameter. It is often rather localised in its distribution and seldom seen in large numbers. It inhabits both running and still water, but is more common in the latter.

The Ramshorn (Planorbis planorbis)

This is a little smaller than the previous species and has a shell diameter of about three-quarters of an inch. This is more common and widespread, being found both in ponds and all types of slow flowing water.

The Keeled Ramshorn (Planorbis carinatus)

This is about the same size as the previous species but can easily be identified by the thickened ridge or keel running all the way around the outside diameter of the shell. They are also fairly common and widespread and found in all types of water.

The Small White Ramshorn (Planorbis albus)

This is a little less common than any of the preceding species but fairly widespread. Likely to be found in all types of water, they have a shell diameter of about half-an-inch.

ARTIFICIALS: During the last decade many snail patterns have appeared but my preference still goes to that excellent cork bodied pattern simply called a Floating Snail which was developed by the late Cliff Henry in the sixties. So far as the Ramshorn species are concerned the only pattern I know of to represent these is one suggested by Taff Price called the Bootlace Snail. This is merely a short length of black, brown or white shoe lace forced into a coil of the desired diameter, glued together, and mounted along the top of the hook shank.

DISTRIBUTION: Snails are very wide ranging in their habitat and at least some or very similar species to those listed will be found in most European countries.

Tadpoles

Strange to relate, these very common creatures are completely ignored by most authorities on trout fishing, yet trout will often feed on them avidly during the early part of the summer when they are present in large numbers in many small fisheries. I first became aware of their importance several years ago when fishing some small dams stocked with trout in South Africa. The immature stage of many different species of frogs, these bulbous bodied, greenish-black creatures with their ribbon like tails, are a familiar sight to most of us either in ponds or in the margins of lakes.

ARTIFICIALS: There is now a choice of tadpole patterns that have been developed in recent years. Despite this I still prefer to use my own pattern which has served me well for many years. This is called the Tadpolly. Dressed on a long shank hook with a wide gape it has a bulbous body formed from Ethafoam blackened with a magic marker or several strands of peacock herl, and a long tail utilising several strands of black marabou and/or three black cock hackles. It is most effective retrieved at a medium pace in long pulls on a slow sink line. I have also used it on occasions later in the summer, with some success even when the naturals are long gone. I think the trout accept the artificial at this time from past memories of the succulent meals they provided.

DISTRIBUTION: Various species to be found in most areas throughout Europe.

Sticklebacks and minnows

Undoubtedly these and the small fry of other fish form an important part of the diet of trout on most stillwaters, and although they are not adverse to feeding on them at any time of the season, the main period is usually late July/August and early September, when these little fish congregate in vast shoals in the margins of most lakes. It is at this time that some trout become preoccupied in feeding on them.

If one can find a fairly secluded stretch of bank on a lake or reservoir at this time of the year it is no uncommon sight to see large trout making sorties into the very shallow edges and harrying the fry unceasingly. Under these conditions it is often possible to find a trout that is making regular forays into one particular area, and providing you fish a suitable imitation in the correct manner, while keeping out of sight, success is usually assured.

However, a situation such as this seldom occurs on our more crowded reservoirs, and consequently the most popular method is to fish the water with a lure, deep, and in an attractive manner. This is most successfully accomplished from the bank. If possible, areas adjacent to weed beds, old hedgerows or shallow banks where fry are likely to congregate, should be searched, but if the water is featureless the angler has little alternative other than to fish the water at random. This can often be productive, for if the imitation is fished correctly there is a chance that any trout in the vicinity will assume that it is a small fish separated from its brethren and is making a dash for the sanctuary of the shallower water near the shore.

Although a lure or imitation fished deep and fast will yield trout at most times, during this period the fishermen who make the heaviest bags of trout will be those who fish the imitation in a lifelike manner. This can be best achieved by spending a little time in closely studying the actions of sticklebacks and then endeavouring to emulate them with the artificial. It is also most important to mount an artificial that corresponds closely in size and colour to the natural fry on which the trout appear to be feeding. For this style of fishing it is usual to fish only one artificial on the point, and a long leader is usually advantageous. Depending on the depth of water being fished, either a high-density, fast-sinking line or a slow sinker should be used, but for fishing the very shallow or weedy water along the shore or for fishing dead or injured fry patterns in or just under the surface a floater is advisable.

ARTIFICIALS: So far as a choice of artificials to represent sticklebacks or fry is concerned, we have a very wide selection. For over half a century various eminent anglers have formulated and recommended patterns, and many of them are readily obtainable from the shops. That well-known angler, Dick Walker, perfected and popularised a series of imitations which he called Polystickles to represent many of these small fish. They are dressed with a wonderfully translucent body and simulate a small fish to perfection. Other good fry imitating patterns are Sinfoil's Fry or the Church Fry and a good general traditional pattern pattern is the Peter Ross. Apart from dressings specifically copying fry in appearance, there are also many artificials available to approximate them, and these come under the headings of streamer or bucktail flies. The former are basically long-feathered patterns, while the latter, though similar, are made predominantly of hair. One other pattern which has proved to be a killer is Syd Brock's Mylar Minnow. There are now several excellent floating fry patterns also available.

The Saw-fly (Order Hymenoptera). Plate 40 (320)
This insect belongs to the same Order as the bees and wasps, although it only vaguely resembles them. There are various families in this group, among them the Poplar Saw-flies, Pine Saw-flies and the Solomon's Seal Saw-flies. They are mainly dark in colour and some have touches of orange or yellow on the body. The darker variety with an almost black body is the one most commonly seen, and in Ronalds' day over a century ago, its artificial was known as the Great Dark Drone. It was probably better known then than it is today.

The Ichneumon-fly (Order Hymenoptera)
This is a most interesting fly, of which there are many types, most of which are terrestrial and of no interest to anglers. However, at least one species, *Agriotypus armatus*, is aquatic in the early stages of life. The adult flies are about half an inch long, wasp-like in appearance but somewhat slimmer, have four semi-transparent wings and longer antennae than wasps. The body and legs are black,

with two or three segments in the middle of the body orange-yellow. These flies are seldom seen on the water or even noticed by most anglers, and the reason for this is due no doubt to their curious reproduction system. After copulation, the female makes her way to the nearest water which she enters covered with a film of air in search of a host, usually a caddis larva, in which to lay her eggs. This she achieves by injecting them into the unfortunate larva's case, and when they hatch the young ichneumons feed on and gradually kill their host. As these flies are seldom actually seen on the water, but are sometimes found in trout after an autopsy, it would seem that the majority are probably taken by trout under water when the females are in the act of searching for hosts for their eggs. Ronalds, in the *Fly-Fisher's Entomology* published over a century ago, gives a dressing for this fly which in those days was apparently known as the Orange Fly. This was tied as a floater, but in view of the foregoing remarks a wet pattern would probably be more effective.

Bees or Wasps (Order Hymenoptera)

These also are of doubtful value to anglers, although trout are not averse to feeding on any that are blown on to the water. As this seldom happens because they are strong fliers, they can more or less be discounted. I remember on one occasion, however, when a friend of mine had an exceptionally good fish on an artificial. He found a trout rising well, and after unsuccessfully trying various patterns, he moved closer to the fish the better to identify the fly it was taking. He noticed a regular procession of wasps entering and leaving a nest through a hole in the bank a little above the lie of the fish, and on those occasions when one fell on to the water and was carried struggling downstream, the fish picked it off without hesitation. Unfortunately he had no suitable imitation with him at the time, but a day or two later, when he had remedied the omission, he offered it to the fish which he netted in due course.

Daphnia

These tiny crustaceans are found in vast numbers in most stillwaters and while they form an important diet of the trout they are much too small to imitate with an artificial. However, they are most important to the angler from June onwards as they can be an indicator as to what depth of water the trout may be feeding in. Broadly speaking, find your Daphnia and the trout will not be far away, as when they are present the trout feed on them gluttonously. Enormous clouds of them can often be observed in the water, but as they are sensitive to bright light, the sunnier the day the deeper they will be found. Fortunately, when trout are feeding on Daphnia they are not adverse to accepting other forms of food.

CHAPTER 10

RIVER FISHING

Having now covered pretty comprehensively the identification of flies and fauna upon which trout feed let us now look albeit briefly at trout fishing on rivers. We will then follow this with a much more comprehensive coverage of trout fishing on stillwater as it is only in the last two or three decades that this has become the most popular venue for fly fishing in Great Britain and where it has now reached in such a comparatively short period of time an incredibly high degree of sophistication.

Generally speaking river fishing is less complex than stillwater fishing as in most cases trout will either betray their location by rising on or near the surface or take up lies, where they can be located if you know how to read the water. In addition to this the insects or flies that the trout may be feeding upon will be carried along by the current to a position where you can observe them. Fly fishing on rivers is by far far the oldest branch of our sport and has been practised for many centuries, unlike stillwater fishing which has only been gradually developed as a serious contender within the latter half of this century. Mind you stillwater fishing has been practised to a very minor degree on many of the Scottish Loch's and Irish Lough's for several centuries but during this period it was mainly confined to fishing from a boat and dapping with a live insect or drifting before the wind with a team of flies, referred to as loch style fishing. The various techniques depolyed by the river fly fisher have been well documented over many years, and there are many hundreds of books that have been published over a very long period that cover all aspects of both dry fly and nymph fishing so we shall not cover these in this volume. Compared to stillwater fishing where there have been tremendous advances in methods and techniques in the last thirty years, little progress has been made on rivers until quite recently, apart from the advent of Frank Sawyer's Pheasant Tail Nymph and the brilliant success of his induced take method of nymph fishing. Within the last two or three years there have been a few interesting advances though, so I feel this information should be recorded within these pages.

First of all let us look at the vision of trout underwater. This is a subject that has facinated fly fishers since the inception of the sport, and since the middle of the last century much as been written on it. Over the intervening years many authors have covered this and subsequently brought to light many new facts which have inevitably provided us with a better understanding of how the trout sees and what he sees. Before Brian Clarke and myself published our book "The Trout & the Fly" we undertook considerable research on fish vision and we were consequently able to provide some new most interesting and enlighting information in the book on this subject. Since then I undertook further research and presented this, in an article for the "Trout & Salmon" magazine which is reproduced here with their kind permission.

TWENTY-TWENTY VISION

"The vision of trout is a subject that has fascinated me for many years as our knowledge of how a fish sees and what he sees is sketchy to say the least. While we may make educated guesses, one thing no one can say is how the brain of a fish interprets the message transmitted from the eyes. However, when it comes to *how* a fish sees we should be able to make some pretty accurate assessments, by combining known scientific facts with carefully controlled experiments and/or observations.

During the late '70s when Brian Clarke and I were working on our book *The Trout and the Fly*, we were both involved in a tremendous amount of research and also carried out a lot of most interesting experiments, many on various aspects of fish vision.

After publication of our book I decided personally to pursue some of these aspects further and, as a result, have now reached certain conclusions which I hope in the fullness of time will prove to be correct.

One of the most intriguing aspects of a trout's vision is the fish's ability to scan an arc of 160 degrees or more on each side of its body while at the same time being able also to observe objects immediately ahead with binocular vision where the arc of the eyes overlap.

Obviously this area of binocular vision must be very important, particularly to a brown trout that spends a large percentage of its time searching for food on or near the surface. Would it not therefore be interesting from a fishing point of view, I asked myself, to find out the precise area that was covered by the fish's binocular vision?

On referring to all the books in my library that cover the vision of fish, little seems to have been written about this aspect. The only reference, which most of them repeat, is that a trout has a narrow arc or band of binocular vision some 45 degrees dead ahead, where the arc of the eyes overlap.

Now it seemed strange to me that a trout which spends much of its time searching the undersurface or mirror overhead would only have binocular vision immediately ahead. I therefore decided to study the structure and position of the eye in the head of the trout. The first point I noticed — and one which seems to have escaped the attention of other researchers — was that not only do the eyes slope inward slightly towards the nose, but they also slope inward to the top of the head. In effect this means that not only does the arc of the eyes overlap immediately ahead but also over the top of the trout's head, so surely this should mean that the range of binocular vision would be very much more extensive than previously suspected?

To find out what area this covered I took a series of close-up photographs of the heads of many trout — both from directly in front and also from overhead. I then measured the angles of the arcs formed by the inward angles of the eyes in front and overhead. While it was not possible with the equipment available to me to measure these angles precisely I am confident that they are probably accurate to within at least a few degrees.

To start with, I found that the arc immediately in front was about 35 degrees, and not, as previously supposed, 45 degrees (see fig. 79). The arc which also extended overhead was a little less and seemed to be about 28 degrees (see fig. 80). Due to the fact that the arcs (or more probably elongated cone) of binocular vision appear to overlap considerably because of the two inwardly converging

185

angles of the eyes, I assume that the overall area covered by binocular vision is about 125 degrees from in front to overhead (see fig. 82). I also assume that the trout's binocular vision at each end of this arc would be less acute, and that its most acute vision would occur where the cone or arcs overlap — which would probably be at an angle of about 35 to 40 degrees from the horizontal in front of the trout's head (see fig. 82). From many hundreds of subsequent personal observations of trout in their feeding lies I noticed that most trout seem to lie at a slight angle with their head up. This in effect means that this optimum angle of acute binocular vision is probably nearer to 45 degrees from the horizontal, which would enable the trout to observe not only the mirror above but also into the edge of its window. During the latter stages of my research in the above I once again contacted Professor W. R. A. Muntz in the department of biology at Stirling University. Professor Muntz is one of the world's leading authorities on fish vision and had been of considerable help to us when we were researching the fish-vision section of our book.

Binocular vision

This time I asked him if he could provide some detailed information on the structure of a trout's eye with particular reference to its binocular vision and focusing ability. The information he provided was most interesting, as he was able to provide accurate details of how a trout moves the lens in its eye by means of a large retractor lentis muscle to adjust its focus. When at rest in the retina, the lens is so positioned that anything in front and overhead is in close focus, which to some degree seems to confirm my research. This lentis muscle when retracted moves the lens both inwards and towards the back of the retina in a straight line away from the nose, thereby providing focus to infinity directly in front and to some degree above.

As a matter of interest, during the vision research for our book we had established with the help of Professor Muntz that infinity occured at about two feet. Having, I hope, established the approximate area of a trout's binocular vision I now wanted to establish, if possible, the width of water overhead and in front that this would cover. First of all we must take the two arcs first discussed: the one in front at 35 degrees and the one overhead at 28 degrees. A rough average would then be 32 degrees. This means that if the trout's eyes were focused at less than infinity he would be aware only of approaching food within a narrow arc no more than 14 inches wide at the maximum focusing distance of two feet. Even with its eyes focused to infinity and concentrating on approaching food within its area of binocular vision, the band of water above and in front covered would be less than 30 inches wide at the maximum distance in water of an average clarity.

Seldom is one able to confirm theories by practical tests or observations in the field, but early last season I was most fortunate to find a co-operative trout in a perfect lie in such a position that, with dense cover behind and partly over me, I was able to lower a dry-fly from directly above him and place it very accurately on the water a few feet in front of the spot where he was rising. To start with I was drifting the fly down to him at predetermined distances to each side, and by this method I quickly established that my theory seemed reasonably accurate, as with the trout lying only about 12 inches below the surface he completely ignored my fly if it were more than 18 inches to either side of his lie. I was about to retire and leave the trout in peace when to my astonishment he broke through the surface in the most perfect arc and took my fly in the air as it was hanging about 16 inches

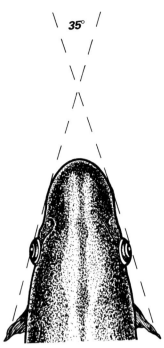

79 The arc of vision immediately in front of a trout is probably about 35 degrees and not, as commonly supposed, 45 degrees

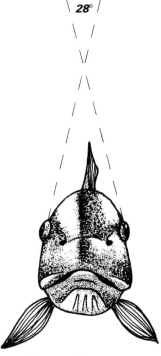

80 The arc of vision overhead is about 28 degrees

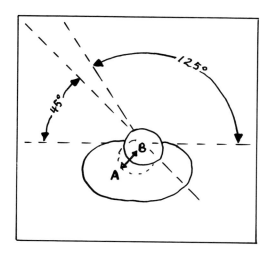

81 Eye seen from above with the nostril to the right. In A with the lens retracted for all around vision to infinity to arc of bonocular vision is probably far less than 25 degrees. In B with the lens extended for close focus in front of the trout the distance from the lens to the part of the retina providing vision to the rear remains constant thereby giving him an arc each side of about 45 degrees that still remains focussed to infinity. However this does leave a grey area of poor vision about 10 to 12 degrees slightly to his rear where his forward close up focus changes to infinity behind him.

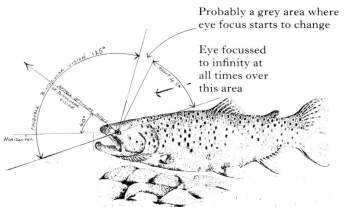

Probably a grey area where eye focus starts to change

Eye focussed to infinity at all times over this area

82 The trouts arc of overhead vision

above the surface and about 20 inches upstream of his lie.

Fly in the air

Now the only way he could have seen this fly in the air was over the edge and in front of his window, and as I was reasonably sure that he had not tilted upwards before jumping I realised that if I could persuade him to jump and accept the fly a few more times I might also be able to prove, or disprove, my first theory that they may indeed have cones of binocular vision to some extent overhead as well as in front. Never have I met such a co-operative trout as during the next 15 minutes or so as I persuaded him to launch himself into the air 17 times!

His reactions were absolutely fascinating as each time I lowered the fly and swung it down towards him I was in no doubt at all as to whether he had seen it. When he did, all his fins — particularly his tail — would start vibrating, and these vibrations would increase in intensity as I swung the fly closer until it was in range of his lie, when he would jump and try to take it in mid-air. I quickly established that he would first see the fly in the air if I swung it to within two or three feet directly upstream of his lie. Now of course what I wished to establish was whether or not the trout was observing this fly over the edge of his window through his close up binocular vision.

If my theory were to be confirmed, he would be unaware of the fly if I positioned it in the air between three to four feet upstream and more than 24 inches off-centre, and so it proved to be. If I swung the fly down to him anywhere near the centre-line he would see it every time, but I could swing it down right past him repeatedly if it were more than about two feet off-centre and not once did he seem to be aware of it.

Now what conclusions can we draw from the above — and how will this help the fly-fisher improve his chances of success?

1. A trout lying and feeding within, say, 18 inches or so of the surface will probably by concentrating through his close up binocular vision and therefore the approaching fly-fisher would probably not register unless he made any sudden movements.

2. A trout lying very close to the surface will probably be focused below infinity so any approaching objects, including the fly-fisher, will be even less likely to be seen. In both cases, however, accurate casting will be necessary, as the fish is unlikely to be aware of any fly drifting down to him on the surface either side of his narrow arc of binocular vision. In view of this I am now beginning to wonder whether this may explain our difficulty in tempting trout during those infuriating evening rises on stillwater when every trout in the lake seems to be rising and yet any pattern we offer is ignored. At this time the trout are usually cruising along almost in the surface so would be unlikely to see any fly less than about 24 inches immediately in front or 24 inches on either side of them. Maybe during this evening rise we would increase our chances if we fished our team of flies much closer together. I certainly intend to try this during the coming season.

Finally, what about those trout that are lying and feeding at a much deeper level? All the angling books that contain a section on trout vision tell us that the deeper a trout is lying the further off he can see the angler as of course the deeper he lies the larger his window overhead.

While this is certainly true, the additional distance he will be able to see is at best marginal, so I am now inclined to think that the more likely explanation for his increased awareness of our presence is due to the fact that at this depth he is unlikely to be concentrating through his binocular vision so everything on each side of his head within the whole 160 degrees arc of his vision will be clearly seen. This also means that when presenting a fly to such a trout even more care will have to be taken with your approach but at the same time accurate presentation of your fly will not be crucial as the fish will be aware of approaching food over a much wider area.

In conclusion, I would add that the detailed information provided to me by Professor Muntz on the structure of a trout's eye and exactly how he moves his lens to provide his focusing ability has thrown up a most interesting new fact. The lentis muscle is apparently so positioned that when it expands or contracts to provide the necessary focusing adjustment to the lens, it moves in and out at such an angle that it leaves the front section of the lens equidistant at all times from the front section of the retina. This means that even when a trout is focusing at very short range on food immeditely ahead of it, an arc of about 45 degrees on each side and to the rear of the fish is still focused to infinity while on each side somewhere between 85 degrees and 95 degrees he probably has a grey area where his vision changes from infinity to close range (see fig. 81).

Close to the surface

This would indicate that a trout feeding very close to the surface and focused at short range would be less likely to see you if you were either opposite him or even slightly upstream, rather than well downstream, where you would come within the range of this 45 degree arc at his rear, which is focused at infinity at all times.

In confirmation of this point I am sure everyone has experienced evenings on a river when there has been a heavy fall of spinner and the trout are all lying so close to the surface that their dorsal fins are often protruding. During this period you can often approach a trout so closely that you are almost casting down on to him and yet more often than not he appears to be completely oblivious of your presence.

Sudden movements

This season when the opportunity arises, try positioning yourself opposite or even slightly upstream of any trout rising very close to the surface over 25 feet away and cast to him from this position as I think he will be less likely to see you, but do remember to avoid any sudden movements and where possible cast with a wrist movement to avoid moving your arms.

Finally one other most interesting aspect of a trout's vision, which I do not think anyone has seriously considered, is whether a trout is able to focus one eye independently of the other. This is extremely difficult to prove or disprove, but while I think it is quite likely, I don't think that this facility would be of very great value to a trout, as most of the time when he is focusing on close-up objects he is utilising his binolcular vision, when both lenses would have to be focused together. As I have already suggested, it would appear that his vision on each side and to the rear is permanently adjusted to infinity so this would leave only a relatively narrow arc towards the front on each side where he could use such a facility — and I really cannot visualise many circumstances in which this would be required.

Another interesting advance that has been made within the last two or three years, is the discovery that midges (Chironomids) can be of interest to the river fly fisher. Their value on stillwater where they provide on many waters the main diet for trout has been know for many years, and subsequently a host of patterns have been developed to imitate then, but it is only comparatively recently that attention has been drawn to these tiny insects on rivers.

I believe the French author Raymond Rocher was the first person to draw our attention to them in an article he wrote for one of our magazines recounting a certain amount of success he was having fishing tiny pupae patterns on many of his beloved French rivers. Since then I have carried out considerable research on some of our own British rivers and have found that several of the smaller species of Chironomids are very common indeed. In fact on some stretches of our chalk streams I understand that these small midges are more abundant and common than many other river species including most of the upwinged flies. I have now had several articles published on this subject together with some very imminent authors such as Dermot Wilson and Timothy Benn who have been carrying out independant and corroborating research. When trout are feeding on these tiny midges they will usually be found lying very close to the surface where it is only necessary to tilt their body slightly to raise their head and sup down the pupae or emerging adults as they drift down in or on the surface film. This rise form is also indicative of trout when they are smutting and it is all but impossible to tell the difference. In fact when they are rising in this manner they are often feeding on both small midges and also reed smuts at the same time. In the past when trout were smutting in this manner I used to give them a wide berth, as I knew they were all but impossible to catch. Not these days however, as I now use one of my own patterns called a "Suspender Midge" which when dressed on a very small hook has proved to be a very killing pattern indeed when trout are feeding close to the surface in this manner. This pattern and the methods of fishing it are fully described in the chapter on Flat Winged flies under the heading "Midge Pupae on Rivers".

The only other significantly new method to appear in recent years is a method now generally referred to as "Indicator Fishing". This first appeared and gained favour in the United States whence it spread quickly to New Zealand. So far this has not caught on either in Great Britain or Europe and little is known about it on this side of the Atlantic. This is a method that has been devised to enable the fly fisher to fish an upstream nymph in fast or roily water where it would under normal conditions be all but impossible to detect a take by watching the top of the leader. A forward taper floating fly line is used in conjunction with a standard tapered leader, the length of which depends upon the depth of the river being fished. A small flourescent wool or plastic indicator is secured either to the top of the leader or end of the fly line, which can then be clearly seen even in the roughest of water. While this method may not appeal to the dry fly purist it is certainly a very effective method of fishing rivers with a nymph that would normally only be fishable with a wet fly. In order to fish the nymph near the bottom where it is going to be most effective, it will be necessary to either fish very heavily leaded nymph patterns or alternatively fish a normal nymph with a split shot secured to the leader 12 to 18 inches above it. An interesting alternative is a method now adopted in New Zealand by nymph fishers on the world famous Tongariro river whereby they fish a small Hare & Copper nymph below a large weighted Bug Eye. This Bug Eye nymph is usually dressed on either a No 6 or No 8 hook and the body is formed from Pheasant Tail fibres, with two large heavy metal eyes tied in at the front. You then take about 8 to 12 inches of six pound nylon and tie this round the bend of the Bug Eye hook, to the other end of which you attach your small nymph. This method is now very popular on the Tongariro and I am sure it would prove equally effective on any similar large and fast rivers. Generally speaking the length of your leader should be about twice the depth of the river you are fishing. If you really want to get your nymphs quickly to the bottom, use one of the new braided tapered fast sink leaders with this outfit.

Finally I should like to mention a little tip that I have found extremely useful. I now tend to favour a forward taper fly line for my dry fly or nymph fishing as I find this gives me a little more control particularly over long casts than the more traditional double tapered line. However, even with this line unless you are an exceptional caster 25yds is about the maximum distance you can sensibly expect to cast a dry fly or nymph. Now on most of the rivers that I fish at least 90% of the trout that I cast to are under 20yds, but occasionally one does come across a trout that is rising under the far bank, this will often be a good fish, and it always seems to be on the widest sections of the river, well out of reach of the normal dry fly outfit. Providing the river is no more than 35 or 40yds wide I now have an outfit that will allow me to cover such distances reasonably accurately. I take a normal forward taper line and cut off the first 14yds. On to this I splice a thin running line of braided nylon. In effect this gives me a 14yd shooting head, which any reasonably competent caster should be able to handle and makes distance casts a piece of cake. The interesting fact with this is that to all intents and purposes it is a normal dry fly outfit as in practise the majority of trout to which one casts are under 14yds.

MONTHLY EMERGENCE CHARTS FOR RIVERS COMMON SPECIES ONLY

The following charts have been provided to enable the fly fisher to narrow quickly the species of fly most likely to be seen in any particular month which should prove helpful to those fly fishers visiting other areas or waters for the first time. There is a chart for each month of the fishing season, covering the more common species found on or near the surface (nymphs and other bottom-dwelling species are not included). Many of the species listed apply to periods longer than one month.

APRIL – RIVERS

SCIENTIFIC NAME	COMMOM NAME	TYPE OF WATER	PERIOD OF HATCH	TYPE OF INSECT	BODY SIZE IN MM	BODY COLOUR(S)	WING colour(s)
Baëtis rhodani	Large Dark Olive	all types	between 12 noon and 3 pm	upwinged fly	9–10	dark olive	pale grey
Ephemerella mucronata	European Species	small stony streams	afternoon	upwinged fly	10	brown olive	grey brown
Ecdyonurus torrentis	Large Brook dun	small fast streams	during day or early evenings	upwinged fly	12–16	dark brown	brown mottled
Rhithrogena germanica	March Brown	medium to fast stony rivers	between 12 noon and 3 pm	upwinged fly	12	dull brown	brown mottled
Leptophlebia marginata	Sepia Dun	slow and acid or peaty	late morning	upwinged fly	9–10	dark brown	pale brown
Bibio marci	Hawthorn Fly	terrestrial species	during day	flat-winged fly	10–12	black	dull white
Brachycercus subnubilus	Grannom	medium to fast rivers	early April morning or early after- noon	sedge fly	9–11	grey and green	brown mottled
Perlodes microcephala	Large Stonefly	stony rivers	during day	stonefly	16–23	creamy yellow	chestnut brown
Taeniopteryx nebulosa	February Red	rivers with vegetation	during day	stonefly	7–11	brown to red brown	red brown mottled
Protonemura meyeri	Early brown	swift flowing	during day	stonefly	6–9	brown	grey brown
Chloroperla torrentium	Small Yellow Sally	stony rivers	during day	stonefly	5–8	yellow brown	yellow

SCIENTIFIC NAME	COMMOM NAME	TYPE OF WATER	PERIOD OF HATCH	TYPE OF INSECT	BODY SIZE IN MM	BODY COLOUR(S)	WING colour(s)
Sialis species	Alder Fly	all types	during day	Megaloptera	15	brown	brown mottled
Perla bipunctata (and similar species)	Large Stonefly	fast and stony rivers	during night or early morning	stonefly	16–24	grey brown	chestnut brown
Ephemera danica and vulgata	Mayfly	medium to fast with mud or silt	afternoon	upwinged fly	20–24	creamish; brown marks	greyish; dark veins
Ephemera danica and vulgata	Spent Gnat	medium to fast with mud or silt	early evening	upwinged fly	20–24	pale cream	transparent; black patches
Ephemerella mucronata	European Species	small stony streams	afternoon	upwinged fly	10	brown olive	grey brown
Baëtis muticus	Iron Blue	most medium to fast rivers	during day	upwinged fly	5–6	dark olive brown	dull grey blue
,,	Little Claret Spinner	,,	during day or evening	,,	,,	dark claret brown	transparent
Baëtis vernus	Medium Olive	medium to fast rivers	during day	upwinged fly	7–8	olive brown	dull grey
,,	Medium Olive Spinner	,,	evening	,,	,,	red brown	transparent
Epeorus sylvicola	European Species	fast rivers	during day	upwinged fly		dark green brown stripes	grey
Centroptilum luteolum	Small Spurwing	medium to fast rivers	during day	upwinged fly	6–7	pale olive brown	very pale grey
,,	Little Amber Spinner	,,	evening	,,	,,	pale amber	transparent
Rhithrogena germanica	March Brown	medium to fast stony rivers	between 12 noon and 3 pm	upwinged fly	12	dull brown	brown mottled
Ecdyonurus torrentis	Large Brook Dun	small fast streams	day or early evening	upwinged fly	12–16	dark brown	brown mottled
Rhithrogena semicolorata	Olive Upright	fast or large stony rivers	late afternon/early evening	upwinged fly	9–10	grey olive brown	dark grey blue
,,	Yellow Upright Spinner	,,	evening	,,	,,	dull yellow olive	transparent
Bibio johannis (and similar species)	Black Gnat	terrestrial	during day	flat-winged fly	5–8	brownish black	grey-blue or brownish
Chironomidae species	Midges	all types	afternoon or evening	flat-winged fly	3–6	green, orange-brown or black	transparent
Rhyacophila dorsalis	Sand Fly	medium to fast rivers	during day	sedge fly	variable 10–15	grey to green	brownish with dark marks
Silo nigricornis	Black Sedge	fast rivers	afternoons early evening	sedge fly	8–10	grey black	black
Isoperla grammatica	Yellow Sally	stony rivers or streams	during day	stone fly	8–12	yellow	yellowish green

SCIENTIFIC NAME	COMMOM NAME	TYPE OF WATER	PERIOD OF HATCH	TYPE OF INSECT	BODY SIZE IN MM	BODY COLOUR(S)	WING colour(s)
Ephemera danica and vulgata	Mayfly	medium to fast with mud or silt	afternoon	upwinged fly	20–24	creamish; brown marks	greyish; dark veins
„	Spent Gnat	„	early evening	„	„	pale cream	transparent; black patches
Siphlonurus spp:	Larger Summer Dun	slow flowing rivers	during day	„	16–20	olive with dark brown patches	grey to brown grey
Baëtis vernus	Medium Olive	medium to fast rivers	during day	upwinged fly	7–8	olive brown	dull grey
„	Medium Olive Spinner	„	evening	„	„	red brown	transparent
Ameletus inopinatus		stony rivers	during day	upwinged fly	9–11	dark brown	dark grey
Baëtis fuscatus	Pale Watery	medium to fast streams	during day/ early evening	upwinged fly	5–6	pale watery olive	pale grey
„	Pale Watery Spinner	„	evening	„	„	golden	transparent
Centroptilum luteolum	Small Spurwing	medium to fast rivers	afternoon or early evening	upwinged fly	6–7	pale olive brown	very pale grey
„	Little Amber Spinner	„	evening	„	„	pale amber	transparent
Rhithrogena semicolorata	Olive Upright	fast or large stony rivers	late after-noon/early evening	upwinged fly	9–10	grey olive brown	dark grey blue
„	Yellow Upright Spinner	„	evening	„	„	dull yellow olive	transparent
Caenis species	Anglers' Curse	mainly slow rivers	early morn-ing or evening	upwinged fly	3–5	cream	transparent
„	Caenis Spinner	„	„	„	„	„	„
Bibio johannis	Black Gnat	terrestrial	during day	flat winged fly	5–8	brownish black	grey-blue to brownish
Chironomidae species	Midges	all types	afternoon or evening	flat-winged fly	3–6	green; orange-brown or black	transparent
Simulium species	Reed Smuts	medium to fast rivers	during day	flat-winged fly	2–3	dark brown to black	transparent
Limnephilus lunatus	Cinnamon Sedge	all types	during day/ early evening	sedge fly	12–14	grey with green tinge	yellow to cinnamon
Serocostoma personatum	Welshman's Button	medium to fast streams	during day/ early evening	sedge fly	10–14	grey to black	golden brown
Silo nigricornis	Black Sedge	fast rivers	afternoons early evening	sedge fly	8–10	grey black	black
Rhyacophila dorsalis	Sand Fly	medium to fast rivers	during day	sedge fly	variable 10–15	grey to green	brownish with dark marks
Isoperla grammatica	Yellow Sally	stony rivers or streams	during day	stone fly	8–12	yellow	yellowish green
Perla bipunctata	Large Stonefly	fast and stony rivers	during night/ early morning	stone fly	16–24	grey brown	brown mottled
Chloroperla torrentium	Small Yellow Sally	stony rivers	during day	stonefly	5–8	yellow brown	yellow

SCIENTIFIC NAME	COMMOM NAME	TYPE OF WATER	PERIOD OF HATCH	TYPE OF INSECT	BODY SIZE IN MM	BODY COLOUR(S)	WING colour(s)
Baëtis scambus	Small Dark Olive	medium to fast streams	afternoon or evening	upwinged fly	4–5	dark olive	medium grey
,,	Small Dark Olive Spinner	,,	evening	,,	,,	dark red brown	transparent
Baëtis fuscatus	Pale Watery	medium to fast streams	during day/ early evening	upwinged fly	5–6	pale watery olive	pale grey
,,	Pale Watery Spinner	,,	evening	,,	,,	golden	transparent
Ameletus inopinatus		stony rivers	during day	upwinged fly	9–11	dark brown	dark grey
Ephemerella ignita	Blue Winged Olive	all types	late evening	upwinged fly	9–10	grey olive	dark grey
,,	Sherry Spinner	,,	evening	,,	,,	sherry red	transparent
Centroptilum luteolum	Small Spurwing	medium to fast rivers	afternoon or early evening	upwinged fly	6–7	pale olive brown	very pale grey
,,	Little Amber Spinner	,,	evening	,,	,,	pale amber	transparent
Caenis species	Anglers' Curse	mainly slow rivers	early morn- ing or even- ing	upwinged fly	3–5	cream to brown	transparent
,,	Caenis Spinner	,,	,,	,,	,,	cream	,,
Rhithrogena savoyensis	European Species	small stony rivers	during day	upwinged fly	7–9	yellow brown	grey
Rhithrogena semicolorata	Olive Upright	fast or large stony rivers	late after- noon/early evening	upwinged fly	9–10	grey olive brown	dark grey blue
,,	Yellow Upright Spinner	,,	evening	,,	,,	dull yellow olive	transparent
Bibio johannis	Black Gnat	terrestrial	during day	flat-winged fly	5–8	brownish black	grey-blue to brownish
Chironomidae species	Midges	all types	afternoon or evening	flat-winged fly	3–6	green; orange- brown or black	transparent
Simulium species	Reed Smuts	medium to fast rivers	during day	flat-winged fly	2–3	dark brown to black	transparent
Potamophylax latipennis	Large Cinnamon Sedge	large rivers and streams	late evening	sedge fly	16–18	orange brown	yellow brown mottled
Limnephilus lunatus	Cinnamon Sedge	all types	during day/ early evening	sedge fly	12–14	grey with green tinge	yellow to cinnamon
Isoperla grammatica	Yellow Sally	stony rivers or streams	during day	stone fly	8–12	yellow	yellowish green
Serocostoma personatum	Welshman's Button	medium to fast streams	during day/ early evening	sedge fly	10–14	grey to black	golden brown
Anabolia nervosa	Brown Sedge	all types	evening	sedge fly	12–15	dark brown	brown
Athripsodes cinereus	Brown Silverhorns	medium rivers	late after- noon and evening	sedge fly	8–10	brownish green	narrow and brown

PLUS MANY OTHER SPECIES OF SEDGE FLIES

SCIENTIFIC NAME	COMMOM NAME	TYPE OF WATER	PERIOD OF HATCH	TYPE OF INSECT	BODY SIZE IN MM	BODY COLOUR(S)	WING COLOUR(S)
Baëtis scambus	Small Dark Olive	medium to fast streams	afternoon or evening	upwinged fly	4–5	dark olive	medium grey
,,	Small Dark Olive Spinner	,,	evening	,,	,,	dark red brown	transparent
Baëtis fuscatus	Pale Watery	medium to fast streams	during day/ early evening	upwinged fly	5–6	pale watery olive	pale grey
,,	Pale Watery Spinner	,,	evening	,,	,,	golden	transparent
Ephemerella ignita	Blue Winged Olive	all types	late evening	upwinged fly	9–10	grey olive	dark grey
,,	Sherry Spinner	,,	evening	,,	,,	sherry red	transparent
Bibio johannis	Black Gnat	terrestrial	during day	flat-winged fly	5–8	brownish black	grey-blue to brownish
Chironomidae species	Midges	all types	afternoon or evening	flat-winged fly	3–6	green; orange-brown or black	transparent
Simulium species	Reed Smuts	medium to fast rivers	during day	flat-winged fly	2–3	dark brown to black	transparent
Potamophylax lapitpennis	Large Cinnamon Sedge	larger rivers and streams	late evening	sedge fly	16–18	orange brown	yellow brown mottled
Athripsodes cinereus	Brown Silverhorns	medium rivers	late afternoon and evening	sedge fly	8–10	brownish green	narrow and brown
Isoperla grammatica	Yellow Sally	stony rivers or streams	during day	stone fly	8–12	yellow	yellowish green
Leuctra geniculata	Willow Fly	medium to fast streams and rivers	during day	stone fly	8–11	brownish black	brown mottled
Leuctra fusca	Needle Fly	all types stony rivers	during day	stone fly	6–9	brownish black	brown mottled
Ecdyonurus dispar	Autumn Dun	large fast stony rivers	during day	upwinged fly	11–12	pale olive brown	pale fawn
,,	Great Red Spinner	,,	evening	,,	,,	dark reddish brown	transparent; brown veins
Ecdyonurus venosus	Late March Brown	fast stony rivers	during day	upwinged fly	12–16	red brown	grey brown mottled
,,	Great Red Spinner	,,	evening	,,	,,	dark red brown	transparent brown veins
Halesus radiatus	Caperer	Medium to fast rivers	afternoons and evening	sedge fly	18–20	orange brown	yellow brown mottled
Rhyacophila dorsalis	Sandfly	medium to fast rivers	during day	sedge fly	variable 10–15	grey to green	brownish with dark or white marks
Potamophylax latipennis	Large Cinnamon Sedge	large rivers and streams	late evening	sedge fly	16–18	orange brown	yellow brown mottled
Sericostoma personatum	Welshman's Button	medium to fast streams	during day/ early evening	sedge fly	10–14	grey to black	golden brown

PLUS MANY OTHER SPECIES OF SEDGE FLIES

SCIENTIFIC NAME	COMMOM NAME	TYPE OF WATER	PERIOD OF HATCH	TYPE OF INSECT	BODY SIZE IN MM	BODY COLOUR(S)	WING colour(s)
Baëtis muticus	Iron Blue	most medium to fast rivers	during day	upwinged fly	5–6	dark olive brown	dull grey blue
„	Little Claret Spinner	„	during day or evening	„	„	dark claret brown	transparent
Baëtis vernus	Medium Olive	medium to fast rivers	during day	upwinged fly	7–8	olive brown	dull grey
„	Medium Olive Spinner	„	evening	„	„	red brown	transparent
Baëtis scambus	Small Dark Olive Spinner	medium to fast streams	evening	upwinged fly	4–5	dark red brown	transparent
Chironomidae species	Midges	all types	afternoon or evening	flat-winged fly	3–6	green, orange-brown or black	transparent
Potamophylax lapitpennis	Large Cinnamon Sedge	larger rivers and streams	late evening	sedge fly	16–18	orange brown	yellow brown mottled
Halesus radiatus	Caperer	medium to fast rivers	early or late evening	sedge fly	18–20	orange brown	yellow brown mottled
Anabolia nervosa	Brown Sedge	all types	evening	sedge fly	12–15	dark brown	brown
Leuctra geniculata	Willow Fly	medium to fast streams and rivers	during day	stone fly	8–11	brownish black	brown mottled
Leuctra fusca	Needle Fly	all types stony rivers	during day	stone fly	6–9	brownish black	brown mottled
Ecdyonurus dispar	Autumn Dun	large fast stony rivers	during day	upwinged fly	11–12	pale olive brown	pale fawn
„	Great Red Spinner	„	evening	„	„	dark reddish brown	transparent; brown veins

PLUS MANY OTHER SPECIES OF SEDGE FLIES

CHAPTER 11

STILLWATER FISHERIES

During the past thirty years stillwater fly-fishing in Great Britain has enjoyed an increasing popularity, undoubtedly due to more water becoming available. We are indebted to the various Water Authorities and Boards for the majority of these, as fortunately for the angler, they have finally realized that a steady and remunerative income is to be earned from the angler for fishing in their reservoirs. This fact, combined with present day thinking by most local authorities to provide as many recreational facilities as possible, means that more and more stillwaters will become available in future.

One of the first and certainly the most famous of these is without doubt Chew Valley lake in Somerset. When this comparatively large sheet of water first opened in 1956 the fishing was incredibly good and within a very short time was advertised as the finest trout fishery in Europe. It retained this reputation for a number of years, and even today the fishing is still very good. The chief architect of the success of this particular venture was Mr Kennedy Brown of the Bristol Waterworks Company, and as a result he was, for many years, in constant demand by other authorities throughout the country in an advisory capacity, and I think it should be realized that fly fishermen in general owe him a considerable debt of gratitude. I have quoted this particular case as an example, but would like to point out there are also many other personalities that have achieved success in this field equally worthy of our gratitude.

More recently we have seen the opening of other waters at Grafham and Rutland in Northamptonshire, where the first two weeks of trout fishing can only be described as fabulous; during this period even inexperienced fly fishermen were taking the limit bag of eight trout, most of which were in excess of two-and-a-half pound. Furthermore, quite a large percentage of fish over four pounds and some over five were taken in this period, and when one considers that none of these fish were more than about three years old, the growth rate can only be considered as phenomenal. Unfortunately, this honeymoon period (some referred to it as the duffer's fortnight) did not last for long and by the end of their first season both waters had settled down to giving limit bags only to those fishermen with sufficient experience to attain them.

From the above it will doubtless be apparent that most new reservoirs which are constructed by flooding agricultural land and stocked with trout enjoy a period varying between several months to several years where the size and condition of the trout are well above average. This variation is usually due to two factors, (*a*) the richness, or otherwise, of the newly flooded land and (*b*) the spasmodic rise and fall of the water, and the subsequent regularity with which any shallow areas are left high and dry to fructify in the open air under the direct rays of the sun, thus reinvigorating its complement of living vegetation. A further contributory factor that usually leads to a quick deterioration in the condition of trout stock is the infiltration of unwanted coarse fish.

It is interesting to note that although the fishing and the size of most of the trout in many of these man-made waters tend to deteriorate, there are occasionally exceptions to this general rule. Three of these in particular that come to mind are: Two Lakes in Hampshire, a private fishery run by that genial expert on trout culture, Alex Behrendt, and his wife Katharine. The size of the trout in this fishery has in fact increased over the years, and in this case it would seem to be due to correct fishery management plus particular reference to the culture of the correct living creatures on which trout thrive. In fairness to other management I would like to point out that these lakes are comparatively small, and to carry out the same type of programme on very much larger waters may be a formidable proposition.

The second exception is Hanningfield reservoir in Essex. This is a very large sheet of water and has now been stocked with trout for several years. In this case also the fishing and average size of the trout has improved tremendously since it was first opened to anglers several years ago. This, at first sight, would not appear to be a particularly promising reservoir as there does not seem to be a large annual rise and fall in water level, and it is therefore a little difficult to acertain the reason for the excellent results that have been obtained here. Originally, the trout were introduced into this water to combat the very large numbers of insects that had become established and which were proving a nuisance to both the water authority and the surrounding inhabitants. Perhaps the fact that the aquatic insect population had become firmly entrenched before trout were introduced has proved to be the answer in this case. On the other hand, a further factor may be the high alkalinity of the water, combined with the extremely large amount that is pumped in daily.

Finally, I would mention a slightly different example. Many of the lakes and reservoirs in Wales are of a barren nature or have waters high in acid content. These conditions are naturally not conductive to the growing of large trout. Consequently, the majority of these waters, although well stocked and providing good fishing, rarely produce large trout. Yet a reservoir opened some time ago near Port Talbot in South Wales has over the past few seasons produced an astonishing number of very large trout!

Apart from reservoirs other potential sources of trout fishing are the growing number of gravel pits dotted around the countryside, and over the past few years many of these suitable for holding trout have been acquired either by commercial operators clubs or private syndicates. As in the majority of cases these types of waters are dependent on constant restocking to provide the maximum sport, it is to the lakes and lochs in the more inaccessible parts of these islands that we have to look for our natural trout fishing. A fair proportion of such waters hold a good head of naturally bred trout, but usually the average size of these is considerably lower than in those waters that are carefully restocked. Nevertheless, there are a few noted exceptions, most of which are either in Scotland or Ireland. Typical of these are such famous waters as Loughs Corrib, Mask, Conn and Loch Leven.

During the last two decades considerable progress has been made in fishing techniques and tactics as applied to stillwater fishing, consequently many new artificial patterns of flies have been developed, and a considerable number of these have now proved to be very popular and killing patterns under the right conditions. In my opinion we are now, like the fly fishermen in the middle of the last century, on the threshold of an era where our whole approach to stillwater fishing may be influenced by discoveries and methods yet to be introduced. In substantiation, the advances in river fly fishing in the last one hundred and fifty years corresponds in no little measure to the vast fund of literature that has been published over the same period, during which, at least until 1953, very little of value had been written on stillwater fishing, with correspondingly little progress being made in its technique.

If anyone should require further proof of this it is only necessary to compare the development of artificial flies since the beginning of the century and up to the last war. Let us first consider river angling. Literally hundreds of new patterns have been published and developed, many of which are now virtually household names. Among these are many that were perfected by such angling giants of their day as the immortal Halford, Skues and Lunn. In contrast, I have been unable to discover many examples of significant lake patterns that have appeared in the same period. Apart from many excellent modern ones developed in the last few years, nearly all the famous patterns of lake flies with which we are so familiar, such as the Peter Ross, Alexandra, Butcher, Teal Blue and Silver, and Silver Doctor — to mention just a few — were developed in the last century. None of these patterns are, or were, intended as close imitations of natural flies or insects, although undoubtedly some of them do loosely simulate certain naturals and are no doubt taken by the trout as such. Before I proceed further, let me assure the reader that I am not in any way decrying any of these artificials as, after all, they have stood the test of time and many are excellent killing patterns under the right conditions. I personally refer to most of these types of artificials as "general patterns", and even today some of them will be found in my fly box. However, I do feel that the future of stillwater fishing probably lies in a combination of close imitation plus correct presentation.

In addition to the types of artificials mentioned above, there are also a few of what I term fancy patterns or lures that were popularized during the same period; I have little time for these, but this is purely a personal viewpoint and I should not like to feel that I am influencing other anglers against their use if they feel so justified. As most of these are very colourful and fairly large, I think that many of them originated from salmon or sea trout patterns, as it must be remembered that our forbears consistently fished for salmon and sea trout as well as for brown trout in many of the Scottish and Irish stillwaters even as we do to this day.

At this stage, I feel that the phrase "stillwater" should be clarified. The modern trend seems to be to refer to all bodies of water, whether they be lakes, lochs or reservoirs, etc., as stillwater. It must be appreciated, however, that this is a generalization, as of course nearly all areas of water, except for small stagnant ponds, have some movement of water, caused by inlets, outlets, wind or temperature.

The modern approach to lake fishing (in future, for the sake of brevity, where applicable I shall refer to all reservoirs, lakes, lochs, etc., as stillwater) really began with T. C. Iven's book *Still Water Fly Fishing*, published in 1953, although I think it only fair to point out that the first tremors probably started way back in 1924 with R. C. Bridgetts' book, *Loch Fishing in Theory and Practice*, in which he constantly emphasizes the necessity of recognizing the food on which trout feed and the importance of applying this knowledge in a sensible way to the patterns of one's choice. More recently we have seen the publication of books by C. F.

Walker entitled *Lake Flies and their Imitation*, an excellent work which I look upon as the first major step forward in the history of stillwater fishing, together with the thought-provoking book *Lake and Loch Fishing* by Col. Joscelyn Lane. However, it is only in the last fifteen years or so that the really major advances in methods and techniques have taken place, starting with the excellent book by Brian Clarke *The Pursuit of Stillwater Trout*. Since this was published in 1975 we have been served with a great number of books which have added immensely to our knowledge of stillwater fishing. Among the many worthy of particular mention are — *Reservoir Trout Fishing* by Bob Church. *Boat Fishing for Trout* by Steve Parton, *Bank Fishing for Reservoir Trout* by Jim Calver, *Fishing for Lake Trout* by Conrad Voss Bark and *Trout from Stillwaters* by Peter Lapsley.

To the beginner, on his first attempt to fish stillwater (unless trout are actually rising), the prospect may appear to be most disheartening, and under these conditions — if he has no one present to advise him and has a blank day — he is often, unfortunately, turned away from this type of fishing for life. I would, therefore, strongly recommend the erstwhile beginner to ensure that at least on his first outing he is accompanied by a fly fisherman experienced in this particular art, although I must point out that even the expert does have the odd blank day. Unfortunately, the image of the stillwater fisherman that has existed over the years is that of either the boat fisherman constantly casting and retrieving a short line along the surface with no apparent rhyme or reason, or the bank fisherman standing up to his thighs in the water all day casting a long sinking line with monotonous regularity. It is not to be denied that in fact a fair percentage of anglers do fish in this manner and catch fish, and if they obtain a maximum of enjoyment by so doing it would be a disservice to influence them otherwise. However, it is a great pity that this image persists, as it is very far from reflecting the true enjoyment that is to be found by or on our stillwaters.

Without doubt, persistence and patience are two very important words in the lake fisher's vocabulary no matter how he fishes, although this applies in particular to anglers who fish by the two methods described above. It is probably true that many of these anglers catch their quota of fish and some, on occasion, may even do better than the expert who endeavours to present an imitation in the correct manner, but on balance my money would be placed on the latter every time. On many occasions I have heard the view expressed that lake fishing is purely "chuck it and chance it", as, except when the trout are rising, the fisherman has no idea of their location. This is far from the truth, as an angler who is familiar with the stillwater he is fishing will know from past experience where the fish are most likely to be, under given conditions. Apart from this, most bodies of stillwater have certain features that to the experienced eye will be obvious lies for fish under certain conditions. These are weed beds, shallow banks in deep water, deep channels or ditches in shallow water, old hedgerows or the flooded roads that often form part of the bed, inlets, outlets or areas in the vicinity of natural springs which feed some stillwaters. The list is unending, but as a typical example I would like to relate a personal experience that happened several years ago. At the time I was on a week's fishing holiday in the West Country, and during most of this period I concentrated on trout fishing on a local reservoir. This was in late summer and the fishing was not particularly good and, although I had managed to get a few nice trout during the evenings, the mornings and afternoons had been disappointing. Despite my own lack of success and that of many other anglers with whom I passed the time of day, it was particularly noticeable that one or two fly fisherman in a relatively restricted area along one bank were enjoying consistently good sport during this dour period. Upon closer examination I observed in this area what appeared to be some tree stumps showing slightly above the surface of the water and determined to return early the next morning to give this spot a try. I was fortunate next day in obtaining a place, and had an excellent day's sport, grassing several very nice trout of grand proportions. My earliest suspicions that they were tree stumps and roots were confirmed, as before I commenced fishing I was able to wade out to within a rod's distance of the nearest of them, to find that they were harbouring vast shoals of sticklebacks. Using an artificial stickleback pattern, success was assured. Many times since I have fished this particular spot in this reservoir, but it only fishes consistently well during the latter part of the summer, when the sticklebacks are most in evidence.

Since the early days of fly fishing, stillwaters have been looked upon as the beginner's happy hunting grounds, and no angler of experience would deny that on a certain days trout in stillwater almost give themselves up. On these occasions the beginner is as likely to do as well or even better than the expert, depending largely on luck. Circumstances such as this seldom, if ever, apply on the river, as the expert will rarely depart with an empty creel, whereas the beginner will often fish hard for days on end with nary a single fish to reward his efforts. No doubt it is this fact, and this alone, that has given rise to this opinion. It is most unfortunate that this appraisal of stillwater fishing still prevails, although in latter years it seems to be on the wane, due no doubt to increased interest in the subject. The fact that most bodies of stillwater do provide occasional days when the fish are easy is just as well, as it does ensure that the inexperienced angler is given a certain amount of encouragement. On the other hand, blank days are far more prevalent on stillwater than on rivers and on these occasions it is usually the expert who will get the odd fish. From the small amount of literature available on this subject it would appear that blank days were far more prevalent earlier in the century than they are nowadays, and doubtless this is due to the progress in recent years in fish culture and in the understanding of the entomology of stillwater which has resulted in many new artificial patterns being developed.

As suggested, it is my view that the slow advance in the technique of lake fishing until comparatively recently can largely be accounted for by the lack of interest in the insects and other fauna which, after all, provide the bulk of food for the trout. It would, therefore, appear that at least a working knowledge of entomology should increase one's chances of success. Some anglers may deem it necessary to make a fairly detailed study of this subject, and although I must admit that this can become most absorbing and fascinating, a little basic knowledge should suffice for the average fly fisherman. Therefore, I trust that this book will provide enough information for the enthusiast without confusing the uninitiated.

In the preface I mentioned that this was to be basically a book on flies and, except for suggesting artificials and fishing methods to be used in conjunction with definite species of insects, I intended to keep it this way. However, in view of the rapidly increasing interest in stillwater fishing I felt it prudent after all to give a short résumé of various facets of stillwater fishing that may be of some interest to the beginner or to those experienced river fisherman who have decided to try their hand at this particular branch of our sport, as much of this information is relatively new. I am sure it will also be of considerable interest to many of our European cousins, as up to comparitively recently stillwater trout fishing was practically unheard of in many countries in Europe.

CHAPTER 12

STILLWATER FISHING TECHNIQUES

BOAT FISHING

Over the years much controversy has raged as to whether boat or bank fishing on stillwaters is more successful. Experience emboldens me to suggest that on average more trout are caught by the boat angler, but the bigger ones are usually caught by the angler from the bank, and this seems to be the view expressed by most competent fishermen. Both these methods of fishing require completely different techniques, and although the boat angler may be rather restricted in the way that he fishes his flies, he does cover during a day's fishing a much greater area of undisturbed water, and is able to fish large areas that are inaccessible to the bank angler; hence his heavier creel on most occasions. Some fly fishers prefer boat fishing and some prefer bank fishing and a few can enjoy both equally. Nowadays I do not mind either, in contrast to my former preference for bank fishing.

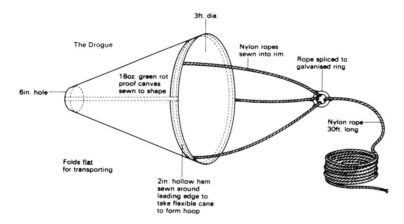

83 The drogue

Perhaps, as one gets older, the little luxuries of life become more desirable, and there is no doubt that the boat is far more comfortable and less fatiguing than the bank. Some hired boats are equipped with a drogue (see fig. 83), a most useful item, as not only does it slow the rate of drift but virtually eliminates yawing. Also the direction of drift may be controlled to a certain extent according to the position at which the drogue is attached to the boat. Normally it is secured to the side of the boat, but in high winds it is a good idea to secure it to the bow or stern. The boat will then drift slower and be more stable. When used in this manner one angler sits in the bow and one in the stern, facing in different directions, each casting at an angle over his right shoulder. In this way each angler will also find he

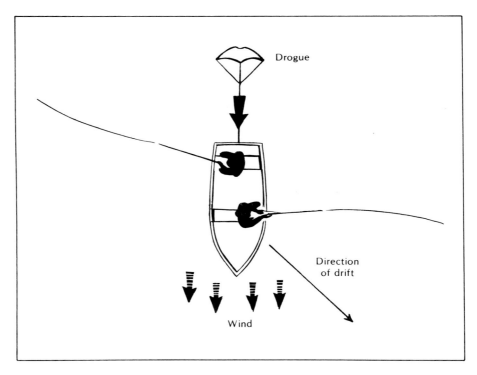

84 When surface fishing with floating lines, cast across the
wind and immediately commence the retrieve

can cover a very wide arc on his side of the boat. This method is equally effective
with sinking or floating lines (see fig. 82).

Most anglers are aware of the frightening effect that vibration has on fish, and
this is particularly applicable when fishing from a boat; for this reason movement
should be minimized as far as possible, and it is a good idea to wear soft shoes. The
use of these also reduces possible damage to your line, as in the process of being
retrieved, it inevitably lies in the bottom of the boat.

It is usual when boat fishing to be accompanied by a friend and, providing one's
sole aim in life is not to catch as many trout as possible in a day's fishing, the
companionship can add greatly to the enjoyment. I would, however, respectfully
suggest that one's companion in a boat is chosen with a little care, as to have an
inexperienced fly fisher in the close confines of a boat with you is, to say the least,
risky, as a team of relatively large lake flies on the end of a cast can be quite
dangerous. It should be made quite clear, tactfully of course, to whomever is with
you that the cast should always be made at right angles to the boat; the only
exception to this rule is during a surface rise, when you may require to cast to a
fish in any direction. Under these circumstances the back cast must be kept high,
and also both of you must be quite certain of each others' intentions. At dusk,
during a late evening rise, this can be a little tricky and it is, therefore, an
advantage to observe a pre-arranged verbal signal which will give advance
warning that one is about to change the direction of the cast.

As previously mentioned, one is rather restricted in the method of fishing a fly
from a boat, and over the years and at least until recently there has been little

advance in technique. The old loch fishers of days gone by usually advocated a long, light rod which allowed them to fish a reasonable length of line without false casting or fatigue, working, no doubt, on the principle that the longer your flies are fishing the better your chances, and so far as any stillwater fishing is concerned this is sound common sense. The long rod also allows you to bounce your top dropper along the surface in a most enticing manner. An expert fishing in such a manner is indeed a pleasure to watch but, unfortunately, nowadays one sees less and less of this style of fishing, the modern trend seeming to favour a shorter rod with frequent false casting to achieve distance, and in many cases you will find an angler standing up and casting from a boat. This presents a much larger silhouette and more movement than a seated angler, and merely puts down fish over a larger radius. Another point which probably only a few anglers realize is that the extra rhythm required for false casting will invariably cause the boat to rock, and this in turn sends out waves in a radius from the boat which is often sufficient to put a trout down. Should anyone doubt this statement, let them take a boat out on a flat calm when fish are rising well, and they will find that the area of water around the boat which often seems empty of rising trout will be broadened considerably when standing up to cast.

The wind is as important a factor in boat fishing as it is in bank fishing. Probably most experienced boat fishers will agree that a steady breeze is preferable to a flat calm, and during such latter conditions it is a good idea to try to locate a slight ripple, which may indicate an area that is receiving a slight breeze from some direction. The edge of such a ripple is often well worth fishing. When the winds are strong, foam or wind lanes tend to form and, as the trout sometimes follow them in their search for food, it often pays dividends to fish along them.

The sun as well as the wind is an important factor in boat fishing, and when it is directly behind you when on the drift, the trout often "come short" and are difficult to hook. A longer, or an across–wind roll–cast instead of one down–wind, will often prove effective in overcoming the problem.

The successful boat angler relies first of all on the correct choice of artificial fly, and combines this with an intimate knowledge of the water he is fishing, particularly where fish are to be found at any given time under any existing conditions.

Finally, it is worth mentioning that a present technique which seems to be gaining converts is the use of a sinking line and a lure cast to maximum distance and retrieved at speed from either an anchored or drifting boat. That this method catches fish is not to be denied, but it has no appeal for me. However, fishing a team of pupae or a nymph from an anchored boat with a floating or sink tip line, can under the right conditions be very rewarding.

BOAT FISHING TECHNIQUES

Since the late 1960s, tremendous advances have been made in boatfishing techniques on stillwater. While one or two of these methods are to say the least somewhat controversial, and in fact are now banned on many stillwaters, I have decided to give full details as on waters where there are no restrictions fly fishers may wish to experiment and decide for themselves which techniques are acceptable to their own personal standards.

204

Trolling

While it is debatable whether or not this method can be construed as fly fishing, there is no doubt it accounts for a lot of trout where it is permissible. Although trolling or trailing a fly from the back of a slowly moving boat is in itself not new and requires little expertise, the same cannot be said about the latest techniques now being employed. Some fly fishermen have developed trolling into a highly skilled operation, making full use of the wide variety of modern fly lines now available. The first requirement is to find out what level or depth in the water the trout are feeding, and this can be established by trial and error or from personal experience of conditions at the time. It will then be necessary to mount the correct fly line — a floating, slow sink or sink tip line if they are feeding on or near the surface, a fast sink line for midwater or for trolling along or near the bottom, in waters of medium depth a HI-D or one of the new super fast sinking fly lines. For trolling in very deep water many anglers now use shooting heads formed from lead cored line, used in conjunction with large lures often in excess of six inches in length. Within the last two years this latter method alone has accounted for many exceptionally large brown trout, which up to a point justifies its use, as these are probably fish that seldom leave the sanctuary of very deep water and are unlikely to be caught by traditional fly fishing methods. Apart from the importance of choosing the correct fly line for trolling, the area or depth of water to be fished must also be taken into account. The movement of the boat in relation to the lines you are trolling must also be seriously considered. For instance, an exaggerated zig-zag course will cover a greater area of water, while a sharp zig-zag will cause the lure to sink and rise again in an enticing way at each alteration of course. It is also worth noting that, under windy conditions, it is often more effective to troll across the wind. The experienced troller will also take into account the type of fly or lure to be used, and his choice will be dictated by the type of food upon which he thinks the trout may be feeding at the time. This may vary from patterns to represent sedge pupae, leeches or fry and small fish up to as much as six or eight inches in length.

Lead Cored and HI-D Super Fast Sinking Lines

In the latter half of the summer small fish leave the shallows and tend to congregate in deeper water along the edges of dam walls, valve towers or any obstructions in the water. These areas are usually inaccessible to bank anglers, and even from a boat it is not possible to present your fly by traditional methods to the large trout that are often to be found feeding in their immediately locality. The answer to this problem lies in the use of the above relatively new lines. Make up a shooting head from either of these lines, very short — seven to eight yards if you are using the lead cored — as it is difficult to cast with a longer length. Mount a very large white marabou type lure (one six inches in length is not too big) on a short leader, and anchor the boat just within maximum casting distance of the wall or tower. Try to cast your lure so that it just hits the structure, and immediately strip off four or five yards of backing under tension. If you have executed the movement correctly your lure will be pulled directly underwater down the front of the wall, and will be taken on the drop. Usually the first indication you will have that a fish has accepted your offering will be the sight of a trout leaping high out of the water. While it is still necessary to watch the backing entering the water from your rod tip it is seldom necessary to strike as most of these fish will hook themselves. For this style of fishing always use a strong point on your leader, at least seven pounds test, as it will often account for some of the biggest trout in the water. These super fast sinking lines may also be used in a similar way from a drifting boat. Utilizing a drift control rudder or drogue streaming from the stern of the boat, cast your line out at ninety degrees to the drift of the boat, and feed out several yards or backing until you feel your line hit the bottom. If you them immediately commence the retrieve the lure will start to come back to you in the opposite direction to the path of the boat for at least a few

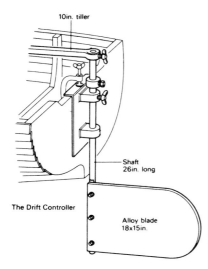

10in. tiller

Shaft
26in. long

The Drift Controller

Alloy blade
18x15in.

85 The drift controller

seconds. It will the suddenly change direction, and this will often prove to be the undoing of many trout, who have been used for much of the season to following the same old lures moving in the same direction.

The Drift Controller
This in reality is a large rudder which is clamped to the transom of the boat, and was originally developed by those two maestros of the stillwater scene, Bob Church and Dick Shrive. Few boats available for stillwater trout fishing are fitted with rudders, and even where they may be found the conventional type is hardly large enough to give the degree of control essential for this relatively new technique. It will therefore be necessary to construct your own. The actual blade of the rudder should be about 18ins x 14ins and this is slotted and riveted into a steel shaft about ⅝in diameter (see fig. 85). Brackets are then formed to take the shaft and these should be welded or riveted onto a plate which is used to clamp the contraption to the stern of the boat. These brackets should be drilled and tapped to take two large wing bolts which may be tightened by the operator to lock the rudder in any desired position, providing the required direction of drift. Finally, a short bar to form the tiller handle is made to clamp on top of the shaft.

A drift controller can only be used in winds of light to medium strength; in a strong wind it is useless, as the rate of drift will be far too fast. The main use of the rudder or controller under the right conditions is to enable the fisherman to gain some semblance of control over the direction of the drift. In more expansive days this was the job of the gillie using his oars. With the rudder this can be accomplished equally well and of course much more silently, and in addition leaves both fishermen in the boat free to concentrate on their casting without the encumbrance of a third person aboard. The amount of control given by the rudder is surprisingly good, and although the basic drift will still be found to be downwind, quite a reasonable angle down or across wind can be accomplished with a little practice. This will enable you to keep the boat roughly parallel to any shore or dam wall a given distance out, and will also allow you to follow the contours of the bank or underwater shoals (see fig. 86).

The Leeboard

This is another idea that came from the inventive mind of that most accomplished stillwater trout angler, Dick Shrive. Like many good ideas it is basically simple, and the only materials required are a plank 5ft 6ins in length, about 12ins in width, and approximately 1in in thickness, plus a large G clamp. The leeboard is clamped to the curved section of the bow on the lee side of the boat (the downwind side), hence its name. When in position, it projects well below the keel of the boat and acts like a centreboard on a sailing boat. The wind blowing into the side of the boat tries to push the boat directly downwind while water pressure on the other side of the board endeavours to prevent it. The net result of these two forces operating against one another forces a compromise, so the boat drifts across and only slowly downwind. With the leeboard in position the wind, often your enemy, can be turned into an ally, as the boat can be held over chosen areas for much longer periods. For example, you may wish to fish a productive section of shallow water immediately offshore. If the wind is blowing directly onto or offshore you will drift over this very quickly, but with your leeboard in position you will be pushed across it, and if you turn the boat smartly and refix the board in the same position on the other side of the bow, you will probably succeed in tacking back again before running ashore or into deeper water.

When using the leeboard, both anglers should fish downwind, but extra care must be taken by the fisherman in the upwind position, as it is only too easy to hook the other angler when casting. For this style of fishing, lures or flasher patterns should be used, as the retrieve should be fairly fast. If you wait too long after casting or retrieve too slowly, your fly line and flies will be swept astern of the boat, and tangle with the keel or other projections. If your retrieve and timing is correct the fly will be presented to the trout diagonally across the path of the wind and will be clear of the disturbed water over which your boat has just drifted (see fig. 86). On occasions this can be a most effective method of fishing, as trout, especially rainbows, seem to take a fly which is moving across their path more confidently than one being retrieved directly upwind, which is more often than not the case from a boat drifting directly downwind in the conventional manner.

A word of warning; a leeboard can be a dangerous tool in the hands of an inexperienced person, so it should never be used unless the following points are strictly adhered to. Never attempt to use one in very strong winds or if there are a lot of other boats, particularly yachts, in the vicinity. Do not stand up in a boat with a board fitted as they tend to be less stable. Never try fitting your board on the upwind side, and above all do not attempt to turn the boat around to go on the other tack with the board in position; remove it, well before you turn and do not reclamp until the boat has been completely reversed. Apart from the above points, care should be taken not to cross the paths of other boats drifting downwind in the traditional style as it is, to put it mildly, most discourteous to

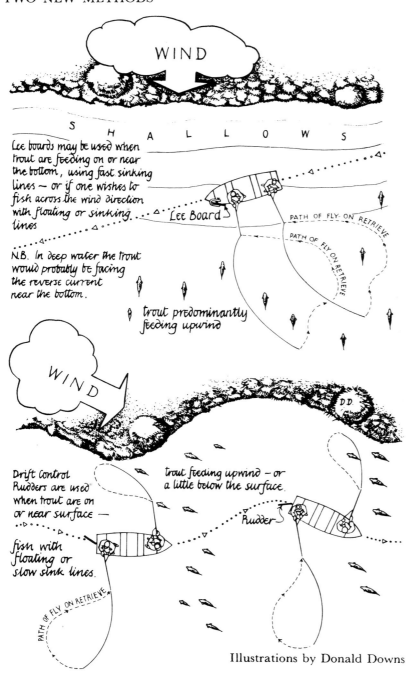

WIND

S H A L L O W S

Lee boards may be used when trout are feeding on or near the bottom, using fast sinking lines — or if one wishes to fish across the wind direction with floating or sinking lines

Lee Board

PATH OF FLY ON RETRIEVE

PATH OF FLY ON RETRIEVE

N.B. In deep water the trout would probably be facing the reverse current near the bottom.

trout predominantly feeding upwind

WIND

D.D.

Drift Control Rudders are used when trout are on or near surface —

trout feeding upwind — or a little below the surface.

Rudder

fish with floating or slow sink lines.

PATH OF FLY ON RETRIEVE

Illustrations by Donald Downs

86 Two methods for boat fishing techniques

disturb the water over which they will shortly be fishing. Leeboards are now banned on many waters, as many authorities now consider they are too dangerous or encourage the illegal practice of trailing which unfortunately is all too easy from a boat on the move in this manner. On those waters where they are allowed, the leeboard itself when not in use makes a most comfortable seat when placed across the thwarts.

Fishing at Anchor

To me the cream of stillwater fishing is to fish Loch style from a drifting boat with a team of three flies, particularly when the trout are feeding on or close to the surface. I think that heart stopping moment when a big trout rises to one of your flies and follows it towards the boat is probably unsurpassed in any form of fishing. Despite this, sad to relate it seems that the modern trend favours fishing from an anchored boat. Certainly at anchor one has far more options, such as fishing deep sunk nymphs or various imitative patters or lures close to the bottom with sinking lines.

At times of course one has little option, as in very heavy winds or flat calms drift fishing can be most unproductive, so let us look at some of the more sophisticated methods that have been evolved in the last two decades.

Prior to this most fly fishers when anchoring were content to fish from a boat anchored amidship, which quite frankly is most unproductive as the boat when anchored thus will yaw from side to side which makes it all but impossible to work your flies properly. Most boats for hire on stillwater are supplied with an anchor of some sort but today most experienced stillwater fly fishers take an additional anchor with with them as two anchors several different options are available. However if you find yourself with only one anchor there are two methods one can adopt that will provide you with a more stable platform from which to fish.

Method 1 is to secure the anchor rope to a corner of the stern and then for each angler to fish from opposite sides of the boat – casting over the right shoulder (see fig. 87) the position one adopts in the boat will depend upon the prevailing current.

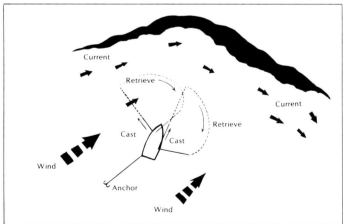

87 With their boat anchored by the stern about 10 yds offshore, these anglers are in the perfect position to make full use of both wind and current which will work their lines around in an arc and cause their flies to cover a large area

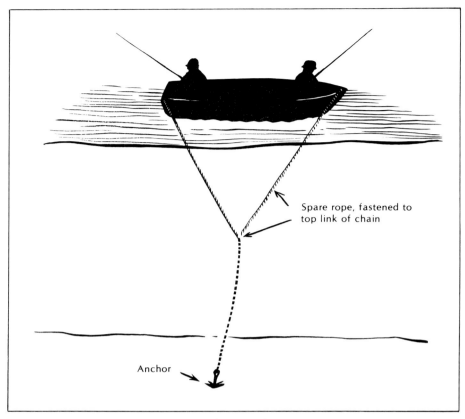

Spare rope, fastened to
top link of chain

Anchor

88 Anchoring broadside on to the wind. Fasten the spare
rope to the chain, using the shackle, to hold one end of
the boat. The other is secured by the double rope. This
will hold the boat firm and steady even in the strongest
winds but it is not recommended for very rough
conditions, when it is safer to anchor bow into the wind

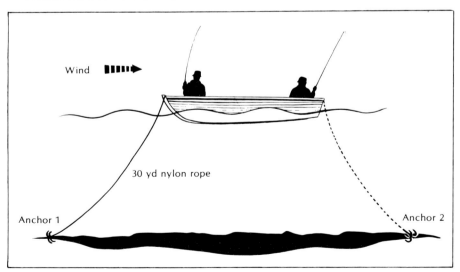

Wind

30 yd nylon rope

Anchor 1

Anchor 2

89 The "Anchor 1" position is the safest in a strong wind
and high wave, and is ideal for fishing lines and for
sinking line techniques in any depth. "Anchor 2" may be
put out over the stern to eliminate swing and provide a
more stable platform. That can be important for slow
nymph fishing when sensitive control of fly line is
necessary

Method 2 requires that you carry a short length of rope which can then be secured half-way up the anchor rope which will then give you two securing points one at the stern and one at the bow (see fig. 88) this will hold the boat much steadier than a single securing point.

With two good anchors a boat can be held with little or no movement at all even in the heaviest of winds, furthermore if the anchors are placed correctly the boat can be held at almost any position in relation to the wind (see fig. 89). While it may be more comfortable to anchor the boat broadside and to fish downwind, it may at times depending upon the prevailing current to position the boat across the wind. The reason for this is that most stillwater trout tend to feed either up wind or up current when it is strong enough, so in this position you are more likely to be retrieving your fly across the path of incoming trout which often proves more effective.

COMPETITION FISHING

Up to the last decade the only trout fishing competitions to be held were the annual boat fishing internationals held between England, Wales, Scotland and Ireland, however since then we have seen the introduction of many more trout fishing competitions including the Benson & Hedges Internationals and more recently the World Fly Fishing Championships which includes a boat fishing section. Personally I am not in favour of trout fishing competitions, as in the first place I look upon trout fishing as a contemplative sport where the enjoyment of a day in the countryside is a reward in itself with the fishing as a distinct bonus. Secondly and even more important competitive trout fishing results in considerable publicity both for the individual and team winners and with no restrictions on limits this usually results in photographs of piles of dead trout killed in the name of sport. This provides lethal ammunition for the various anti-angling lobbies, animal rights groups and the league against cruel sports. I believe at the moment their is talk about fishing all these competitions in future under catch and release rules which would I think make them acceptable. It is interesting to note that under the very strict international boat fishing rules which limits the various techniques rather drastically, some competitors have now developed some new and interesting techniques within these rules that have proved to be very effective. Unfortunately I am unable to elaborate on these new methods as I have to respect my source of information.

BANK FISHING

These days, with the increasing popularity of stillwater fishing, the banks of our more popular waters are often crowded with lines of fishermen, sometimes barely twenty yards apart. Wading, which is fairly general, has created a paradox because the disturbance sends the fish further from the bank, thus making it necessary for the angler to wade out still further, which in turn drives the fish still further away; this consequently has created a necessity for casting greater distances in order to be successful. This seems a great pity, because if bank anglers could be pursuaded not to wade at all it would be possible on many occasions to catch trout quite close to the shore. Unfortunately, human nature being what it is, one or two anglers in a crowd will always be found disregarding a code of behaviour, and naturally if one or two wade, all must wade.

Many times in the past, when I have been fortunate to find a secluded section of bank, I have fished from and along it without entering the water and caught some very big trout. This can be particularly rewarding in the latter part of the season when there are not so many anglers about, and the larger trout are feeding on stickleback or corixa. It is significant that I have caught trout in water so shallow that it barely covers their backs as they voraciously pursue the shoals of fry right into the margins of the lake. When fishing the banks in this manner the angler should always be watchful of his movements and where possible utilize any available background to obscure his whereabouts, or he will find he is putting down more fish than he is able to cover.

The bank fisher, when wading, should always remember that it is a very easy matter to scare the fish out of casting range either by careless wading or clumsy casting. One often observes the bank angler walking out into the water as if he has a train to catch and, on doing so, sending out a bow wave like a barge! Not content with this he then commences to cast, laying the line down on the water so hard that every self-respecting trout departs for the other side of the lake. Wading should always be executed very slowly, carefully placing one foot in front of the other with the minimum of disturbance. It is also circumspect to transfer your weight slowly to the forward foot, or alternatively to use a specially made wading net fitted with a long shaft, as many lakes have potholes or areas of soft mud and it is a very simple matter to take one step forward and find oneself submerged.

It is a good practice, when commencing to cast from whatever position has been selected, to start off with a short line and while fishing between casts to gradually lengthen it successively until the desired distance is attained. Simultaneously one should cover a frontal arc to ensure that the maximum area is thoroughly worked with your flies. Furthermore, an angler's silhouette is so reduced when standing in the water up to his thighs that it is not surprising that, with care, rising trout can be approached quite closely. Of course, care should also be taken in casting and, particularly when fishing a short line, to use a side cast to reduce the movement of the rod against the skyline.

During the evening rise, which is often of short duration, it is a good idea to carry spare flies and accessories in either a haversack over the shoulder or, better still, a hip bag on a belt which can be slid around to the front when required. In addition to this it is necessary to provide some means of retaining any trout caught, and this can be accomplished by fashioning a simple wire hook and hanging it from the bag ring or belt. The angler, thus equipped, obviates the necessity of returning to dry land after netting a trout, thereby creating a disturbance and also wasting precious time. Unfortunately, in some cases, part of this operation may be in vain if you have anglers on either side of you who do not observe the same care.

It has already been stated that the bank fisherman has far more scope in the presentation of his flies to the trout, but I do not intend to elaborate on this for the moment. The different techniques to be used for relating natural creatures to their imitations has already been covered.

Due to variable conditions it is difficult to suggest any set pattern of rules to assist the bank fisher in the locating of fish throughout the season or even during a single day, but to generalize I would venture to suggest the following. During the early spring, before the water has warmed, it is usually better to concentrate in the areas of deeper water. The same applies if the weather turns cold towards the end of the season. On hot summer days it also pays to fish the deeper areas during the day and concentrate on the shallows in the early morning and late evening. Many lakes, or particularly reservoirs, are deep at one end and shallow at the other, and in most cases the shallows fish better in the evenings during the warmer weather of summer. Some lakes, lochs or more often reservoirs, are featureless and offer few, if any, obvious trout-holding areas. Despite this, waters of this nature often have very localized favourite spots for no apparent reason; these can usually be located by excessive wear on the bank in such places, and are always well worth trying.

The direction of the wind can also play an important part in the movement or location of trout. In most lakes trout tend to face or travel upwind against the surface drift of the water, because any insects in or on the water surface are being brought towards them. It will, therefore, be apparent that in a cross-wind both trout and their food are continually moving across the angler's front, and this presents him with first-class opportunities. However, the majority of anglers prefer to fish with the wind behind them, as it requires less expertize and in any case it is less fatiguing. Unfortunately, this can often prove to be bad tactically as, particularly in strong winds if the lake or reservoir be deep, the colder deoxygenated water may be forced up on to this shore off which the wind is blowing. Consequently, it is unlikely to hold many trout for the angler to catch. Under these circumstances the fisherman would be well advised to try one of the other shores. When the wind is blowing towards the bank and bringing food and the hungry trout with it, the angler who has mastered the knack of casting into the wind may have not only a fishing advantage but the boon of sole possession of a large stretch of bank. Occasionally the direction of the wind may change at short notice from that described above, and when it does may prove the exception to the general rule as many insects, terrestrial and aquatic, that have been congregating along the shoreline or among the bankside vegetation, will then be gradually blown into the lake, and when this happens the observant angler will

90 Trout will often patrol the outside edge of coloured water. The diagram shows the perfect positions for intercepting them ▶

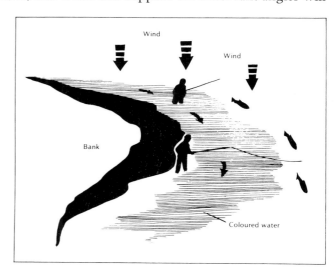

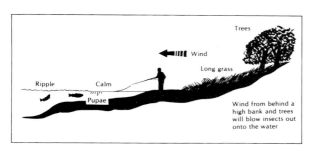

91 Trout will feed along the edge of the ripple where most pupae will gather to hatch, or will cruise along the edge of a shelf looking up to the surface for any insects blown off shore

213

derive much benefit from it. Wind can also form eddies, particularly if the lake has any prominent headlands, and these are always good spots to fish.

Under windy conditions shorelines along which the wind is blowing are subject to wave action which will often stir up mud off the bottom and this will drift along the shoreline with the wind or current. Where this occurs this coloured water is rarely worth fishing as the trout are unlikely to spot your fly in such poor visibility. In most cases you will find this coloured water extends too far offshore for you to fish over it. However, where points or headlands occur one will often find quite a narrow band of coloured water passing across them where it is possible to fish over it. The area where the coloured water meets the clear will often hold patrolling trout and is a good area to fish (see fig. 90). Also under windy conditions if you can find a high bank or one that is protected by trees on the windward side where the water is not too deep a good place to fish is where the calm water meets the rough (see fig. 91).

Finally, it is worth remembering that for evening fishing a west bank is often favourite, because the sun will be off the water first along this bank, and the rise if it occurs will start earlier.

CASTING

There are several excellent books available on this subject and I do not intend to discuss technicalities, but from the tactical point of view there are several points worthy of mention.

In the first place, false casting should always be kept to a minimum, whether boat or bank fishing, particularly in bright weather when the line throws its inevitable shadow on the water, as at times this may scare fish into believing that one of the many natural winged predators is in the vicinity.

The boat fisher relies mainly on the floating line, although the present-day trend is to use, on occasions, a sinking or slow-sinking line, but whichever type of line is used it is sensible to use as light a line as possible to allow delicate presentation and also in an effort to eliminate the sag which tends to form on the retrieve between rod tip and flies, particularly when boat fishing, with consequent loss of touch.

The bank fisher is at home equally with either the sinking or floating line, although most have a preference for one or the other. In addition to the sinking line which is used for retrieving along or near the bed of the lake, and the floating line for fishing the surface or sub-surface, there are also sink tip or intermediate lines available which are very useful for fishing in midwater, or along the bottom in shallower water.

Many discriminating anglers prefer to use a floating line, and use a sinker only when the conditions are such that it is absolutely necessary. A floater gives far greater control of the artificial flies in use and enables waters of depths up to the length of the leader to be successfully fished. Indeed, the only time it is essential to use a sinking line is when fishing into deep water or during the colder weather or on very hot, flat, calm days when the trout are lying deep, and also when retrieving fast and deep, flies or lures such as imitation sticklebacks or fry. The length and type of leader used will vary from situation to situation, but a good average length is about 15ft. Some authorities suggest one style of leader, while others another, and as there are many variations from a standard tapered leader to fancy double or even braided tapered leaders that one can now purchase, the

214

choice must be dictated by personal preference. If the leader is required to float, a light application of mucilin is recommended. A heavy application, which will cause a noticeable wake when the leader is retrieved, is a mistake. When fishing a sunken fly it is highly desirable for the leader and flies to sink as quickly as possible, and to this end I have yet to find a better medium than ordinary commercial Teepol. This can be carried in a small screw-top bottle, and when fishing commences the flies on the leader are immersed in the liquid one at a time, and the liquid can then be spread from the flies along the leader with finger and thumb. An excellent alternative is to treat the leader and flies with a mixture of Fullers Earth mixed with Glycerine. Modern fly lines require little attention or dressing, although it is a good idea to wipe down occasionally a sinking line with Teepol or a floating line with mucilin.

Apart from the normal double or forward tapered fly lines in use today, there is a type of line that is still gaining in popularity for stillwater fishing, and this is called a shooting head, made in both sinking and floating styles. Although these lines are now commercially available, for many years anglers have made these themselves from part of a standard fly line. In this latter case the head is composed of the front section of a standard fly line, and can vary in length, according to personal choice, from 8 to 12yds or more. The cut length is then whipped on to a nylon monafilament backing of about 20lb test. These shooting heads, in vogue in this country since the early sixties, have been used in the U.S.A. for a longer period and undoubtedly originated there. I myself have been using one since 1956, and in the intervening years I have occasionally come across others using them but, of course, they are now very common. My own preference at times is for a head of about 10 to 11yds in length and preferably cut from the front part of a forward taper line, as opposed to a double taper which, in my opinion, does not turn over so well as a forward taper. In addition, I find I can put it down more lightly on the water, particularly against a wind. The length of head used will vary from person to person, depending on the type of rod and a combination of physical and casting ability. If the head is too short the distance you are able to cast will be rather limited but, on the other hand, if the head is too long, while distance can be achieved it will be at the expense of fatigue and poor presentation. With a well-balanced shooting head distances in excess of 30yds can be maintained all day without too much effort, or 40yds if used in conjunction with the double-haul technique, but in spite of this and other advantages some fly fishermen look upon them with disapproval.

These days a certain percentage of anglers use a shooting head for all apsects of lake fishing, and I have even seen them used all day from a boat. Under the right conditions they are an extremely useful weapon in the bank fisher's, or on occasions boat fishers, armoury, but where distance casting is not absolutely necessary they should not be used, particularly when fishing the dry fly, or on very bright, calm days, as they have grave disadvantages compared to a normal fly line owing to the difficulty of the inexperienced caster in laying a shooting head lightly and delicately on the water. This is not to infer that it is almost impossible, but it does require considerable expertise. However, two of the most important benefits of a shooting head lies in the fact that it practically eliminates false casting, and allows you to fish areas where your back cast is restricted.

The shooting head should be spliced to not less than a 100yds of about 20lb test monofilament backing. Some types of nylon are preferable to others, but the choice must be left to the personal preference of the angler. Some anglers use a plastic bucket strapped to one leg, in which they coil the nylon backing, while others use a line raft, or tray, and although undoubtedly their use does increase the distance you can cast, many anglers do not consider the inconvenience caused by these gadgets worth while.

Finally, I should like to mention four methods of attaching your leader or backing to the fly line. Methods A and B show you how to permanently attach the leader to a silk or plastic line, then attaching or detaching your flies as required. Method C and D are intended for the fisherman who prefers to tie and detach the leader, complete with flies, from a selection of leaders carried in a cast or leader carrier. This latter method has much to commend it, particularly when a quick change of flies is required, or when a bad tangle occurs at dusk. You can now purchase the relatively new "airflo" braided tapered leaders complete with a small plastic steeve which enables you to attach or detatch them to your fly line as required.

Another alternative which I also practice is to carry a spare rod with me. During the day this is very useful particularly when bank fishing for either alternative use with a sinking or sink tip line or another floating line similar to that fitted to the main rod but with a different selection of flies. In the late evening once I have decided upon the method of fishing and type of flies, I fit the spare rod up in the same way. I then have a duplicate outfit ready for instant use should I require it.

Unfortunately even the best fishermen acquire some dreadful tangles as the light goes for various reasons. Probably the most common cause is the small rainbow that takes a fly on a dropper — this nearly always results in a wonderful birds nest of leader and flies by the time he is netted. When this type of incident occurs the full benefit of a spare rod or made up leaders will be appreciated.

I have already discussed leaders earlier in this chapter but it is worth noting that during the mid sixties we engaged upon some interesting research into these and also fly lines. So far as the former are concerned I now use much longer leaders 18 to 22ft overall and according to the records I have kept, my catches have been better since using the longer leaders. Of course, it is almost impossible to prove or disprove any theory such as this conclusively, but apart from improved bags of fish it seems logical to have as long a leader as one can manage thereby allowing maximum distance between artificials. Using standard 9 or 10ft leaders I now feel the artificials are too close together or too near to the fly line and this may appear suspicious to a trout.

I have a friend who had access to certain laboratory equipment, including an extremely delicate unit for measuring decibels of sound through water. He fitted this to a long tank of water and carefully tested various sounds made by the fishermen and his equipment. The most astonishing results of all these tests was the relatively high proportion of sound or vibration made by a fly line hitting the water after the angler's cast. The worst offenders were floating lines particularly bug or forward tapers in the heavier weights. Naturally the lighter the line and the smaller the diameter the less the noise.

Following on from this he then carried out a series of tests between the new plastic coated lines and the old fashioned type of silk lines. This seemed to prove that the smaller equivalent diameter of the silk fly lines made less sound when hitting or alighting on the water. We had, previously carried out a series of carefully controlled tests over a whole season using modern plastic coated lines

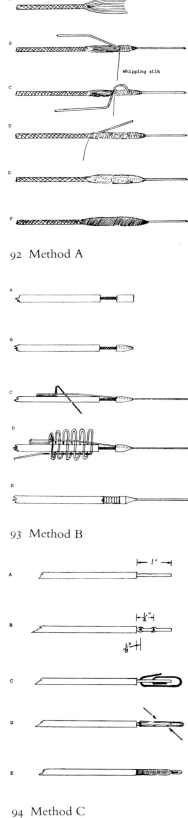

Whipping silk

92 Method A

93 Method B

94 Method C

216

and the old style silk lines, and the latter certainly accounted for far more fish particularly from a boat. I am sure we can all recall calm still days with plenty of trout rising, but no matter how careful one is every fish you cast near goes down. I am now reasonably certain that this is due to this line slap as I call it, and although it cannot be avoided completely it can most certainly be minimised by using as light a line as possible. Following this train of thought we have also found that the longer leaders we now use for the reason previously discussed also assist to minimise the sound of the line hitting the water to the trout, as naturally the longer the leader the further the actual fly line from the trout and the less noise it will hear.

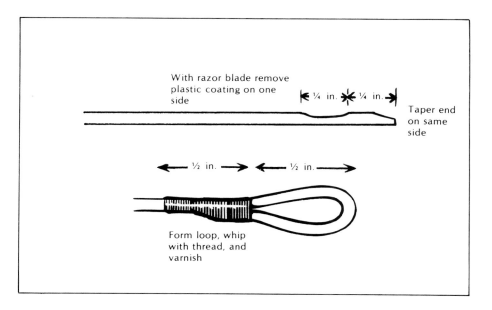

With razor blade remove plastic coating on one side

¼ in. ¼ in.

Taper end on same side

½ in. ½ in.

Form loop, whip with thread, and varnish

95 Forming a small whipped loop at the end of a fly line. Method D

CHAPTER 13

FLY FISHING METHODS ON STILLWATER

Artificial flies may be fished in many different ways, but the two basic ways are wet and dry.

Broadly speaking, most lakes or reservoirs may be divided under either of two headings: upland or lowland. Such waters as Chew Valley, Blagdon, Ravensthorpe and Eyrebrook, are typical lowland waters and, being of an alkaline nature, often based on rich limestone or other subsoil, have an abundance of underwater life, harbouring large quanitites of shrimp, snail, corixa, caddis larva and other forms of life. In waters of this nature the trout wax fat and often grow to a very large size, but they are basically bottom or midwater feeders and it consequently requires an abnormal amount of insects on or in the surface film to bring about a general surface rise. Under these conditions the wet fly is usually the better proposition, except when surface activity is fairly widespread. The upland lakes and lochs in the hilly country of Wales and the North, on the other hand, are often of an acid nature. These waters are not so rich in bottom or midwater fauna, and consequently a relatively small amount of surface hatching or even terrestrial insects blown on to the water will often bring the fish up, and on these waters a dry fly may often prove as effective as a wet fly.

THE DRY FLY

This style of fishing may be practised equally well from a boat or the bank, but in both cases succes is usually dependent on some surface activity. It must be appreciated that there are many different types of natural insects to which trout will rise, and as the artificials of many of these require individual techniques, this aspect must be taken into account. It will doubtless be realized that when trout appear to be feeding on the surface it does not necessarily mean that they are actually doing so, as they may well be taking nymphs or pupae hatching in the surface film. In most cases it is possible for the experienced lake fisherman to tell the difference by the rise form, but it is seldom easy and the beginner is liable to have a little difficulty until experience provides the answer. To a large extent the best dry fishing is dependent upon the right weather conditions as well as a rise of fish to surface food. A gentle breeze which provides a good ripple on the water, especially when the air is crisp and when the sun occasionally peeps through the fleeting clouds, will probably prove ideal. Bright, sunny or heavy overcast days seldom provide good bags, and very bright, hot cloudless days with a flat calm are certainly not conducive to good fishing with either the wet or dry fly. While wet, windy conditions often favour the wet fly fisher, they are not the best medium for good dry fly fishing as even with liberal use of floatant it is no easy matter to keep

218

the fly on the surface where it belongs, and from a boat where one has a fast drift to contend with it is generally impossible. On sunny days it will be particularly noticeable that the most likely time for a trout to rise will be when an odd cloud covers the sun for a brief interval. Over the years I have found this situation to be so consistent that I always expect activity when the sun is covered briefly in this manner.

When stillwater fishing, if possible, it is always a good policy, whether from bank or boat, to have two rods made up, one for wet fly fishing and one for dry. Most boat anglers prefer the floating line and in consequence both rods are usually equipped with normal double tapered lines, while for bank fishing one rod is usually equipped with a shooting head. It is also a good idea to have various leaders made up with flies or nymphs ready for use; should a tangle occur, particularly in poor light, lengthy unravelling time can be avoided if the spare leaders are held on a leader or cast carrier, available for instant use.

Some authorities advocate the use of wet flies in conjunction with a dry fly on the leader, but it seems the majority of anglers prefer to fish a single dry fly. Another choice facing the fisherman is whether or not to use a floatant on fly or leader. When fishing with a dry fly it is in most cases important that it cocks well and floats high in the water. To achieve this the leader can be greased with a floatant such as lanolin or mucilin, and the fly can also be treated with one of the many floatants or sprays available from tackle shops. Mucilin, which can be lightly applied with finger and thumb, is also a good medium for anointing the fly, particularly for some sedge patterns which have to be fished with movement, which drowns a dry fly far quicker than anything else and which to a large extent is prevented by an application of mucilin. The use of floatants, which form a film of oil around the fly and leader, in calm conditions may well cause a taking trout to refuse at the last moment and is avoided by many experts. If one is of this school of thought, the answer lies in frequent false casting, combined with the occasional use of amadou to dry your fly thoroughly. A compromise between the above methods is to use floatants sparingly only when conditions make their use essential, and this is probably the best solution.

When dry fly fishing in stillwater, observation of the movement of trout on the surface is of utmost importance. Providing the actual rise is observed it is often possible to tell in which direction a trout is travelling. In some cases, particularly if the fish shows its head and tail, it is quite easy, and in other cases, if the trout is moving along just under the surface fairly fast, the direction can be ascertained by the shape of the rise. On many occasions, however, it is exceedingly difficult and only experience will tell. Some fly-fishermen of my acquaintance have this talent to a very high degree, and can forecast the direction with uncanny accuracy, but for myself I am quite elated if I prove to be correct twice out of three. This problem is most complicated during a widespread general rise, and at its simplest when a solitary trout on a beat is observed rising in a more or less straight line at frequent intervals. In such a situation as this, if the fish is in range the fly can be cast to alight in the estimated position of the next rise. Most authorities seem to believe that in stillwater trout tend to move up-wind, and my own observations so far substantiate this, and therefore if one is uncertain of the direction being taken by a rising fish it is always a sound proposition to cast a few yards up-wind of the last rise. However, there are exceptions to all rules, and some trout seem to favour a more or less stationary position a few feet under the surface, waiting for wind or surface drift to bring food into their window before rising. Consequently, when I am uncertain of direction, I always drop my fly as speedily as possible near the centre of the rise, and with practice it is amazing how quickly this can be achieved. If this does not produce a take within a couple of seconds I then re-cast and drop the fly about five yards up-wind, but experience teaches that even when we feel we can estimate the position of the next rise, our cast should be somewhat short in order to prevent lining the fish and putting it down, which will almost certainly happen when the surface is calm or unruffled. Remember, if it is not put down you will probably have two or three chances to cover him before he is out of range.

Without a doubt, one of the most difficult features of the dry fly on stillwater is to know when to strike. Over the years much argument has raged on this point and, as no two anglers seem to agree, I venture to suggest the following. On stillwater, trout generally take a fly on the surface in a much more leisurely fashion than on a river and, consequently, the fisherman would be well advised to hesitate for a second or so before striking. The larger the artificial being fished, the longer the hesitation. Alternatively, if one's eyesight is good it is an excellent plan to watch the cast or line a few feet from the artificial or rod tip and strike when you see a positive draw. This delayed strike is one of the most difficult features for a river angler — who is used often to an instantaneous strike on fast water — to master. There is good reason for the longer hesitation on stillwater compared to running water, for on the latter the insect is very quickly removed out of reach by the current, and so the trout must act quickly; whereas, in contrast, the stillwater trout is well aware that its prey will probably await its pleasure, and that therefore it can take its time.

No description of dry fly fishing would be complete without a mention of dapping, or blow line fishing as some call it. Apart from informing the reader that this can sometimes be a very thrilling form of fishing, demanding the use of a very long light rod in conjunction with a live insect and a floss silk line, I feel I can do little better than make reference to that excellent book *Loch Trout*, by Col. H. A. Oatts, where a whole chapter is devoted to this particular style of fishing.

THE WET FLY

While some anglers prefer to use a dry fly on a lake whenever possible, most are confirmed wet fly fishers and in many cases rarely consider even using a dry pattern; this is, of course, a pity, as the successful fisherman should be prepared to alter his method of angling at a moment's notice according to conditions. As the dry fly is usually restricted to periods when trout are rising, it will be appreciated that its use is far more limited than the wet fly, which can virtually be fished at all times under all conditions and, furthermore, it can be fished at varying depths, just under the surface, midwater or along the bottom. For this reason, and also because it embraces not only general wet flies but also nymphs, lures and varius other patterns, its scope is exceedingly wide. From the above it will be quite apparent that the claim for wet fly fishing as the most efficient method of killing trout in stillwater is not without considerable justification. This form of fishing may be practised equally well from a boat or from the bank, although, as previously stated, the boat fisher is very much more limited with his style of presentation and corresponding range of patterns that can be successfully used. In most cases the boat angler favours the use of a floating fly line with his wet flies, while the bank fisher sometimes prefers a high density fast sinking or slow sinking line, although I myself favour a floater on most occasions. When fishing from a boat in rough conditions the wet fly angler, due to his flies fishing in or near the surface because of the inevitable fast drift, will probably find himself limited to the use of mainly general patterns. On the other hand, on calm, windless days, he has almost as much scope as the bank angler, and many methods may be used. Another alternative is to anchor the boat, when, in theory at least, it should be possible to emulate the style of the bank angler. In practice, however, this does not seem to work out, and personally I never feel I have the same control or fish so well using bank techniques from a boat.

The bank angler has far greater scope both in respect of methods of fishing and varieties of artificials he can use, though many of these artificials are tied as imitations to represent specific insects and must be fished in a certain way. The methods of fishing standard or fancy patterns also varies greatly. With nearly all stillwater imitations animation is of utmost importance, and this can only be imparted by the way they are fished, although it must be pointed out that the type and quality of materials from which they are tied can assist in this respect. This fact has no doubt led to the present popularity of hair, marabou or fur-dressed patterns, as these have more built-in life than tinsel or feather. Some anglers rely on the surface ripple to impart animation to their flies when being retrieved, but others accomplish this eaither by movement of the rod tip or by variation in speed of retrieve. Other factors also play a part, such as the depth at which your flies are fished or whether you retrieve in a series of small jerks or alternative long and short pulls, or by sink and draw, which is a very effective method. Whichever way is adopted, some anglers seem able to impart a little extra something to the flies which will produce a trout where other fail. In practice the above methods should be regulated according to the specific pattern being fished, but if a general pattern is being used, each of the methods may be tried over a period, devoting sufficient time to each until success is achieved. When the taking method has been discovered the angler should persevere with it until such time as conditions have obviously changed or a period has elapsed with no results.

As mentioned above, the depth at which one fishes can also be of importance, and the following system can be adopted. Cast out your line and allow your flies to sink while slowly counting to, say, five, then slowly retrieve and examine your flies carefully for particles of debris or weed, which should confirm, if present, that maximum fishing depths has been reached. If your flies are clean, repeat, but increase your count by two, and keep on increasing till bottom is located; alternatively, if the bed of the lake is weedy, constant plucks on the line as you retrieve will tell you that your flies are as near bottom as it is possible to fish. Once bottom has been located by this counting method it is a simple matter to predetermine the depth at which you fish your flies by the number to which you count before the retrieve is commenced. By this same counting method it is also possible to ascertain and maintain the fishing depth at which the trout are found to be feeding.

When fishing the dry fly it is seldom necessary to fish more than one artificial on the leader, but when fishing wet it is often desirable to use two or three patterns. Some waters do have restrictions in this respect, and insist on a one-fly-only rule, which in this case must be observed. On the other hand, on many of the Scottish lochs it is sometimes the practice when boat fishing to use four or even more artificials. When fishing with more than one general wet pattern most authorities on the subject insist that these should be attached to the leader in a predetermined position. In a few cases many experts are in agreement over the position of certain patterns, and good examples of these are the Peter Ross on the point, and the Mallard and Claret on the top dropper. In most cases the experts are far from unanimous, and for this reason it would be of little value to pursue this subject further. The distance between flies on the leader is also another controversial point, and is best left to the discretion of the individual angler, although this aspect, in addition to length of leader, has already been dealt with in relation to specific artificials.

The wet fly fisher should be on the alert for a take at all times, and for this a high degree of concentration should be maintained, particularly when bank fishing. Unlike fishing the dry fly where the take on the surface is obvious, the take of the wet fly underwater is usually impossible to observe. In some cases the take is quite savage and the trout will literally hook itself with little or no assistance from the angler, but at other times the take can be so gentle that only the experienced angler will know that a trout has, in fact, accepted his fly. In the latter case the only indication is a slight drawing of the line, and this is rarely felt. Probably the best answer to gentle takes such as this is to watch the fly line on the surface of the water, and to strike immediately any check or movement is noticed. In conditions where the light is not good it is advisable to watch the loop of line hanging down from the rod tip to the water.

One little hint which cannot be emphasised too strongly is, never to hold your rod pointing directly along and parallel with your fly line. How often the stillwater trout fisherman is heard to state, "and I was broken on the take by a huge trout", and in nine cases out of ten it is due to the above fault; and furthermore, if the truth were to be known, it was probably only an average sized trout anyway. When the rod and line are in one straight continuity, a trout may break the cast with little effort, and I have indeed observed personally a leader with a 12lb point broken with ease because of it by a trout of about 3lb. This is largely an oversight of the bank angler, as when retrieving, seated in a boat, the angler's rod tip is pointing slightly upwards automatically. It is surprising how how many fly fishermen are in fact guilty of this fault, including many experienced reservoir fishermen. It is no uncommon sight to see a whole line of bank anglers fishing in this way. The answer is quite simple. When retrieving, always stand at a slight angle to the direction in which you have cast, so that your rod forms a slight angle to the line. This will allow the natural flex of the rod to absorb the initial shock from a fast moving trout should it take your fly. At the same time whenever possible, always hold the rod with the tip ring as near to the water surface as possible. Under windy conditions I prefer to hold it just below the surface. I do assure you fewer takes will be missed if this method is adopted.

LURE FISHING

Today this style of fishing has become very popular on many of our stillwaters, and it is no uncommon sight to see a whole line of bank fishermen so engaged. Depending on the depth of water and presumed location of the trout, either a floating, slow sinking or sinking line may be used. It is usual to fish only one fly or lure on the point. This method of fishing is regarded by many fly fishermen as tantamount to spinning, and while I am personally inclined to agree that its use can be abused, I feel it can be justified when fishing a lure that is meant to represent some specific form of food such as fry or sticklebacks on which trout are obviously feeding. To fish such a lure correctly requires considerable art and experience.

Unfortunately, such lures, even when fished incorrectly, prove to be attractive to some trout by virtue of their size and the speed at which they are usually retrieved. This fact undoubtedly accounts for their popularity among some anglers and it is a fact that, providing persistence is maintained, it usually results in a fairly high quota of takes. This applies particularly after restocking before the trout have become educated, and even more so on a new reservoir for the first season or so. Generally speaking the older and more established, or harder fished a water, the less effective lure fishing becomes. In any case it is a very monotonous method of fishing and unless used selectively requires little imagination or technique.

Many of the lures in use today come under the heading of Bucktail or Streamer flies and are not really tied to represent any particular living aquatic creature. Some of them have double or even treble hooks tied in tandem and are really fearsome looking creations. When one considers that some anglers fish three or more of these lures on the same leader, either from the bank or from a boat, it will be realized why in certain circles this style of fishing is frowned upon. Personally, I derive too much pleasure from the pursuit of natural representation of flies, on which the fish may be feeding, even to consider this style, and I am inclined to believe that trout take this type of lure only either out of irritation or because of the primeval or predatory urge to pursue a creature endeavouring to escape. The technique of fishing these lures is a combination of distance casting and physical endurance, hardly the proposition for the thoughtful angler.

However, this method should not be condemned out of hand purely on these grounds, as we are all entitled to enjoy our selected style of fishing. What is objected to is the fact that a method based largely on physical prowess and little else lacks interest and is capable of little development and, consequently, kills the desire in many anglers to pursue the imitative style of fishing where there is so much to be learned and so much to enjoy.

By the Waterside

Many of us have an enquiring mind and are keen to improve our catches, and although there are many ways in which this can be achieved, one of the most important and certainly one of the most interesting is to undertake a study of the insects on which trout feed.

Undoubtedly, the quickest way to further one's knowledge in this direction, provided the angler has the basic will to learn, is to make a habit of regularly collecting a few specimens at the waterside on every outing, and then take them home for study and identification at leisure. Within a comparatively short time it will be found tht you will be able to recognise the more common species at the waterside as you encounter them. Once an angler has learnt to identify most of the more prolific species of insects, and to match the corresponding artificial to the natural, his chances of success must obviously be increased.

The collection of the natural insects need take little of the angler's time, and in any case it will often provide him with an added interest during those dour periods that are often encountered. The only equipment that the budding collector needs is a small, fine mesh net for capturing specimens either in the water or on the wing. This can be purchased at any aquarist shop and can quite easily be adapted to screw into a landing-net handle. A watertight screw-top jar for retaining acquatic species of insects and a second screw-top container for adult winged specimens. For these latter insects the inside of the jar should be lined with blotting paper to absorb moisture which would otherwise damage these relatively delicate winged flies. As it is difficult to retain more than three or four specimens in an open-top jar at a time, due to the fact that the original captures tend to escape as fresh specimens are introduced, I have adapted a very simple item to solve this problem. Purchase a small-size plastic paraffin funnel from an ironmongers, cut off the long spout at the base of the funnel and trim off the top section until it is a press fit into the top of the jar. Your collecting jar will then operate as a minnow trap. The insects can be tapped into the container, but it is virtually impossible for them to escape.

One other aspect that is closely allied to the collection of live specimens and also of considerable value, particularly to the stillwater trout fisherman, is the spooning out of captured trout to study their stomach content. This, of course, is done in an effort to discover on what particular species of insects the trout are feeding at the time, and can be of considerable importance in deciding the choice of pattern to be fished. Of course, in some cases the stomach content will be nil, but it takes so little time to spoon a trout that nothing is really lost by so doing. From the dry fly fisherman's point of view it is, of course, rarely necessary to carry out this operation, as in most cases the insect on which the trout is feeding can be observed on the water. On lakes or reservoirs, however, where various forms of underwater life are often the order of the day, it can often mean the difference between a good bag of fish or an indifferent one and, therefore, the first fish caught should always be spooned out even if subsequent fish are not.

It is possible to purchase a proper marrow scoop, although they are not always easy to locate. Alternatively, it is fairly simple to make one or, temporarily, a long-handled teaspoon with the sides of the spoon trimmed can be used. The spoon or scoop is pushed down the trout's gullet as far as it will go, and is then twisted from side to side or completely turned over and then withdrawn. The contents of the scoop should then be emptied into a shallow container of water for examination. In many cases it will be found that much of the stomach content is digested beyond recognition, but insects that the trout have most recently fed on will usually be recognisable, and these, of course, are of prime importance and the specimens to which the artificials should be matched.

On small waters where the trout are difficult to catch but free rising it is often good practice to bide one's time and only cast to individual rising fish rather than to fish the water. For this style of fishing concealment is of utmost importance and it is essential to use a light rod and line with a fine cast and point in conjunction with a single fly. This also applies on all waters when trout are rising and feeding in a flat calm. Under these conditions at certain times of the year trout become preoccupied feeding on *Caenis*, smuts or exceedingly small midge pupae and are often notoriously difficult to tempt. It seems the best chances of success are assured by using the above mentioned method combined with a general pattern such as a Hare's Ear, or specialised patterns like my own Last Hope or Small Hatching Midge tied on the smallest of hooks. It should also be mentioned with this style of fishing correct presentation and very accurate casting are essential.

224

To grease or not to grease

Finally let us look closely at one particular aspect of stillwater trout fishing that is of the utmost of importance. I am still surprised at the comparatively large number of trout fishermen I have encountred over the years that seem unaware of the importance of oil or line grease, or lack of it, on their leader or flies. This can often mean the difference between success or failure and is essential under most conditions.

Let us first of all take a quick look at some of the preparations available to fly fishermen today. There are several different brands of line grease on the market and most of these have a mucilin base. Personally I use the plain mucilin in the little green tin, as this is freely on sale and I have always found it perfectly satisfactory. This is supplied with a felt pad for application to the leader, but it should be applied sparingly. Oil or floatant for flies is offered either in bottles or aerosol type sprays and there are many different brands on the market each one claiming to be superior to any other. I prefer the preparation first recommended by Dick Walker in *Trout and Salmon* many years ago, called "Permafloat", as I find this far superior. It is in liquid form and is supplied in a wide mouth screw top bottle, so that the whole fly no matter how large can be dipped in the liquid, but this should if possible be carried out some little time before use to allow it to dry out thoroughly. Flies treated with this oil float beautifully for several hours. There are several preparations one can obtain for degreasing leaders or flies from ordinary liquid glycerine to thick mud from the edge of the water which will suffice if nothing else is available. Liquid detergent is very good, but I prefer glycerine mixed with fullers'earth.

A basic error made by many anglers is to apply grease too liberally to the leader in an effort to ensure that their dry fly does not become waterlogged. This is a mistake, always apply lightly, and always leave the last six inches completely free of grease. Some fishermen do not realise the amount of disturbance a greased line creates as it is retrieved on the surface; under calm conditions this will be immediately apparent, but in rough water this is not noticeable to the angler, but may be to the trout. A similar situation can apply when using wet flies or nymphs on a floating line, if you require to fish these at any depth it is essential to thoroughly degrease both flies and leader before fishing commences. It should also be appreciated that the application of grease to different sections of the leader can predetermine at what depth various flies on it will fish.

For example, from midsummer onwards where there are a lot of sedge flies about, an extremely effective method is to use, in conjunction with a floating line, a dry sedge pattern on the dropper with a sedge pupae artificial on the point. In this case the leader above the dry fly is greased whilst the remainder down to the point fly which must be retrieved just below the surface is thoroughly degreased. In another instance you may wish to retrieve a dry sedge, invicta or similar patterns in the surface film. This can be a very killing method when trout are feeding on the adult sedge, as they will often completely ignore a dry sedge fished on the surface, but readily accept the same pattern fished in the film, as they seem to take this for a sedge fly hatching. To ensure that your chosen pattern fishes in the correct position it is necessary to degrease the leader and very sparsely oil the artificial. Too much oil and it will float too high, too little and it will sink too far below the surface.

To illustrate the importance of this aspect of fly fishing I should like to recount an actual incident I was personally involved in a few seasons ago. The time was early July and I had arranged to take a friend out for a day's boat fishing on one of our larger reservoirs. Fairly new to this style of fishing he asked me if I would be kind enough to guide him on which patterns to use and how to fish them. Upon arrival at the water I was informed that few, if any, fish were rising and anglers were having most success fishing deeply retrieved lures. Observing several sedge-flies fluttering in the margins I felt it should be possible to take a few fish on the surface despite the complete absence of rises. Under these conditions I knew it would be necessary to attract the trout to our flies, so it was therefore essential to use a large dry, well oiled sedge on the dropper with an invicta fished just below the surface on the point. I explained this to my colleague and also advised him to well grease the leader above the dry sedge. We then commenced a nice drift, over water not too deep where the trout should be able to see the disturbance created by the sedge on the dropper even if they were lying near the bottom. Sure enough this proved successful and during the next two hours I boated four nice trout and also rose several others which came short. The disturbance created by the sedge attracted them to the surface where most accepted the invicta. Despite the fact that my companion was fishing the same method with similar flies he only rose one fish in this period. I checked his flies, leader and even the distance between flies, but could not account for this, we also changed places in the boat but all to no avail, eventually I suggested we exchange rods and the reason for his lack of success was immediately apparent. The flies were fishing incorrectly as he had greased the leader between the two flies instead of the section only above the sedge on the dropper. I immediately corrected this for him and within five minutes he was delightedly playing a fine plump trout.

This demonstrates the extreme importance of this aspect of fly fishing.

CONCLUSIONS

As it is not always easy to pick out the more important points from a mass of other information, I am listing them below in the hope that they will provide a quick reference of do's and dont's for the newcomer to stillwater fishing.

1.   Choose one's fishing location carefully, taking advantage of any natural holding areas.

2.   When fishing from a boat avoid noise and excessive movement.

3.   Do not stand up to cast from a boat, unless absolutely necessary.

4.   Avoid unnecessary false casting.

5.   Never wade unless you have to, but it you have to, wade carefully and quietly.

6.   Always take advantage of background or cover, where possible, when bank fishing.

7.   A cross-wind is usually most favourable for the bank fisher.

8.   Use floatant sparsely on flies and leaders when necessary.

9.   Do not strike too quickly when fishing the dry fly.

10.   When wet fly fishing watch the line on the water or at the rod tip for indication of a take.

11.   Never point your rod directly along your line when retrieving your fly, but always hold your rod with the tip as close to the surface as possible.

12.   Periodically check your hook for damage and *always* after losing a fish.

SPECIAL STILLWATER ARTIFICIALS

In the preceeding chapters on stillwater fishing I have discussed the many different methods and techniques one may use, and I have also briefly mentioned some of the more popular artificials that may be used in conjunction with these. However there are often occasions when little activity is apparent and one is at a loss as to which artificial to use. In such situations the use of a general or special attractor pattern will often pay dividends. The following artificials come within this category.

The Muddler Minnow
This is an old but often very effective general attractor pastern that was originally perfected in America to represent a small minnow or fish, but in fact looks like many other forms of underwater life. This can be fished slowly on or near the bottom or it often proves very effective indeed if retrieved very fast just beneath the surface on very windy days when their is planty of wave action.

The Dog Nobbler
This is a more recent pattern that was originally introduced to this country about ten years ago by Trevor Housby. It is a lead headed lure that is very similar indeed to the American Bass fly rod jigs that have been in use for many years. It is dressed with marabou in different colours which gives it the illusion of life and is fished near the bottom with a sink and draw action. Loved by some, hated by others it is often referred to as the most deadly lure ever devised for trout.

The Boobies
Any pattern of wet fly, nymph, or lure can be turned into a booby by adding two foam beads trapped in stocking mesh immediately behind the eye of the hook. This is quite a modern innovation first introduced by Gordon Fraser which he based on my suspender principal. The foam makes the flies buoyant and unweighted patterns are fished slowly just beneath the surface, but it is most effective when weighted patterns are used in conjunction with a sinking line. This proves an attractive and unusual action as when the line is retrieved the fly sinks, but when you pause the fly rises. That excellent fly fisher Peter Lapsley recently described a method he has found to be very killing using a high D fast sink line. He secures a 12 inch length of nylon to the bend of the hook on the Booby and at the end of this ties on a very tiny unweighted nymph, when he pauses on the retrieve the tiny nymph attached below the Booby pops up from the bottom and many trout find it irresistable.

The Clouser Deep Minnow
This is a new general attractor pattern recently introduced from the United States. A pair of lead eyes arte tied in behind the eye of a long shank hook and the body is formed from Bucktail in two different colours plus a few strands of Sparkleflash. Very simple to tye the secret is to dress it very sparcely indeed with little more than half a dozen strands of Bucktail in each colour. this is an extremely killing lure for all manner of game and saltwater fish as well as for trout. For trout I have found the most effective method is to fish it quite slowly on a floating line with a sink and draw method of retrieve.

The Pursuader
This is one of my own patterns I developed as a general attractor as it must appear to the trout as a representation of many different forms of underwater life. In water up to about ten feet in depth it is best fished with a long leader on a floating line very slowly along the bottom. In deeper water use it in conjunction with a sinking line. This pattern has taken a lot of big trout in recent years particularly brown trout, which are often less inclined to come up to the surface than rainbows.

CHAPTER 14

MONTH BY MONTH ON STILLWATERS

As previously mentioned, on occasions popular general artificial patterns prove to be as killing on stillwaters as those tied as specific representations of the natural. If this situation always applied, there would be no point in writing this book, but this is not always the case as often the trout become preoccupied when feeding upon a particular form of aquatic fauna, and will be caught only on an artificial that is a close imitation. This is no drawback as it provides a constant challenge to the angler, and keeps his interest alive, in what otherwise could become a rather dull and uninteresting branch of our sport.

One of the most difficult problems to overcome in this respect, assuming the angler is provided with close artificial representations of the natural insects, is when and at what time to fish them. To the novice this may appear to be an insurmountable problem, and on occasions even the expert may be perplexed, due to the fact that we are seldom able actually to see what the trout are feeding on underwater. Naturally, the problem is never quite so acute when trout are feeding on or in the surface, but even then it can be tricky, as at such times the fish often have a large variety of food to choose from.

There are, of course, plenty of clues which may assist the reader to come to a decision, and I hope I have covered most of them within the various chapters of this book, but as it will take time and much experience for the novice to absorb all these various factors, I feel it is necessary to limit the field to a certain extent. It seems to me that the easiest way to do this is to give brief details of the more common insects and other fauna which may be expected throughout each month of the fishing season, and furthermore, for quick reference, also to present this information in concise table form at the end of the chapter.

Before giving this information, however, there are several other factors that must be taken into consideration, and I feel it would be wise to present them before proceeding. In the first place, it should be pointed out that weather conditions from day to day affect the emergence of insects quite considerably. In really adverse conditions the emergence of a complete species may be delayed by as much as a week or even two. Under these circumstances it will be appreciated that at times it is quite possible that certain species which would normally be anticipated one particular month, may not turn up till early the next month.

Another important factor is the distribution of different species of insects, for I am sure it will be readily understood that only the very common varieties are likely to be found on all stillwaters. Therefore, readers should tailor the monthly lists to include only those species known in their localities. Should the angler be fishing a water with which he is unfamiliar, information regarding the insect population may be gleaned from other fishermen, but it is sometimes best for him to rely upon his own judgment from observations at the waterside.

In some cases the field may be narrowed still further, due to the fact that certain fauna in stillwater, with which we are concerned are broadly speaking normally confined to known areas or localities. To quote a few examples, such creatures as Water Lice, Shrimps or Corixa are unlikely to be found in deep water. Pond Olives nymphs are usually found in shallow water, while the similar Lake Olive often prefers the deeper water. Adult Sedge-flies are more likely to be found in the vicinity of bank-side vegetation or adjacent to trees or copses than in open water. Certain species or Orders of insects often show a preference for thick weedbeds, or for muddy or perhaps hard or stony bottoms. The list is endless, but as this aspect may be difficult for the beginner to observe, I only mention it as it can be of considerable value as his knowledge increases.

I intend to commence the season from the month of April, as the majority of stillwaters open either during this month or in May. Localised or uncommon species are not included.

APRIL

During the early part of the season the fishing is usually patchy, as there is little insect life to tempt the trout, and therefore throughout this month a Black Lures or general attractor or flasher patterns, such as a Butcher or a Dunkeld, will often prove effective when there is nothing apparent for the fisherman to imitate. Two species of fauna that are present in most waters at this period are the Shrimp and the Water Louse, and where concentrations of these are found it is always worth trying the appropriate artificial. The first of the Upwinged flies, the Sepia Dun, appears on some waters usually in mid or late April and although it is sometimes possible to take trout on a floating artificial to imitate the Dun or Spinner, the sunk nymph is usually most effective. In areas where they occur a few species of Stoneflies may be in evidence and also at least two species of the more common Midges. They are the Black and the Grey Boy Midges. Hatches of the latter are seldom seen in large numbers so early in the year, but sometimes a reasonable emergence may occur late in the afternoon, and may produce a fair rise of trout to the pupae. The other common species, the Black Midge, is a very useful early season insect. In Wales and Scotland it is very common during March and April and in these areas it is often referred to as the Duck fly; it emerges during the middle part of the day, and the appropriate artificial should be fished on or just under the surface. The Blagdon Green Midge may be encountered at this time also, but it is of little consequence so early in the year.

MAY

By this time of the year the better weather should be with us, and it may be possible to take fish regularly in the latter half of the month, early in the morning and late in the evening, as well as during the day. Many of the species that first appeared in the previous month are still with us, while many new ones are about to emerge. The Sepia Dun is often very prolific early on in certain localities, but by the middle of the month except for stragglers, will be seen no more till next season. Hatches of the Blagdon Green Midge are now on a larger scale, particularly during the day, and some trout may commence to feed on the pupae as they do at spasmodic intervals throughout the rest of the season. During the late evenings, and occasionally in the very early mornings, good buzzer rises to the

Grey Boy or Olive Midge may be expected, particularly in the latter part of the month. At the very end of April or early May the Alder larva should be much in evidence, and an artificial to represent it is often killing; also about this period we are likely to encounter the first hatches of Lake Olives and, later in the month, Pond Olives. A less common Upwinged fly, namely the Claret Dun, should be encountered in some areas towards the end of the month, while at the same period on certain waters, particularly on the Irish loughs, the Mayfly, the largest Upwinged fly of all, will be making its début. During this month two new Orders of insects, Beetles and Sedge-flies, join the assembly. Among the former Order the Cockchafer, a large terrestrial insect, may be encountered on windy evenings, and so may some of the aquatic members of this Order in both larval and adult stages. By the middle of the month certain species of the Sedge-flies may be observed in fair numbers, particularly the Small Silver and the Small Red Sedge, but this early in the year the trout are usually a little reluctant to come to the surface for them.

JUNE

Without a doubt this is the most pleasant month of all by the waterside, as the warmer weather is now with us, and early morning and late evening rises are of fairly regular occurrence. Hatches of most of the Upwinged flies are now at their maximum and it is often possible to find odd trout cruising about during the early evening sipping down the spinners of the various species, or taking the ascending nymph in the mornings. Many types of Sedge-flies are now on the wing, and close attention by the fisherman should be well rewarded, particularly by fishing appropriate artificials of the pupae of those insects which can be successfully imitated. Various species of Beetles are also commonly encountered in certain areas, including the Coch-y-bonddu and the Soldier and Sailor Beetles, as well as many aquatic species and their larvae. Other fauna that are with us throughout the season, such as the Shrimp, the Water Louse and, on a few localized waters, various species of Stoneflies, should not be forgotten. Heavy hatches of many of the Midges (Buzzers) are now to be expected in the early morning as the sun rises, and again in the very late evenings, the predominant species being the Olive or Golden Dun or Grey Boy Midges, although the latter usually disappears by the middle of the month. One of the smaller species also appears for the first time during June; this is the Small Brown Midge, and the angler will be well advised to keep in mind the rather unusual rise form of the trout to these small insects which usually takes place during the day. Towards the end of the month Corixa and Damsel nymphs are likely to be in evidence in sufficient quantities to interest the fish, and often in the late afternoons emergence of fair numbers of the Large Red Midge are likely, and will often bring about a spasmodic rise of trout to the pupae in the surface film. In late June the first hatches of the Angler's Curse (Caenis) are fairly certain, usually in the early evenings.

JULY

The early part of this month is often very pleasant and producive of trout, but by the end of the second week, particularly during a spell of hot weather, conditions deteriorate, and the trout usually become dour and disinclined to feed; at least during the hours of bright sunshine. However, there are certain compensations as by this time of the year many species of Sedge-flies are prolific, and it is timely to commence fishing the artificial Sedge on the surface as a dry fly. Around this period, Crane-flies are beginning to appear in ever increasing numbers and in some areas an artificial representation fished dry is killing. The Upwinged flies are now seldom encountered, except for odd hatches of Claret Duns or Pond Olives, but emergence of the Angler's Curse is now likely in ever-increasing numbers. Many of the species previously mentioned are still likely to be seen and of these the following are of particular interest during July; Damsel nymphs, Corixa and some species of Beetles. Two types of fauna that often appear for the first time in July, particularly, should be the weather be very hot, are floating Snails and ants, and as the appropriate artificials can be extremely effective when these are about, a careful watch should be maintained. In the early mornings and late evenings occasional buzzer rises are still encountered, but towards the end of July heavy rises are again likely to the pupae of the Large Green Midge. During the day, if the sun is not too fierce, trout may sometimes rise to the Small Brown or Small Red Midge, and later on in the afternoon to the pupa of the Large Red Midge. About this time of the year, in the evenings, emergence of the very tiny Black Midge, often in incredible numbers, is to be expected, and in localities where they occur they are likely to be encountered at spasmodic intervals throughout the remainder of the season. Although a rather difficult month, July provides one further item on the menu of the trout, this is the Stickleback, and by the middle of the month the fry of these or other fish are usually in sufficient concentrations to provide both interest to the fish and the angler.

AUGUST

Often referred to as the "dog days", the month of August is usually very difficult, although not hopeless, as if the fisherman is fortunate enough to pick a cool, or even better, a wet day, sport can be most rewarding. By this time many species of insects are on the wane, and consequently less volume of food is available to the trout, and the effect of this, combined with high water temperature and bright sun, seems to make the fish dour and disinclined to feed. However, should a few days of cooler wet weather come along, the trout may recommence feeding, and at this time a dry sedge or a stickleback imitation will often provide the angler with an unexpected heavy bag. On the other hand, should the weather prove unkind, the best chances of killing a few fish are undoubtedly during the very early mornings or late evenings, as there is often some activity at this time, with artificials to represent Sticklebacks, Corixa or Midges offering the best chances of success. Finally, under favourable conditions, a rise to floating Snails or Ants may be anticipated, and should provide an unexpected bonus to the observant angler.

SEPTEMBER AND EARLY OCTOBER

By this time of the year the trout are often very wary and difficult to catch, and in addition natural food is becoming increasingly scarce. Fortunately for the angler the fish apparently anticipate the lean months of winter, and consequently a comparatively small amount of insect activity will often bring the trout particularly big browns on the feed, and provide the more experienced fishers with fair bags. For a brief period in late August and September, spasmodic hatches of Pond and Lake Olives are likely, and during this same period the Olive Midge is the predominant species among Buzzer rises. Early in the month it is still possible that rises to the Ant or floating Snail may be observed, and also at this period it is still worth while fishing an artificial Corixa. On some waters Sticklebacks and other fry are still about, and may even extend into early October. During the whole of September the Small Red, Small Brown and Small Black Midges are again quite common, the latter extending well into October. It is to the Sedge-flies that the angler should look for his best chances during the closing stages of the season, as September is undoubtedly one of the peak months of the year for the emergence of a great variety of these insects. On some occasions during the warmer periods the dry artificial will still prove effective, but artificials to represent the various pupae of these Sedge-flies are usually most productive under average weather conditions. On those waters that remain open until the middle of October, general attractor patterns again give good results, for a similar reason to those of the early season fishing in April.

SUMMARY OF SEASONAL METHODS

This is only a general guide and does not take into account specific techniques required when fishing certain patterns.

Spring

In the early part of the year, before the temperature of the water rises significantly, the trout will feed in deeper water and it will therefore be necessary to fish your artificials on or near the bottom. Choose your fly line according to the depth to be fished: floaters with long leaders for shallow water, sink tips or slow sinkers for water of minimum depth or fast sinkers for very deep water. During this period slow retrieves give the best results.

Early summer

As the temperature of the water rises, surface activity will increase, particularly during the early evenings, when good hatches of chironomids (buzzers) may be anticipated. During the day however, most trout are still to be found on or near the bottom, but a faster retrieve is to be favoured when using lure type artificials.

Mid-Summer

(Calm Conditions)   With a high water temperature and little wind, lure or attractor patterns are best fished slow and deep, while nymph and imitative patterns seem to be most effective retrieved very slowly in midwater during the day, or near the surface early mornings or late evenings, particularly in the shallower areas.

Mid-Summer

(Windy Conditions)   Trout, particularly rainbows, at this time are likely on or just under the surface, so it is seldom necessary to fish your artificial deep.

Late Summer

As the temperature begins to drop it will once again be necessary to seek your trout in deeper water. However, surface activity may still occur on odd days, particularly when weather conditions favour late hatches of fly.

USEFUL TIPS

Coloured Water

In windy conditions a good place to fish is in areas where clear water meets coloured.

Wind

Where possible, fish the bank or shore onto which the wind is blowing, but if it is too strong, move to the bank which the wind is blowing along.

Fishing at Anchor

Unless there are special circumstances, move the boat at frequent intervals until you find the fish.

Algea and Wind Lanes

Always be on the lookout for these particularly when boat fishing, as food tends to congregate along these lanes and the trout will not be far away.

Early Season

Black and white lures are often most productive at this time of year, but you will have to find out which is the taking colour of the day as they seldom produce trout at the same time.

Drift Fishing

If the trout are continually coming short, try altering the size of your artificial, speeding up your retrieve, or both.

Colour

Orange seems particularly attractive to trout during July and August.

Inlets–Outlets

Any such places where there is an unusual movement of water are likely to attract trout and are well worth trying.

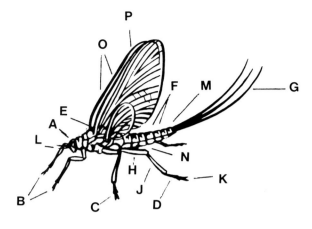

A. Oculi.
B. Anterior legs.
C. Median ,,
D. Posterior ,,
E. Thorax.

F. Tergites.
G. Cerci.
H. Femur.
J. Tibia.
K. Tarsus.

L. Antennae.
M. Dorsum.
N. Venter.
O. Costa.
P. Pterostigmatic area.

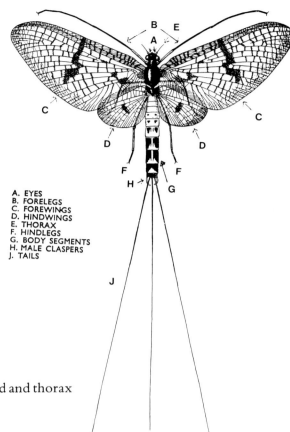

A. EYES
B. FORELEGS
C. FOREWINGS
D. HINDWINGS
E. THORAX
F. HINDLEGS
G. BODY SEGMENTS
H. MALE CLASPERS
J. TAILS

BODY PARTS OF FLIES

ENTOMOLOGICAL NAME	ANGLER'S NAME
Abdomen	The main body below head and thorax
Antennae	Feelers
Anterior leg or wing	Foreleg or forewing
Caudal filaments	All three tails
Cerci	Two outer tails
Costa	Leading edge of wing
Costal process or projection	Spur on leading edge of wing
Cuticle	Skin encasing dunn or nymph
Dorsum	Top of main body segments
Femur, Femora	Top part of legs
Forceps	Claspers of male fly
Intercalary veins	Small veins between main veins
Maxilla	Mouth parts
Median leg	Middle leg
Mesonotum (Mesothorax)	Central section of thorax or wing cases
Oculi	Eyes (compound)
Posterior leg or wing	Back leg or rear wing
Pronotum (Prothorax)	Shoulder of nymph or fly
Pterostigmatic area	Area near edge of wing apex
Sternites	Base of abdominal segments
Terminal filament	Centre tail of three
Tarsus, Tarsi	Feet or claws
Tergites	Upper abdominal segments
Thorax	Shoulders, chest or wing cases
Tibia	Middle part of legs
Venation	Veining of the wings
Venter	Under part of the main body

POSTSCRIPT – THE BARBLESS HOOK

RE-PRINTED FROM 'THE TROUT AND THE FLY'
BY BRIAN CLARKE AND JOHN GODDARD

We want to close this book with an appeal on behalf of the trout.

The use of the barbed hook is almost universal in fly-fishing, and yet we believe that on both practical and aesthetic grounds it could be replaced by the barbless hook tomorrow, and nothing would have been lost. Nothing perhaps, except by the opponents of angling.

The barbed hook in angling serves two purposes: in many forms of fishing, it does the practical job of helping to keep a bait on the hook. In all forms of fishing – including our own – it serves a second purpose: it gives the angler peace of mind. The thought that a hook is in beyond the barb and *cannot* come out save in the most extreme circumstances, gives the angler a glow inside. It is an insurance policy against him losing fish.

But is it? For many seasons now, we have used barbless hooks – either because we bought them without barbs, or because we have filed off the barbs from our conventional hooks or pressed them flush with tiny pliers – and have found no increase in the numbers of fish we have lost.

Of course, we have lost *some* fish. It is a rare angler indeed who does not lose some fish. But certainly we have not lost *more*, and JG is sure that he has lost far fewer.

How can this be?

The jaw of the trout is for the most part very tough. When the hook with the barb comes unstuck it most often does so because the point has failed to penetrate far enough: the barb just hasn't gone in. If the hook does not simply come away during the fight, a fish is often enough lost for another reason: the immense leverage that is exerted upon the very tip of a hook that has failed to penetrate, causes either the hook to straighten, at the bend if it is undertempered or break if it is overtempered, or for it to snap at its weakest part – at the point where the barb is cut.

With the barbless hook, it may well be the case that the odd fish comes away because the hook slips out. But the barbless hook in normal circumstances goes *in*, every time: there's simply nothing to stop or to slow it. And because any pressure is then exerted upon a fully-sunk point, we do not have our hooks straighten or snap. In fact, neither of us can remember a barbless hook *ever* snapping or being pulled straight. So if the occasional barbless hook does slip out, the balance is more than made up by the advantages outlined above. We do not believe that the barbed hook – and certainly the hook with the enormous barbs of today – lends any practical help in landing a higher proportion of fish.

All of what we have said so far, concerns practical considerations. But there are also aesthetic considerations.

Most experienced fly fishermen would agree that the moment of deception is *the* moment in the practice of their Art: that the rise to the dry fly or the take to the nymph or wet fly is the one moment which provides them with the greatest satisfaction. The hunt and the stalk are exciting, but they are merely the precursors of the cast; the playing and the landing can provide moments of excitement and triumph – but they are moments that are dependent upon the take.

It is the *deception* that consummates the skills. And when that moment is achieved, many anglers are content to play the fish out, and then return it.

But before the trout can be returned, the hook has to be removed. And often enough, as every one of us knows, that is not easy. It has to be worried out – sometimes tearing a hole in the fish's mouth, sometimes causing the fish to bleed.

Often enough, when damaged fish are returned to the water, their condition declines, as research in the United States has shown. Frequently, when a bleeding fish goes back, it dies. And what point is there in returning to the water a fish that is doomed to be stunted from that point on, or that is condemned to die?

There is no point at all.

The barbless hook makes all of that unnecessary. It comes out with the merest twist of the fingers. There is little more damage to the trout, than would be caused by a pin-prick in a human. And there is almost *never* bleeding. Indeed, it is often a practical proposition to set the fish free, without ever handling it – and many fish are damaged by the handling alone. By holding the rod far back with one hand, and sliding the other hand down the leader, the trout can often be set free without ever having been taken from the water. This is particularly easy to do – and of particular importance – when returning undersized fish, the sport of tomorrow.

For ourselves we kill very few fish indeed, even sizeable fish. In well-stocked fisheries, where the return of trout is possible)and most often, on still waters in the United Kingdom, the returning of trout is against the rules) we kill little more than a dozen or so fish a year for consumption, from a total of some hundreds caught. On wild fisheries which are not stocked, we kill no fish at all, unless the water will obviously stand the loss, and we very much want one to eat.

Indeed, where circumstances allow, we would support the establishment of special no-kill fisheries – or at least the keeping of parts of fisheries where all undamaged fish could be returned. Certainly, this would make the business of deception more difficult: but it would reduce the burden of stocking costs, and would make the moment of triumph more memorable still, for those who care to pursue it. In practice, it would merely be an extension of the size–limit principle which operates with considerable success, in many of our northern and western rain-fed streams. (There is one other point of no-kill fisheries that we would make, and it is this. There is no sense in using a barbless hook, if the trout is condemned to die because of the way it has been played. Many fish die, or suffer from oxygen starvation and brain damage, because the fight has been long drawn out. *Always* play your fish hard – and if they are to go back, get them back as quickly as you are able.)

But let us end on the point of substance.

It is obvious to anyone who walks the banks of our rivers and lakes, and who has the interests of our sport at heart, that much is done in the name of angling that most of us would abhor.

Not the least of our shortcomings as a group is that we do not care as much for our quarry as we might. And those who seek to deny us our sport – and their numbers are ever now increasing – will alight on our shortcomings first, when cobbling together their case.

It behoves each of us to raise the standards of behaviour on the bankside, while there is yet time. The avoidance of unnecessary cruelty to fish, however caused, must come right at the top of our list of priorities. And the general introduction of hooks without barbs would be no bad place to begin.

P.S. It is interesting to note that on many American and even some European trout streams the use of barbless hooks is now obligatory. Or even more significance is the following recent press release 'Manitoba a Fishing Enthusiast's Paradise, has become the first province in Canada and the first North American region to ban the use of barbs on hooks. The barbs must be pinched or filed off. The intent of the new regulation is to improve the sport fishing resource in Manitoba and to encourage catch and release angling. It is stated the no barb rule makes it easier to release fish to be returned and minimizes the damage particularly to unwanted immature fish'.

BIBLIOGRAPHY

BOOKS

BRIDGETT, R. C. *Loch Fishing*. Herbert Jenkins.
BROWN, E. S. *Life in Fresh Water*. Oxford University Press. 1955.
BUCKNALL, G. *Fly Fishing Tactics on Stillwater*. Frederick Muller Ltd. 1966.
CLEGG, J. *Pond and Stream Life of Europe*. Blandford Press Ltd. 1963.
CLEGG, J. *Freshwater Life of the British Isles*. Frederick Warne & Co. Ltd. 1952.
COLYER & HAMMOND. *Flies of the British Isles*. Frederick Warne & Co. Ltd. 1951.
FROST, W. E. and BROWN, M. E. *The Trout*. Collins Clear Type Press. 1967.
GAIDY, Charles. *Ephemeras Mayflies*. Edicom.
GODDARD, J. *Trout Fly Recognition*. A. & C. Black Ltd., 1966.
GODDARD, J. *Trout Flies on Stillwater*. A. & C. Black Ltd., 1969.
GODDARD, J. *Waterside Guide*. Unwin Hyman. 1988.
HARRIS, J. R. *An Angler's Entomology*. Collins. 1952.
HENZELL, H. P. *The Art and Craft of Loch Fishing*. Phillip Allan & Co. Ltd. 1937.
HICKIN, NORMAN E. *Caddis Larvae*. Hutchingson & Co. Ltd. 1967.
IMMS, A. D. *Insect Natural History*. Collins. 1947.
IVENS, T. C. *Still Water Fly Fishing*. Andre Deutsch Ltd. 1952.
KITE, OLIVER. *Nymph Fishing in Practice*. Herbert Jenkins, 1963.
LANE, COL. JOSCELYN. *Lake and Loch Fishing*. Seeley Service & Co. Ltd.
LINSSEN, E. F. and NEWMAN, L. H. *Common Insects and Spiders*. Fredk. Warne & Co. Ltd. 1953.
LUMINI, Piero, *Imitazioni di Effimere*. Editorial Olimpia.
LUMINI, Piero, *Imitazioni di Tricotteri*. Editorial Olimpia.
MACAN, T. T. and WORTHINGTON, E.B. *Life in Lakes and Rivers*. Collins. 1951.
MELLANBY, H. *Animal Life in Freshwater*. University Press. 1938.
MOSELY, M. E. *The British Caddis Flies*. George Routledge & Sons Ltd. 1939.
NEEDHAM AND NEEDHAM. *Fresh Water Biology*. Constable & Co. Ltd. 1962.
OATTS, COL. H.A. *Loch Trout*. Herbert Jenkins. 1958.
OBESO, Rafael. *Moscas Para La Pesca*. Editorial Everest.
PHILLIPS, E. *Trout in Lakes and Reservoirs*. Longmans Green & Co.
PRICE, TAFF. *The Anglers Sedge*. Blandford Press.
PRICE, TAFF. *Stillwater Flies, Book 1*. Ernest Benn Ltd.
PRICE, TAFF. *Stillwater Flies, Book 2*. Ernest Benn Ltd.
PRICE, TAFF. *Stillwater Flies, Book 3*. Ernest Benn Ltd.
VENIARD, J. *A Further Guide to Fly Dressing*. A. & C. Black Ltd. 1964.
WALKER, C. F. *Lake Flies and Their Imitation*. Herbert Jenkins. 1969.
WILLIAMS, A. COURTNEY. *A Dictionary of Trout Flies*. A. & C. Black Ltd. 1949.

BOOKLETS AND PAPERS
Fly Fishing on Lakes and Reservoirs — John Henderson. Private Printing.

FRESHWATER BIOLOGICAL ASSOCIATION
SCIENTIFIC PUBLICATIONS
No. 15. *Adults of Ephemeroptera*. D. E. Kimmins.
No. 16. *British Water Bugs*. T. T. Macan, M.A., Ph.D.
No. 17. *Nymphs of the British Stoneflies*. H. B. N. Hynes, D.Sc.
No. 19. *Crustacea and Malacostraca*. Hynes, Macan and Williams.
No. 20. *Nymphs of the Ephemeroptera*. T. T. Macan, M.A., Ph.D.
A Key to the Adults of the British Ephemeroptera by Elliot and Humpesch.

BOOKLETS BY THE ROYAL ENTOMOLOGICAL SOCIETY OF LONDON

Vol. IX. Part 1. *Diptera. Introduction and Key to Families.* H. Oldroyd.

Vo. IX. Part 2. *Diptera—Nematocear.* Coe, Freeman and Mattingly.

Vol. 109. Part 5. *Ecology of Chironomidae in Storage Reservoirs.* J. H. Mundie.

Vol. 112. Part 12. *A Study of Trichoptera.* M. I. Crichton.

Vol. 113. Part 6. *Diurnal Variation in the Emergence of Some Aquatic Insects.* N. C. and A. B. Waddell.

Vol. 116. Part 15. *Diurnal Periodicity of Flights by Insects.* T. Lewis and L. R. Taylor.

Vol. 119. Part 10. *Study of Limnophilus lunatus.* A. M. Gower.

TRANSACTIONS OF THE SOCIETY FOR BRITISH ERNTOMOLOGY

Vol. 14. Part 11. *Studies of the Larvae of the British Chironomidae.* D. Bryce.

BOOKLETS BY THE FRESHWATER BIOLOGICAL ASSOCIATION

Vol. IV. No. 4—1952. *Taxonomy of the Nymphs of the British Species of Leptophlebiidae.* T. T. Macan.

Vol. III. No. 1—1951. *Taxonomy of the British Species of Siphlonuridae.* T. T. Macan.

NATURALISTS HANDBOOKS

No. 13 *Mayflies* by Janet Harker.

BOOKLET BY THE ZOOLOGICAL SOCIETY OF LONDON

Series A. Vol. 108. Part 4—1938. *The Growth of* Caenis Horaria, Leptophlebia vestertina *and* L.marginata. P. H. Moon.

OTHER PAPERS

A Species of Caenis new to Britain—D. E. Kimmins—reprinted from *The Entomologist*, Vol. LXXVI, 1943.

A Key to the Nymphs of the British species of the Family Caeidae—T. T. Macan—*Entomologists Gazette*, Vol. 6, 1955.

British Midges—B. R. Laurence—*A.E.S. Bulletin*, Vol. 11, 1952.

Some Ephemeroptera and Trichoptera collected by mercury vapour light trap—P. H. Ward—*Entomologists Gazette*, Vol. 16.

Insect Emergence from a small Scottish Loch—N. C. Morgan, 1958.

Diel Periodicity of Pupal Emergence in Natural Populations of some Chironomids—E. Palmen, University of Helsinki, 1955.

The Biology of *Leptocerus alerrimus*, with reference to its availability as a food for trout—N. C. Morgan, The Brown Trout Research Laboratory—Pitlochry, 1955.

Some observations on the Biology of the Trout in Windermere—K. R. Allen, The Freshwater Biological Association Laboratory.

Survey of a Moorland Fishpond—T. T. Macan, the Freshwater Biological Association Laboratory, Wray Castle, Ambleside.

A Key to the Adults of the Chironomidae No. 1. V. C. Pinder.

A Key to the Adults of the Chironomidae No. 2. V. C. Pinder.

A Key—Check Lists (Distribution) of Ephemeroptera in Europe. Dr Joachim Illies.

A Key—Check Lists (Distribution) of Trichoptiera in Europe. Dr Joachm Illies.

A Key—Check Lists (Distribution) of Plecoptera in Europe. Dr Joachm Illies.

Index